Tokyo Notes & Anecdotes: Natsukashii

Bruce McCormack

TRAFFORD PUBLISHING

Copyright © 2000 by Bruce McCormack

All rights reserved. No part of this publication may be reproduced, stored in a retrieval system, or transmitted, in any form or by any means. mechanical, photocopying, recording, or otherwise, without the written prior permission of the author.

Cover and Calligraphy by Mitsu Ikemura
Contact the author through Trafford

Canadian Cataloguing in Publication Data

McCormack, Bruce, 1952-
    Tokyo notes and anecdotes

Includes bibliographical references.
ISBN 1-55212-320-0

1. McCormack, Bruce, 1952- 2. Canadians--Japan--Tokyo--Biography. 3. Tokyo (Japan)--Social life and customs. I. Title.
DS896.2.M32A3 2000   952'.135049   C00-910096-2

TRAFFORD

This book was published *on-demand* **in cooperation with Trafford Publishing.**
On-demand publishing is a unique process and service of making a book available for retail sale to the public taking advantage of on-demand manufacturing and Internet marketing.
On-demand publishing includes promotions, retail sales, manufacturing, order fulfilment, accounting and collecting royalties on behalf of the author.

Suite 6E, 2333 Government St., Victoria, B.C. V8T 4P4   CANADA
Phone   250-383-6864   Toll-free   1-888-232-4444 (Canada & US)
Fax   250-383-6804   E-mail   sales@trafford.com
Web site   www.trafford.com   TRAFFORD PUBLISHING IS A DIVISION OF TRAFFORD HOLDINGS LTD.
Trafford Catalogue #99-0070   www.trafford.com/robots/99-0070.html

10   9   8   7   6   5

This book is dedicated to my friends (both old and new), in Japan and elsewhere. I sing their praises, because it's their companionship and encouragement that made this long journey all worthwhile.

Oh Tokyo -
I never can sleep in your arms
Mind keeps on ringing like a fire alarm
Me and all these other dice
Bouncing around in the cup
But did you have to show me that accident scene
Didn't I get enough shaking up?
Still I'm gonna miss you . . .

                         Bruce Cockburn

TABLE OF CONTENTS

Acknowledgments		ix
Preface		1
Chapter 1	Claustrophobics Need Not Apply	5
Chapter 2	Settling into the System	45
Chapter 3	The Honeymoon Draws to an End	107
Chapter 4	Up Against the Social Contract	179
Chapter 5	Coming to Terms with Japan	227
Chapter 6	Still I'm Gonna Miss You	301
Epilogue		379
Glossary		383
Notes		391

ACKNOWLEDGMENTS

There are so many people who have encouraged me, stimulated me and helped me along as I wrote this book. I wish there was space to thank them all in print. I trust they know that I offer my heartfelt thanks to each and every one of them. Without their support, this project might never have gone beyond my laptop computer.

Some have been of such great assistance that their names must be mentioned with special thanks. I extend my appreciation to Bruce Batchelor, Tanis Toope, Terry Lussier and everyone at Trafford Publishing for guiding me through the final process of getting the book into print.

I'm also very grateful to Jude Rand, Gretta MacIlvaine and Elliott Dainow for reading early drafts and giving me invaluable feedback. Many thanks go to Helen Dunbar and Dhyani Jo Sinclair for editing later drafts and urging me to persevere.

I wish to acknowledge Bert Almon, Douglas Barbour and the late W.O. Mitchell, for sowing seeds of inspiration in me all those years ago in their creative writing classes.

A special thank you goes to Richard Young for his photographs, and for the many laughs he and his wife Jan and I shared together during our years in Japan.

I extend my sincerest thanks to Mitsu Ikemura for drawing such a lively cover for the book, adding calligraphy to each chapter, and being a supportive and enlightened friend. Mitsu-san has lived in Canada since the 1970's, having grown up in Kyoto. When we met through our choir in Victoria, B.C., we quickly discovered that we share many cross-cultural affinities. We both understand what it's like to be a *foreigner* in a land we weren't born in. Our experiences are mirror images of each other: I was the Canadian in Japan; Mitsu-san was the Japanese in Canada. We also share the belief that we're all universal travellers on this planet, regardless of our cultural and geographical origins.

Special thanks go to my sister, Dory Nicoll, for endless support, to Sam Neal for invaluable computer support, and to Tressa List and Kelly Jarvis for boundless encouragement when I needed it most. I also wish to thank the many supportive friends I've made while attending programs offered by P.D. Seminars, held at Haven By-the-Sea on Gabriola Island, B.C.

In Japan, I've been helped and aided by countless people along the way. I owe a debt of gratitude to them all, most especially to Hanae. Though many of my Japanese and foreign friends, colleagues and students are pseudonymous here, these are their stories as much as they're mine.

PREFACE

Japan is a remarkable country, and it's been very good to me. But blasting around like an overheated molecule in the pressure cooker of the Tokyo subway system does not come naturally to a Canadian used to blue sky and wide open spaces. Eventually, I began to feel like I was evolving into some kind of mutated hybrid rat/robot, rehearsing for the next sequel to *The Fly*.

I wrote *Tokyo Notes & Anecdotes: Natsukashii* because living in Japan changed me dramatically, and I needed to continually process what I was going through. I also realized that I wanted to share my often wonderful, sometimes zany and occasionally bizarre experiences, as well as the many changes in my feelings about Japan. But it's not just a book of my own impressions. It also includes those of many friends and colleagues I met and worked with during a decade in Tokyo.

On my trips back to Canada and the U.S., I always found that everyone - friends, acquaintances, barbers and bank tellers - was intensely curious about life in the Land of the Rising Sun. Most people on the West Coast knew someone who was working in Japan - a cousin, a neighbor's daughter, a friend of a friend - or they'd hosted a Japanese homestay student. They often hadn't read any of the excellent academic books now available on Japan's society and economy. Though they were very interested in all of that, the question they almost always asked was simply, "What's it like living there?"

This book is a long answer to their question. It's a chronicle of my journey – amusing incidents, everyday routines, reactions to inexplicable happenings, and wonderful encounters. It's also the story of my volatile evolution from infatuation through waves of culture shock, and on to a sense of acceptance and appreciation of a country and people I've grown very fond of.

Wonderful books have been written about life in rural areas of this great country by people who might as well have been on a different planet from me, so different are the stories we have to tell. In actual fact, many Japanese would probably say that Tokyo is not the *Real Japan*. That being the case, perhaps this is a book about the *Unreal Japan* – especially the one inhabited by a *gaijin* (foreigner) like myself. But I wasn't alone in this unreal place called Tokyo; thousands of others shared it with me, and our experiences were certainly real to us.

I trust these stories will give the reader a very real sense of what it's like to wander the subway labyrinths of this enormous techno-megacity and endure its horrendously cramped trains. I hope it will shed a bit more light on what it's like to live and work as a *gaijin* in this complex society, one in which you will always be an outsider, however long you stay. I trust it will convey some vivid impressions of Tokyo life, of what it's like to ride on its urban and social roller coaster, to come home utterly exasperated one night, and totally delighted the next.

I also hope it makes a contribution towards showing a Japan with a human face, a face that can be very hard for outsiders to see. To a considerable extent, that's because the Japanese people are so concerned about saving face – their public face, that is. Knowing this, I have often used pseudonyms to safeguard the privacy of friends, colleagues, and even employers.

For Westerners, this concern over 'face' can be quite a challenge. Many eventually leave this country with a great sense of frustration, and I might have done so as well had I left at an earlier time. But on the other side of the formidable cultural barriers that have confronted me in Japan, I've been privileged to discover many endearing qualities in the Japanese people. Given how stressful their lives are – dealing with a system that binds them in so many ways – I consider their kindness and generosity to be a small and wonderful miracle.

One more thing – I chose the word *Natsukashii* (naht • su • kah • shē) as the book's Japanese title because it came to me in a dream one night that the title should include that word. It refers to a sentiment much valued by Japanese people, who often say *natsukashii* when remembering something nostalgically.

It evokes both pleasure and a measure of sadness, and there's no word in English that better describes my feelings about Japan.

I'm afraid I've gone on so long that we're going to have to run for the train. But that just means it's a normal day - on your marks, get set, Tokyo!

4 • TOKYO NOTES & ANECDOTES: NATSUKASHII

youngphotography

1

CLAUSTROPHOBICS
NEED NOT APPLY

Japan the Cultural Blender

On the evening of my arrival in Japan in the fall of 1987, my destination was a city called Sendai, two hours north of Tokyo by *shinkansen* – the famous 'bullet' train. Krista had already been living there for a year, and we weren't sure at that time where we'd locate. I might join her in Sendai until she finished her contract, or live in historic Kyoto for awhile. But succumbing to the frenetic magnetism of Tokyo was a fate I imagined I could avoid.

Even though I was exhausted from the flight, my memory of that first night in Japan is crystal clear. Signs in *kanji* (Chinese characters) were everywhere. I was entering an alien universe.

In those days, you had to take a five-minute bus ride from Narita Airport to catch the train to Tokyo, because the last stretch of the train line hadn't been finished yet. The authorities were doing battle with farmers whose land they'd appropriated to build Narita Airport, a fight that still goes on in one form or another to this day. I remember that the bus was packed, and the silence was like that in a reference library.

I then took the *Skyliner* – a one-hour express train into downtown Tokyo – and soon found myself in Ueno Station, an enormous maze filled with people going every which way. Up to that point, things had been relatively easy. Now I was suddenly swimming in *kanji* signs and at a total loss as to which way to go.

A complete stranger kindly went out of his way to walk me a great distance through a sequence of passageways and staircases right to the entrance of the *shinkansen*. He then dashed off, quite unaware that one day he'd wind up in my book, having been instrumental in forming a very favorable first impression of his country in my mind. It was early in my time in Japan that I first heard the expression, "You've only got one chance to make a good first impression." In my case, Japan passed that test with flying colours.

Feeling safe and excited, I hopped aboard this country's high-tech ironhorse marvel for the first time and headed for Sendai, so Krista and I could plot our future together in the *Land of Wa* (meaning 'harmony').

Unlike Tokyo, Sendai is a fairly manageable size, and I liked it immediately. Krista normally rode a bicycle to work, but if she chose, she could walk home in 45 minutes. In Tokyo, walking home from work would probably take most people a couple of days.

So on the morning after my arrival, Krista gave me a key and dashed off to work on her bicycle. I puttered around her apartment for awhile, captivated by how tiny everything was. The minuscule bathroom brought the expression 'water closet' to life. But soon I, too, was out the door, eagerly awaiting more first impressions of Japan and Japanese life.

I didn't have to wait long. Barely had I gotten onto the nearest street when something came around the corner and embedded itself in my memory for all time. It may well be the best image that's ever crossed my path of the cultural incongruity a Westerner encounters here. On my first morning in Japan, no less – very Zen.

At first there was just this familiar song – the melody without the lyrics – which I couldn't quite make out, but which was drawing nearer and nearer. I stopped walking and glanced down the road towards the next corner, to where the sound was coming from.

Then two things happened at once. Just as I recognized the melody – *Camptown Races* by Stephen Foster – around the corner came this huge garbage truck loaded up with what seemed, thanks to the mood created by the music, to be a kind of cartoon caricature of happy-go-lucky workers, like you'd see in a kid's storybook.

Everyone – including the Japanese I guess – knows this familiar upbeat melody with the "doo dah" chorus: "Camptown ladies sing this song, doo dah, doo dah ... Camptown racetrack five miles long, oh, doo-dah-day ... !"

Into full view now came six Japanese garbage men – smartly dressed in crisp blue uniforms – hanging onto the back and the sides of their truck, while this very un-Japanese melody blared across the neighbourhood from a static-plagued loudspeaker on the dashboard.

The truck suddenly stopped. The men jumped off and diligently collected our neighbour's garbage, working with a great sense of purpose.

Every 30 seconds or so, the melody would come to an end, and then start right up again. I was mesmerized, and watched in total fascination as these guys made their way down the street, house by house. After the fourth or fifth round of their musical accompaniment – "Oh doo dah day" – the truck, its workers and its upbeat melody rounded the corner and disappeared from view. The song hung in the air a few more moments and then faded away.

It was my first contact with the cultural blender of modern Japan. You come here with your head full of images from books and movies and expect things to be Japanese. Instead, what you encounter is this curious mix of traditional Japan superimposed on cultural motifs like heritage Americana.

I was later to learn that the purpose of the song is to alert people to the truck's presence, in case they've forgotten to put out their garbage. "Of course," I thought, "just like ice-cream trucks back home play a melody to draw the attention of children." But on my first morning in Japan, I actually concluded it was designed to keep up the workers' spirits. It seemed to be doing a fine job of it too, the way they were going at that trash like men on a mission. Talk about diligence.

As for the *Camptown Races*, it's a good old song, though it beats me how they could listen to that melody hundreds of times a day without going berserk. I suspect that from now on, whenever I hear it, I'll see those Japanese garbage men in my mind's eye, hanging onto the back of their truck in the light of a Sendai morning.

Get the Lead Out!

I can honestly say that I came to Japan without the slightest intention of working in Tokyo. 'Anywhere but Tokyo' was the refrain of many of the Westerners I spoke with, and I felt much the same. Yet here we are, Krista and I, well and truly caught up in the workaday world of this amazing city. As that most Japan-friendly of Westerners, Laurens van der Post, might have put it, "I had no plans for Tokyo, but Tokyo had plans for me."

Nor did I get right off the plane and look for a job that started the next day. In fact, for my first three weeks, I had a Japan Rail Pass that permitted unlimited travel throughout the country on JR trains. That allowed me to job hunt in cities all over the country. It also gave me a chance to get a feel for Japan before settling down somewhere. It's definitely one of the world's great travel bargains.

Armed with one of these, I calmly zipped around Japan on its incredible *shinkansen* express trains and watched everyone else racing around, caught up in their workaday worlds. It gave me a terrific introduction to the Land of the Rising Sun.

Osaka was clearly a close rival for Tokyo's sprawl and speed. But smaller cities like Hiroshima in the west of Honshu, and Sendai in the north were obviously more relaxed places to live. Kyoto was lovely, flanked by green hills, filled with temples and rich with history. Yet everywhere I went, there was the same steady hustle and bustle, an orderly and methodical approach to getting things done.

Some of my first insights into Japanese efficiency and use of time came courtesy of the Higashiyama Youth Hostel in Kyoto. Being an old hostel aficionado from away back – I can say that the Kyoto hostel was an eye-opener, quite unlike anything I've ever experienced in Europe or North America.

At mealtimes, identical servings were all laid out on plates perfectly arranged on banquet-length tables. All you had to do was show up, sit down and eat, but you had to keep to the schedule or you'd go hungry.

At nighttime, the doors to the outside world were shut up tight at 10:00 p.m. This, in itself, is not so unusual – hostels around the world often run a fairly tight ship. But in Kyoto, the regimentation was ironclad. The fluorescent bedroom lights were turned off at precisely 10:10 – all of them. You might have been engrossed in a spellbinding novel – too bad. 10:10 p.m. sharp was bedtime, and there were no lights on bedside tables. It reminded me of cub camp when I was a kid!

I remember lying in bed until about 10:20 assessing the situation. Wide awake and full of energy, I eventually wandered out into the hallway and stumbled into the men's room, squinting against the fluorescent lights that were still blazing away in the washrooms. To my astonishment, I discovered the place was filled up with Italians and Germans knocking back whiskey (a very definite Japanese hostel no-no) and shooting the breeze. They were all cursing their fate at the hands of these stringent regulations.

It was the next morning, however, that provided me with my most memorable object lesson in Japanese social procedure. We were suddenly woken up by the sound of four ascending xylophone-generated notes – a tonic, a third, a fifth and an octave, coming through a loudspeaker on the wall – ping, pong, pong, pong!

Then came a classic moment. Having been startled awake with this musical overture, we then heard the voice of an elderly gentleman speaking Japanese. His voice, though it had a gentle quality, boomed loudly through the crackling speaker. Suddenly, he spoke a few words in English, minus the 'l's - "Six o'crock, parease take showa." [sic]

This was followed up by the same four notes on the xylophone, but this time in descending order - Ping, pong, pong, pong!

I have since come to know that these sounds, signaling the beginning and ending of a message, were manually produced by somebody playing an actual xylophone in front of a microphone. My company in Tokyo was still using this technique when I first started working there. What with Japan's worldwide reputation for technological prowess, it felt like an endearing throwback to a simpler time.

In any event, this exhortation to action did not have the desired effect on the Germans, Italians and Canadians in the hostel that morning, at least not in my dorm room. Not a body moved.

At 6:30 he came on with the second assault. Ping, pong, pong, pong! Rambling on in Japanese - this time for about three or four minutes - he then switched to English, at which point I realized he was translating the weather report. Still wrapped up in the illusion that I was going to be able to ignore all this and get a few minutes more sleep, I tried to tune it out. But two words from that weather synopsis impaled themselves forever on my brain: "Dangawus tundacrouds" (dangerous thunderclouds). It was just too funny to be believed.

He finally finished up and signed off, with one final round from the xylophone: "Ping, pong, pong, pong!"

Not 30 seconds later, at precisely 6:40 a.m., a young Japanese guy, obviously well trained in the art of handling recalcitrant Westerners, came in and did an amazing thing. He tugged at my sheets to indicate he was going to pull them out from under me right then and there, which he soon proceeded to do with one swift yank! Seems we were all supposed to have gotten up, showered, piled up our sheets for the laundry and, for all I know, memorized fifty *kanji* characters and done a hundred push-ups by 6:40 in the morning, in time to be the first ones downstairs for breakfast.

The Japanese people don't mess around getting the day started. I later came upon the *Higashiyama Youth Hostel Timetable* and there it was, all spelled out: *Closing time 10:00 PM.; Light Off 10:10 PM; Shower time 6:00 - 7:00 AM; Rising 6:40 AM; Clean your bed and room 6:40 - 7:00 AM; Breakfast 6:40 - 8:00 AM.* The brochure was entitled: *How to have a pleasant stay.*

Downstairs, identical breakfasts were waiting for us on identical place settings right the way down the banquet-length tables. No other choices were available. Our job, again, was just to sit down and eat the meal that was all laid out for us.

A group of us, foreigners from various places, sat together. There was plenty of mirth around the breakfast table as we all shared our experiences of the hostel. Japan was different - that was abundantly clear.

After breakfast, I checked out and wandered around Kyoto, marvelling at its ancient shrines and temples, but keeping my eyes open for signs of a major typhoon. As I recall, there wasn't a hint of rain all day, nor was there a dangerous thundercloud to be found.

Welcome to Tokyo

I almost got crushed on the *Odakyu Line* again this morning. The knuckles of my right hand felt like they'd crack open, pulverized against the train door window, my fingers boring into my ribcage. A gray-haired Japanese gentleman had laughed kindly, watching from the platform as the station guard crammed the last of my body parts into the train car. It must have amused him to watch an obviously green foreigner undergoing this most routine of Tokyo rituals - routine, that is, for the Japanese who have grown up in this city. But who - outside of those veterans and the rest of us initiates - could ever fully appreciate the well-managed intensity of this drama without actually living it?

Scene One is your basic rush hour train car - stuffed to bursting with human bodies, many in contorted positions. By anyone's definition of the word, it's full beyond capacity. In the eyes of most monster-city dwellers on the planet, the train is packed.

Then comes Scene Two. Thirty or forty more bodies pile in through every door, moving as one solid mass and looking more like members of a determined rugby scrum than mere commuters. With arms bent at the elbows for leverage, the most eager push like fullbacks with me seeming to be in the center of the scrum, the station guard bulldozing up behind the whole pack of us, straining with his full body weight and brandishing his people prod - pressing, forcing, squeezing ... then the doors slam shut on my headline. Welcome to one of the world's great urban pressure cookers, Tokyo.

The Favorite Pastime

Tokyo is home now, and my footloose first weeks in Japan seem like ages ago. After a three-month stint working in Kyoto, I was finally lured to Japan's largest city by a better job offer. Now Krista and I have fallen in step with Tokyo's marching hordes, and live by the clock and for the weekend. But although Tokyo can be crowded and stressful, we've discovered that it's got a lot going for it. We've also learned a few things about how people here deal with sleep deprivation.

At least once or twice a month, I have to work a full day on Saturdays, and Krista usually works a six-day week. But on a Friday night when a two-day weekend is ahead of both of us, we sometimes feel positively giddy. If you ride Tokyo's *Yamanote Line* on a Friday night, you feel a sense of relief in the air. It's a sharp contrast with the grimness on the rails the rest of the week. People are chatting and laughing and lightening up in a big way. It's a heartening thing to witness.

The Japanese work hard, and they play hard. I've taken to saying that compared to what I'm used to as a Canadian, the way they live may not be a difference of kind, but it's definitely one of degree. Japanese society swings more between extremes. People keep a sharper dividing line between work and play. Work time is more serious, and play time – in scarcer supply – is more frivolous. But Friday night is definitely play time.

"So what else is knew?" one might say, "Friday night is the same everywhere."

Yes and no; it's the phenomenal intensity of life in Tokyo that's surprised us. During their first weeks in Tokyo, most new foreign residents undergo a battery of identical experiences: one is discovering that Tokyo is an incredibly exhausting place; another is being astonished by how many people sleep on the trains. Then there's the response you get when you ask Japanese people about their weekends.

When I first queried my Japanese company colleagues about what they do on Sundays, more than half offered the same response, "I sleep."

Most *gaijin* admit to the same surprise on hearing this again and again. Assuming it's kind of a joke about being overworked, we probe further, "O.K., but what do you do after you wake up?"

There's often an embarrassed laugh and a pause, followed by something like, "I sleep all day. I don't get up."

Months of curiosity later, you eventually conclude they're telling you the truth. I now assume that millions of Japanese men and women spend Sundays just recuperating. Since six-day work weeks are still very common here, it's not really all that surprising. I don't pretend to have any great insight into how

Japanese companies work; I'm a simple rewriter (a proofreader of often incomprehensible English), as well as a teacher. I toil away on the fifth floor of an annex across the street from our company's main building. But on any given weeknight when I've stayed late in the office, I can peer across to our central fortress near Tokyo Station and see men in their creased white shirts scurrying about with ties askew, fluorescent lights blazing until 10:00 p.m. and much later.

I know from speaking about it with my Japanese colleagues that they sometimes work through most of the night, because at 10:00 p.m. Tokyo time, American buyers in New York are just waking up and reaching for their phones. Tokyo *sarariimen* (the *salaryman* being a male white-collar company employee on salary) – and a few of their indispensable *office lady* helpers as well – are waiting for them in their offices, ready to make a sale.

One cannot live and work here for very long without forming the impression that to a great extent, Japan roared to success economically in the 1980s on the strength of long hours of conscripted workaholism.

Outside of national holiday periods, Tokyo's *salarymen* and *office ladies* (O.L.'s for short) – and most everyone else as well – work quite relentlessly. Apparently the Japanese always have, there being accounts of this by Western observers dating from the 1890s. In fact, when it comes to sleep, there's nothing much new there either. Writing in the 1940s, the cultural anthropologist Ruth Benedict, in her classic study of Japan, *The Chrysanthemum and the Sword*, described it as being "another favored indulgence. It is one of the most accomplished arts of the Japanese. They sleep with complete relaxation, in any position, and under circumstances we regard as sheer impossibilities."

So it is that the hard-working Japanese sleep whenever and wherever they can. I took a one-hour evening train trip on the Odakyo Line in which the woman sitting next to me quickly nodded off. As often happens on Tokyo trains, her head soon fell on my shoulder. Since I wasn't particularly bothered, it didn't occur to me to disturb her much-needed sleep. But to my surprise, her head remained there for the entire hour. As I read my newspaper, she dozed to her heart's content.

Newspaper Technique

Since settling down in Tokyo, we've discovered that morning rush hour commuters on the subway system often have to fold their newspapers in a manner I'd seldom seen before coming to Japan. They don't fold them in half or even quarters – there's not enough space. Many people fold them in eighths.

I have followed suit, but I've learned that this doesn't leave you with much in the way of reading material. So in Tokyo, if you know you're going to be standing on the train, you pick your story carefully before you get on. That's because you may be stuck with your choice for 15 minutes, or even for the duration if you're on a horrendously crowded train, which is an hour to an hour and a half for most commuters.

The problem is that once you've chosen your one-eighth of a page, you may not have the chance to change your position for long stretches of time. Your upper arms may be pinned to the sides of your torso. Your elbows will be bent with your hands clutching the thick wad of newsprint floating a few centimeters away from your eyes.

You can forget about unfolding your one-eighth of a page to search for another interesting article – that's usually an impossible task. You can also forget about locating a button on your Walkman. I'm now convinced that the Tokyo subway system is the reason the Japanese invented the automatic reverse. In fact, even reaching down to get a pen out of your pants pocket would involve more wriggling and struggling than it's worth.

To live comfortably in Tokyo as a morning train commuter, your best approach is just to give up the idea of voluntary movement of limbs. Space in this city is too limited to keep it empty for any length of time. The wise commuter learns to accept the fact that their physical body is temporarily immobilized in a solid ocean of other bodies. Pressed up against them, you just learn to relax. There's simply no going anywhere.

One trick I've learned is to keep inventing new ways to savour my chosen newspaper article. I translate as many words as possible into Japanese, or I practice a trick I learned from the sci-fi writer Ursula Le Guin – reading everything backwards and inventing new words. If I find myself reaching the limits of endurance, I try mentally refuting everything the article says as a way of expressing my frustration with my imprisonment.

When I've exhausted these techniques and the train still races on, I work on that speed-reading technique I never quite mastered. As a last resort, I try memorizing the whole article to see how well my brain is standing up to the commuting pressure.

Such is morning rush hour on the *Odakyu Line*, the *Mita Line* ... most any line, Tokyo. There's simply no choice but to abandon the notion of personal space and create a mental zone of your own. I also find it helps to keep as lighthearted about the situation as I can, and to do as the Japanese do – practice my imperturbability.

Only in Japan

Fortunately for a *gaijin* company employee like me, there are many bright sides to life in Tokyo. This is especially true on a weekend when you've slept your way back to a relaxed state and find yourself feeling *genki* (upbeat and happy) and ready for some leisure time in your newly adopted country. For one thing, you seldom have to go far afield to find something interesting, unusual or bizarre.

I love that aspect of our lives here – the novelty of everything around us. I just have to wander down any one of the hundreds of side streets I haven't explored yet and little discoveries abound. Even if what you discover is totally off-the-wall inane, it's unlikely to be dangerous. Compared to most other urban behemoths its size, this city still deserves the label, 'Tokyo the Safe.'

That's worth a great deal in a world in which, early in our time here, I remember reading that Detroit was imposing a Halloween curfew for four nights to curb violence and mayhem. The contrast with the safety we were experiencing was so astonishing.

In the late '80s in Tokyo, secretaries routinely trundled across the street here with the equivalent of $20,000 in cash tucked nonchalantly under one arm. Come payday, many people were still getting paid in cash – great wads of yen in unsealed brown paper envelopes. For many, this practice still continues. Occasionally, you read of commuters forgetting shoulder bags with enormous bundles of cash in them on overhead luggage racks. They often get them back.

One suspects that this may all slowly unravel, but glacially slowly, the way most things change in Japan. For the time being, foreign residents can continue to marvel at the relative safety of this city compared to wilder urban centers like L.A.

From my point of view, this positive aspect of Japanese society can't be downplayed, though the actual degree of safety is sometimes exaggerated to mythic levels by the Japanese themselves. Within my first six months in Japan, I had 30,000 yen ($250) stolen from my wallet. So thoroughly had I absorbed the notion that the Japanese were completely trustworthy that I left my wallet and money in my pants pocket, in a wicker basket in the locker room of a *rotenboro* (outdoor hot spring). Half an hour later, my money was gone, though my wallet and all my cards were untouched. Even in Japan, I've learned to adhere to the wise Islamic adage: trust in Allah but tie your camel.

Still, the Japanese have good reason to be proud. Whatever the complex collusion of social forces accounting for it, this high degree of everyday personal safety in an enormous megalopolis the size of Tokyo is a major success story. It's possibly without parallel in the other great cities of the world.

So, nestled in this womb of safety, one learns to handle the bizarre here with confidence and calm. And watch open-mouthed as life imitates, what? ... television? The theater of the absurd?

It was much like that one Saturday night when Krista and I were feeling energetic and looking for a little cultural enrichment, Tokyo-style.

We had just surfaced from the Chiyoda Line at Nogizaka Station in search of *The Cavern*, a replica of the Liverpool club where the Beatles incubated in the early '60s. It's a venue complete with live music by Japanese Beatle look-a-likes. We got there, eventually, and had good fun, enjoying what the stereotype says the Japanese do best: it was definitely first-class imitation.

But this story lies en route – just up and out of the subway at Nogizaka Station. Suddenly, out of nowhere, two Japanese couples approached us, all talking at once in Japanese and broken English. They were in their early 20s.

"Wiru you puray parutii gamu parease? (Will you play a party game, please?) Please? Five, ten minutes only."

"What on earth can this be about?" we mused, stalling but finally giving in, curious and knowing it would be harmless fun, whatever it was. After all, it was 1989 in Tokyo, a city whose people felt so innocent to us. This evening was no exception. Our acceptance generated expressions of childlike glee and hand clapping all round!

Without delay, our gentle captors whisked us into the elevator of a classy-looking building nearby. Up we went to the second floor, surrounded by a coterie of excited Japanese, there being no predicting what would happen next.

Krista and I exchanged looks of bafflement and joy. How do you prepare for something totally out of your cultural frame of reference? In Japan, you just surrender to it, and see what happens.

The elevator doors opened onto a huge ballroom filled with hundreds of people dressed in tuxedos and long gowns. The instant they saw the two of us – total strangers to them – they burst into sustained applause laced with shouts of approval as though we were Robert Redford and Meryl Streep, just off the set and into a reception being held in our honor! It was truly twilight zone.

Krista and I exchanged a glance that said, "Can you believe this is happening?" as we were shepherded up onto a stage, having been armed with a couple of microphones while making our way there. Pretty quickly, the *yen* dropped – so to speak – and we figured out the game. It was a wedding reception. The challenge was to find a few 'foreigners' out on the street and get them to come up on stage, just to wish the bride and groom well, or perhaps to sing them a song.

Regrettably, we did no justice to Redford and Streep, but the wedding guests hooted their approval just the same, gave us gifts (New York City calendars) and – true to their word – escorted us back to the elevator inside of 15 minutes.

Just as quickly as we'd been swept upstairs, we were back on *Gaien Higashi Dori* (Street), laughing incredulously, "Did that really happen, or did we just dream it?"

Events like this help explain why Westerners often feel the world of Tokyo is fantasy-like, detached from real life.

"This money feels like 'play money,' someone once said to me. "I still can't believe it's real."

It was the Tokyo of the late '80s – a quite amazing place. After years of discipline and struggle, the Japanese had risen to the top of the world and were revelling in their success. Yet, young Tokyo Japanese were so much more innocent and naive than their American counterparts. They felt no qualms about wandering out onto the safe streets of their city, fully expecting to find willing non-Japanese strangers like us to play their party game with them.

By and large, they were quite infatuated with Western culture (meaning American, for most). They wanted to imitate it, imitate us, receive our approval and include us in their celebration of their rise from the ashes of the war.

I smile at the memory of that night. It will always speak to me of something I've encountered in many Japanese and grown fond of. Call it a trusting nature, a guileless spirit, an absence of overt cynicism.

And hey, in what other city on the planet could I possibly be mistaken for Robert Redford and Krista for Meryl Streep? Our 15 minutes of Japanese fame behind us, off we went to enjoy the Tokyo version of the Beatles' Liverpool Cavern.

Day One at *Soulful Software*

If I live to be 100, I think I'll always remember my first day on the job at my Japanese company. To protect the innocent, I'll call it *Soulful Software* – every good company can use a little soul. It was January 4, the first day back on the job for all company employees following the New Year's break.

One hears a great deal about the frenetic pace of Japanese company employees, but on that day, the atmosphere at my new office was calm and unhurried. We only worked until about 11:30 in the morning, at which time everyone in our department (Personnel) gathered for a short speech by our department head to inaugurate the New Year. Being a new employee, I was introduced and asked to give a brief speech myself, which I struggled through in my pigeon Japanese, to enthusiastic applause. Everyone was very warm and welcoming.

I distinctly remember noticing how quiet the atmosphere was, how relaxed and congenial everyone seemed. Of course, they'd just come back from some time off, but still, it was striking - noticeably different from a Canadian office setting. It was my introduction to some of the nuances of the Japanese character I'm growing to appreciate.

We then had lunch, laid on by the company, and at about 1:00, to my surprise, we were all told that that was it for the day! It was no surprise to anyone else - it turns out that this 'half day' in early January is an annual event. Like so many others in the Japanese calendar, it's unvarying from year to year. Clearly, it was not all drudgery here at Soulful Software.

What a happy camper I was, taking the uncrowded train home in the early afternoon sunshine to enjoy this unexpected gift of time to myself. I'd felt a lot of inner resistance to taking this job, because it meant living in Tokyo with its tremendous stress and mobs of people. But Soulful Software had graciously bent over backwards to accommodate my needs, and on that day in January, I came to terms with my situation and decided that life in Tokyo was going to be all right.

Looking back to that first day, I see now that it offered my first valuable lesson in the simple equation of Japanese company life, as lived by the Japanese. Provided you accept that the company holds your life in a virtual vice grip - more completely than most Canadian or American companies could ever dream of doing with the lives of their employees - it will be consistently good to you in small but significant ways. Management will, for example, provide a free lunch and give you half a day off at the beginning of January, every single year of your working life. You can count on it.

Human Magic

To varying degrees, many foreign residents of Tokyo seem to shut themselves off in a cocoon of resentment. They lock onto cultural anomalies and perceptions of unfairness towards non-Japanese people and complain ad nauseam. I know about this because I've already done my share. I've had to rein myself in and regain perspective on a number of occasions.

As a *gaijin*, it can be difficult to steer clear of such reactions. In itself, the frequent use of this word is a trigger point for many Westerners. Some say they prefer *gaikoku-jin*, meaning 'foreign country person,' but *gaijin* is the expression most commonly used for Caucasians.

After you've been perceived as an 'outside person' for awhile, you begin to understand how resentment and negativity can become a chronic condition. At its most challenging, Tokyo is an intensely crowded, stressful, and alienating city - for Japanese and foreigners both. Riding the trains everyday, you're forever dealing with the constant jostling for the limited number of seats. Young teenage boys are notorious for getting a seat, and then spreading their legs as wide as possible for their own comfort.

Japan also presents the 'foreigner' with a society replete with unfamiliar cultural protocol. There are countless social trip wires and barriers visible only to the Japanese, not to mention the huge linguistic hurdle. Sources of confusion and misunderstanding abound on a daily basis. Not the least of these is the illusion that Japan is 'very Westernized.' Kentucky Fried Chicken outlets, 7/11 stores and the golden arches of McDonald's are everywhere. When I first got here, Michael J. Fox's smiling face used to look up at me from vending machines every time I bought a drink.

As a Westerner, you can easily find yourself harboring a subconscious expectation that things are or 'should be' the same as you're used to back home. You get lulled into forgetting that beneath the Americanized surface of Tokyo lies a labyrinthine network of social rules of conduct which the Japanese have internalized from an early age. When we first arrive, we know next to nothing about any of them.

As a result, living and working here often calls for extraordinary stamina, patience and tolerance on many levels. It's unfortunate when a cycle of complaining gets started with you and your foreign friends, because you can focus on the negative anywhere and have a continually unpleasant time of it. And unless you completely turn off, and just stop seeing what's around you, you can't help but notice many positive aspects to life in Japan that help balance out the negatives.

Japanese politeness is legendary for good reason, though some longtime residents of Tokyo will often tell you much of it is a facade. That was perplexing to me at first, because this is a country where I've encountered many unexpected and quite extraordinary acts of kindness from total strangers. From my own experience, I'll always know that what is often said is true – the Japanese people can be extremely courteous and obliging.

Take the other night, for example. I actually got a seat coming home on the *Odakyu Line* for a change. I then nodded off, like half the population, perpetually exhausted as usual. Catching forty winks on the commuter train is truly a civic pastime here. You've never seen so many people 'out like lights' on a train in all your life! But then I should talk – I've taken to it like a politician to polls.

Anyway, at one point in the journey, I reentered the zone of semi-conscious awareness and decided to have a glance at my *International Herald Tribune*. Absorbed by a story on my home and native land – imperiled as usual by Quebec separatism – I suddenly realized my train was now immobile and waiting at a station which might well be mine. Leaping to my feet with an adrenaline rush, I dashed to the doors before they slid shut. Then I caught a glimpse of a station sign, and realized home was still about ten minutes down the line.

My seat, of course, had been instantly filled by another commuter – one of hundreds standing and packed together for the long journey home. I glanced back at my former place and saw a gray-haired gentleman, probably in his 50s. He was now comfortably settled in. He was wearing the large white-gauze mask that many Japanese wear over their mouths and noses when they have a cold. They put them on to protect others from catching it. Is that incredibly considerate? Or quite bizarre? I've had both reactions, depending on my mood. Last night, I simply noticed that he was wearing one, knew he must be under the weather, and didn't give it any thought.

"Oh well," I mused, "it's only another ten minutes to my station." I set about finishing my article standing up.

Meanwhile, the Japanese gentlemen with the white mask had seen what had happened. He understood that I'd mistaken my stop and was now forced to stand, while he occupied my former seat. He himself had been standing for as long as I'd been on the train. He could not possibly know how much further I had to go on my journey home. Ten minutes? Forty-five minutes? An hour? All were possible from that point on the *Odakyu Line*.

I have to conclude that all such considerations were irrelevant to him. As was the fact that he had a cold, and may well have been feeling awful as a result of his condition. Without any hesitation, he bounded to his feet, suggesting that I sit down again. I politely declined, but he persisted. I resisted, and he insisted. We continued this dance for about a minute, until I finally laughed appreciatively and sat down, knowing I could return the seat to him before long. I then read for ten minutes more in comfort, with this wonderful Japanese gentlemen hovering contentedly above me, holding on to the commuter strap for support.

When I got up to leave, he graciously took my seat. I could not see his mouth, of course, covered as it was with the white-gauze mask. But I won't soon forget his eyes. They were sparkling, shining eyes – generous and friendly eyes. This, from a tired, overworked company man with a cold to boot, who might well have felt entitled to his seat. It was a warm and special moment I will not forget – made in Japan.

My Work in Tokyo

Perhaps it's time I explained more about what I actually do in my job. Though I've been a math and English teacher most of my life, four-fifths of my time at my current company is spent *rewriting*: re-working correspondence, proposals, academic articles and promotional material for Soulful Software's products, and turning them into readable English.

The rest of the time I teach company employees – salespeople, engineers, secretaries and receptionists – helping them develop the English skills they need to do their jobs. It can be disconcerting to be a trained English teacher in Japan; the country is filled with fly-by-night teachers who happen to have blonde hair and blue eyes.

Soulful Software is a traditional and well-respected Japanese company, and I like my job very much. The work is interesting and challenging, and I'm always learning something new. By Tokyo standards, it's also reasonably well-paying, though the high cost of living in Tokyo takes care of plenty of my salary. Still, it's a good living, and I'm happy to have work. Fortunately for me – and for all those of us plying the language trade in Japan – many Japanese can read English very well, but writing and speaking are another matter. Far fewer can write coherently, and fewer still can speak English well enough to clearly convey what they mean to say.

Working as a rewriter, I've discovered that my Japanese colleagues can almost all write some English, and the best of them write very well. Even the most disjointed stuff I've read reminds me that I'm an absolute beginner at *Nihongo*. *Hiragana* – a phonetic system for writing things like the endings of adjectives and verbs – is manageable. *Katakana* – another phonetic system used to transcribe foreign words into pronounceable Japanese – can also be mastered without too much difficulty. But learning *kanji* – thousands of Chinese characters – is a monumental undertaking.

Still, much of the so-called *Japlish* (Japanese English) I'm asked to rewrite is riddled with grammatical and semantic problems. The Japanese seem to have every bit as much difficulty with my language as I have with theirs. I've obviously been hired with good reason.

So I often have to talk to the writer – in my still primitive Japanese – to find out exactly what he's trying to say in his writing. This can be a daunting task when the topic is a technical device about which I know precisely zilch. There's a lot of quick learning involved. Rewriting in Japan is seldom just easy proofreading – dotting the i's and crossing the t's. Sometimes what you've been presented with is so discombobulated that you've little choice but to scrap it and start again.

As Soulful Software is an international company, they send out an enormous quantity of correspondence and promotional material in English. That's lucky for me. Japanese companies, universities and schools have given employment to tens of thousands of grateful Canadians, Americans and nationals from many other countries.

On the teaching end, the employees I work with need practice with many skills: writing to foreign companies, speaking on the phone with English-speaking company reps, meeting with foreign visitors and doing face-to-face business in English.

Some are getting ready to head overseas to an American, European, Asian, African or Middle-Eastern destination. They may be going for a week or a month, or they may have been told last week that they're going to Ecuador on a three-year assignment. They come to me, or one of my British or American colleagues – sometimes in a semi-panic – seeking help to prepare for culture and language shock.

On Saturdays I work with managers – all male – many of whom have travelled overseas frequently. They have extensive cross-cultural experience and second language skills. Working with these men can be fascinating. They'll sometimes come out with very provocative observations. One manager who's been to the States dozens of times talked knowingly about his experience. At one point, he made the comment, "Americans never say they're sorry." I've taped some of their conversations as they share these perspectives – often in near-fluent English. They have a lot to say about the various countries they've worked in for Soulful Software.

These men are far more internationally-minded than one might ever imagine from stereotyped media accounts of Japanese company men. When we work together through the long hours of an all-day Saturday workshop, I'm always impressed by the breadth of their knowledge. Then there's their seeming indefatigability. Their diligence and dedication to their company goes a long way in accounting for Japan's economic strength and success.

The Tale of the Cantaloupe

Ah yes, the price of things! As most everyone in North America learned long ago, one of the first things you notice in Tokyo is the outrageous price of just about everything: the price of clothes, the price of restaurants, the price of a cup of coffee in exclusive coffee shops. Surveys consistently list it as the most expensive city in the world, with Osaka normally coming a close second.

But the story that bears repeating – perhaps you've managed not to hear it – has to do with cantaloupes. In a sense, the tale of this fruit is the story of the Japanese economy in the late eighties – disengaged from reality, orbiting in space.

I should first let you know that I'm very partial to cantaloupes. I love cantaloupes. They were always a favourite in my family, especially with vanilla ice cream.

So naturally the first time I saw one, I wanted to check out the price. In Tokyo, you quickly learn that you can't just buy everything you like. You have to make serious choices if you really want to save any money, and some things have to go. But give up cantaloupes? I'd rather not.

So it is that I clearly remember the day I first saw a cantaloupe in Tokyo. It was perched on a sidewalk display outside a Tokyo grocery store. Salivating on sight, my eyes took in the price tag – the amount of hard-earned yen I'd have to part with to savour one of those lovely fruits.

You couldn't miss it – the price was written in big, bold black letters. The cantaloupe itself was comfortably positioned on a bed of shredded green paper strips in a smart-looking wooden box. The price tag was prominently displayed beneath it.

I remember being flabbergasted by what I read. I was with my colleague Kieran, but he'd kept walking up the street as I stopped to gape openmouthed at what I'd seen. The mathematical part of my brain was struggling to make contact with my tongue, to pass on the unbelievable results of its exchange-rate calculations.

"Hey Kieran, look at this, can you believe this cantaloupe? This can't be right – do you know how much they want for this cantaloupe? They want 80 bucks for one cantaloupe!"

There was no mistake. It was highway robbery at the fruit stand! On that day in 1988, with the U.S. dollar at 120 to the yen, the asking price for one cantaloupe in a box was *ichiman-en*, (10,000 Japanese yen). Or – if you preferred twins – it was *niman-en*, 20,000 yen, or $160 U.S., for two boxed cantaloupes on a twin-size bed of shredded green paper.

On the spot, I went cold turkey on cantaloupes in Tokyo. I also began trying to figure out what it was about cantaloupes that made them so outrageously overpriced.

Finding Relief in the Labyrinth

Last night's stress attack appears to have subsided. It struck at about 3:00 a.m. I awoke from a Tokyo dream drama, my brain pulsating with thoughts, all tied-in with that editing job I did yesterday. I never cease to marvel at how the human mind can sift through the events of the day – no matter where on the planet they take place – and come up with an original star-studded cast, a setting and a plot to represent the whole thing on the stage inside the skull.

It was the earthquake that did it, and that unflappable general manager.

One moment I was working diligently through his fractured written English – a letter to Boeing – and suddenly the whole room was rocking like it was going to come undone, the walls flapping like cardboard.

"It's an earthquake," I stammered, trying to stay cool through my first experience of Tokyo's famous seismic volatility. I imagine I looked at him expectantly, hoping at the very least for an echo of my concern.

Instead, he directed a deadpan gaze my way and repressed a sigh. Revealing a touch of exasperation at this obviously oversensitive foreign neophyte, he briskly announced, "Come on, we're wasting time."

The quake, for this corporate Trojan, was an irrelevancy. It was just a blip on the screen of life, a distraction from the work at hand – not even worthy of comment. Of course – these shakers happen all the time in Tokyo, and time is *yen*. I repressed a nervous laugh at my own timidity and the contrast in our reactions.

We actually continued our work without the slightest pause, with the walls and windows still trembling and me along with them. Within a few seconds, the quake was history – likewise any lingering doubt I may have had about how this economic juggernaut shook the world in the 1980s.

As I lay half-awake recalling the moment – lightning bolts of pain streaking from my neck up to my head – Bruce Cockburn's refrain about this city, "Oh Tokyo, I never can sleep in your arms," circled round and round in my skull. At 5:00 a.m., Krista, my very significant other, soothed my aching neck with her magic Minnesota hands before the clock plunged her into the shower and out into the early morning light. She leaves a bit before me these days. I lay in bed for a few more delicious moments, feeling revived and ready, revving-up for my own plunge back into the frenzied vortex of the Tokyo subway system.

Winter Interlude

It's snowing today in Tokyo, though nothing serious by Canadian standards, just light fluffy flakes. But since I still harbor a love of the white stuff from my childhood, the 'first' snowfall of winter is not something I ignore, especially when it comes in March!

I take a few precious moments off to gaze out the office window. I marvel at how the sky here is suddenly filled with what seems like *color*, even though it's just a wash of white. A colorless city like Tokyo starts to stultify your eyes after awhile. Buildings, suits and subway walls – bland and cheerless – are mostly what you get to see, day in and day out, with relatively few splashes of vibrant red and brilliant blue to offer visual relief. Then along come these magnificent white crystals hurtling through space, whirling and whooshing through the urban canyons carved out of the office blocks, buffeted up and down, and this way and that, following no rules set down by human kind.

A childhood memory stirs within me – of windowpanes covered over with cutout paper snowflakes. I get completely absorbed in this freak five-minute interlude in the routine, a reminder of the phenomenal aliveness of nature, this ecstatic dance of frisky crystalline beauties – no two alike.

I glance up the road a stretch. The street is like a clean, white sheet of music paper, crisscrossed with nonsensical black lines going every which way, right on up to Tokyo Station. My childhood reverie yields another memory – 'Every Good Boy Deserves Favor,' or was it fudge? – that's how we learned to remember the lines on the musical staff that went with the treble cleff.

Living in Tokyo, one is too seldom reminded during a normal working day of the spontaneous splendor of nature. So I savour this fleeting wonder a few moments longer. Then almost as quickly as it began, the sky resumes its gray pose, as if this ephemeral event had all been in my imagination.

"I could have ignored this," I think to myself. "But these are the moments that keep you alive in Tokyo."

I turn back to the word processor to help my Japanese company please a few more customers.

Thoughts in Telephone Limbo

When I first used phones here, at work or at home, it was hilarious to be put 'on-hold.' For a long time in Japan, computerized melodies of the same four tunes were the standards: (1) *Home on the Range*, (2) *Greensleeves*, (3) Beethoven's *Fur Elise*, and (4) *Red River Valley*.

This is in Tokyo, you ask? It's occurred to me that maybe it's all aimed at soothing overseas buyers while they wait. In other words, the whole country is making the sacrifice of listening to these foreign melodies, so that no American business person will be put off when they're put on hold. Instead, they'll be immediately soothed by familiar melodies with deep roots in their past.

When you're on the phone here dozens of times a day, it's not surprising to find yourself humming along under your breath to phrases like, "Where the deer and the antelope play." You find yourself reflecting on the fact that you haven't sung that song since you were eleven, sitting on a wet log somewhere in time gazing at a campfire. At such times, life in Tokyo can seem dreamlike.

While waiting to be connected, I also find myself pondering things like the incongruity between life in Tokyo and the lyrical content of some of these tunes.

Take *Home on the Range*. I finally concluded that the words probably speak to the Japanese of the wide open spaces most have never known, and will certainly never know here in Tokyo. The American West with its vast oceans of prairie grass must seem like Shangri-la to hard-pressed Tokyo Japanese.

For those of us lucky enough to have experienced such unrestrained, open spaces, where the skies 'are not cloudy all day,' it can get quite bizarre listening to a computerized version of *Home on the Range* 20 or 30 times a day. Especially while you're staring into the brick wall across the road from your desk. The sad truth is that most Tokyo Japanese may never even see an open range, let alone have a home there. It's easy to understand the fantasy appeal of this song and the spacious sense of freedom it evokes.

For Westerners like me, endless repetitions of these electronic on-hold melodies can get mighty tiresome. Fortunately, I've found a finer musical side to Tokyo. My local 'import' grocery store plays Beethoven symphonies, not neutered muzak versions – the real Ludwig! The other day I reached the tail end of my shopping list just after the thunderstorm in the *Pastorale*. It was mildly transcendent.

It's not that you don't hear muzak in Tokyo. A *kissaten* (coffee shop) treated me to a horrendous string version of *Ticket to Ride* the other morning that made me want to howl a lament for John Lennon.

Yes, muzak is ubiquitous, but it hasn't completely taken over yet. You find relief in the most unexpected places. One day waiting for a friend in the enormous sprawl of Ueno station, I was treated to authentic Vivaldi, Mozart and Debussy.

It was a pleasant surprise. Back home in Canada, I used to daydream about what could be done with music to bring cities alive. I imagined malls and subway tunnels enlivened by Bach organ music and triumphant Beethoven symphonies. Japan is the last place I expected to find a bit of this. It remains one of Tokyo's simple pleasures.

Earthquake #2

We had another earthquake early this morning – at 5:35 a.m. I can see this is going to take some getting used to. I was jolted into semi-consciousness to witness what looked like a bedroom adrift on moderately rough seas. The walls and ceiling of our 60-year-old house seemed to curve like a belly dancer as they rode the shock waves.

Ten seconds later everything was still – except my thoughts, which had started up where the quake left off.

"We're going to voluntarily live in this danger zone for how long?" came a shaken inner voice.

After a few more unsettling thoughts, the inner quake also subsided and

I got up, followed my normal routine and headed off down the hill to catch – as always – the 7:24 a.m. morning train. Trains are on time 'to the second' in Tokyo, and most people follow the same commuting schedule everyday.

Being a novice when it comes to earthquakes, it hadn't occurred to me that normal life might be seriously disrupted by such an event. One glance at the train station, and it began to dawn on me.

The platform was pandemonium. Wall-to-wall commuters were all packed together, waiting for trains that were 45 minutes late. The expired train times on the electronic timetable boards meant nothing. There was total disruption of the normally precise schedule.

An express pulled in and my eyes did a somersault in their sockets. There were already a substantially larger number of people on board than I'd ever seen before, and this is a train that had always struck me as filled to beyond bursting. It's simply indescribable how crowded those cars were!

What happened next was even more amazing. Somehow, the sliding doors managed to open, but nobody on the inside budged, though it's very likely that somebody wanted to get out. Escaping from a maximum security prison couldn't have been much more difficult.

Then, without a second's delay, the mob waiting on the platform began surging forward. I stood back and watched, astonished at what I was seeing.

"There's just no room," I thought to myself, "there's not enough space for one more human being in there!"

Yet, as I had that thought, throngs of people at every entrance began exerting all their strength to get on that train, as though it were the last available way out of a disaster area that was about to explode into flames in ten minutes time.

As a last resort, a few young *salarymen* – no doubt extremely concerned about making a bad impression by being late for work – began trying to launch themselves bodily up and over the assembled mass. They were trying in any way they could to get to the other side of those doors before they slid shut. I swear I'm not exaggerating; it's a Tokyo scene I'll remember forever.

In spite of all their efforts, few were successful in getting aboard. Nevertheless, the scene was repeated with every express train that came through. These guys looked like salmon spawning at Hell's Gate Canyon on the Fraser River, leaping into the air to get upstream against the current.

Not knowing what else to do, I positioned myself next to a thick metal pole, one of many that serve to hold up the roof of the platform. It gave me some protection from the frenzied jostling, and allowed me to just take in the whole drama. I had no idea how I would get to work, but I knew that the later it got, the worse the situation would get. Peak rush hour normally begins at about 8:30, and it was only 7:45. At one point, I laughed out loud, shaking my head in disbelief. Then a startling thing happened.

When your Japanese is as basic as mine is at this stage, you get so used to not being able to speak to people that it doesn't even occur to you to try. If I do manage to meet someone in public who speaks some English, most of the time it's as elementary as my Japanese.

So imagine my surprise, in the midst of all this tumult, to hear a Japanese voice, calmly and with much joviality, quietly remark, "It's a madhouse, isn't it!"

It was a middle-aged Japanese man whose English was very good. He'd spent a lot of time in Chicago on business, I was to learn. We chatted amiably about the earthquake and how crazy the whole scene was. It was such an unexpected relief to be able to talk to someone about what was going on, that most of my stress just dissolved into amusement.

"Take the local train," he suggested. "It'll take longer, of course, but you'll get there. Everybody's going to be late this morning, whether they like it or not."

I thanked him for his kindness, said goodbye and took his advice. Stepping onto the local train, I noted that it was almost as crowded as the express train 'normally' is.

Little did I know what lay ahead. After a long delay, we finally pulled out, stopping at every single station on the way to Shinjuku in central Tokyo. The closer we got to our destination, the more people began to adopt the same idea the Japanese gentleman had recommended to me. Being inside that train got crazier with each stop.

To make matters worse, as you get closer to Shinjuku, the express train no longer stops. So the local train is the only option for those at the last three stations. That meant that each time we stopped, everyone on the platform was trying to get on our train.

There finally came a point in time when I honestly felt like I was fighting for my life and in some danger of being trampled and/or squeezed to death, or both. Claustrophobics definitely need not apply.

In the end, I lived through that experience and got to work an hour late, and the next morning the train seemed just a tad full. The commute has never seemed quite so bad since that day – the morning of earthquake #2. It's amazing what contrast can do for your perception of things.

International *Salarymen*

Some of the men I've met through my job are remarkable people. No doubt many of the women are equally interesting, but I get fewer chances to meet them at work. Not to mention that the gender barrier seems more formidable, and that prevents easy communication.

During a seminar on cross-cultural experiences, I interviewed male company employees who'd been stationed abroad at some point in their careers. I quickly learned that Japanese love to talk about their overseas experiences, and it's a real icebreaker.

As part of this work, I spoke with a group of men in their early thirties who'd been sent by the company to Libya some years before on a three-year assignment. They had – they told me – no choice in the matter, except to go or to resign. (One of their colleagues did, in fact, resign rather than be subjected to Libyan hospitality.)

They had harrowing stories to tell, about social circumstances and rules that changed from one day to the next. I immediately felt able to relate to their experiences, having passed the better part of 1978 in Iran. At that time, I was working for the British Council in Meshed, in the days leading up to the revolution there.

In Libya, they lived in a company dorm with a checkpoint entrance, manned by guards with machine guns and unpredictable temperaments. One day, as they prepared to exit their compound, the guard demanded that they fix his heater before leaving for the pier where they worked – processing company products as they arrived from Japan, and dealing with Libyan customs. The Libyan guard had spent the whole night freezing in his checkpoint cabin, and he was not happy about it.

At first they attempted to explain that this was not their responsibility. His mounting fury and menacing machine gun quickly assured them that this was the wrong tack to take. They soon set about fixing his heater for him, which took most of the day.

Another time, on entering the customs pier in the morning, they were asked to leave their official security clearance cards at the entry point. They'd never had to do this before, but were assured it was necessary on that day. In the evening, when they attempted to pass through the checkpoint to leave the pier for the day, a different guard was on duty. He demanded to see their clearance cards, and claimed to know nothing about what had happened in the morning. They were immediately held under suspicion, and it took them hours to get the situation sorted out.

I came away from these interviews with plenty of respect for the courage, tolerance and sense of humor of these men, as well as with a good feeling that I had much in common with them. We felt a connection through our shared experiences. Clearly, they were lucky to get out unscathed, as I'd been in Iran.

Others were not so lucky. They told me that during their stay in Libya, another Japanese company employee made a grave mistake. While on a domestic flight, he pulled his camera out and took a photo out the plane window. He was arrested for spying after the plane landed, and he'd been in jail for nearly three years at the time we did the interview. All appeals by the Japanese consulate to release the man had fallen on deaf ears.

Still another poor fellow they heard about (not a Japanese) was arrested on entering Libya for possession of fruit bonbons. He hadn't noticed that they contained a tiny quantity of alcohol. He was kept in prison for 11 months.

Encounters with international Japanese businessmen who have been out of the country and can recount fascinating stories like these for hours on end, are enlightening for foreign residents like myself. We might otherwise form a very skewed view of Japanese company men, given that those who have never left Japanese soil can all too often come across as uninspired, lacking in personality or enthusiasm for life.

This impression has to be handled with care, because it can simply be a reflection of cultural differences. A great example of this comes courtesy of my neighbours in Setagaya, a wonderfully friendly Japanese couple who recently got married. When they were showing us the photos of their wedding – 'us' being a group of their *gaijin* friends who know and love them both – Jeannie, an Australian, burst into laughter. She howled with amusement, and got us all going, because Toshi was not smiling in any of the photos. "Toshi, it's your wedding," Jeannie teased, "not the beginning of the end!"

From a Western perspective, it looked like he was attending his own funeral. Even though his new wife, Kimiko, was smiling radiantly, Toshi looked grim and anything but happy. But we know this guy well for the sweetheart he is. He's just very low-key, and can appear to be somber when he's not at all. This experience helped me greatly in learning to deal with, and not pre-judge, the emotional flatness I often encounter in the men at Soulful Software.

Some are natural introverts, no doubt, much as you'd find anywhere. Others may be typical Japanese guys, though I have to say that a lot of the men I meet do not seem much enthused about their lives or their work, or at least they don't express it. It's hard to get a sense of how they feel, and it's easy to conclude that they don't feel all that good about life.

So it's refreshing to meet others who defy this norm and are very much alive, conversationally engaging and internationally minded. A high percentage of the time, you discover they've spent time outside Japan. As a result, they've adopted a more Western-style personality which is, naturally, more what I'm used to as a Canadian. Admittedly, that's also my bias.

With many of the younger men I work with in classroom settings, a passive and emotionless response to what we're working on together is quite common. I admit that this impassivity is something I have difficulty accepting as a natural and normal response to life. But I'm aware that I may just be struggling with the age-old differences between the Orient and the Occident.

At the very least, for many of these men a good vacation or change of scene seems long overdue. I often think that getting sent overseas is the best thing that could happen to them, even if their destination is Libya.

I'm finding that this emotional lassitude can be challenging when you come up against it everyday. I've noticed that many of my *salarymen* colleagues come to life and are much more personable one-on-one, when we're working on a letter or a contract. My best hunch is that it's in settings that resemble a school environment that this listlessness really kicks in.

Of course, living and working in Tokyo for years on end must have something to do with it, and the men with international experience are the lucky ones, in my view. Returning from their ordeals in Libya, they give renewed meaning to the Japanese expression *Genki des* ("I'm doing great"). It's the upbeat response to the question, "*O genki desu ka?*" (How are you?), and when they say it, I know they mean it. They ought to give lessons in 'seizing the day' to their less inspired colleagues, the ones who usually tell me they're feeling *ma ma* ("So so") on any given day.

Advantage Japan

One of the great things about Tokyo is the virtual absence of street hustlers and confidence tricksters. When I reflect on that, life here becomes immediately more pleasant and bearable, even at the most stressful of times. Generally speaking, Japanese people just leave you alone. On a normal day, nobody ever bothers you.

In many countries in Asia and Europe, targeting tourists and foreigners is a growth industry. By comparison, you can walk down any street in Tokyo without ever being approached by young hustlers trying to sell you a 'copy watch' - a fake Rolex. In cities like Hong Kong, this is a regular event.

Tokyo would be still more stressful if this were an everyday occurrence here as well. But there are very few street solicitations, at least for non-Japanese. Many companies hire people to hand out flyers and free packages of tissues with advertising on them - but you can take them or just pass on by. There's nothing 'in your face' about it at all.

There are also very few people walking around trying to scam tourists in Tokyo. On my first day in Paris years ago, my friends and I were approached by a talkative Frenchman who offered to take us to a 'good' restaurant where the food was excellent. He ordered a large meal for himself, wolfed it down and then excused himself to go to the restroom. He never returned, and we had to pay his bill. Bad luck? I hope so. But such experiences can leave you with a rotten feeling about a country.

In Tokyo, it's very unlikely that such a thing would happen. I can stand on a busy street corner here with a map open – broadcasting with my blonde hair, blue eyes and dazed look that I'm a lost foreign tourist – and the only person who approaches me will be someone offering to help me find my way.

What you do occasionally get is young people – allegedly cult members of one kind or another – approaching you with clipboards, but only at major train stations in Tokyo and Kyoto. They ask for donations for the oddest causes, but you just have to look away and they're off to petition someone else. I gave a hundred yen once in a weak moment and received the reply, "Next time, give more."

In India, you can sample the delights of architectural wonders like the Taj Mahal, but you also have to deal with the constant harassment of con artists and rickshaw drivers who want to take you to their brother's rug shop, instead of to your destination. When we were in Agra it became so irritating that I finally asked somebody how to say, in Hindi, "I don't want a rickshaw, thanks." That didn't change a thing; the incessant pestering continued unabated. I was finally driven to learn "*Kootch nei chaiyei!*" – "I don't want anything!"

That just provoked raucous laughter, and the harassment resumed. It's been much the same for everyone I've ever spoken to who's visited Agra, and it's put a damper on many a visit there.

You encounter no such problems in Tokyo, one of the world's largest cities. If you take the train three hours north to visit the great temples of Nikko, you'll find the same thing – virtually no harassment of any kind. In fact, you can travel the whole length and breadth of the country and seldom be bothered by anyone trying to hustle you. It's a truly remarkable fact of life in Japan.

In Amritsar, on my first day in India, a cashier in a train station tried to take advantage of my unfamiliarity with the currency by giving me change for a 50-rupee note instead of the 500-rupee note I'd given him. Such a thing is an absolute rarity in Japan. On the same trip to India, I met a couple in New Delhi who'd been conned into giving away all their traveller's checks in hopes of getting a cheaper rate. In Japan, nobody ever approaches you with an offer of this kind – it's unheard of.

In Thailand, travellers are warned not to take offers of food or drink from Thai people. How sad it is to have to heed such a warning in a land with so many sweet people, but you're foolish not to. Stories abound of con artists slipping heavy-duty sleeping potions into drinks, and then robbing their victims. I personally know several people to whom this has happened, and it nearly happened to me once. In Japan, you'd be more likely to be attacked by aliens with three heads than to fall prey to such a scam.

In Jakarta, two good friends were on a crowded city bus with their two children when they were surreptitiously robbed. At the moment they realized something was missing, half a dozen passengers said in unison, "He's getting off now, that's him!" They quickly jumped off to chase whoever it was, at which point Rich's young son - who'd seen it all happen - said, "Daddy, that's not the man who did it, he didn't get off." As the bus pulled away, they realized they'd been *had* by a very organized group of thieves.

There are pickpockets on the Tokyo transport system, that's for sure. They seem to operate independently and furtively, although the newspapers sometimes report that a 'Korean gang' is currently operating on the trains. Still, the kind of conspiratorial theft my friends were victims of in Jakarta would be a freak in Tokyo.

People generally have their wallets stolen here out of cavalier carelessness, by leaving them in an exposed pocket or backpack. Many Japanese, lulled into a false sense of security by exaggerated reports of the safety of their country, do not even take basic precautions. But if you're mindful and careful, your wallet is far safer in Tokyo than in any city this size that I know of.

As for taxis, the Japanese are very precise. The sooner you can learn how to say exactly where you're going in *Nihongo*, the better. Drivers may get angry out of a kind of panic or frustration if you're vague, or if you can't give clear directions in Japanese. But if you know your way and can direct the driver, *masugu* (straight) *migi* (right) and *hidari* (left) are pretty much all you need to say.

It took me some time, and a few uncomfortable experiences to learn this, but once I did, my problems with taxi drivers basically ceased. It may be expensive, but the price is fixed. You'll never be cheated, a rare thing in the great cities of the world. I've taken plenty of taxis here now, and it's an extremely uncommon thing in Japan for a cabbie to take you on a roundabout route to increase the fare. Meanwhile, if the driver's been to Canada, I usually have a great chat with him about the places he visited. One such man even gave me a discount to show his good will towards me.

I compare this with ripoffs I've experienced in the U.S., such as arriving late for a flight at an airport, giving the driver $15 for an $11 fare and being told he had no change. Not only will this *never* happen to you here, but the driver does not expect a tip. Advantage Japan.

Japanese Women: Feminism Not

It's now well known in the West that from the point of view of women's rights, Japan still seems to resemble '50s and '60s America in many ways. At Soulful Software and most other large Japanese companies, women continue to do all the routine work like photocopying, answering phones, greeting guests and serving tea. They still serve as receptionists, they serve as computer typists, and above all, they serve the men in whatever way the men need to be served.

In the working world, Japanese women are very much second-tier citizens, and suggestions that it's 'rapidly' changing are fanciful, with exceptions proving the rule. Most women here have little hope of climbing the company ladder to managerial positions at anytime in the foreseeable future. For the most part, they occupy the lower rungs in corporate settings, a gender-determined underclass.

In Canada, women now comprise upwards of 50% of middle managers, though they've made much less headway with upper management positions. No such change of this magnitude is occurring in Japan. An enormous pool of untapped energy lies in waiting for male-dominated Japan to recognize its power.

The traditional corporate expectation still holds sway – women are not to be taken as seriously as men in the working world. Despite evidence to the contrary, it's still expected that female university graduates will stick around for about five to seven years, then get married and leave the company to have children. Those who fail in this quest, or choose not to find a man to support them, may end up as lifers – like their *salarymen* colleagues – but with major differences. Their chances at significant promotion are not great. The faces of directors and managers in publications such as my company brochure are exclusively men, mostly gray-haired, promoted to the top by seniority that's based on age and years of service.

Even as Japan has taken quantum leaps forward in terms of increasing its power and wealth, the message Japanese women receive remains fairly constant: career paths are for men; the company a woman has worked for is not interested in rehiring her once the children are in school; Western feminism doesn't apply to Japan; the choices American and European women have fought for don't fit with the Japanese way of life.

This would be a bleak fate for a gifted and ambitious Western woman who wants a career, and seeks the same opportunities for advancement as men. Krista, like most of the American women I know, can get livid when she talks about what women in Japan put up with.

But there is a baffling side to all of this. Many Japanese women don't seem angry or bitter at all, at least from what they show you of themselves. I've helped one group of about eight young office women in our company with their English at lunchtime. I've found them to be consistently lighthearted, cheerful and pleasant to talk with, albeit very conservative - dressed immaculately in their blue and gray uniforms

One day, a young woman announced that she's going to have a baby and will be leaving the company soon. The others laughed and clapped their hands like schoolgirls to share their congratulations, though I could see the woman on the spot was embarrassed. Perhaps that was because a man was in their midst, a foreign guy no less, hearing this personal news about her pregnancy. But they were one happy bunch of women that day - there was no doubting that - and they were very pleasant to have lunch with.

I know little, as yet, about how the women of Tokyo really feel about their lives. But one thing has already been brought home to me. When you make cross-cultural comparisons, you're covering a lot of uncharted territory. Approaching another culture from a starting point that yours is right is a surefire way to learn nothing about that culture.

Rivers of Money in Bubble Japan

In the *bubble* years of the late 1980s, it was often said that Japanese people actually 'preferred'' to pay more. At the very least, they certainly weren't worrying about 'getting a good deal.' Rivers of money were gushing around the country, and ostentatiously spending large sums of it was a living demonstration that you were part of the action.

During my lunch hour, I used to wander around the Nihonbashi *Takashimaya Departo* near my office and just gape openmouthed at the prices. While women's purses, priced at 575,000 yen ($4,750 U.S.), were causing my eyeballs to turn into slinkies, the Japanese appeared to be taking it in stride. It all seemed to be announcing: move over America - Japan has arrived! What an amazing time it was to be in Japan.

I remember working one day with a group of my company's businessmen and discussing the Gross Domestic Product (G.D.P.) of various nations.

"Who has the largest?" I asked.

"Japan," said Mr. Honda, an up-and-comer in his mid-twenties.

"Ah, no," I said, a little surprised, "the U.S. is still the largest, but Japan is second."

We compared the numbers. At that time, Japan, in U.S. dollars, had become a strong second, way ahead of other nations.

Out of curiosity, I remember asking, "And who will have the largest G.D.P. in ten years' time?"

"Oh, that would be Japan," said Mr. Honda without a moment's hesitation.

It was a reflection of the times. You could cut the underlying brashness with a knife. In Mr. Honda's mind, it was a given that Japan would soon declare economic victory over America.

People had money, and they had 'attitude,' which revealed itself through Japan being a nation of prestige seekers. If there was logic involved, perhaps it went along the lines of, "If it costs more and has a brand name, the quality must be better," coupled with, "Now that we're on top, we buy only the best as a demonstration of our status."

On a trip to Bali, Krista and I discovered that Japanese tourists were being bussed to jewelry stores set up especially for them. We checked and found that the prices were up to a hundred times more than the local price! One ring I'd priced at 125 rupiah in the market was 10,000 rupiah at the tourist store. Being international neophytes in the travel world, many Japanese just paid without a care, especially since the prices seemed comparable to yen prices they would pay back in Japan.

But price differentials between Japan and North America could be shocking. On a trip home to Canada, I bought a good quality raincoat for $75 U.S. after seeing its equivalent in a Tokyo *deparo* (department store) for roughly ten times the price - 73,000 yen. I also took notes on the price of rice. In B.C., a 20 kg. bag of my favourite long-grain brown rice was $12 U.S., whereas in Tokyo, a *one* kg. bag of brown rice was only slightly less, 1,240 yen ($10).

Japan's political firecracker, Shintaro Ishihara, provided an explanation for his country's exorbitant prices. In his words, "Japan's complex wholesale and retail distribution channels are a knotty problem. An army of middlemen drive consumer prices sky high."

I remember spotting, in Nihonbashi's *Daimaru Deparo*, the same Seiko travel alarm clock I'd bought in Montreal for $45 U.S. just before coming to Japan. Curious, I checked the price. Had I paid more in Canada than I would have in Japan? After all, the clock had been made here. How much were the Japanese paying for their own company's product?

The price tag was a shock: 12,000 yen, or $100 U.S. at the rate of the day. So, the Japanese were paying more than double what I'd paid for a Seiko clock made in their own country. I later spoke to a Seiko dealer in Canada who confirmed my finding with the simple comment, "Oh yeah, everything's double in Japan."

If the sharp rise in the value of the yen in the '80s had increased costs for Japanese exporters, it seemed the Japanese people themselves were the ones to pay for it, unknowingly and uncomplainingly.

I later told my Seiko alarm clock story to Japanese university students and found they were incredulous. But then, how would they know such things without traveling abroad? In a similar vein, most Canadians were oblivious to huge discount incentives my American collegues were receiving for flying to Tokyo through Canada on Canadian carriers.

In the midst of learning about these marketplace anomalies and coming to terms with Japan's exorbitant prices, a baffling thing happens to a newcomer to Tokyo. You experience the remarkable 'money's-no-object generosity' that many Japanese extend toward newly arrived Westerners visiting their country. You may want to respond, but you often don't know how to do so appropriately. Nor do you necessarily have the money to reciprocate in kind.

After awhile, you pick up that as a new foreign 'guest,' you're not expected to know anything about Japanese social rules of obligation and reciprocation. You're out of the loop, and that's one of the things that attracts some Japanese to Westerners – they don't have to engage in relations and exchanges based on *giri* (obligatory social duty) with us.

Giri is a formalized and systematized approach to social relations and the obligations that come with them. In *Nihongo*, my brother-in-law – my *older* sister's husband – would be my *giri no ani*. He's someone with whom I have a *giri* relationship. If I were Japanese, I would have very specific obligations to him because he married my sister. In Japanese culture, these obligations are very important, and they sometimes seem to be like chains that bind people to required behavior.

It's my sense that the natural inclination of many Japanese to give freely and unconditionally finds an outlet with Westerners. For once, they don't have to worry about protocol. I've come to believe most Japanese don't really care if we reciprocate or not, and when we do, it can actually cause problems. Once you give something back, your Japanese hosts may then feel obliged to reciprocate again, just as they would if you were another Japanese with whom they had a *giri* bond.

One American friend, Marianne, a longtime Japan resident, told me of an experience she had with the owner of a local flower shop, someone she passed every day on the way from the station to her home. The florist, a middle-aged Japanese woman, kept giving her small potted plants for free. One day, Marianne decided to return the favour and brought something to the florist, who promptly recoiled in horror and refused to accept it. Sadly, after that their relationship basically dissolved.

All of this can lead to major cross-cultural confusion on the part of clueless *gaijin*. Many Westerners just opt out, accepting gifts with a gracious thank you or declining them altogether. You learn not to talk too much about things you really like, because a Japanese who overhears you may go right out and buy it for you.

Krista has been very careful to explain her feelings about gift giving to her Japanese friends and students.

"Please don't bring me gifts," she told them bluntly. "It's not necessary."

In spite of this, during one gift-giving season – Ōseibo in mid-December – one of her students in Sendai brought her a huge basket of fruit.

"You're not including me in gift giving, Tomoko, are you? You know I explained how I feel about it."

"Oh, I know," replied the young woman, unruffled. "It's just that my father's a professor and the house is piling up with fruit. Please, take some of it – otherwise, it's all just going to rot!"

'Waste' alone often seems like a good enough reason for opting out of the Japanese gift-giving rituals.

As for the exorbitant price of things, Krista and I are typical North Americans. We'd just as soon pay less if we can find a bargain that doesn't seriously sacrifice quality. Speaking of bargains, since my first sighting of a cantaloupe in Tokyo, I now know that those high-priced boxed fruits are intended to be gifts for the fulfilling of *giri*. You'd never buy them for yourself for dessert. It turns out that when you take away the wooden box and the green shredded paper, the price of cantaloupes in this city plummets to 2,000 yen – a big improvement. But that's still 16 bucks a melon.

I kept looking. Eventually, I found that in many stores, there's always a mound of less-than-perfect specimens – meaning there's a little discoloration, or they're a bit bruised. There's an obsession in Japan with external perfection in fruit – among other things – but on the inside, these melons taste just as good as their high-priced cousins.

And how much are they, these poor, delicious mutants? They're a mere 550 yen ($4) each at our local grocery, and that's as good as it gets. If you want cantaloupe melons in Tokyo, that's the bottom line.

And what's the bottom line for foreigners like us? Probably the same as most Americans and Canadians. Give us the option to pay 20 times less, and we'll manage just fine without the box and the fancy paper.

This is Service!

For me, one of the really pleasant aspects to life in Japan is the quality of service you get. It's so consistently first rate. Many proprietors, especially small-business people, will often go the extra mile for you unhesitatingly.

There's very little of the "I'm just doing this job" attitude here that we've often witnessed back home. People working in a department store or restaurant almost invariably give you their best. It's clearly an area of life in which Japan excels. One wishes they could upgrade the quality of service around the world, the same way their competitiveness forced an improvement in American car quality.

Noticing the negative effects of the company work ethic on the Japanese people in Tokyo is easy – so many look exhausted and overworked during the commute. But when you're their customer, the 'service ethic' in place when people are on the job offers a refreshing counterbalance. It's one of the positive features of the Japanese devotion to their working lives that I quickly came to respect.

Take the other day, for example. I'd just bought a second-hand ten-speed bicycle from a Canadian friend who's returning home. It's a bike he brought over from Canada when he came to Tokyo two years ago.

I went looking for some kind of headlight so I could ride the bike at night, and I soon found one in an accessories stall outside a small department store. Without my even asking, the proprietor immediately offered to hook it up for me. I happily agreed, because I don't have any bicycle tools with me in Japan, and it was an unusual type of light I'd never used before. It's the kind that operates on the energy you generate in riding the bike – the faster you pedal, the brighter the light. Nifty, but it might have taken me an hour to put it on myself.

He promptly whipped out a tool box, and had it ready to go within five minutes. Not only did he not charge me for this, but he smiled, said *sabisu* (meaning 'free service') and proceeded to give me the equivalent of a $5 discount off the list price, because it was my first visit to his store. That, it turns out, is a common practice in Japan – designed to make a good first impression, no doubt.

It makes quite an impression, especially when it happens to you again and again. I've quickly become enamored of this aspect of Japanese life. How could you not? You encounter it everywhere, and it makes life easier.

You drive a car into a gas station and watch with amazement as male and female attendants, in brightly coloured uniforms, pore over your vehicle like you were the King of Thailand. Eventually, they run out onto the street to stop traffic and help get you back on the road, bowing to those who have stopped to let you by.

It's quite a sight when you first see it. I'm still asking myself: What accounts for this unforced courteousness, this emphasis on good service, this willingness and desire to do one's job so well at all times?

It's probably a combination of things: the deeply rooted emphasis on fulfilling one's social obligation, and a fear-based sense that you must do your best or risk social ostracism and loss of face. But I believe it's also an honest expression of good will.

In Japan, I find myself reminded of encounters I had in the Middle East. Travelling through Turkey in the 1970s, nine of us - all Westerners - stopped at a tea shop one afternoon. When it came time to pay, the proprietor gently waved us off. He pointed to a man sitting quietly in the corner, who put his hand over his heart when we turned to acknowledge him. He had paid for us all, the owner told us.

Later, working in Iran, I was often invited into Iranian homes for a meal and treated very sweetly. It was there that I learned the phrase *Guest is God*. Sometimes in Japan, I think they've got their own version: *Customer is God*.

After thanking my bicycle repairman for his help, I hopped on my newly equipped two-wheeler and headed home. The experience must have been the crowning moment in a series of similarly positive experiences, because along the way a little poem by Rabindranath Tagore sprang to mind. It's one I learned years ago when working for a charity service organization in Montreal: "I slept and dreamt that life was joy, I awoke to find that life was service. I served and lo! Service was joy."

Perhaps many Japanese know something that a lot of us in the West have forgotten. I'd like to think so. The experience of half-hearted or mediocre service has become too common an event back home, and my intuition tells me there is genuineness in what I'm experiencing here.

Some longtime foreign residents in Japan will find me starry-eyed, no doubt, believing that this widespread service ethic basically reflects something much more mundane - the ingrained social requirements of master/servant relationships or meeting the demands of competition.

There's no doubt truth to that as well. But that doesn't put a damper on my appreciation of people such as my bicycle shop man. He and many others like him have shown me a civil side of Japanese life I greatly admire.

Let me state it here and now for the record: Service in Japan is consistently excellent, more reliable and carried out with more grace than back home in Canada or the U.S. For that matter, I've now visited nearly 30 countries in my travels, and I put Japan pretty much at the top of the list.

Excuse me, What's this Language?

Well documented by now is the fact that all visitors to Japan are instantly struck by the ubiquitous presence of a language on T-shirts, handbags and the sides of delivery trucks that bears a striking resemblance to English, but turns out to be a mutant form.

You quickly realize that this unique vernacular should not be probed for meaning, especially when you live here and you're exposed to the stuff on a daily basis. Most of the time, there's no meaning to be had.

Occasionally, I realize my mind is trying to deduce what *might* have been intended if the expression had been concocted by a native speaker. But since this is seldom the case, looking for meaning is a dangerous practice. It opens up a semantic black hole into which I've recklessly plunged many times.

A characteristic sample from slogan-enhanced T-shirts I've acquired along the way as gifts explains it best: *Earth: A judgment on anything cooly maintain your composure to enable you to form.* [sic]

Absurdly, you find yourself pondering these ludicrous little pronouncements for a few seconds, and trying to wring meaning out of them. That's a ridiculous pastime, because the stuff is everywhere, and most of it's nonsensical. If you let yourself do this every time you see a blurb in English, you'll wind up feeling crazy. But it's hard to completely avoid because your mind recognizes the English words and automatically searches for meaning.

Occasionally, the feeling comes over you that you're living in a home for blithering imbeciles – of which I am one – a linguistic nether world where English is still used but has been stripped of all meaning – rendered idiotic. You're drifting in a kind of semantic daze through streets of what seems like a futuristic movie set, confronted on all sides by madhatter T-shirts, signs for LOVE hamburger chains, train station kiosks called LET'S and hotels named WITH.

When I get like this, I quickly make my way to an English movie theater for cultural reorientation.

Here's one on a shoulder bag: *Men's Bats: Gives life and grace to life's unquiet dreams.*[sic]

Before you can stop it, your mind asks the question: Are we talking baseball bats here? You have to train yourself not to start the inquiry. If you live in Tokyo and spend time dwelling on these ludicrous proclamations, you may end up unhinged and mumbling to yourself in subways.

The best approach is to immediately dismiss the nonsensical fragments, all the while keeping an eye open for the gems. They're easy to recognize – you don't have to think twice about their meaning.

At lunch one day, we saw a noticeably plump teenage girl whose T-shirt shouted at us in large red letters: 'Fatty potamus.'

The poor girl is surely oblivious to how this sounds to an English speaker, or she'd never be wearing it. Fortunately for her, it's safe to assume that few Japanese will ever understand the connotations either.

For young Japanese, snippets of foreign languages on T-shirts have a strong appeal, but the actual meaning of the words seems to be irrelevant. It's the 'foreignness' itself that holds the attraction. Meanwhile, gibberish is king. It's an odd phenomenon.

Sometimes, you read one that does have a clear meaning, but that doesn't mean it's understood. I saw another teenage girl whose T-shirt message was in French. It translated as, "I'm available anytime." Curious, I asked her if she knew what it meant.

"No," she replied, in a manner that showed it hadn't occurred to her to wonder, but seemed to reveal her embarrassment at not knowing.

"Would you like to know?" I asked.

"No," she said again, looking flustered. I left well enough alone.

But my favorite to date, author unknown, shrieks to any English-speaking passerby in need of a good laugh from a small, china cup in the window display of a restaurant near our office: "Once upon a time, when the man was the man and the woman was the woman – they had to elegant ferocity with each other." [sic]

Ah yes, those were the days, my friend.

Joke-Jitsu

Ever since I joined Soulful Software, I've been studying Japanese for an hour and a half, two afternoons a week. The lessons are provided courtesy of the company. They're great about assisting you to learn the language to help you do your job. I have to confess, however, that I haven't been the best of students. I do my three hours of study a week, and that's about it. For one thing, I'm overwhelmed by the complexities of the writing system, not to mention the fact that this is a language that conjugates adjectives. I thought French verbs were tough until I started studying *Nihongo*.

Nevertheless, I can say a lot of things in Japanese now, and I do my best to speak when opportunities arise. It's essential when I need to rewrite a rough draft of a letter by an employee who speaks no English – but has writing ability – and I need to seek an explanation of what he's trying to say in order to get the meaning right.

I always greet the *kanrinin* (guard/doorman) in the lobby and pick up the key if I'm the first one at the office. He's very obliging, though somewhat somber.

His female co-worker, a caretaker, is much more expressive when she's there, sometimes offering me a warm smile.

Both of them must be in their 60s and as of yet, I know nothing more about them. Every morning at 8:10 when I arrive at work, we say *Ohaiyo gozaimas* (Good morning) to each other; this and an exchange of short bows has become a simple morning ritual. Even as my *Nihongo* got better, I wasn't sure what else it would be appropriate to say.

Recently, as we headed into late November and the weather started to cool down, they introduced me to a new refrain, a followup to *Ohaiyo gozaimas*. I'd long ago learned the words for cold (*samui*) and hot (*atsui*), so I understood them right away.

"*Samui des ne!*" he said, with some concern. (It's cold today, isn't it?)

The expected reply to this comment is simple agreement: "*So des ne!*" (Isn't it though!).

The function of this little interaction in Japanese is not to initiate a dialogue. It's just intended as a formulaic greeting. It's phatic speech – for social purposes only – the universal exchange of comments on the weather.

Being, however, a contrary Westerner on occasion, I admit to being unwilling to always accept the protocol of such scripted interactions. Sometimes, okay, but every day? My impish impulse is to break out of the mold if my tongue can manage to find the words. So after a few rehearsals of this new routine, I responded one morning by explaining in my broken Japanese that, in fact, I didn't find it cold at all. (*Jitsu wa, samukunai des, Kanadajin des node. Kanada no tenki wa, hontō ni samui desu.*) As a Canadian, I explained, I found this winter weather to be comparatively mild and pleasant. By contrast, Canadian winters got *really* cold!

"*A so des ka?*" (Oh really? Is that so?) was his somewhat startled response.

The next day, he reverted to the old and simpler refrain of *Ohaiyo gozaimas* and left it at that.

But the weather kept getting colder, and soon the *kanrinin* tried the same refrain again, believing that I must surely be finding it cold by now.

"*Samui des ne!*" he said emphatically. Again, I ducked the expected response, explaining that this *still* wasn't really cold for me. After that, he completely stopped using the expression.

Weeks went by, and the weather got progressively colder. Then a few days ago, a February morning, it was really freezing, the coldest day of the winter so far. Walking from the station to the office, I found myself shivering and hurrying to get there.

"If this were Canada," I thought to myself, "I'd be wearing a sweater, a hat and a much warmer coat."

But I didn't have a warmer coat, and I was damn cold and happy to get to the office. I came in the front door, rounded the corner and saw the *kanrinin* and his female co-worker, both looking at me with twinkling eyes. I noted an unusually playful expression on their faces. As I signed the book to pick up the key, the old gentleman quipped, "*Atsui des ne!*" (Hot today, isn't it?). Then they laughed and laughed!

It was a great moment. I suspect they'd be waiting for weeks for the day when they could spring it on me. With a single stroke, these two playful, elderly Japanese had shown me I had to throw out all my premature conclusions about the seemingly rehearsed nature of Japanese life and scripted language use. It was perfect timing, especially coming just when I'd begun deluding myself that I had Japan all figured out.

author's collection

2

SETTLING INTO THE SYSTEM

At Home Over New Year's

Over these lazy days of the New Year's holiday, we're making space for Japan's English dailies. By that, I mean we're reading newspapers opened up wide in the quiet and comparative spaciousness of our miniature living room. It's a big improvement over struggling to absorb the news of the world in the midst of our normal newspaper-reading environment – the subway mob.

Krista and I are news hounds. It's a treat to be able to examine page three while still looking at page two, with our newspapers spread out in front of us. We sip our hot mugs of coffee and share snippets of the stories we're reading, savouring simple pleasures in our adopted foreign land.

From the dozens of articles and photos I've perused today, one in particular – in *The Japan Times* – leapt to the fore and demanded to be read. It's just a black and white photo of an orchestra, together with a very large choir, but below the picture is a short descriptive caption which reads as follows: *Japan Air*

Lines personnel, flight and cabin crew members perform Beethoven's Symphony No. 9 in a concert held Sunday to deepen mutual understanding among them on the occasion of the airline's recent privatization.

How about that! The photo conveys a sense of the Rock-of-Gibraltar company solidarity, the extended family of Japanese life. I pause and try to imagine employees of a typical North American or European Airline Company pulling together to rehearse and perform a piece like this, let alone doing so to 'deepen mutual understanding.' Somehow, I don't think so.

It would now be an anomaly in the West for people to join a full-sized choir and orchestra made up of their company colleagues, though there must still be such companies. I know an elderly Canadian woman who worked in Woodward's Department Store in Vancouver in the 1940s and sang in a choir made up of Woodward's employees. She told me they used to rehearse in the morning before the store opened, though their managers looked unfavorably on the whole thing. Perhaps their singing was an expression of worker solidarity.

Nowadays, people who love to sing would normally join a private choir, whose members are people from many backgrounds sharing only a passion for singing.

The Japanese, however, live with great social pressure to socialize within whatever group they're in, at any given stage in their lives. So if a company forms a choir or a baseball team, employees will join.

It's also a practical decision. A typical Japanese company employee can't easily join a private choir that rehearses on Tuesday and Thursday nights, because they can't count on being available. What about overtime? What if there's a company dinner? Since there's no escaping these obligations on any regular basis, it's just easier to go with the flow and get together with your fellow employees to sing or play baseball, or do whatever the company's organizing.

That way, you get credit for loyalty, as well as getting to do something you enjoy. There'll also be no uneasiness over not conforming, a heavy issue for Japanese people. Only a rebel would join a private choir when the company has its own.

As I look at this photo and imagine myself in this choir – a company man for life – a memory stirs. It's of a short story called *Life in the Crystal Palace*, required reading for a university course I took at age 19 on the *Psychology of Alienation*.

The story described an ideal company life in America, with the company as lifelong womb, protecting and supporting you on every level, requiring only your loyalty. Yes, the writer concluded, it was comfortable and tempting. But wasn't something fundamental missing? Life as a journey and adventure to shape for oneself? Life as uncharted territory? As I recall, the story concluded with open-ended questions.

All these years later, life in a Japanese company is as close to the *Crystal Palace* as I've ever gotten, and I readily admit that the benefits of 'belonging' often feel very good.

My colleagues and I recently cheered on the Soulful Software rugby team, watching the game in a stadium with a few thousand employees from our company and that of the opposing team. It felt like we belonged to a sports team rather than a company. That's probably all part of the corporate formula for holding everybody tightly together. At times, I felt like I'd been granted extended tenure on my high-school years. It was a happy afternoon out in the sun and away from our desks. Oh, and we won, as usual – cause for toasting our company's superiority.

All of this togetherness is very effective in fueling identity with your corporation. Cheering on your sports team with your colleagues, or rehearsing and performing Beethoven's Ninth (an annual December event for many orchestras here) functions as a kind of superglue, bonding you with your co-workers. My company has a very comfortable *onsen* (hot spring) getaway in Hakone, just north of Tokyo, that Krista and I have stayed at for 1,500 yen a night, an incredible bargain in a resort area that could otherwise run you 25,000 yen. Everyone staying at the resort was a Soulful Software employee, and on the coffee tables in the lounge area, there were company brochures and product portfolios.

"And how would I feel," I ask myself, "if this were my job for life until retirement?"

Personally, I don't welcome the thought, though I know I could probably stay here for twenty more years if I chose to. But I've never sought one job for life, especially not in a city as crowded as Tokyo.

For many Japanese, however, their country's model of the *Crystal Palace* is their life's anchor, and I've witnessed an enviable amicability between the Japanese at work. They enjoy a deep sense of connectedness through their membership in the same corporate family, their homogeneity as a people and their shared values about social harmony. The trade-off is that the greater good far outweighs the individual's right to choose.

It's not all peace and love, that's already clear to me. But if I compare it with the overt conflict and backstabbing I sometimes witnessed in the workplace in Montreal, the more harmonious Japanese office ambience comes out looking pretty good.

Our discussion about cultural differences continues on into the afternoon. Krista and I talk endlessly about Japan, bouncing our evolving understanding of the country off her American and my Canadian background. Krista went to school with Japanese students in Hawaii, and came to Japan armed with a knowledge of the language and culture that I didn't have. We relish the chance to lounge around and chat, take a stroll around the neighborhood, and then come back to make tea.

We thrill at the prospect of not having to catch a train for four undemanding days in a row. We ponder what it must be like to be a Japanese working for JAL and to play and sing Beethoven's Ninth, but only in the company choir. Above all, we relish these quiet hours of our private life and the freedom to spend them as we please.

Laundromat Surprise

We had such a huge pile of clothes to wash last Sunday that we decided to take it all down to the local coin laundry, instead of doing it one load at a time at home.

My first visit to a Japanese coin laundry was in Sendai, and it was memorable for my astonishment at how tiny it was - the floor space was three strides long and one stride across, flanked on either side by washers and driers.

It's an experience shared by everyone from North America who visits Japan; one of the strongest first impressions you have of this country is the lilliputian dimensions of things - train station lockers, seats on buses, the pocket mirrors the young girls use to check their eye liner on the trains.

An American friend who first came here with the armed services in the late sixties recalls that at that time, when he rode on a train, he was a head taller than everyone else. Jim told me he could look right down the car he was in and gaze over the heads of the men; the women were shorter still. There was remarkable uniformity in terms of height, and the Japanese were uniformly tiny. Tailors must have had a great time - one-size-fits-all!

On this front, things have since changed dramatically. The young men now come in all sizes and some of the 18-year-olds look to be in a position to try out for the N.B.A. Meanwhile, many laundromats, apartments and coffeehouses have remained tiny, as space has become ever more precious and expensive in Tokyo.

One effect of this is that over time, your concept of space undergoes a radical shift. Take, for example, our Sunday visit to the local coin laundry here in *Setagaya-ku*. Small by comparison with anything back home, it's quite roomy compared to the minuscule laundromat I first encountered in Sendai.

Occasionally you find yourself marveling at the spaciousness of such a place, a laundromat the size of a medium-size living room as opposed to a walk-in closet. It's at such moments that you realize how accustomed you've become to a downsized universe.

But our local coin laundry, it turned out, was not only larger than most. It has much more than washers and driers to offer its customers. It also has three narrow 'coin shower' booths – eight minutes for 100 yen, less than a dollar.

Surprised to find the place empty, we filled up four or five machines (which was most of them) and went across the road for a bite to eat in a local 'video' restaurant. Elton John escorted us through lunch on a big screen, belting out "I'm still standing" and leaping over his white grand piano on a beach on the other side of the world. After lunch, we went back to shift the clothes to the dryer. The place was still empty, but not for long. We were soon to discover another popular use of our local laundromat.

In came a couple, dressed in *yukata* (light cotton *kimono*), giggling and obviously delighted with each other. Unlike us, laundry was not what they had on their minds. They hurriedly popped 100 yen into the coin shower slot and excitedly plunged in for, perhaps you guessed it, a quickie! For eight stimulating minutes, while our clothes tumbled away in the dryers, we were treated to the sounds of what is surely Japan's most inexpensive *love hotel* experience.

One can only guess what the situation of these lovebirds is, but there's an excellent chance they live in a tiny apartment bursting with in-laws, and they seldom have a moment of privacy. For them, the coin shower is probably a godsend – eight minutes of intimate space just around the corner from home.

The whole country is flooded with so-called *love hotels* that cater to the same need for private space, and they often come with a fantasy theme setting of your choice. I've read that upwards of half the visits to *love hotels* are by married couples seeking a private love nest of their own. In these establishments, two hours is the going time frame, and that will usually cost you between 5,000 and 12,000 yen.

Our laundromat lovers had found a stand-up alternative at a bargain price. Suddenly, the shower machine shut down, and out they came – flushed and refreshed. With no embarrassment that we could detect, she giggled and he laughed, and they headed off down the street. Tokyo's full of surprises. Even on a Sunday afternoon, if you keep alert, there's usually more going on than you'd ever imagine.

Company Life in Japan

There are many favorable things to be said about how traditional companies like Soulful Software treat their employees, especially foreign ones like me. The once clear-cut promise of lifetime employment, largely for men, was surely highest on the list of positives for those who welcome that kind of security. As the West came to know, most Japanese companies offered their 'lifers' a guarantee of a job and salary right through to pension. It seems like a mighty good deal from the outside.

But seen from the inside, the downside of this arrangement soon becomes apparent. I'm grateful for the opportunity of working here for a time, but living the corporate life my male colleagues are obliged to follow for thirty-five years is not imaginable to me, nor would most Westerners I know want it, whatever the benefits.

Working for a Japanese company, I've learned firsthand what it demands from those human beings who work within it. My comments about the Japanese company system come mostly from my experience at Soulful Software, but this company does nothing to warrant my singling it out as being especially inhumane. They definitely treat their Japanese employees significantly better than some I've had dealings with, especially smaller companies struggling to survive. As for the way they treat their foreign employees, they've generally been very fair to me. So it's not my intention to be anything but fair-minded in assessing my experience working for them.

That said, from a Western point of view, company loyalty is not a rationale for whitewashing or glossing over the downside of a job situation. Most of us would agree that praise is rendered meaningless if it comes alongside a ban on criticism.

From the point of view of a Japanese company, however, gratitude is expected to lead to loyalty. This means that you *do* gloss over the negatives in public, for the sake of the company's reputation.

My decision to use a pseudonym reflects my willingness to defer to this Japanese cultural norm. Like some other foreign writers, I've chosen to be culturally sensitive on this issue because I don't wish to cause any offense to my employer. This choice actually leaves me freer to say what I wish and to attend to the bias of my own culture: namely, that a self-censored account of my experience is a waste of time. As one Canadian woman I met who'd been in Japan for a year told me, "Well, I'd never read your book if you weren't going to tell the truth."

Constructive criticism often falls on sensitive ears in Japan, however fair and well-informed it might be. Critical commentary levied at specific Japanese companies – or even at society in general – is socially unacceptable for the most part, and it can quickly get you labeled as a malcontent. A good case can be made that the Japanese have a real problem with this issue, and it gets in the way of their progress as a nation. They're much less comfortable thrashing things out in the open; a disagreement can more easily lead to the severing of a relationship.

An American journalist told me about writing a critical article about a particular company's practices, only to be told by his Japanese editor, "The story's great, and if you could just delete the name of the company, it'll be fine."

Japanese are taught not to be confrontational or to directly question authority. One picks this up quickly – the expectation is that you'll be patient and not complain. It often seems as if complaining publicly is the biggest taboo of all. As a Westerner, you learn that criticism on your part will be instantly labeled as 'Japan bashing' by some people. It sometimes seems like a kneejerk method of preventing the *gaijin* from speaking his or her mind.

This is not to suggest that Japanese don't engage in criticism – they can complain with the best of us – but they're usually more discreet about it. Some of my overworked Japanese male colleagues have confided their criticisms of the Japanese company system to me in private conversations. It's pretty clear, however, that little in their educational experience has encouraged them to feel they have the right to speak up about it to someone like their boss, let alone petition for change.

These are men and women I'm growing to like and respect very much. Like people everywhere, they hope foreigners will like them and speak well of their country. And though I have critical comments to make – believing that the Japanese, like people everywhere, are best served by the truth (i.e. what foreigners really think) – I also have many positive things to say about them and about Japan. It's my intention to always strive to strike a balance between the two.

The Rat Race Japanese-Style

The Japanese social contract involves sacrificing considerably more of what would be free time for Europeans and Americans. We like to view our time as our own. We're willing to give over a reasonable percentage of it to our employer, but it's taken for granted that a fixed portion ought to be ours to manage as we choose. Basically, this is not how things work in Japan.

One of the first clichés you hear when you arrive is that, 'Westerners work to live; Japanese live to work.' There's a lot of truth to it, though it's hardly that people want it that way.

Whatever their initial resistance, most Japanese men with a lifetime position eventually comply with the needs of their company, and learn to always put them first. It's understood that *giri* (social duty) must win over *ninjō* (what your heart would do). The social contract calls for you to sacrifice yourself to your company and submit to its demands.

Japanese women must also work tirelessly for their company. But for Japan's *office ladies*, there are glass walls as well as glass ceilings. Although it's slowly changing, corporate Japan continues to view most female employees as expendable – they're not expected to stick around beyond their twenties.

Overtime work and after-hours obligatory drinking sessions are a habitual part of the work routine for my colleagues in Tokyo. If their co-workers are going out drinking after work, there's strong social pressure – especially for the men – to join the group, and there's a clear element of ritual to it.

It's the norm to conform, and you don't easily opt out for personal reasons. One often hears of golf widows here who basically raise their children on their own, because their husbands are on the links every weekend with their customers. None of this is going to change dramatically anytime soon.

It can certainly be viewed as being more a difference of degree than of kind. Americans and Europeans obviously face similar pressures from their companies, but more is expected in Japan, and less is accepted as an excuse for opting out. If you're a lifetime employee, there's not much other than illness that comes ahead of a demand on your time made by your company.

Soon after joining Soulful Software, I learned that there's a welcome or farewell dinner for every employee who enters or leaves our department, and everyone is expected to attend. Since interdepartmental transfers are not infrequent, and Soulful Software has upwards of 20,000 employees, obligatory dinners – usually starting at around 7:00 p.m. – are a regular event. As are the late, intoxicated train rides home, because most of these dinners are followed by a visit to the bar. For many of the people I work with, the term 'corporate party animals' seems to fit.

Personally, I had a very pleasant time at the first few of these dinners I went to, what with the novelty of the whole thing. I sampled the *sushi* and *tempura*, marvelled at their aesthetic presentation, practiced my Japanese, and started to get to know other people in our department. I felt really comfortable.

When you're inside a Japanese *circle* – foreigner or not – you're considered to be part of the group for events like this. It's something I really appreciate about the Japanese. Many foreigners complain of exclusion, but in my experience we often exclude ourselves. In settings such as my company's dinners, the Japanese have shown themselves to be consistently gracious, welcoming and tolerant of Westerners.

After three or four of these 'welcome' and 'farewell' dinners, however, I began to realize that my Japanese colleagues, although making the best of it, were simply there because they had to be. It was hardly out of some sense of excitement at the prospect of continuing to socialize on into the night with the people they'd just worked with all day. After all, many have been attending these obligatory dinners for years, and such events are usually not free. In fact, they may cost as much as 5,000 yen ($40).

But it's all approached with the attitude of *shōgenai* (it can't be helped, there's nothing you can do about it). It's something that must be accepted, and in Japan everyone just gets on with what's required of them.

Back at their apartments by 11:00 or 11:30 – or even later for long commuters (young men in low-priced apartments have to visit their local *sento* – or public bath house – once they get to their local station) – millions of salaried people in Tokyo live their lives this way.

I've discovered that many people stay up until 2:00 a.m. to get stuff done around the house and enjoy some free time to themselves. Japanese often tell me they only get four or five hours sleep most weeknights, and I believe them. The next day, they get up early and do it all over again. Their stamina is quite astounding, though the phenomenon of people catching up on lost sleep by napping on the trains reveals the strain of it all.

Many of my colleagues seldom have evenings free. Compared with them, I'm a pampered pussycat. I rarely have to attend more than two or three evening outings a month, and overtime – for me – is by choice.

It's not at all that Japanese people wouldn't rather be doing other things. Their *ninjō* (the dictates of their hearts) are surely akin to ours. They'd love to have more time and more choices in life, but the rules of Japanese corporate life curtail such freedom. American companies have their share of parties, social dinners, overtime hours and after-work drinking sessions. But these events occur less frequently, and there's not as much pressure to *always* attend. If you really need to opt out of a company event in Canada or the States – for whatever reason – you usually can.

If there's a consolation for a Japanese company employee in Tokyo, it's that everybody's doing it. When they're working late in the office, or out bonding with co-workers at a company function, the whole city is doing the same thing within their own 'circles.'

Japanese people define themselves by their company, department and section affiliations much more than by their sense of a unique individual identity. This is all a reflection of their culture. To most Westerners, the social gridlock they live with would be far too constraining. We lack the social ethic of holding like glue to a group that demands so much of us. For better or for worse, we insist on a far looser structure that allows us more personal freedom and choice.

Low-Tech Earthquake Prep

Tucked beneath my desk at Soulful Software is a small duffel bag with a draw string; inside the bag is my emergency earthquake kit. For the longest time, I never bothered to check out the contents. I finally smartened up and did so. After all, Tokyo is big-time quake country.

The bag is stamped with the bright red Soulful Software insignia. On top of it rests a plastic helmet with a blue cloth chin strap, again stamped with the same logo. Children in major quake zones in Japan all walk to school with their helmets on; I've seen this in quake-prone Shimoda on the southern tip of the Izu Peninsula southwest of Tokyo. It's quite a sight – hundreds of little boys and girls looking like tiny construction workers off to the job site. That's genuine earthquake preparedness!

In 1923 there was a mega-quake in Tokyo. My friend Ken and I went to an earthquake information center near Tabata on the Yamanote Line, and lived through a reenactment of the actual quake. It was a sobering experience. When we first arrived at the center, we were given a choice. We could either sit at a dining room table in a kitchen or on an adjacent *tatami* (thick straw) mat. We chose the *tatami* so we'd know what most Japanese would have experienced during the quake. The simulated household was all on a raised platform with some kind of hydraulic system underneath.

For 140 seconds we went through the quake of '23, exactly as it transpired at the time. As our guide pulled a lever to regulate the intensity of the quake, he held up fingers – now five, now seven, now six – indicating the severity of the tremors, since they varied throughout the long cycle of the quake. Just when you thought it was over, another booming tremor came along. At times, the *tatami* shook violently, bouncing us six or eight inches in the air. It was very humbling; there but for the grace of God go we when living on fault lines.

We stumbled out onto the street, aftershocks of 'inner' tremors still resonating within. Did we really want to live in this city a day longer? Wasn't it a bit like playing Russian roulette?

At Soulful Software, one glance under my desk in the morning serves to remind me that life in many parts of the Japanese archipelago – Tokyo being a site of major volatility – is founded on a prayer. The Japanese people live with the reality and terror of it from early childhood. Small quakes happen here in the *Kanto* (the greater Tokyo region) all the time. Just after there's been a tremor, you can flick on your television and within minutes a written description of the quake's intensity in all regions affected will appear on the government channel, N.H.K. It's reassuring to be able to get immediate feedback on what's happened.

Less reassuring, I discovered, were the contents of my earthquake kit at the office. I stayed late one night to finish a rewriting assignment, and decided it was time to check it out. One or two items at a time, I pulled things out of the duffel bag. The most disconcerting items were as follows:

- a small can of corned beef, which, eaten with the water, would seem to promise instant botulism
- a package of an unidentifiable substance which I presume to be rice yellowed with age
- a non-functioning flashlight
- a bottle of water in a green plastic container wrapped in a cellophane bag and dated *Showa* 60.8 by the Japanese calendar (approximately three years old at the time of writing)
- a tin of biscuits with a pull ring, on the wrapper of which is a Scottish bagpiper strutting through what appears to be a biscuit hailstorm.

In an odd kind of way, I found my Soulful Software earthquake kit to be reassuring. It offered living proof that Japan, renowned for its high-tech wizardry and superior quality products, is not always on top of things technical. Company earthquake kits – unlike cars, elevators and junior-high-school children – can go uninspected for years at a time.

So what is one to do if a major seismic shake-up happens while we're at the office? At this point, I know only two things for sure: one, nature holds all the cards; and secondly, my earthquake kit seems not to require a cyanide pill. A lethal dinner of ancient corned beef and rice, served up in a tinfoil tray along with three-year-old water, would probably finish me off in short order. Sayonara!

Apparently, one-tenth of the world's earthquakes take place in this country, a major battleground for warring tectonic plates. Foreign residents in Tokyo talk about feeling reassured when there are frequent small ones. Fact or fantasy, word has it they're supposed to relieve the pressure and reduce the chances of a big one (though the totally unanticipated Kobe quake of '95 showed that nobody really knows).

A lot of the time, you don't even notice small quakes in Tokyo. I'll be on a subway in a tunnel under the city, and it'll suddenly stop for a few minutes. There's been a quake – they're waiting to hear about its intensity before continuing. You don't even want to think about what a nightmare it could be for commuters in Tokyo if a major quake struck at rush hour.

At other times, we'll be at work and the building will begin to sway, or there'll be a jolt straight up, depending on the type of seismic activity. You don't give them much thought after awhile. Sometimes, I'll be aware of one during the night; it's like a dream, and I just drift back to sleep, even as the walls are still vibrating. After our experience at the earthquake center, I now figure if it's a big one, there'll be no mistaking it.

Though the authorities work hard to raise awareness about what to do if a catastrophic rumble should occur, you can't dwell on an everpresent peril that's beyond your control. I've known foreign residents who have left Japan because they can't handle the fear. Most Japanese have no such option. Everyone knows the designated place to go if a big one hits – usually the nearest open public space. Meanwhile, life goes on, and the danger of earthquakes is just part of it, as it is in many other cities around the world.

Maybe there's a reason for the neglect of my office earthquake kit – it reflects a secret wish on everyone's part that it'll never be needed. So I'm putting it all back under the desk and forgetting all about it. I never could stand corned beef.

Company Dilemmas

Company life in Tokyo seems a lot like a sub-culture to me. Much more than just being a job, it's a way of life with its own special rules of conduct and compensation, rules that totally shape lives. While still negotiating the terms of my contract with Soulful Software, I learned early on about one of these rules and the resulting dilemma it poses for my Japanese colleagues.

It started with a call I made to my immediate superior, Charlie, to ask him a few questions I had after reading the company handbook.

"I'm wondering about sick leave, Charlie," I queried. "I see from the company handbook that we're entitled to 12 paid holidays our first year, but there doesn't seem to be any mention of sick days."

"Oh," he replied, with a somewhat embarrassed laugh, "we don't get sick."

What he meant was that at Soulful Software – and many other companies who use the same approach – Japanese workers who fall sick are obliged to use their paid holidays as sick leave. At the time of my hiring, new company employees received 12 paid holidays in their first year, 16 in their second year and 20 from then on, till retirement at age 55. Interestingly, nation-wide statistics consistently reveal that 60% of full-time salaried workers routinely take less than half of their allotment of paid holidays.

At first glance, I'd imagined this to be entirely out of loyalty to the company and the departments that people work in. Everyone's so conscious of not putting others out in Japan, especially when they're within your 'circle.' Taking a long holiday is best avoided, because it would mean others would have to work doubly hard in your absence. On your return, you'll face the obligation to make up for having left others holding the ball while you vacationed.

Faced with this bind, many full-time workers just settle for the public holiday periods. Thanks to these, the Japanese do get blocks of time off work. Over New Year's - with a weekend sandwiched between public holidays - most people get at least four or five consecutive days off.

So-called *Golden Week* in late April is usually interrupted by a couple of days back at work, but many Japanese now use several of their paid vacation days to get a full week off. On a lucky year that has two overlapping weekends, this can mean nine days off, with minimal risk of making waves at the company. Japanese people shrewdly plan these vacations eight months to a year in advance.

In August, during the *Obon* period, when homage is paid to the spirits of ancestors, many companies now effectively shut down, allowing their employees a continuous stretch of time off. Thanks to such holidays, Japan is definitely not all work and no play.

During these nation-wide holiday periods, tens of millions of people pour onto the highways leading out of Tokyo, and airline tickets double and triple in price. Much the same situation exists in North America during Christmas and New Year's, but people stagger their summer vacations. That's not the case in Japan, where the majority of people take all their vacations simultaneously.

As for the annual 20 days of paid holidays available to full-time employees of Soulful Software, these can't be accumulated beyond a two-year period. So you can build up a two-year reserve, but after that you start to lose it, which is exactly what happens in many cases. Almost all of the male Japanese employees we know never take anywhere close to their twenty days off in any given year. Seven days is about average but, except in the case of new or younger employees, even those are often not taken consecutively. A 'business day' here and there is quite common.

For one thing, the pressure to stay on the job is too great. But since paid holidays have to double as sick leave, many people view them as 'sick leave' days. With no other safety net to catch them, my Japanese colleagues save their vacation days partially out of a need to have a line of defense for themselves and their families, should they become ill. It's a necessary strategy.

At the point where a Soulful Software employee who becomes seriously ill has exhausted any remaining vacation days, his or her salary is cut to 60% for any additional time off, and their twice-yearly bonus is also cut proportionately. The loss of income for a family with monthly financial obligations in a city as expensive as Tokyo could be quite drastic. Fortunately, almost all Japanese have national health insurance, which puts them in a much better position than millions of Americans.

Still, a stressed-out family man contemplating a holiday that would eat up his twenty-day vacation allotment, faces a dilemma. He must ask himself, "Do I use up my only line of defense against sickness, in order to take some time off to relax? Or do I just keep working as I have been, and rely on national holidays, knowing that if I get sick, I'll still have my vacation days to fall back on?"

A majority make a smart compromise, it seems, by taking seven to ten days of their vacation allotment and saving up the rest as sick leave, should they need it.

One downside of all this is that those employees who intend to use their paid vacation days to take a longer vacation – lasting 10 days or two weeks – often drag themselves to work, even when they're sick – coughing, sneezing and looking grim. The only alternative is to forfeit their vacation by staying home.

For an increasingly large number of young Japanese – particularly women – travelling overseas is not something they're prepared to forego. If they have to haul themselves into work when they're sick to hold on to their vacation days, they'll do it. I actually take it as a very healthy sign, a recognition of the importance of a real and well-deserved holiday.

Perhaps the term 'vacation days' is just a misnomer. In *Nihongo*, the word *yasumi* is a catch-all expression covering holidays, sickness or time off for any reason. A clearer interpretation of the term may be that companies like Soulful Software offer an 'all-purpose' 20 days off a year, which is meant to cover every eventuality. For those who would take a European-style holiday, vacationing can be a risk. You have to bank on staying healthy until your next 20-day allotment comes in.

The Totaled Salaryman

Many middle-aged male employees who seldom take paid vacations – out of a sense of responsibility and loyalty to Soulful Software, or fear of losing their illness buffer – have most of their vacation allotment – 40 days accumulated over two years – in the bag at all times. For these men, life is totally centered around their work, and paid vacation days are simply thought of as health insurance.

Sometime in his working life, however, a '40-day-in-the-bag' company man may be asked to check into a hospital for upwards of a month of tests. For a man who values his position in the corporate hierarchy, this constitutes the most socially acceptable way out for an extended block of time.

Such a man could not easily cash in 20 vacation days, spend three weeks in Hawaii, and hope to show his face in the office again with the same expectations of promotion down the road. But a hospital stay will not be a problem, since it's out of his control; the hospital authorities will determine how long he must be there.

Visiting my own friend in hospital here, I've sat with the middle-aged company men watching *sumo* wrestling on the lounge T.V. in their hospital gowns and slippers. Some are undoubtedly ill and in need of extended hospitalization. But in Japan, a lot of people you run across have spent a few weeks – or even a month or two – in hospital for 'tests' at one time or another.

A report in *The Economist* revealed that hospital stays in Japan are statistically the longest in the world – averaging an incredible 40 days, "even after excluding people receiving long-term treatment." This compares with five days in America. A skeptical observer might point out that the Japanese medical establishment benefits handsomely from the test fees, in addition to prescribing more drugs to patients than any other country in the world. As for hospital visits, doctors seem all too willing to book people in for long periods of time.

However it came about, it's socially acceptable for them to require this, and most people don't seem to question it. Though admission rates are much lower than in the West, once a doctor has told you to come into a hospital for tests, it's usually time to pack a large suitcase. Doctors are still much more god-like in Japan, so the lengthy stays are simply accepted as being in your best interests.

Besides, for a hardworking company man, a socially sanctioned chance to kick back and watch *sumo* for a month may be just what the doctor ordered, so to speak – the best available antidote to accumulated stress. An extended holiday in the tropics might well rejuvenate his health better than anything the hospital can give him, but that's seldom an option.

So it's just as well that this release valve exists. It provides emergency relief for a stressed-out *salaryman* or a beleaguered *office lady*, who may otherwise be a candidate for serious stress-related illness, or even *karōshi* (death from overwork). A month of napping and shuffling around in slippers to watch *sumo* is not a beach in Hawaii, but it's still a total break from the intensity of Tokyo's helter-skelter corporate life.

The men and women at my company live life at full throttle. Yet despite the incredibly demanding conditions of their working lives, I would describe most of the Japanese I've met at Soulful Software as being friendly, considerate and likable people. I reiterate this, because it continues to strike me as remarkable, considering the circumstances of their lives.

I try to imagine selling a lifetime corporate position in Tokyo to your average Westerner – myself included – if it were actually spelled out: "Right, you'll be working at our company from age 21 to 55; you'll often work till late at night on weeknights for all of those 35 years. You'll have to commute long distances daily on unbelievably crowded trains. Oh, and by the way, in addition to being in this full nelson for life, you'll only ever have short vacations if you take any at all beyond statutory holidays – we certainly discourage anything longer than a week at a time, especially if you seek major promotion. You start tomorrow."

Just shoot me now, thanks, would be the likely response of most Europeans. Americans allegedly work much harder – even rivaling the Japanese – and some might be more willing, but only if the salary was fantastic and they had a chance to retire early with a huge nest egg.

I mention again that those Japanese *salarymen* who get to travel, or live abroad as part of their jobs, seem much more well-rounded and content, whatever the hardships they've endured overseas. Two or three years elsewhere offers a company employee a radical break from Tokyo and a whole new perspective on their lives once they get back to Japan. The men I've met who have done this are much more willing to talk about their work and experiences. For those who have been to places like Libya, of course, the positive side to Tokyo life is now far more apparent.

The fact that these men are very interesting – like people anywhere who have experiences to relate – bears repeating, because the stereotypical portrayal of the *salaryman* is invariably negative. Regrettably, it's easy to see why. But I've found that there's life, variety and great humanness inside many of these gray and blue suits, among men of all ages, those who have traveled and those who haven't. At Soulful Software, it's been my pleasure to meet them and learn from them. They are survivors of an extremely tough system.

But there's no denying the existence of the 'totaled salaryman.' He's the late middle-aged male human being you see on the trains in Tokyo, the one who looks like he's been run over by a steam roller. In fact, he has. His face is seemingly fixed in a perpetual scowl, and his skin is often pale, jejune and sickly-looking. That's the result of too many years of smoke-filled offices, fluorescent lights and alcohol abuse. His life force and energy have provided the human fodder for the Japanese economic machine, and he seems in permanent need of a month in the detox tank.

Perhaps his view of the obligations of life and work is much as Ruth Benedict noted years ago, "The fact that a man often suffers intensely in living up to his obligations ... is not more than they expect. It makes life hard but they are prepared for that."

Looking at these men on the trains every night, I have to confess incomprehension of the Japanese worldview on this issue. Japanese are renowned for believing Westerners can never understand Japan. Perhaps they're right. For the life of me, I can't see why such total sacrifice is still viewed as necessary in a modern and industrialized country such as Japan. It seems closer to the kind of sacrifice we demand of men in times of war in the West than anything in civilian life.

All of that said, for me the unexpected thing was this: However burned out some of these fellows look, I'd bet a month's salary that if any one of them were to invite you over to his home, you'd experience generosity and gracious hospitality that would leave you feeling deeply appreciative. Much as I experienced in Iran, I've found that when you're invited into someone's home in Japan, you are the honored guest, and they treat you wonderfully.

It's a remarkable thing about the Japanese people - if they share some part of their life with you, you can count on their good-naturedness. Equally predictable is this: If you were to imagine that a man with this kind of work regimen must hate his life, you'd probably be wrong. In that sense, Ruth Benedict's observations still seem correct to this day. What he's enduring is definitely extreme - from a Canadian or American point of view - but it's not more than he imagined he'd have to put up with. He may not like it, but his society has prepared him well, which better allows him to make his peace with it.

And hey, it's Sunday and you're their foreign guest! So it's a special day for your Japanese hosts. Of course, he'll want you to drink with him. Alcohol is like soda water in Japan, drinking being the primary means your *salaryman* friend has had for releasing his inhibitions all these years.

The man's wife will dote all over you, feeding you a spread of delicious and aesthetically beautiful dishes she's worked hours to prepare. At one point, the couple will ask to show you their honeymoon photos - their seven days in Hawaii 25 years ago. Traveling was a big deal for the Japanese back then, and his work may not have permitted them to travel overseas again since then.

He'll prove capable of dropping the scowl and having a good laugh, and you'll end up admitting that he's a lot more personable than you'd ever imagined when you saw him on the trains, just a human being after all. As you say your goodbyes and express your gratitude for their warm hospitality, you'll find yourself feeling that he's a really nice guy and his wife is a lovely woman.

He's the quintessential Japanese *salaryman*, the product of a system that conscripted - rather than hired - him into the workforce years ago. You'll see him passed out on the late-night trains or on station platform benches, drunk and exhausted. American female friends tell me young Japanese women say they detest his type, perhaps because he represents a fate they intend to avoid in their futures, namely, taking care of 'Son of Salaryman' while he heads down the same self-destructive company trail.

And how do the young men feel? Well, some are clearly not happy about what they see in their fathers and company men in general. One night walking near Ochanomizu Station, I saw three young guys pass a man who looked about 50. He was staggering along, very drunk. One of them belted him in the face as they passed, right here in safe and civil Tokyo! The older man went straight down, hit the pavement, and then slowly got himself back onto his feet.

The young men just kept walking without a backwards glance – taking who knows what resentment out on this stranger and what he represented to them. The older man said not a word to them. Despite being very intoxicated, he managed to stand up and carry on, stumbling towards the subway station, home to his wife and his nightly *o-furo* (hot bath).

There he was, the 'totaled salaryman' on public display, this foot soldier in Japan's economic army who's given his life to his country and family, and is just letting off steam in a socially acceptable manner. Adding to his woes, he'd now been beaten and humiliated by members of a younger generation that has little appreciation for his sacrifices.

From a traditional Japanese perspective, such men are just fulfilling their *giri* as they understand it. It would be mighty presumptuous of me to imagine I can pop over to Japan on a jet plane, struggle with the basics of the Japanese language and culture for a few years, and come away understanding how a man like this feels about his life and the requirements of his social duty. I'm the first to admit that I can only ever make an educated guess.

My Canadian upbringing tells me that this man is a victim of a system that is often not on the side of its people, but many older Japanese may not see it that way at all. They may view him as a hero. After all, it's his sacrifices and those of his wife that have been the foundation of Japan's rise from the ashes to a position of great economic strength in the world. Whether such total sacrifice will continue to be demanded of Japan's company employees in the future remains an open question.

Fools and Buffoons in Their Midst

My colleague Chris once told me a story that has surely been repeated in one form or another by half the foreign residents in this country. It's something that's happened to me a few times, but his particular anecdote is the best version I've heard.

Chris was one of the few foreigners at a Japanese wedding he'd been invited to, and he was enjoying himself and mingling with the many guests. Everyone was dressed immaculately, this being a wedding in clothes-conscious Japan. The liquor, of course, was flowing, and Chris – like all the guests – was having his share. Perhaps because of that, an unfortunate discovery awaited him as he chatted away and enjoyed the reception.

At one point in the evening, he glanced downwards and realized that for the previous couple of hours, he'd been wandering around wearing bright red plastic slippers with the word TOILET written in large, black letters on each slipper!

In Japan, most washrooms have special slippers like this which are intended to be put on while you're using the facilities. You then take them off before you leave, and put your in-house slippers back on. But it's an easy thing to forget when you're not used to doing this, and after a few drinks, it's inevitable that it sometimes slips your mind.

The slipper slip-up serves as a metaphor for the behavior of Westerners in Japan. To the Japanese, we must often look like fools and buffoons, walking blindly through their social rituals without the slightest notion of the error of our ways. To their great credit, they don't draw attention to it, which helps to make the embarrassment less acute when you learn what you've done.

Later, you sit around and laugh for hours, comparing social transgressions with your foreign and Japanese friends. There are, happily, no serious consequences for wearing the TOILET slippers at a wedding. You didn't know any better – end of story. For a foreigner in Japan, ignorance can indeed be bliss.

Sento Heaven

Ah, *sento* – traditional public bath houses. They're one of the things I've really learned to love about Japan, so much so that I think I'm changed forever – the Japanese have got this one right.

In recent years, *sento* owners have had trouble attracting customers. *Sento* traditionally served as bathing facilities for people who didn't have an *o-furo* in their homes. As Japan got wealthier, people started renting apartments that had *o-furo* in them, and there was less incentive to trundle on down to the local *sento*.

Fortunately, many *sento* are surviving. Lots of older Japanese still hold onto this tradition, and young company workers living in low-priced housing without an *o-furo* or shower have to use them. People living with large or extended families sometimes prefer the *sento*, because they don't have to wait their turn for the *o-furo* in their home. At the public bath house, they can also take their sweet time. Business is always quite brisk in the *sento* I've been to.

If you haven't heard, the Japanese bathing system requires that you get scrupulously clean *before* slipping into clean, hot water just to soak. This approach now just seems like normal hygiene to me, infinitely better than getting into a bath, washing the dirt off and then sitting in it.

On the other hand, most apartment *o-furo* in Tokyo are half the size of a bathtub. You have to bend your legs at the knees, and the tubs are too small for real comfort. So one major advantage of the *sento* is that you get to stretch out in a huge tank of steaming, hot water, like in a Jacuzzi.

My first trip to a *sento* was in Kyoto, where I lived for a few months before moving to Tokyo to work at Soulful Software. I didn't have a bath in my little Kyoto cabin on the slopes of the hills of *Higashiyama-ku*, so going to the local *sento* quickly became my evening ritual. I had plenty of company – the Japanese traditionally bathe at night. I learned to love it.

When the *sento* is open, some beautiful strips of cloth called *noren* will be hanging out front. These and the script written on them (usually the *hiragana* character *yu* for hot water) identify the establishment as a *sento*, and from a glance up the street, the *noren* will signal that the *sento* is open for business. At the entrance, you part the *noren*, go through a sliding door, take your shoes off in the *genkan* (entranceway) and lock them in a wooden locker with a key attached to a large wooden key ring. It's a bit rustic, taking you right back to the old Japan.

My *sento* cost 380 yen (about $3). You pay an attendant and pick up anything extra you need at the front counter, like a towel or a bar of soap, though many people bring their own toiletries in a small, plastic bowl that you use to pour water over your head.

Women then go to the left and men to the right, and you end up on opposite sides of a matronly lady, who sits on an elevated seat inside a wooden boxed-in area that looks like a raised witness stand. She presides over the *sento*, perched on top of an eight-foot high partition running the entire length of the facility and cutting it in half. Her position affords her a full view of both the men's and women's bathing areas – an interesting vantage point.

You first undress in a *tatami* mat locker room, then go through a sliding door into the bathing part of the *sento*. On my side, naked men are sitting around on plastic stools. The voices and laughter of women come wafting over the wall just next to us.

Then you get yourself a plastic stool and a bucket next to a faucet, which is also equipped with a shower hook-up. Everyone is busy pouring water over themselves and scrubbing like mad with long cloths, working themselves up into a great lather of suds.

At that point, you pour still more water over yourself until you're squeaky clean, after which comes the essential experience of the *sento*. You slowly climb into a very large tank of exquisitely hot water and slip below the surface up to your neck.

In the Kyoto *sento*, the water is sometimes so hot that the first few times, it took me up to five minutes to fully submerge myself. I remember once having finally done so after many partial and temporary immersions, only to watch in mild horror as a father casually dunked his screaming one-year-old boy straight in and out a few times. Hell's bells, dad!

I should add that I've never since encountered such near-scalding water –

it must have been especially hot that night. Lest you've already concluded from this description that *sento* are not for you, I should add that most of the time the temperature is just right (or shall I say, you get used to it), and stress evaporates from your body like a puddle in a desert at midday. It's ecstasy, Japanese-style, and later in the evening, you feel so fresh and clean, and you sleep so well.

All *sento* have a cold tank as well as a hot one, and believe it or not, some have an electrified tank called *Denki Furo*. I stuck my leg in one once and felt the weirdest vibrations. Much later, I began thinking I must have imagined it, until I came across a story by a guy named Jeff Greenwald, who wrote about having the same experience. Read it if you need proof, and I also serve as witness – electrified water, only in Japan.

Personally, I steer clear of the *Denki Furo*, choosing to move back and forth between the hot and cold tanks, like the Swedes are reputed to do between saunas and snowbanks. Most *sento* lovers seem to prefer the hot tank, but they often get out and scrub a second time before climbing back in. I think the Japanese must be the cleanest people in the world, a good thing considering the close contact everyone has during their daily commute on the trains.

The day will come when I leave Japan, and *sento* are something I'll definitely miss. Going back to traditional baths is just not an option. I suppose I'll have to use showers again – and Jacuzzis when I can find them – and wax nostalgic about the heavenly side of Japan.

Hearing Impairment from the Right Wing

By and large, most Japanese people seem to be quite apathetic about politics. I've found it to be nearly impossible to engage my Soulful Software colleagues in a political discussion of any kind. They avoid committing themselves to a position, and appear to be largely disconnected from the political process.

It sometimes seems as if the government is just another corporation with rules of its own. Government ministers seldom resign and go back to the private sector here; they just take up a new position within the government apparatus.

When I arrived in Japan in 1987, the L.D.P. (Liberal Democratic Party) had been in power since 1955, so this apathy is perhaps understandable. When I try imagining more than 30 continuous years of Republican or Conservative administrations in the U.S. or Canada, my eyes glaze over.

So I remember my surprise at seeing a long protest march in front of our office at the time of the famous *Recruit* scandal in the late '80s. I watched it with my British and American co-workers, one of whom commented that it was the largest he'd seen in his 13 years in Tokyo, though I've since read that in 1960, hundreds of thousands marched in Tokyo and elsewhere in Japan to protest the signing of the new U.S./Japan security agreement.

We watched as what looked like several thousand people quietly filed by, protesting insider stock trading between members of the L.D.P. and *Recruit Corporation*. The sight of a demonstration in Tokyo jogged my memory. I recalled another protest I'd once witnessed from an office building in a very different foreign land. The recollection lent me some perspective; this Tokyo march was small potatoes compared to that one. It had happened in Meshed, Iran in September 1978. I had also watched that protest with co-workers, but from the second floor of the offices of the British Council, where I was working at the time.

During that incredible protest against the Shah's rule, an estimated one million people streamed past us on the street below, led by their religious leaders, the *mullahs*. What made it truly impressive was that the *mullahs* had called for the march to be held in 'total silence,' and the people had all complied. It was the most powerful display of disciplined solidarity I suspect I'll ever witness.

I remember the awe and trepidation we all felt, gazing down at that eerily silent curb-to-curb phalanx of people stretching for miles; we spoke in hushed whispers near the open windows to ensure we didn't attract attention to ourselves. This was real people power! You could sense that these Iranians would have their way, that there was really no stopping them now from getting what they wanted – an end to the Shah's rule.

But that was Meshed, and this is Tokyo. The *Recruit* protest, however large by current Japanese standards, was absolutely tame by comparison, both in terms of the numbers of people involved and the power behind the protest. Yet unlike Meshed, it turned out to be anything but quiet.

Our Tokyo office is very centrally located, and it so happens that quite a few organized marches and rallies take place on the street right below us. Perched on the fifth floor, we see and hear them all.

In subsequent years, I've only ever seen one other comparable protest rally in Tokyo (against U.S. bases in Okinawa). Japan is a complete contrast with its neighbour Korea, where students protest regularly and often get into violent clashes with police. But at the time, watching the protesters stream by, I took it to be a healthy sign that these people were concerned enough to organize on such a scale. Carrying placards, they strode along the sidewalk on the far side of the street in a very orderly fashion without even disrupting traffic. There was nothing radical about it, and the participants were very subdued, unlike Western-style protests where people would have been shrieking, "What do we want? When do we want it?" There was none of that.

Then along came the trucks and Tokyo's mobile right-wingers. It soon dawned on me that they were the organizers of the whole thing – staging noisy protests is their forté.

The rallies frequently staged by right-wing nationalists in Japan are quite shocking to many North Americans when we first see one, or more to the point, hear one. Incredibly loud military music blares through loudspeakers, which hang from a line of rapidly moving army-style trucks flying Japanese flags – the red Rising Sun. A man with a megaphone-magnified voice often rants and raves like a bona fide zealot, exhorting all Japanese to do I'm not quite sure what – reclaiming the 'true national spirit' of Japan seems to be the gist of it.

Japanese will tell you that the right wing is just a fringe group which is put up with, but totally ignored. Virtually no one pays them any mind, you are assured. In fact, you learn that this is the case when you watch people's reactions out on the street – they don't react at all. Looking at their faces, it's pretty much as if it's not happening. They seem oblivious to the rhetoric being screamed at them. It can be a 'twilight zone' event at first, because you have the sense that you're the only one experiencing it.

Sometimes, a right-wing truck will park outside a major train station like Shibuya, and a man will stand up on a platform and screech his throat out through a megaphone, his shrill voice booming off buildings – not to mention your eardrums – at a truly deafening volume. Yet, just about everyone will scurry on by, carrying on their shouted conversations as if he wasn't even there.

A few times, when this megaphone mania has been drowning out our conversations at the office, I've asked my Japanese colleagues exactly what these ravers are shouting, but they never want to tell me. They mumble excuses about not being able to understand the old-fashioned expressions. They say *chotto* to convey that "It's hard to explain," or *muzukashii* ("It's difficult"). More to the point, they'd just rather not talk about it. In fact, most of the rhetoric is about 'Japan the Glorious' and 'America the Hideous.' For my colleagues, the whole thing is very embarrassing.

Providing I can continue to subdue my impulse to shout back at these loudmouthed gentlemen when they take over a street and threaten everyone with hearing impairment, I guess I'll learn to live with it like everyone else. But I know I'll never succeed at tuning it out as the Japanese seem able to do. Nor do I wish to just ignore something that's so 'in your face.'

One has to wonder what role right-wingers would play here during a time of grave national crisis. In many ways, they seem quite tame compared with extremist groups in the U.S. and elsewhere. One article in the Tokyo English press suggested most members of the mobile right wing are just regular Japanese guys you could have a drink with.

That may well be true, but the most fanatical among them have a reputation for intimidating, threatening and even shooting people who disagree with their views. (Motoshima Hitoshi, the mayor of Nagasaki, was shot, though not killed, for stating that the Emperor bore responsibility for the war.) Their presence on the streets can be menacing, and their style maintains a direct link with Japan's authoritarian military past. That such bombast – however benign much of the time – is so commonplace here at a time of social peace and prosperity is certainly a surprise when you first encounter it. It's not the image most North Americans or Europeans have of Japan before they come here.

All things considered, I've actually come around to the view that allowing these marginal voices to express themselves and show their true colours is much better than trying to muzzle them, if that were even possible. They get to vent, and they just get ignored by the vast majority of Japanese.

I am, however, equally convinced that Tokyo residents ought to carry ear plugs and silently protest the noise by popping them in every time a megaphone approaches. Otherwise, your eardrums will get periodically hammered in this city. In my case, that used to be worth it for Led Zeppelin, but Japan's right-wingers have yet to show signs of musical talent. You'd think they'd notice that everyone ignores them. Perhaps if they stood up on their trucks and crooned *karaoke* tunes, they'd get more satisfaction.

Thoughts on Pachinko Land

Another battleground for the ears in modern Tokyo is the famous chain of pinball arcades that stretches right across the country. These venues are largely under the control of the *yakuza* (Japanese underworld), with many Japanese-born Koreans being in the business. In fact, the *yakuza* are widely known to have strong links with the right wing, and often to be one and the same.

Known as *pachinko* parlors, these architecturally garish arcades got their start after the war, because there were literally tons of ball bearings lying around and nobody knew what to do with them. In Canadian singer Bruce Cockburn's song *Tokyo*, the strangeness of pachinko found a place in his lyrics.

This is not surprising, because as most every visitor to Japan will tell you, pachinko parlors are everywhere, and you can't fail to notice them. If you manage to miss the mirror-multiplied barrage of flashing lights and wild neon, the decibel level will be sure to grab your attention. American pinball establishments, by comparison, seem pretty quiet.

Most of the time, once you're within range of a pachinko parlor, your ears will be pummeled by a recognizable melody that serves as a pachinko signature tune. Two of these have been standbys for years, endlessly repeating themselves to passersby on Tokyo streets: (1) The horse racetrack tune that tells you, "They're at the post!" and (2) A blaring military refrain known as the *Gunkan March*.

These pieces are played loudly enough that you can hear them half a block away. Standing right in front of a pachinko establishment for the first time, I remember my initial reaction to this barrage.

"Who'd ever go in there voluntarily?" I wondered.

Millions of people, apparently, and if you do go inside, the decibel level of the cacophonous wall of sound will escalate dramatically. Not only do the musical refrains keep replaying endlessly, but you'll also be subjected to the din of hundreds of tiny metal balls bouncing around off buzzers inside the parlor's vertically positioned machines. It's not everybody's idea of bliss, but Japan has many true pachinko believers.

In the midst of this auditory chaos, sitting on swivel stools arranged in long rows in front of the pachinko machines, you'll find hundreds of men and women of all ages. Many are adolescents, with more boys than girls. But in the evening, the stools fill up with off-duty company employees of both genders looking for some diversion. Whatever their age or sex, they all sit glued to their board, spellbound by the movement of the tiny, metal balls.

One estimate I read was that 28 million Japanese pass hundreds of hours a year this way, spending vast sums of their hard-earned *yen* on this quite mindless game. But there is a monetary incentive behind it. If you should get lucky and "get into the machine" - as my Canadian friend Kathy describes it - there's a payoff. Balls will start pouring out like manna from pachinko heaven.

Curiously, since this kind of gambling is supposedly illegal in Japan, you have to play another game - a bureaucratic one - in order to collect your winnings. You exchange the balls you've won for one of a variety of gifts, all of which have a coded value. You then take the gift out of the pachinko parlor and around the corner to a small secret window, where it will be exchanged for cash. I like to call it 'Japanese fuzzy logic.'

As far as skill goes, the only activity required of a pachinko player is the movement of a lever, which adjusts the speed at which balls enter the board. Kathy tells me you can get good at this maneuver and win consistently as a result, but minimal brain wave action is needed to play nonetheless.

One day, passing yet another of the umpteen pachinko parlors in Tokyo, I thought of a line from Paul Simon's song, *The Big Bright Green Pleasure Machine*: "We can neutralize your brain, you'll feel just 'fiiiiine' now!"

But the thousands of pachinko parlors in Japan obviously fill a need. As much as anything, they serve as central gathering places in overcrowded cities like Tokyo, and provide a way of killing time. For those who do become pachinko addicts, these venues seem to me to be more like techno-wastelands where human potential idles in neutral. Obviously, I'm not their biggest fan, though as a social phenomenon, pachinko continues to intrigue me. I keep asking the question, "Why do these places thrive?"

Pachinko Nation

I suppose it shouldn't be all that surprising to me that a form of mindless escapism like pachinko is so widespread in Tokyo. Most people's lives here are bound up in a very rigid routine. Many are perpetually stretched to the limits by their jobs and social obligations. By contrast, pachinko parlors demand nothing; they're a place to zone out.

They're also a place to sit undisturbed. Space costs money in Tokyo. You have to sit somewhere to get out of the crowds, be it in a coffee shop, restaurant or movie theater. If you're by yourself, pachinko gives you a stool to sit on, without the uncomfortable feeling that you're the only one who's alone. Many lonely people must find some kind of comfort and security on those stools - often the expensive kind if they play for hours.

There's also no overlooking the simple fact that in the awful, muggy heat of a Tokyo summer, an air-conditioned pachinko parlor promises immediate relief. When you walk past one of these places on a steamy August night, you're hit with a beckoning blast of icy, cool air. It can be enticing.

But many people clearly dislike pachinko, or at least want nothing to do with it. There may be millions of Japanese who shake their heads with disbelief, and wonder how on earth the culture which produced calligraphy, aikido and the aesthetic beauty of the tea ceremony ended up with mind-numbing pinball arcades on every street corner.

As good a reason to avoid it as any is that pachinko becomes a serious gambling addiction for many who play it, and they squander a lot of hard-earned cash. You can see the long lines of unemployed and retired men of all ages waiting for the doors to open in the morning. In fact, Kathy confessed to me that she went through a phase here in Tokyo where she was going all the time and couldn't stop herself.

Occasionally, there are stories in the local paper about *salarymen* who have blown their entire paycheck in one night of pachinko. They've then gotten caught stealing, in an attempt to avoid having to explain what happened to the rent money to their wives.

Every summer, Krista and I have read a few tragic accounts of fathers - even both parents - leaving infants in cars to go play pachinko for a few hours during a hot summer day, only to return a couple of hours later to find their children dead from heat prostration.

In a country with millions of overworked people, there are always going to be such stories in the papers - press bias everywhere being towards the horrific. And I think it would be unfair not to mention in this context that the tales of aware and responsible parents, who would never let such a thing happen, seldom get told.

But the stories do astound us when we continue to come across them in the newspaper. We read one about three young children who'd been left in a parked car. They then released the emergency brake, and ended up drowned in a river. All the while, their father sat mesmerized in pachinko land.

Japanese pachinko addicts spend many hours a month amidst the deafening roar of pinball dissonance and the endless repetition of the *Gunkan March*. At one point, I found myself wanting to know more about that military melody. Out of curiosity, I asked around: Did anyone know the background on that piece of music?

A Japanese professor who works with a friend of mine filled me in. It's called the *Gunkan* or *Battleship March*, *gun* meaning army, one possible translation being 'many cannons.' It was very popular in the 1930s, back when Japan was on the march militarily.

The practice of choosing a piece of music and repeating it on an endless cassette is hardly unique to pachinko parlors. Many stores like *Bic Camera* play their thirty-second signature tune over and over again all day long. In Shibuya Station in downtown Tokyo, an endless cassette has been playing *Love is Blue* for as long as I can remember.

Occasionally, I've pondered the fact that the repetition of the *Gunkan March* delivers a continual reminder of Japan's military past to the entire population, whether they like it or not. But the right-wingers do that anyway with their military parades through Tokyo - they're not about to let anyone forget it - and after you've been here awhile, the use of this melody seems inconsequential.

But a few times early on I had an experience that unnerved me, and I can't be alone in having been shaken up by it. A walk past a pachinko parlor playing the *Gunkan March* coincided with a deafening loudspeaker volley from 15 right-wing trucks rumbling by at the same time, all flying the Rising Sun. Just in itself, the noise was horrendous. But I can easily imagine that for an elderly foreign visitor with wartime memories, being confronted with this out of the blue could be frightening and traumatic.

Personally speaking, three months of living under martial law in prerevolutionary Iran in 1978 - scurrying through downtown squares ringed by tanks and young soldiers wielding bayoneted machine guns - left me wary of military displays, whatever their purpose. But expert commentators I've read - though less sure that Japan could never again militarize and threaten its neighbours - would describe as alarmist the view that Japan poses a military threat in the near future. For one thing, Article 9 of the American-imposed constitution – Japan's renunciation of war – still stands in the way.

For another, the unimaginable horrors brought about by militarization, culminating in Hiroshima and Nagasaki, left behind a people deeply suspicious of war. That's hardly surprising. One day I flipped perspective and thought about it this way: What if New York and Toronto had been hit by the A-bomb in 1945, if the West had been defeated, and Canada and the U.S. had been taken over by an occupying force of Japanese for seven years, instead of the other way around. How completely and utterly that would have changed us as people. Imagining this reverse scenario helped me begin to fathom the impact it must have had.

Official Japan's evasion of its own wartime aggression aside, the ceremonies every August, marking the anniversary of the atom bomb blasts in 1945, serve to remind a forgetful world of the destruction and death they brought about. They remain a vitally important remembrance, and the memory of no other nation but Japan can serve to recall and warn us of the total hell of nuclear war.

Sakura in Bloom

Spring is coming, and it's a wonderful time in this city. *Sakura* – delicate cherry blossoms – are exploding to life everywhere, a stunningly beautiful change from the gray drab of Tokyo winter.

Snow only once graced the skies of Tokyo this year, but it never covered the landscape as it did last winter for a few days in February. That's a perennial feature of Canadian winters I never thought I'd miss, but the pure white stretches of prairie snow and glazed ice still have an appeal in my memory's eye. Trudging through snow in Tokyo – watching the Japanese children let loose their joy in snowballs and snowmen with carrot noses – is a treat, especially because it's only for a few days.

But thoughts of snow are long past this year. It's early April now, and exquisite explosions of white plum and pink cherry blossoms are enlivening the boulevards in *Setagaya-ku* and throughout Tokyo. It's a delight!

To celebrate, there's *Hanami*, cherry-blossom-viewing season. Once these beautifully scented April blossoms appear, virtually the entire Tokyo population sets off to the nearest park, in groups both large and small, throughout a one-week period.

Each group lays out a tarpaulin to reserve a space amongst hundreds of others, congregating in a very orderly manner in places like Ueno Park and *Aoyama Reien* – a sprawling cemetery, no less. They bring *yakitori* (grilled chicken), *onigiri* (rice – often with fish – wrapped in a seaweed called *nori*), salad, *soba* (buckwheat noodles) and plenty of beer and *saké* (Japanese rice wine).

And under the *sakura* of spring, they drink and relax, Japanese-style, together in their 'circle' from the office, along with the great leveler – alcohol. If you're a moderate drinker, as I assumed I was by the time I came to Japan – despite having been a drinker with the best of them in younger years – this is an issue you'll have to deal with in this country.

Some Japanese, especially the women, drink moderately or not at all, but almost all of the men drink, and many are a rival for the Russians and the other renowned drinkers of the world. No small number of company men imbibe until they're well and truly drunk. During *Hanami,* restraint is not the order of the day. Savoring the delicate scents of the blossoms, whose fleeting presence has spurred the revelers to celebrate, is cause for Bacchus to rule.

It's easy to understand. It's a party in the park in the warmth of spring, often on a weekday. I ride the cattle car express everyday with millions of these hardworking *salarymen* and O.L.'s , whom I currently see sitting out under these splendid trees. If I knew I were totally locked into the Japanese way of life from now until retirement, I suspect I'd be knocking it back indiscriminately with the best of them.

But when Mr. Hamada asked me ever so sweetly to join his *Hanami* group this year, I politely declined, with misgivings. On the one hand, I really appreciated his invitation to be part of the group, and I wanted to join them.

On the other hand, I didn't want to face the inevitable pressure to drink too much that comes with most social situations here. I've learned that this – along with the social coercion to sing *karaoke,* which many would rather not do – is an issue for lots of Japanese as well. I knew I'd feel uncomfortable being with my colleagues in a party atmosphere where I wasn't letting go along with them, in the way they understand 'letting go' best. I also knew that they might feel self-conscious with my not drinking.

One dilemma is that Japanese pour alcohol for each other, so someone is always filling your glass when it gets low. Actually, I like the sentiment behind this custom. The problem is that you can get drunk awfully fast if you don't keep an eye on yourself. The Japanese are very eager to oblige their foreign guests, and you can easily lose track of how much you've drunk when your glass is always being kept full.

I remind myself that Westerners often feel excluded by the Japanese, but sometimes it's quite the opposite. For whatever reason – not wanting to drink being a very common one – we opt out ourselves.

But if you're an unabashed drinker and find yourself in Tokyo in the first week of April, you may love *Hanami.* If you go to *Aoyama Reien,* you'll see people leaning against tombstones – it's no sacrilege here – laughing and sharing food, playing guitars and singing. If you're polite and respectful, you could wander up to just about any group, join them and be welcomed. There's an extension of trust to 'foreign guests' on the part of the Japanese that can be very endearing.

Hanami is a life-affirming celebration in the park, and a reprieve from the dreary sameness of the routine. Knowing how hard they work, who would begrudge these company warriors this socially sanctioned release, whatever the toll on their livers? With *saké* in the bloodstream, everyone can drop, for a time, the constraints of age, hierarchy and social position which rigidly guide workaday life in Japan.

But my image of a contemplative, mystical nation, musing philosophically on the ephemeral April magic of the *sakura* and the transitory nature of life, has had to be modified somewhat.

Yes, that's all still there, I have no doubt – deep in the Japanese soul. But in the green spaces of modern Tokyo during *Hanami*, it's a lot more down to earth than all that for the legions of Tokyo's working men and women. It's a Dionysian afternoon in the park, with everyone freed for a brief spell from the stringent requirements of being a member of the corporate rank and file. And winter is finally over!

Undoubtedly, the wonders of their beloved cherry blossoms are savored by the Japanese people every April. They follow the march of the blossoms on T.V. as they move from Kyushu in the south to Hokkaido in the north. Meanwhile, in Tokyo's parks, there are days of intoxicated revelry and joy, and amidst choruses of *Kampai* (Cheers!), a nation of gung-ho drinkers welcomes spring.

Tama River Crossing

The April 29 to May 5 *Golden Week* holiday has arrived. With two vacation days added on to make it a continuous stretch of time off, we're busy exploring our new neighbourhood on the western edge of Tokyo. Today, we wandered down to the Tama River, just a five-minute walk from our *manshon*, a three-story walk-up apartment. We'd actually lived here a few weeks before we even discovered the river was there. It was like emerging from a jungle – this one being concrete, of course – and stumbling upon the great western plains!

It's nothing spectacular as rivers go, but since it's the first real expanse of open space you get to as you head west from Shinjuku in the heart of Tokyo, it was quite a sight that first day – open nature in a nature-deprived city. Even though we're less than a half-hour from Shinjuku by express train, our hardcore city friends now say we live in the boonies, to which we reply: Happily!

In the early afternoon, under the warm sun of May, we went wading in the cool water in bare feet, with my pants rolled up and Krista's skirt tied in a knot above her knees.

Golden Week is one of those times of the year when noticeable numbers of Japanese men can be seen strolling around in open-necked shirts, spending time with their families, and unwinding from their stress.

Millions leave Tokyo and head off on overloaded trains and freeways to other parts of the country. We read that many spend entire days in 60-kilometer traffic jams, but eventually get to where they're going – usually a hometown – and hang loose with relatives for a few days. Then they face the same trek back to Tokyo. From our perspective, it looks like a lot of wear and tear for a brief respite, but that's modern life in Japan.

Families for whom Chofu is home, with no obligation to go elsewhere, would seem to be the lucky ones – along with any others who have just elected to stay put for *Golden Week*. They were all down by the Tama River today, passing leisurely hours in the great outdoors. Everyone looked quite transformed, especially the casually dressed men drifting along with their smiling wives and laughing children.

I admit to being surprised. I'd gotten it into my head that men in Tokyo never stop working long enough to really let go with their wives and children. I now know that's not the case for some, and it was a great sight to see.

Some were flying kites or playing catch with their kids, while their wives basked in the family togetherness; others were playing around with mechanical helicopters. A couple of dozen were fishing for catch you'd never want to eat, but having fun anyway. This area must have been a great fishing spot thirty years ago, long before Tokyo's sprawl encroached and engulfed it. There's still an old tackle shop just up from the river selling rods, weights, nets and bait – the whole kit and caboodle.

All along the river, people were sitting on blankets, snacking and sipping beer, chatting and laughing, and soaking up the warmth of family.

It's hard to convey why this is so special, given that it's not at all unusual back home. But in Tokyo, it's easy to get the impression that nobody ever really slows down long enough to savor the simple things of life. It was a small revelation to see families just having a picnic in the sun. In fact, it was sobering to realize just how out of touch with natural surroundings we'd gotten. Our move further out of town has spawned immediate benefits.

We waded down river along the far bank, eventually reaching a place below a dam, just on the other side of which, children were wading around in six to eight inches of water. Here, it appeared to be shallow enough to walk right across the river from one side to the other, without going in above your knees. There were little islands of land dotted about with people here and there, so we knew it was pretty safe, though the water was flowing fairly swiftly. We decided to cross over.

Nevertheless, being the cautious type around water, I still felt a little unsure, given how broad the river is at this point, and because I've heard of drownings here. So to allay my fears, we asked five or six boys – probably ranging in age from about 8 to 13 – the best place to cross over safely. They laughed at my concern and leapt at the opportunity to personally guide a couple of foreigners across their river.

It was great fun. We felt genuine excitement at simply being in such an open space again – in a spot where we could see for a couple of miles in all directions – perhaps even fifteen miles upstream, stretching our eyes towards the distant hills of Chichibu-Tama National Park. Everywhere, the sun sparkled and danced on the flowing water. It seemed aptly named, this *Golden Week* in the glory of May.

As a train on the Keio Line thundered over the bridge half a mile upstream, I pondered the toll that a life of jam-packed trains and inner city office towers must take on the Japanese of Tokyo over a lifetime. After less than two years of living in the core of Tokyo without ever experiencing this kind of spaciousness, we felt drunk with delight being reunited with it again, and very grateful that our new home made this possible. Commuting a longer distance is challenging, but at least it allows us some access to nature.

We splashed our way across the Tama River, amused by the little human universes we passed on the way. Just down river, we were treated to what appeared to be a convention of small pirates. A group of six-year-old boys were triumphantly flying a black flag, chattering conspiratorially amongst themselves, all stripped down to their underwear and sitting on their haunches around a campfire they'd started. This self-contained world was all happening on a spit of sand, right in the middle of the river that was flowing rapidly around them.

Our trustworthy guides accompanied us right the way across, putting us again on the Tokyo side of the Tama, this river that forms the great city's western border.

"I'd love to give these kids 1,000 yen ($8 U.S.) for helping us," I whispered to Krista, "so they could buy themselves some chocolate bars or something."

"Better not," she replied, "that may just teach them to expect money in this kind of situation. Besides, they're not looking for it; they were happy to help us."

"Yeah, you're right," I said, "but it's really too bad, 'cause I'd love to show them their kindness is a good thing. They need to know how much we appreciated their willingness to help us."

Not 10 seconds later, as we reached solid earth at the edge of the river, my gaze fell on a cleft in a rock on a small patch of ground. There, sparkling in the sun, was a pile of Japanese coins amounting, it turned out, to almost exactly 1,000 yen! They'd probably fallen out of a fisherman's pocket while he sat on the rock fixing his bait.

I love those moments in life when providence or synchronicity, or whatever name you want to give it, seems to intervene to allow good things to happen. I waved the boys over and pointed to the mound of coins. Their inquisitive expressions quickly changed to glee as nimble fingers grabbed at the coins with lightning speed.

One more little surprise awaited us on this altogether pleasant day. Ten seconds later, most of the coins had vanished into wet pockets, but not all. Twelve or fifteen coins remained on the sandy crevice, unwanted. These were one-yen coins, plus a few five-yen coins, worth slightly less than a penny and a nickel respectively, amounting to about a quarter altogether.

"Strange," I thought, "would American children in the same situation leave pennies and nickels on the ground, passing them over as though they were worthless?"

Somehow, I doubted it.

"I wonder what this tells us," I said to Krista, "about the messages Japanese children pick up about money."

Was it something about not taking it all because that would be greedy, just as Japanese seldom take the last portion of a shared plate of food? Was it a sense that groveling after the smallest coins would also imply poverty? Perhaps it was a value they'd learned about leaving something for others. We couldn't be sure.

They waved goodbye enthusiastically for at least a minute, then splashed their way back across the river in an excited frenzy to spend their loot – that is, if the little pirates didn't get them along the way. As we made our way home to our new abode, the sun was slowly setting on one of the most relaxed days we'd ever passed in Japan.

Psychic Gyrations

Perhaps the most puzzling thing about living in Tokyo is the roller coaster nature of our feelings about the city. We swing back and forth about the people, their perceptions of us as 'foreigners,' the social constraints Japan places on us, and the overall gestalt of the society.

One month, it's a remarkable country. There's the low crime rate, and the fact that people are considerate and helpful if you really need some assistance. The transportation system is efficient and reliable. The trains are packed, but they're almost always on time. Despite its crowds, Tokyo can be an exciting place. There's the exhilaration of coming up out of the subway and discovering a fascinating new part of the city, and there are the endless choices available for night life. During good periods, I find it easy to downplay the unpleasant side of life here.

On a bad day a few months later, the whole city becomes a minimum security institution for unsmiling prisoners, of whom I am one. During these periods, Tokyo feels like a highly regulated work camp - however benign - where no one gives you any clue as to what they're thinking.

At such times, I experience myself as an underworld denizen on a treadmill, who responds on cue to a plethora of mechanical signals on train platforms - buzzers, bells, alarms and whistles. Tokyo becomes a scene out of *Blade Runner*, a city run from central control, chewing up interchangeable workaholics like us.

The worst of these thoughts usually come when I'm crushed on the express train at rush hour. It's the most demanding aspect of life here. A few years of this and - as B.B. King would have it - the thrill is gone. On a bad day, I think of us as the intimate zombies, expressionless and hovering a few centimeters from each other's faces. Tokyo can seem unbearable at such times.

A week later, things have turned up, and my inner dialogue is often full of self-recriminations.

"All right, so Tokyo's incredibly crowded - but how would people fare in New York, Toronto or San Francisco if things were this intense there? There'd be fist fights or knifings in every subway station! Besides, subways back home aren't exactly warm and fuzzy human settings. You can't find another city of this size anywhere with as high a percentage of well-mannered, tolerant and considerate people. And they're paying you well. So what's your problem?"

In interacting with my Japanese colleagues, my experience can, on occasion, be similarly rocky. One day, I'm viewing them in a totally positive light and appreciating their amiability, dedication and good will. A few inexplicable interactions later, and I'll be thinking thoughts of inscrutability and duplicity.

Invariably, I later retreat from that as well and chastise myself: "Relax, you're just getting caught in a stereotyped view – probably the one you were taught as a kid in *Bridge Over the River Kwai*. You're reacting to cultural differences – you're experiencing culture shock. Lighten up."

And so we swing, many of us, back and forth – in our perceptions of Tokyo and the Japanese we meet – as sure one month of what we're feeling as we are the next in pondering the opposite. It's such a common *gaijin* experience that it's even been given a name: the 'Seidensticker syndrome,' courtesy of the writer Edward Seidensticker.

My good friend, Maggie, explained her experience to me by saying that one month she feels Tokyo is the greatest city she's ever lived in, and the Japanese people are unbelievably sweet. A month later she's hard-pressed to find anything positive to say about living here. Later she flips back the other way again.

Of course, there are also *gaijin* who move towards one viewpoint and stick with it; they hate most everything about this country or, conversely, Japan can do no wrong. In his well-written book, *The Outnation: A Search for the Soul of Japan*, Jonathan Rauch wrote about a friend of his who also flipped back and forth in his views. Then Rauch commented: "Among other foreigners I found a polarization to a degree that was altogether unsettling."

There's something about Japan that brings this on. In fact, I suspect the Japanese experience a similar ambivalence about Westerners. One day, we're delightfully unique and enviably casual human beings. Several cultural misunderstandings later, and we're unpredictable, loudmouthed individualists with no sense of loyalty!

Placed in close proximity, we appear destined to have distorted perceptions of each other, at least some of the time. Our differences can seem intergalactic. But there's a Japanese proverb I find most pleasing and helpful: *Ura ni wa, ura ga aru* – 'The reverse side has its reverse side.' No matter how sure I get about what I think of Japan, I can usually count on it to flip over after awhile to reveal the truth of its opposite.

Rocky Cross-cultural Terrain

It would be enlightening to be a bilingual and bicultural fly on the wall, in a room where Japanese are lampooning the foreigners in their midst. I'd love to hear what they find most incomprehensible, hilarious and insufferable about us. There's plenty for them to laugh and be exasperated about, no doubt.

On the other side of this cultural divide, most Westerners have experiences with Japanese people that keep recurring again and again. Krista and I feel that some Japanese character traits – such as their patience and phenomenal willingness to extend a helping hand – are worthy of much praise. There are many examples of this. Early on in our time here, Krista's best friend, Gail, came to visit us from Minnesota. It was her first trip to Japan, and a middle-aged man named Mr. Suzuki met her on the plane and drove her right to our door – a two-hour drive through the jungle of Tokyo!

At the same time, other traits – such as the cultural penchant for scheduling everything, always having a *purpose* and being reluctant to leave much to chance – can get tiresome. Gail was perplexed by one thread of the conversation she had with Mr. Suzuki, during their ride from the airport.

"He kept asking me what my plan was," she explained, "and I kept saying I didn't really have a plan, that I was just going to meet my friends and take it day by day. He must have thought I hadn't understood his question."

We laughed and shared more such stories. There are standardized question hoops everyone jumps through repeatedly in Japan, old-faithfuls like: "Can you use chopsticks?" and "Can you eat *natto* (a soy bean dish with a strong taste)?" Then comes: "Do you like Japan?" and "How old are you?" (age being such a critical matter here, since hierarchy is largely based on who's older). I'm quite sure it doesn't occur to most Japanese that foreign residents are being asked these same questions wherever they go. I suspect that when Japanese visit Western countries, many go through a similar routine, with their hosts asking them questions about Japan.

But the magnanimity of the Japanese towards Westerners makes our lives here much easier than they would otherwise be. This generosity is reflected in the many invitations we've received to visit people in their homes on Sundays, where culture gaps of one kind or another usually come right along with the pleasure of the get-together.

When we were first invited to people's homes, we were pleased and grateful. Our hosts were so gracious, and we were happy to spend the better part of a Sunday enjoying the hospitality that many Japanese have extended to us as guests in their country. We were new here, and it was very comforting to feel included in their families.

We spent many Sundays in this way, even though it usually required two or three hours of commuting time on the trains. But the invitations just keep coming, often from people whom you meet for a few minutes by accident, and with whom you may have little in common. Your would-be Japanese hosts may think otherwise, however, as was the case with Mr. Suzuki, who generously invited us all over to his home.

Some foreign friends of ours talk about the '*gaijin*-groupie syndrome' – middle-aged couples who seem to be 'collecting' *gaijin* – but I now think that's uncharitable. One couple we got to know, the Takeuchis, rent apartments to

Westerners, and then invite them over on Sundays, probably because they enjoy our company.

They were a very friendly couple, a dentist and his wife with two daughters, and we were introduced to them by an Australian friend who'd already spent a few Sundays with them.

We were also invited over, and found out they'd been entertaining one foreign couple or another most Sundays for years. No doubt the routine they followed with us - pulling out the photos from their honeymoon trip to Mexico 20 years before and explaining each one - was a routine they knew well, and one they could comfortably deal with in English.

During the first few Sundays we spent with the Takeuchis, we worked hard at communicating and finding things to talk about. It was always a struggle, but that's part of intercultural exchange, and they kept inviting us back. I guess we kept accepting because Tokyo can be a lonely place for newcomers, and we appreciated the warmth of family which they extended to us. Their two teenaged daughters were sometimes at home during our visits, and though they were extremely polite and pleasant, they showed clear signs of boredom with mum and dad's *gaijin-guest* pastime.

After a while it dawned on us that if we took up every invitation we received, we'd be spending all of our Sundays in Japanese homes or on the trains getting there and back. We also realized that until our Japanese improved considerably, we'd be having the same minimalist conversation every weekend.

Eventually, we started declining invitations, in part because we were exhausted. We also began to feel somewhat less comfortable with each new encounter. It began to seem as though we were the 'showcase foreigners' - on display every Sunday.

Our discomfort led us to the conclusion that our own relationship was going to suffer if we kept this up. It was too unsatisfying a way to spend our precious one day a week off, and we needed this time to reconnect with each other.

No doubt the Takeuchis have since found other foreign residents to take our place, and newly arrived Aussies, Americans and Canadians - bewildered as we were by the vast strangeness of Tokyo - will certainly benefit from their remarkable kindness.

We would be ungrateful wretches if we did not appreciate the good will that's been extended to us here in Japan, strangers that we are in this foreign land. The Japanese have a well-earned reputation for self-effacing hospitality. However, we realized we absolutely had to strike a balance between time spent in Japanese homes and time spent by ourselves, because living in Tokyo can put you under such tremendous stress.

We eventually determined that we'd just try to deepen our connection with those Japanese couples and families we already felt a rapport with, and make polite excuses the rest of the time. So when we go up to Sendai, we visit the Kumagai family whom Krista knew when she worked there, and here in Tokyo, the Takano family have become our good friends. I trust the day will come when we can return their warm hospitality.

Land of Formality

In addition to growing weary of the well-intentioned courting of *gaijin*-befrienders, many foreign residents find themselves challenged by the greater formality of Japanese life. Whenever you're introduced to someone, you have to go through the ritual routine of exchanging and discussing the details of each other's *meishi* (business cards) for the appropriate amount of time. It's part of the fabric of daily life. In Japan, you've gotta learn to love it.

Most Americans and Europeans are used to a much more laid-back approach to meeting and getting to know people. Far more than we realize, our style is a shock to many Japanese. A university teacher friend of mine told me about taking a group of his Japanese students to Seattle for five weeks. One day on a train in Oregon, Jim struck up a conversation with an American guy for the duration of the trip, at the end of which one of the students, a 20-year-old Japanese male, asked Jim who the man was. On hearing that Jim had only just met him, that the man had been a complete stranger, the student was flabbergasted!

Jim laughingly told me that after they'd all returned to Japan, the young man kept repeating this story – nothing had had more impact on him during his time in the U.S. The fact that Americans talk to total strangers without having been introduced, and before exchanging business cards and learning each other's relative social positions, was mind-boggling to him.

That's not so surprising, given that this is a hierarchical society whose language requires the use of a feature called *keigo* – the inflection of verbs to show appropriate deference. Basically, this means that Japanese people need to know each other's social rank, in order to know how to speak to each other appropriately.

On another level of formality, Japan must surely be one of the few countries in the world where many young women go around perpetually dressed to the hilt in nylons and skirts with not a hair out of place, even on Sundays in outings to the park. American women are generally blown away when they see this. Perhaps for those Japanese women who consider finding a man an economic necessity, round-the-clock vigilance regarding their appearance seems perfectly natural. In a society that places such importance on dress and external appearance, I suspect it's perceived as greatly increasing one's chances of finding a husband.

As for the men, many company men wear a suit and tie religiously, seven days a week. I heard one story about some Canadian guys who came over to Japan to build log cabins for Japanese clients. Their Japanese co-workers showed up to do drywalling, dressed in suits and ties.

Men can also be regularly seen in tux, tails and starched white shirts on Sundays, attending one official function or another. My guess is that many wouldn't feel comfortable dressed any other way. 'Formal' is easier because it's the default style – it's always going to be socially acceptable.

I suspect that some serious climbers of the corporate ladder are ever-vigilant. They never know when they might meet a superior unexpectedly, an event that always calls for a ritualistic round of bowing, with the lowest on the totem pole bowing the deepest. Perhaps the thought of being caught off guard, and having to go through that routine in shorts and a T-shirt, is more than most self-respecting Tokyo businessmen can bear.

I remember receiving a postcard from an American friend in 1985, at a time when I was still only considering a move to Japan. Doug was on a research trip, having been offered a job in Tokyo, but feeling a need to have a look around before leaving his job in Montreal and accepting a position here.

"Land of the blue-suited businessman," he wrote back. Doug declined the job without a second thought, and headed off to Tibet instead. The styles and trials of Japan are clearly not for everyone.

But make no mistake, Japan has its rebels. Our local bar, *Heartbeats*, is a small oasis for non-conformists. It's owned and managed by a laid-back Japanese reggae lover with braided hair halfway down his back. There'll be no formal company life for him.

Westerners Under a Microscope

The longer you stay in Tokyo, the more you become acculturated to Japanese formality. This can lead to many altered perspectives on your own culture. Against the backdrop of Japanese norms, it's as if the ways of other cultures are written in bold relief.

Take dress codes, for instance. It was a bizarre experience for me to see a couple of American backpackers on a Tokyo subway the other day, and to find myself pondering how unkempt and disheveled they looked.

These weren't grubbies who hadn't washed or shaved for three days, just your average young Westerners on the road. It was strange because a few years ago, I'd have just thought, "Oh, backpackers passing through Japan."

I could see that my perceptions had undergone a shift, that I'd started to see my own culture through Japanese eyes.

It was a Tuesday when this happened, and that partly explains it. On a weekday in Tokyo, pretty much everyone dresses impeccably because that's the norm. You're on your way to work - you dress the part. Work is serious business. Westerners in jeans and backpacks, struggling to get on the Tokyo subway on a Tuesday morning, look like freaks from Mars with giant appendages. At least, they do now; I'd come around to this way of seeing without even realizing it.

The required conformity of Japanese society can be prescriptive and judgmental. To many older company employees on their way to work, foreign backpackers look like homeless ragamuffins, social untouchables. After all, this is a society in which women wearing short-sleeve 'summer-appropriate' blouses a few weeks into autumn receive disapproving stares - subtle pressure to get back in line. Slovenly Westerners on weekday morning trains are quite beyond the pale.

Some Americans I know who live and work here couldn't care less about all this. They dress the way they would back home, and sometimes stand out like strippers in a Sunday tea salon. Conformity be damned is their attitude, and because they're *gaijin*, they can usually get away with it.

The Japanese can be very tolerant of behavior from Westerners that they would never accept from each other. Occasionally, I witness the most astonishing things here. At a driver's license bureau near Shinagawa, I listened to a wacky German guy - attempting unsuccessfully to procure a motorcycle license - rave and shout non-stop at the female clerk for a full 45 minutes! I actually started timing the episode because I found it so unbelievable.

None of her numerous co-workers wandering around in the back room came to her aid, or attempted to intervene. She was on her own dealing with this wild man. Waiting to pick up my own license, I offered to help at one point, but he would have none of it, and showed signs of shifting his fury to me. So I sat back down and watched to see how long his tirade would last and what would happen. Nothing happened, nobody took any action, and nobody called the police. He eventually left the counter, and went away empty-handed.

After a few minutes, the cross-cultural paramedic in me felt the need to go up to the counter and say something to console this poor woman, in hopes that she wouldn't swear off *gaijin* forever. She was visibly shaken and averted eye contact at first, not knowing what to make of me. Another lunatic? How was she to know?

I tried to convey that I'd felt sorry watching her go through all that, told her I was Canadian, and tried to make conversation in my faltering Japanese. I eventually reached for props – Canadian money – and ended up giving her a one buck coin – the so-called *loonie* in Canada, because it has a *loon* on it.

The hilarious connotations of that little gift escaped me at the time. I hoped I'd calmed her somehow, but more likely I just confirmed her view that Westerners are predictable in only one way – we're all quite mad.

Extra Latitude for Westerners

Besides television and movies, the behavior of Westerners living in Japan is the main thing most Japanese have to go on to deduce what we're *actually* like. But there's a complex combination of forces at work that can radically alter our behavior while we're in Japan. Simply by virtue of our being out of our own countries – stumbling our way through a foreign language and culture – the way we act is sometimes very different from what it would be back home.

Expats can be an unusual bunch to begin with, quite atypical, and yet our behavior is viewed as being perfectly representative of our culture. What's a 'so-called' Westerner? We're it! The same is true in reverse for many Japanese who go overseas – say to America – and stay for a few years. But by so doing, they are already social renegades in their own country, being very unlike your average Japanese. Yet it's from knowing them that most Americans will form their impression of what Japanese people are like.

It's usually a distorted perception, a bit like looking in the funny mirrors at the circus. When you're out of your own culture for an extended period, you're on unfamiliar ground – your own cultural support and references are in short supply. There's often a sense of liberation from cultural constraints you've left behind, a shifting of boundaries as to what is acceptable, and a removal of inner barriers to taking risks. There can also be a feeling of being completely at sea in a raft with no oars.

Your hosts, meanwhile, see none of this, and take your actions to be the normal behavior of people from your cultural background.

I recall buying a train ticket one day for 140 yen, and then going a single stop to Shinjuku Station. At Shinjuku, the man in the glass booth insisted that I pay again. As he said this, he kept repeating *Okyaku-sama* (venerable customer).

At the time, I could not for the life of me figure out what was going on. I knew I'd paid exactly the right amount, because he didn't simply want another 20 yen – he wanted the whole amount again!

He kept on with the *Okyaku-sama* routine, and my explanations in *Nihongo* were getting nowhere. I remember starting to get very annoyed, and I had the absurd thought, "If I'm so blippin' honorable, why are you making such a big deal out of this?"

It went on for some time without resolution, and I finally grew exasperated. One final *Okyaku-sama*, and that was it. I put down my ticket on his counter and said three words in English very slowly, enunciating each one: "I have paid."

I passed by his window feeling distraught, my hands physically shaking, knowing I was breaking some rule I couldn't understand, not absolutely sure I wouldn't end up being chased by uniformed men with whistles, hauled off and deported. But I had to get to work, I couldn't argue with him all day, and I wasn't about to pay twice.

It's not something I would have dreamt of doing back home. But then, in my own country, I'd never have had to do it. I'd have understood his explanation immediately.

In fact, he let it pass, and only much later did I find out that I'd bought a ticket for one of two train lines - run by separate companies - that pass through the same station. Everything's written in *kanji* on ticket machines, so these kinds of things are unfathomable to foreigners who can't read Japanese. To not pay again, I would have had to go back to the station where I got on, get a refund on my ticket, purchase another ticket from another machine whose *kanji* I couldn't read, all so I could take the same ride again and come right back to Shinjuku. Or I could have kept the ticket and switched train lines, assuming I could have figured out which train was which.

I've no doubt at all that newcomers to Tokyo make these kinds of mistakes on a daily basis. I'm also certain that many Japanese station employees who have to deal with us have a negative impression of Westerners as being stubborn, aggressive or just downright crazy! That is surely how we sometimes come across in our fumbling attempts to communicate in this new world we're inhabiting.

But there's a lot of latitude given to Westerners, along with an understanding that we don't 'get it.' It's easy to capitalize on this by feigning complete ignorance and playing the helpless dependent. In my subway scenario, I might well have been better off just smiling and bowing all the way past the man in the glass booth, repeating over and over, "Ah, *sumimasen* (Sorry), no speak Japanese." At times, it's tempting to want to do that.

Japan, despite its ambivalence about the West - and Westerners in general - still shows partiality towards Caucasian foreigners, something that can make you uneasy if you think about it. I've discovered since coming here that Asians such as Korean residents are routinely viewed in a much less favourable light.

I suspect that Caucasians get preferential treatment largely because of Japan's special relationship with America. The U.S., after all, became Japan's conquering master after 1945, and former American ambassador E.O.

Reischauer's famous words that Japan and the U.S. constituted "the most important bilateral relationship in the world bar none" spoke loudly to the Japanese as to where their security lay.

If advertisements in the U.S. had as many Japanese in them as Tokyo subway ads have Caucasians, you'd conclude that there'd been some kind of cultural paradigm shift. Billboards in Tokyo are a parade of "who's who" in the American entertainment industry, and apparently most of them have it written into their advertising contracts that these ads can never be shown outside of Japan. An American audience would find the Japanese portrayal of its stars to be hilarious and strange.

One long-running advertisement all over the Tokyo trains is for a wedding package. It shows two extended families dressed in tuxes and bridal attire – bride and groom, parents, little brothers and sisters on both sides. Everyone is white – all foreign models, no doubt. Obviously, *white* and *foreign* sells in Japan.

I feel uncomfortable looking at ads like this one on the trains. I wonder why images of Caucasian Westerners have more appeal to the Japanese than images of themselves, especially given how beautiful Japanese women are. Considering how bizarre some of the behavior of Westerners in Tokyo must seem, it can sometimes be hard to fathom what it is they want to emulate about us anyway.

Comic Relief

Ah, my favorite bank in Tokyo – may it prosper. For Westerners, its services are by far the most convenient. Having said that, it's come to my attention that it has a small problem with its name.

That's because in the Japanese language, there's no phonetic equivalent for the third letter of the English alphabet. Instead of saying 'a, b, c,' anyone reciting the English alphabet who's not mastered the pronunciation requirements of this letter, invariably comes out with 'a, b, shi.' This is the case with many Japanese speakers of English.

This leads to some very amusing pronunciations of words borrowed from foreign languages. One of my favourites is *shiruba*. This word, with its three syllables, demonstrates three classic stumbling blocks encountered by the Japanese tongue struggling to speak English.

Shiruba is how Japanese pronounce the English word *silver*. It works like this: 'c' becomes 'shi,' 'l' becomes 'r' with a vowel tacked on, and 'ver' is pronounced 'ba': *shiruba* – so close, and yet so far from being recognizable as an English word.

Explaining my bank's problem is as simple as 'a, b, *shi*.' When I first got to Japan, colleagues told me right away that most foreign residents get an account at this well-known foreign banking institution.

Having been subjected to some bureaucratic quagmires at two Japanese banks, I didn't have to be persuaded for long, so I gave them a call to check out their services. Greeting me on the other end of the line was the voice of an enthusiastic female receptionist, who confidently identified her employer to me:

"*Shittibank*, may I help you?"

I should add that since opening my account, I've had nothing but terrific service from Citibank. In fact, they usually answer the phone with flawless English now. Something tells me that management caught on, and provided everyone with a crash course in pronunciation practice.

The Mystic East Repackaged

I was at work at 7:00 p.m. last night, finishing off a rewriting assignment. Our section is a small group of mostly American, British and Canadian *gaijin*, all cloistered together in a self-contained office - just us and our Japanese secretary, Miki. But everyone else had gone home. I was alone and it was quiet - dead still, in fact.

My line of thought was suddenly broken by the sound of the *yaki imo* man, though I never mind being disturbed by the soothing quality of his voice. Sitting in his pickup truck in the early evening hours, just outside our building five floors down, his presence conjures up images of the Tokyo of times past.

His chant uses a plaintive minor third and has a haunting quality - *Yaaa-ki-i-mo-o*. To my ear, it speaks of melancholy combined with courage - very Japanese.

Alone in this silent, modern building in central Tokyo, I pause to listen. The voice hovers in the air, this seven or eight-second refrain offering up a touch of twilight beauty to the urban landscape: *Yaaa-ki-i-mo-o* beckons his message, over and over, summoning up memories for me of invocations to prayer, wafting from minarets throughout the Middle East.

But what this Japanese man is offering is something much more down to earth, a gastronomic treat - sweet potatoes, baked in a wood-burning stove roaring away right on the back of his pickup truck, his recorded message crackling through a megaphone while he tends the fire.

Yet it does provide me with a kind of spiritual sustenance, sitting alone in this sterile office. I succumb to the dreamy sound of his voice, chanting away as if Japan has not changed one iota in 100 years. I could hear that beckoning call in my mind 30 years from now, and I'd be instantly pulled back to a sense of something authentically Japanese. In Kenji Mizoguchi's classic film *Gion no Shimai* (Sisters of the Gion) – made in 1936 – you hear almost the same call, but for roasted chestnuts.

But there is more. This, after all, is modern Tokyo. The *yaki imo* man's recorded chanting soon gives way to speaking. He chats away for a while in animated tones, telling passersby how delicious his baked potatoes are and encouraging them to partake. Then, as if a spell has been broken, the message comes to an end – with a xylophone version of Mickey Mouse! M-i-c-k-e-y M-o-u-s-e, M-i-c-k-e-y M-o-u-s-e.

Soon the haunting melody again fills the twilight air – *Yaaa-ki-i-mo-o*. The tape repeats again and again, accompanying me through my rewriting job, a remnant of a bygone and timeless Japan, wedded to fairy-tale America.

Yes, I Have Understood

I was reminded today about what is expected of Japanese on the bottom end of the company ladder. It came in the form of a phone call yesterday from my new boss, a very friendly American woman, Cressie, whose Japanese is excellent. Charlie from Indiana recently quit the company after 13 years to move back to the U.S. – to Hawaii to be precise – having sold an apartment purchased in the middle '70s for five times its original price. It's an example of how Tokyo has made a lot of things possible for those in the right place at the right time.

Cressie let me know that a subsidiary of Soulful Software wanted some photos of a male foreigner for the cover of a brochure. It sounded simple enough. They would come to our office at 1 p.m. tomorrow, and just take some shots of me at my desk. It wouldn't take a minute they assured her, and I scribbled it in my calendar.

This morning I came in to learn that the plan had been changed. Instead of their coming to me for a quick photo at 1:00 p.m., now I was to go to see them, half an hour across Tokyo, at 3:00 p.m., for a *videotaping session*.

The man who'd called to notify us had simply informed Cressie of the change, without bothering to ask her whether it was still convenient. Cressie chose – in the interests of maintaining good relations with the subsidiary – to acquiesce, but she informed me of this change by saying that the man had spoken rudely to her.

She suspected gender bias, something she often encounters. For some Japanese men she's unusual and threatening – a foreign woman in a position of authority who speaks Japanese very well. Being married to a Japanese man, Cressie probably knows the territory well, though the rudeness could just as easily have been a reaction against foreigners in general. With Westerners, Japanese men sometimes ignore protocol in ways they'd never do with each other.

This was off to a bad start, and it put me in a funny position. My boss was annoyed, and now so was I. I had to accept her decision not to check with me first – that was her call. I should probably have asked her to okay such a change with me next time, and left it at that. Instead, I focused my displeasure on them, as she was doing.

The new timing meant rescheduling my afternoon appointments on short notice, jumping on a train and spending the afternoon across town. Even though our contracts spell out that we're rewriters and teachers, other tasks – such as posing for brochure covers – also end up being a part of the job.

With my boss's blessings, I called up the subsidiary and said I'd be there at 3:00 p.m., adding brusquely that next time, I would appreciate being asked about a change in the schedule and the plan.

A Japanese in my position would never dream of doing such a thing. After all, my own boss had okayed the change in plans! But given Cressie's feeling that the discourtesy they'd shown her stemmed from her being a woman, she was quite happy to have me dress them down a bit. Call it gender politics, Japan-style.

On arriving at the subsidiary, I soon began to suspect that the request for a photo session had simply been a ruse anyway, that they'd really wanted me to come to their office all along. You're often stumbling blind in Japan trying to figure out what's actually going on. On top of that, you're walking on eggshells so as not to be culturally insensitive. All of this puts Westerners at a distinct disadvantage. There was no way I could know what their initial intentions had been, but the place was clearly a studio, all set up for videotaping.

Of course, it's entirely possible that someone had said, "Well, we've got someone now, so let's make a bigger production out of it." But it didn't look like that and besides, I hardly felt like giving them the benefit of the doubt after the disrespect we felt they'd shown.

There's the cultural rub – our sense that they were being insensitive or disrespectful. This holds very little weight in Japan if you're at the bottom of the hierarchy. As a subordinate (in the case of *gaijin* like ourselves, we're pretty much everybody's subordinates), my involvement was surely viewed as being open-ended. The mindset of the men at the subsidiary is that I would do exactly what my boss asked me to do. Having been chosen to help them, I was at their disposal. A change of time and place was not mine to question.

Most young Japanese at the bottom of the hierarchy in a Japanese company just accept this. They know that at this stage of their careers, following orders well and without hesitation is enormously important. Obviously, many

American and European employees are subjected to a fair bit of pushing around by their superiors, but there are limits to what people will take. In Japan, the attitude seems to be: I know I have to get ordered around now, but the better I can demonstrate my acceptance of that, the sooner I'll get to be the one who does the ordering.

At Soulful Software, I often have occasion to overhear one side of phone conversations between a Japanese subordinate and his boss. These men come to us to have a letter rewritten, and then they call back across the street for their next assignment. The one-sided nature of these dialogues demonstrates how the hierarchical chain of command is just taken for granted in corporate Japan. Very frequently, the side of the exchange I get to listen to – with the subordinate speaking – consists of absolutely nothing more than an endless refrain of the same phrase, "*Hai, wakarimashita,*" meaning, "Yes, I have understood." At our end of the phone line, nothing more is said.

A Japanese acquaintance, Akiko, told me she watched such a performance on a *shinkansen* one day, listening to a brow-beaten young *salaryman* intone those same two words, over and over again, for nearly one solid hour!

"He sounded," she despaired, "like some kind of robot parrot."

Obviously not a fan of such mandatory obedience, Akiko is one of the few Japanese women I've met who's not afraid to share such viewpoints.

From the traditional Confucian point of view, giving and following orders like this is efficient and makes good sense. It's sensible because you work with a proven model. Knowing the model, the teacher leads and the student just follows; the boss directs and the subordinates obey. In Japan, the *sempai/ kohei* (senior/junior) relationship defines much of social interaction at work and in school.

One Japanese guy I spoke to had no qualms about it. He said, "One day, we'll get our turn to boss around the ones beneath us."

At the studio, my subsidiary colleagues did the videotaping with me – the recalcitrant foreign guy. When the session ended, they gave me a tie clip with the company logo on it and a $5 telephone card. They also sent me back to my office in a taxi, extra compensation, no doubt, for putting us out.

I felt some discomfort about having made waves, but from our perspective in our tiny section in the company, the prevailing viewpoint is that if we let things like this happen without comment, we'll be treated like lapdogs. Forty-page rewriting assignments are sometimes submitted in the late afternoon, with a request that they be ready the following morning. If we were loyal Japanese employees, we'd just accept it and work all night to finish the job. Instead, we choose to set reasonable limits for ourselves.

As for the reaction of the Japanese men at our subsidiary, I suspect they were as mystified and put out by my behavior as we were with theirs. After I left, the comments probably ran along the lines of: "These damn foreigners, they're so stubborn."

Perhaps it's just so deeply ingrained – someone lower down the hierarchical ladder doesn't question a superior. After all, they didn't question things when they were subordinates.

Perhaps it's ingrained in Japanese men that women like my boss are always beneath them, so there's really no need to be courteous; it's the woman's role to be polite and yielding.

Then again, perhaps this is simply one man's approach to telephone communication. In his view, we all work for the same company, and we're trying to get a job done as expeditiously as possible.

Perhaps. These cultural gaps between us sometimes feel like chasms. We fill them up with guesses.

Reverse Culture Shock, French-Style

I've learned firsthand that when you live in a foreign culture, you change in ways that are not readily apparent until you step out of it again. Experts say that reverse culture shock – encountered when you return home – is, in fact, more challenging than culture shock itself. You go back home expecting life – and yourself in the old situation – to be the same. But both have changed, and that can produce some hilarious moments.

This was brought home to me on a recent return to Montreal, the last city I lived in before moving to Japan. I flew in at about 10:00 p.m. and arrived at a friend's near midnight on an overnight stopover. Stewart had kindly offered me the use of his place, but he wasn't in town. So I just went to bed without having had a verbal exchange with anyone, and I got up early the next morning to catch a bus to the U.S.

At the bus station, I had the sudden thought to make a quick trip to a *depanneur* (convenience store) and pick up a few things for the journey. The French ambience of the store was immediately familiar, but completely different from Japan. Enjoying the experience of reading French – instead of *kanji* – on the packaging, as well as the excitement of being in travelling mode, I picked up some juice and a few packaged sandwiches, and I headed for the counter.

The female voice that spoke to me instantly turned my brain to mush. I speak French pretty well, and understood immediately what was being said to me: "*Est-ce que c'est tout, Monsieur?*" (Is that everything for you, sir?)

But what automatically popped out of my mouth without a second's hesitation was the Japanese word "*Hai*" (yes).

The word "Hai" is spoken rather sharply and abruptly. As it parted my lips with a will of its own, the woman's eyebrows arched and her face reflected a strange surprise, but she quickly replied, "*Bonjour*," concluding that I was a friendly English speaker saying "Hi!" in a very bizarre way. My intonation was distinctly odd, but she took it in stride. I'm sure she meets all types at a *depanneur* near the bus station. Meanwhile, my brain was doing cartwheels trying to locate the French hard drive buried somewhere in its circuits.

I put a $20 bill on the counter, which quickly prompted another question, "*Est-ce que vous avez quelque chose plus petite, Monsieur?*" (Do you have a smaller bill, sir?)

In spite of myself, it happened again. I was clearly not in control of my own mouth.

"*Hai*," I piped up again, feeling like a complete idiot. The woman's eyes glazed over at this point. I was now – in her mind – squarely in the category of wild card or nutcase. The only important question was whether or not I was dangerous.

For the life of me, I could not find the French words I needed to communicate my situation, to tell her that I was just off a plane from Japan where we all say "*Hai*" all day long. I tried formulating the words in my head, but the English and Japanese and French parts of my brain felt like the ingredients of a smoothie put together in a blender.

I knew if I tried to speak again, I'd probably just dig myself in deeper. Obviously, my mouth was currently out of order. What to do? I left the store knowing I was being seen as a guy who wasn't playing with a full deck. As people often say in Japan, *shōgenai* (it can't be helped).

Back in Japan, I'm now following the lead of my secretary, Miki, who routinely uses another word to say 'yes.' It's a more polite form of *Hai*, is pronounced like 'eh' in the English word *said*, and has no English equivalent to muddle my brain. I've also acknowledged that being in Japan is affecting me more than I'd realized. I wonder if saying "Hi" will ever be quite the same again.

The Tokyo I'm Very Fond of

If there's a balance to the Japanese work ethic, it's in their love for food and the ceremonial side of eating. Tokyo has an incredible variety of restaurants, and I especially love eating in traditional family-owned establishments. In most of them, the people serving you are very good-natured.

At such times, I'm reminded of the traveler from Austria whom I met in Kyoto just after I'd arrived in Japan, when I was wide-eyed and impressionable. He'd been working here for nearly a year, and he'd absolutely had enough. The *salarymen* were awful, he'd complained – cold and unfeeling – but the working people were another story. He'd learned to love them – construction workers, small restaurant owners, everyday folks. He could relate to them, and they made an effort to relate to him. They laughed, smiled and shared small talk with him.

At the time I met him, he was about to leave Japan. Unsure of his future plans, he commented, "Well, at least now I know what I don't want!"

I always remember his impressions, because I now share his affection for those who are 'the salt of the earth' in Japan. Like white-collar workers, they, too, are usually overworked and under constant pressure. Yet many small restaurant workers remain gracious, lighthearted and considerate.

In an area in the heart of Tokyo called *Ochanomizu* (meaning 'Green Tea Water'), I love to go to a very narrow, little restaurant where they serve *tempura teishoku* (deep-fried seafood and vegetable set). The food is so good that around lunchtime, there are always people waiting. Customers sit on stools along an L-shaped counter, while others wait on a wooden bench that's about six meters long and runs the entire length of the shop.

As someone leaves, the people at the top end of the bench get up and take their place. The others who are waiting slide down the bench, making room for those who are standing at the entrance. It's quiet like a library, and everyone patiently waits their turn. Such social order I'd never seen before coming to Japan.

Behind the L-shaped counter, the restaurant workers go about their work with total diligence in a calm and unassuming sort of way, and I feel very welcome in their presence. I also get to eat their delicious food, which I've grown to love.

The proprietor of the shop keeps busily dipping the vegetables and seafood in the hot tempura batter, seeming to get a lot of pleasure out of his work. Two cheerful women busily take orders and immediately pass them on to him verbally – no pen and paper necessary here. Throughout it all, they keep up a ritualistic chorus – a common feature of many Japanese restaurants and stores – their sing-song voices serenading every new customer who enters the shop – "*Irasshai Irasshai*" (Welcome! Come in!)

It's everyday Tokyo at its very best. These people are lovely. I will sing their praises long after I've left Japan.

As for the white-collar *salarymen* the Austrian traveler had grown to detest, I have my own view, and it's different from his. I get to meet dozens of young men (and some women) when they first enter our company. Many are active and very much alive – windsurfing on weekends and doing what twenty-one-year-olds do back home.

I've come to believe that the *salaryman* world is a totally unnatural habitat for human beings to dwell in. These young men would turn out completely differently if they weren't compelled to conform to their company's punishing work regime.

Unlike the Austrian traveler, I haven't come to detest *salarymen*. Many whom I've met at Soulful Software are very likable people. They manage to steel themselves to cope with what Japan Inc. demands of them and still be civil and good-natured; they've got more guts and stamina than I do. It's true that others get totally burned out, but they seldom give me reason to actually dislike them for it.

Not working for a company, my Austrian friend had no such encounters, nor did he benefit from what, in Japan, is all-important – an introduction. Many *salarymen* you've never been introduced to and have no social connection with – such as those you see in the streets or on the trains – can definitely come across as aloof, arrogant or condescending.

To my way of thinking, there's nothing so unusual about this – it's corporate life in the big city. The unique element is that Japanese are generally much less comfortable at making a connection with complete strangers, at least when they're sober. When they're drunk, some *salarymen* exhibit totally bizarre behavior, as with the middle-aged man who literally cosied up to me on the Yamanote Line reeking of sweat and alcohol. With a delirious Cheshire grin on his face, he attempted to rub cheeks with me! The young Japanese couple sitting opposite were embarrassed out of their minds, watching this crazed performance by one of their intoxicated countrymen.

Still, if you worked in the same office with one of these characters, he'd probably be sane and humane all day long. I suspect that if I had to work as a company man for 35 years in Tokyo, I, too, would be crazy as a loon at midnight.

As for the proprietor of the little *tempura* shop, I sometimes sit and watch him go about his work, as I wait my turn on his long wooden bench. I imagine he lives upstairs just above his restaurant and has no commute. His relaxed and amicable nature is a welcome contrast to much of what I see in the men of Tokyo. But then, he escaped the company hamster wheel – no wonder he's so at ease.

Getting Out of Town

Living in this compressed urban sandwich has deepened my appreciation for a lot of things I used to take for granted. Space is one of them – namely, the vast stretches of open land that we Canadians and Americans have in our own backyards.

Being confined to Tokyo for a lifetime would be a tight fit. A junior-high-school teacher friend told me her students say they've never seen anything close to a real horizon – that is, an uninterrupted view as far as the eye can see. Other than the standard three-day trip to Kyoto, which just about every young person takes around grade seven, millions spend most every waking day in Tokyo. And there's precious little gazing across a natural, unblemished landscape to limitless horizons to be found on a Tokyo commuter train.

Doubtless, a comparable situation prevails in other huge cities around the world, especially for poor and disadvantaged kids. When I worked in a children's home in London in the '70s, many of them had never set foot outside the concrete enclave of Ladbroke Grove, let alone the city of London itself. They'd rarely been to a big park – even though London has plenty of them – and when I drove them to Hampstead Heath, they felt uncomfortable and out-of-place and didn't know what to do with themselves. Later in the day, they were visibly relieved to get back home to the familiar concrete walls of Portobelo Road.

For those who can appreciate them, London does have enormous parks and sprawling commons, with far more green space and less concrete than Tokyo. But it must be noted that there are many thousands of splendid little parks in Japan's capital and some large green spaces as well, more than you first realize. *Inogashira Koen* (park) is my personal favourite.

Space is definitely much harder to come by, though, and everything is more tightly packed together. Tokyo's narrow and compact high-rise parking lots are a classic example. Your car is put on a ramp and moved around like cargo on an oblong ferris wheel, according to who wants to get their car out next. It's all done to maximize the small amount of space available.

If you try to get out of Tokyo for a day trip on the weekend by any means other than the pricey *shinkansen* – which will rocket you out of town in no time at all – you soon learn that the urban sprawl seems to go on forever. If you take a regular express train from the center of the city and head towards nearby Yokohama – a 30-minute trip – you'll eventually reach the city limits of Tokyo. But you'll never know it from what you see out the train window. If you're looking at a map, the names will change en route, as one city gives way to the next, but the monolithic urban cityscape will keep relentlessly rolling by. The residential and industrial octopus of Tokyo has stretched its tentacles in all directions.

As a Canadian, I grew up knowing the euphoric feeling that comes with seeing a sign that reads 'End City Limits.' From that point on, we'd leave the boundary of the city behind and move on into wide-open spaces of land and sky. Bruce Springsteen's early lyrics revel in the feelings of freedom that come over you when you hit the highway, and the spatial limitations of everyday city life dissolve. To think I used to take it all for granted.

It's not so easy to find an equivalent experience on the outskirts of Tokyo, should you decide to get up one Sunday morning, rent a car and drive till you're out of town. What you'll probably discover is that getting beyond the boundaries of this extended mega-city is one challenging undertaking.

It can be done, of course, and if you go far enough you can get to some fabulous places. But if you take an ordinary non-toll road (like the so-called 2-4-6 starting in the heart of Tokyo), you'll sometimes crawl along for hours. Even after you've driven for 50 kilometers, what confronts you is what we've dubbed as 'somewhat less of more of the same.'

So people who really want to get out of town pay to use a high-priced toll road – such as the *Tomei Expressway*. If you plan it well – and you get on the road no later than 5:00 a.m. on a Saturday that doesn't fall in a national holiday period – you may be having something akin to a Springsteen-style experience by 7:00 a.m.

Despite the challenges involved, trips of any kind are better than not getting out of this city at all. A steady diet of viewing only what can be seen from Tokyo's commuter trains and office windows will not keep body, mind and spirit together.

Fortunately, there are beautiful, green hills just beyond the chain of cities and towns Tokyo has recently engulfed. A two-hour bus ride from Shinjuku Station will put you in the heart of Hakone, where you'll find mountains with impressive views, lush vegetation and good hiking trails. Of course, if you've got three or four days and plenty of cash to play with, and you're prepared to go really far afield, the rest of Japan offers the foreign visitor a wealth of impressive natural and historical sights.

Friends of Tokyo

For unprepared day trippers, the tentacles of the Tokyo octopus will probably reach you – in some form or other – wherever you go. This was certainly the case with Krista and me, on our first few attempts to escape this city. Even up on a sleepy hillside – several hours of train and bus transportation away from central Tokyo – you'll still be within range of a train station whistle, or a siren announcing the noon hour, or the voice of some guy with a megaphone hooked to his van – cruising a street somewhere far below you – his sales pitch booming off the surrounding hills.

Fortunately, it's possible – with help from those who know – to get just a little further afield and discover beautiful settings that delight you with their rural charm, especially given their proximity to Tokyo. *Chikyu no Tomo* – the Japanese branch of 'Friends of the Earth' – organizes terrific hikes here, taking people on the best possible sojourns within a day's commute, about two Sundays a month.

Invariably, it takes about three hours, by some combination of trains and buses, to get from our apartment to the group meeting point in Tokyo, and then on to the starting point of the hike on the outskirts of town. Five or six hours of hiking later, you're faced with the return journey home. An average hike, therefore, entails about five or six hours of commuting time in addition to the hike itself. So to undertake one of these urban exoduses early on a Sunday morning after a grueling week at work, you have to be pretty eager to commune with the natural kingdom.

Yet, in our experience, it's always worth the effort required, either to go on an organized hike, or to explore the surrounding area on your own with a good guidebook on daytrips near Tokyo. As far as we're concerned, if you're going to subject yourself to living in this urban pressure cooker, it's an absolutely essential release valve.

Besides, in nearby sites such as the extraordinary town of Nikko, or in the hills above the historic town of Kamakura, you make magical discoveries. You can wander timelessly through historical temples that make it easy to completely forget - for a day - that you live in Tokyo. Along with all the other daytrippers, you'll likely snooze peacefully on the train home, exhausted but renewed.

There are many other reasons for joining 'organized' hikes. The makeup of participants is usually a stimulating mix of Japanese, Swedes, Swiss, Americans, Koreans and Australians - like a small United Nations. Most everyone has a great time chatting, strolling and struggling along the best trails to be found within a day's reach of town. There are a surprisingly large number of them.

I've found that just looking at the smiling faces of the friendly, rural Japanese hikers you pass along the way makes these excursions worthwhile. After suffering a daily diet of Tokyo's tired and expressionless faces, I sometimes feel like I've died and gone to heaven on these hikes. Smiling Japanese, smiling at me? *Sugoi!* (Terrific!)

Some hikes end with a visit to an *onsen* (hot spring spa) - Japan at its most luxurious. One we encountered had huge wooden tubs that faced a green hillside through broad, open windows. After our long hike, we thrilled at being able to soak in the steaming water, soothe our aching muscles, and then follow that up with a delicious Japanese meal, sitting on *tatami* mats in the *onsen* dining room.

These are heavenly moments in Japan. My memories of our visits to that *onsen* are exquisite. By the time you get home after such a day, you're in a state of 'natural' exhaustion for a change, and you fall into a deep sleep. The next morning, you're rejuvenated and ready again to do battle with Tokyo. The Japanese adore their *onsen* with good reason.

These excursions offer nature-lovers trapped in this city the sanest way to spend a Sunday. However, you have to accept the facts of life when you're living in a city as huge as Tokyo. I remember the hike where we all ate lunch under a microwave tower on a green mountain slope – all forty of us. That aside, we were still free for a day from that omnipresent sense of confinement which – as a Canadian accustomed to a far greater sense of space – I struggle with daily.

My appreciation for the natural parks and wilderness areas of my own country has soared since living in Tokyo. Memories of sitting undisturbed on boulders next to swiftly flowing Rocky Mountain streams seem idyllic. Watching a bald eagle float across an enormous, silent mountain valley is even more inspiring after a few years of seeing only the narrowed horizons of Tokyo's commuter trains.

Whenever I go home to the west coast of Canada, I try to get up to the top of Mount Maxwell on Saltspring Island. On that lofty perch, the fresh ocean breeze buffets my face, and I reflect on the fantastic view of the horizon offered up by that magnificent cliff face. On a clear day, it stretches forever into a vast blue sky with the ocean as a floor. During my last visit there, I found myself pondering the fact that Japanese economic success – however great it has been or will be – can never buy a spectacular horizon for Tokyo's kids. It's no wonder they flock to Whistler to ski.

I could not fully appreciate that fact before my years of living in Japan. I sometimes wonder how many of today's young Canadians and Americans – despite being blitzed by satellite T.V. images from around the world – are any closer to grasping how incredibly lucky we are. I somehow doubt it, and suspect that deprivation is an excellent teacher.

Let's Compare Geographies

Consider that you could fit 51 Japans into the combined land area of the United States and Canada. Consider also that Canada is about 26 times larger than Japan with slightly less than a quarter of the population. These comparisons bring the phenomenal density of life in Japan into focus.

Japan would fit comfortably into California. The mind boggles at the idea of 125 million people living in that state! Yet, there's room for more than two Japans inside British Columbia and three and a half inside Quebec.

Of Japan's four main islands – Honshu, Hokkaido, Kyushu and Shikoku – Honshu is the most populated. The city of Tokyo is situated in the southeast corner of Honshu in a region known as *Kanto*, an area about the same size as Canada's Vancouver Island, which has a population of under a million. But *Kanto* has a population of 39 million! For another comparison, shrink New York State to a quarter of its size, then more than double the state's population.

Kanto is three-fifths the size of Nova Scotia, which has a population of under a million people. Getting a feel for the density of *Kanto* requires imagining the entire population of Canada – approximately 30 million – plus an extra

10 million thrown in for good luck, huddled together in three-fifths of Nova Scotia. Then picture the whole area crisscrossed every which way with hundreds of kilometers of rail lines packed with commuters. There you have *Kanto*, the heart of which is the great city of Tokyo.

If you lived in this city, you wouldn't wonder for a minute why those Japanese with the money to do so have bought up land and property in the U.S., Canada, Australia and other locations renowned for their vast space. You need buckets of cash to buy space and beauty of that kind in Japan.

For millions of Japanese people living in Tokyo, the possibility of owning a house or land in their own country – let alone outside of Japan – is a remote one, given the exorbitant cost of real estate. At one point, I even heard that 60-year mortgages spanning two generations were being offered to entice buyers.

Many Japanese in Greater Tokyo have given up the idea of ever owning their own home in this city. Some have a hometown to return to someday, and wouldn't want a house here anyway, but millions could just never afford it.

In lieu of ever having the money to buy a home, an ever-increasing number of Japanese (easily surpassing 15 million per year now) content themselves with spending their disposable income on overseas trips, to the great benefit of tourist destinations everywhere. At least that way they get to spend part of their time in more spacious and beautiful settings than Tokyo can offer. Others head to rural *onsen* – scattered throughout Japan – to enjoy the home-grown beauty of their own countryside.

Of course, for a country this size, Japan has accomplished extraordinary things. The comparisons with that other small group of northern hemispheric islands are too striking to be ignored. In fact, the United Kingdom is only two-thirds the size of Japan. Yet between them, these two nations have had an enormous impact on the world. Perhaps that little saying, "Good things come in small packages," has geographical implications. It also seems to help if the packages come tightly packed.

Hilarity on the Rails

There's no evidence of sloth in the men who work the Tokyo train platforms to secure the safety of commuters. They sometimes charge up and down the platform just before the doors shut, blowing their whistles and showing real hustle. In the rush hour, they're doing this every three or four minutes, each time another totally packed train pulls in to unload and then reload its human cargo. But despite their ardent efforts to get everyone aboard, sometimes one thing or another doesn't quite make it into the train.

If you stand back – as the sliding doors shut – and watch this performance, from time to time you'll see parts of jackets, briefcases, purse straps and the heels of shoes protruding from between the rubber grips of the doors. It can be a real circus.

The conductor will then sometimes open all the doors with the flick of a button, to give people one final chance to suck in their breath and reclaim those stray skirt hems, accessories and limbs. But it's often to no avail, since nobody inside can budge an inch. As a bystander on the platform, you'll see the oddest sights as the train pulls away.

I once saw nearly a foot of long, black hair waving in the breeze outside the train, while an astonished woman on the inside came to terms with her situation. I trust she was able to reclaim her locks at the next stop.

On another occasion – from inside the train – I witnessed a comic scene in which a frantic *salaryman* with part of his suit jacket caught in the door was yanking on it, like it was the proverbial sword in the stone, to try to pull it free. Why the frenzy? The problem was that he wanted to get off at the next station. He'd realized to his shock that only the doors on the opposite side of the train would be opening at his stop.

Our British neighbour, Mike, once recounted a similar sighting, but the ensnared appendage was a businessman's tie. His description of the scene had us crying with laughter, because we've all seen variations on this little drama.

If this happens to someone on an express train, it's a major inconvenience, because the doors on the offending side of the train may not be opening any time soon. So someone in this predicament could easily end up going 15 to 30 minutes beyond their stop before they can liberate themselves. Then they'll have to cross the tracks and wait for the train back. That could be a long wait, since fewer trains are heading back towards Tokyo late at night. After a long day as a *salaryman* or *office lady*, who needs it?

As Mike recounted his story of the poor fellow struggling with his tie, someone laughingly suggested it might be a public service for station workers to start carrying around big scissors for this kind of emergency.

"Excuse me, ma'am, if you don't mind parting with some of that hair, we'll have you out of here in no time."

It can be awfully dreary on these trains – full as they are with tired and sullen strangers – with not a lot to alleviate the torpor, save a book or a Walkman and your own personal inner universe. But there are these occasional moments of hilarity that just crack you up, break the monotony, and make for tales that deserve to be told.

It's a good thing, too. Hours a day on these cheerless caravans would be a long time to go without a laugh.

Humor to the Rescue

When I sit down to write, trains continually come up as a topic. They're such a big part of people's lives and conversations in Tokyo. We're dependent on the iron horse here, so there's always train-related stuff happening and more stories to tell.

Living in traumatic Tokyo, it can be hard to remember that overall, Japan's rail system easily warrants the use of the word 'awesome.' Throughout the entire length and breadth of the country, trains operate right to the second 99.9% of the time. Considering the phenomenal number of trains that zip around the country every day, there are very few accidents. As for the *shinkansen*, since its inaugural journey in 1964 there has not been a single fatality. When it comes to safety and efficiency, Japan's train system leaves Amtrak in the dust.

But once Tokyo has swallowed you up, it's easy to forget all that. Commuting everyday on packed trains, you gradually lose perspective. To use the term that Japanese government spokesmen routinely employ to describe calamitous situations, conditions can start to seem 'regrettable.'

Most of us have been on crowded trains at one time or another. I once spent 17 hours sitting on the floor of an overcrowded steam train in northern India, going from Varanassi to Delhi. Japan hardly has a monopoly on train ordeals.

But this country does put its own special stamp on *commuter* travel, as it does on most aspects of life. People spend two to four hours a day inside these mobile metal boxes, so there's lots of time for things to happen.

Living in Tokyo, you begin to notice that some of your most bizarre experiences occur during your commute. These can be very stressful events, or moments of levity, depending on your mood or how you're able to handle them on a given day. What happens during the morning battle to get to work can shake you up for the whole day if it gets to you - so you have to devise effective strategies for coping.

Besides, after awhile it begins to dawn on you that coping with Tokyo's trains provides a pretty good metaphor for the most challenging aspects of Japanese company life: freedom of movement is restricted; you get pushed around a lot (upper management is excluded since they often take cars, not trains); and there are constant deadlines to meet. This latter point is brought home by the fact that running breathlessly for the next train is an everyday Tokyo pastime, even though there's almost always another one coming in three to five minutes.

So I seldom pass up an inspiration to write about the twice-daily ordeal on the rails. The simple truth is that in trying to convey what life is really like in Japan's capital, the physical and psychological battle on the trains is center stage.

After a while you begin to think you've experienced the worst, and nothing can surprise you. Then along comes a new train trauma. Such debacles offer the possibility of raising your blood pressure to new highs, or the opportunity to learn how to maintain your equanimity under extreme duress. It seems to me that when you're a toothpick in the ocean, a humorous perspective is definitely the preferred option.

I've discovered that crazy things most often happen when you break your daily rhythm, as I did a few mornings ago, taking a subway line I'd never been on before at 8:40 a.m. – peak rush hour – on my way to an assignment at an unfamiliar location.

With well-travelled routes, at least you know the ropes. You line up at the same time in a pre-selected spot in a familiar station, and then at your destination you merge into one stream with the mob going out the same exit. It can be intense, but at least you're in the flow, you know where you're going, and everyone else is heading there too.

Ah, but when you're on unfamiliar turf during rush hour in Tokyo, you're in for it! You may have no idea which end of the platform you want to exit from, let alone – in larger stations like Ohtemachi or Shinjuku – which of fifteen possible external exits you want to move towards, with labels like A3 or C9.

With no advance plan in such a situation, you're destined for a ride in a spin dryer once the train door opens. Put another way, you'll quickly find yourself in the midst of a stampede that *knows* exactly where it's going and isn't about to stop for you, the wayward buffalo. You are seriously out of step with the herd.

So it was the other morning. I was on a ten-car train, chok-full, heading for a destination on the Mita Line, a station whose platform was new to me and undoubtedly overflowing with would-be commuters. It was a normal Tokyo morning – operation straitjacket.

While trying to formulate a game plan for how to respond once we got there and the doors opened, I found myself in an extremely contorted position, pulling on the overhead strap in an effort to maintain an upright stance. In order to do so, I was having to use all my might to resist the pressure from the 15 people behind me, who were slowly forcing me down onto the heads and laps of the seated passengers, with my knees buckling under the strain.

It's nobody's fault when this happens; no one was actually pushing me – it's just the combined pressure of everyone all packed together and tilting en masse. There's usually nothing much anyone can do, because there's nowhere to move. The floor is wall-to-wall feet, and nobody has any more control than you do.

But should you be ignorant enough, as I was that day, to raise your foot for an instant to relieve some pressure on an imperiled leg muscle, you may find – as I did – that when you try to put it back down, the space you'd assumed was yours to reclaim is gone, not two seconds later!

The only truly useful weapon at your disposal in such moments is the Monty Python perspective on life, the red alert question spoken inwardly, "Now, how would John Cleese handle this?"

Here I was, standing on one leg on a Japanese train, my torso at a 60-degree angle bent over the seated passengers, my right foot dangling in the air. I held on as tightly as I could to the overhead straps and quickly recognized that this was the chance I'd long been waiting for – a primer in advanced stork imitation, something I'd been putting off for long enough.

It got me through it. Moments later, the train lurched to a stop at my unfamiliar destination, *Shibakoen*, and a new horror challenged me as I braced myself for whatever was coming next.

The sliding doors sprang open, relieving the pressure and spilling out a gusher of those nearest the exits. Seconds later, finally disengaged from stork posture, my body was also twisted and swept towards the train door and disgorged along with the outgoing mob onto the station platform. That platform was already packed with the incoming mob, members of which were jockeying for position, readying themselves for the big push onto the train.

It must be noted that they were doing this in a very orderly fashion, lining up as best they could in queues, the Japanese of Tokyo being extremely civilized about organizing the overcrowdedness imposed upon them.

Train platform decorum is a sight to behold. The outgoing mob goes first while the incoming commuters – in lines flanking the doors – patiently wait their turn. Only the last stragglers exiting the train get caught up in the crosscurrent of incoming arms, legs, torsos and heads when the flow reverses. By contrast, I recall that one train I rode in Bombay was a total free-for-all, with people fighting tenaciously to get both on and off the train the second the doors opened.

That said, the whole procedure in Tokyo is still an exercise in controlled bedlam. My strategy, not having any bearings, was to get into a stream heading close to the nearest wall, flatten myself against it and wait out the exodus. This would give me about three minutes to locate a subway wall map, get oriented, and then head out the appropriate exit before the next train pulled in. Inevitably, I had to go against the grain to carry out this plan, squeezing myself between people into spaces that didn't exist, all the while provoking consternation and a few startled looks. Eventually, I reached the wall running parallel to the train track and pasted myself on it. I just stood there looking out into the torrent of people, trying to express with my body language to everyone squeezing by me that I wasn't planning to move along with them.

A few glances from my fellow commuters – traversing familiar routes no doubt – told me they wondered what on earth I was doing. It's awfully easy to look strange in Tokyo when you're a *gaijin* going against the norm. You feel like a strange spectacle sometimes.

"And not one iota stranger than the spectacle that passes for normal in these trains every day," I thought to myself, impaled on the wall as if it were a boulder in a canyon beside a swiftly-flowing river.

I stood my ground as the platform cleared out. The train I'd gotten off soon filled up to bursting, and a frantic-sounding voice yelled warnings through a loudspeaker – the conductors can really sound hysterical at times. No doubt they know from experience the dangers involved in moving all these millions of people around everyday.

A couple of train employees darted from door to door, stuffing in an arm here, a leg there, trying to keep Japan moving on time. Occasionally, one of them vigorously leaned his full weight against the communal body of commuters, squeezing a final shoulder and a last briefcase in behind the sliding doors.

A whistle blew, and the doors slid shut. I dashed along the platform in search of a wall map of the area. I had at least two minutes before the next mob arrived, time enough to plot my course, plunge down a few tunnels and up a few staircases, then out into the light of day.

Chuckling, I chalked up one more Tokyo train drama, endured and survived, a tale to share with Krista and friends at our next party. On a daily basis, living in Tokyo sometimes presents you with a simple choice: You develop a sense of humor, or you go bonkers.

∞

youngphotography

3

THE HONEYMOON DRAWS TO AN END

This is It?

In the course of doing my job, I get to look around every day at my young *salaryman* and *office lady* colleagues. As always, they're stoically slogging it out for the greater good of Japan Inc., as dedicated a workforce as there ever was. Recently, a cartoon crossed my path that spoke to me about their predicament.

Though the context is different, the cartoon describes for me what many young, white-collar Japanese males must surely feel at some point along the line, once the reality of their situation really sinks in. Although the number is gradually falling, millions of male university graduates still wind up as lifers with the same company, a fate with mixed blessings. We get to meet these new recruits every April 1, the day when Soulful Software and companies across Japan hire new employees who have been recruited during the previous year.

The young people we meet come straight from four years of taking life a lot easier at one of Japan's universities. These institutions are noted for being a kind of oasis, providing a buffer zone between the intense pressures of the school years (Japanese use the phrase *examination hell*) and the years of hard work that begin once the university phase is over. But the flexibility ends right there – few young Japanese take a year off to see Europe or do Peace Corps-style work; that might well sabotage their careers.

On my own, and accompanied by my boss from Indiana, we've taken groups of these new male recruits on field trips to Kamakura and on day hikes near Tokyo. Soulful Software gives them to us for weeks at a time in their first summer with the company for 'English Intensives.' We get them to do the research and preparation for these trips, and then spend the whole day with them out of the company setting. By so doing, we establish rapport and get to know them quite well. Generally speaking, these 21-year-old young men are extremely pleasant, well-mannered and have the feel of innocence about them. They're very nice guys.

We then get to watch and see how they adjust to the rigors of Japanese company life, which is where the cartoon comes in. It's a Gahan Wilson cartoon, and it shows two Japanese monks, robed and sitting on meditation mats. One character looks to be in his 60s. His forehead is severely wrinkled, and his face looks as if it assumed a permanent scowl years ago. These days, I interpret this character to be a well-weathered *salaryman* rather than a Zen monk. Life has clearly been tough on this guy.

Sitting next to him with a somewhat distraught and quizzical look on his youthful face is a novice monk. The older monk is speaking. The caption reads: *Nothing happens next. This is it.*

It must be a sobering moment when this realization comes to a 23-year-old Japanese male on a lifetime track, once the initial excitement of being a salaried company man has begun to wear off. The young man's brief flirtation with a freer lifestyle, permitted during his university years, is now distant history. That's been supplanted by a quasi-military company regimen: the intense work schedule for which the Japanese are famous worldwide; the breathless running for trains and the carrying out of the company's relentless demands. For most men (and women) in this position, there's nothing much to do but bite the bullet and keep on biting.

For years, Japanese men more or less accepted that this was the tradeoff required, in exchange for the lifetime job security their companies were able to offer them and their families. Recently, with this no longer being a given, the door is opening to the possibility of considerable social change. Perhaps it's one many Japanese will welcome. Lifetime employment has a definite downside, as the young novice in my modified cartoon has figured out.

Women working for a company like Soulful Software are presented with immensely challenging constraints of a different kind. We had only one female recruit in our summer program last year, a quiet and self-possessed young woman whom the guys basically ignored. The gender divide separating her from them was enormous.

It was clear that some felt she was on male territory and should have been placed with the O.L.'s (office ladies). Newly recruited O.L.'s do not participate in our summer program, however. This young woman had undoubtedly been recognized for her talents by somebody in administration and recommended for our program. There she sat, calm and poised in the midst of this male club, seeming to me like some kind of modern Japanese suffragette. Yet, tradition will conspire against her being promoted along with the men.

Meanwhile, foreign male free agents such as myself are in an enviable position. Since we're not Japanese, we're not constrained by Japanese social and corporate norms, yet our skills are often in demand. So we have a variety of options, and that is one more thing Japan has taught me not to take for granted.

Grateful though I am to Soulful Software for helping me get started in Japan, I've recently begun to exercise my options by planning a move. It dawned on me one day that if I didn't watch it, I might end up drifting into a decade of working for this company as a commuter *salaryman*, just as my former boss from Indiana did. For me, that was a most disturbing thought.

Of course, some Americans, Brits and other foreign nationals do choose to work here for many years with the same corporation. Many have families, and they appreciate the job security companies like Soulful Software offer them. They manage to adjust to the routines and compromises of company life, as well as to the stressful demands of Tokyo. My hat goes off to them.

Some *gaijin* find a non-corporate niche and thrive in Tokyo, people like the American art dealer I met who sells the work of Japanese artists. I suspect these are the *gaijin* with the best chance of forging a long-term link here that brings them a sense of contentment. They have a calling that connects them with Japanese culture.

Then there are the disgruntled ones, people like the German fellow I heard raving at the driver's license bureau, who end up belonging in straitjackets, but stay on in Japan anyway!

With no intention of ending up like him, I'm trusting my instincts. The Gahan Wilson cartoon taunts me to undertake something new. Perhaps it's just my Canadian frontier genes that prompt me to move on from time to time.

On the Lower Rungs of the Ladder

Americans, Canadians and Brits who make a lifetime commitment to a Japanese company, in the hope of Western-style promotions to positions of real responsibility, may be courting major disappointment. This has certainly been the experience of some of my Western colleagues at Soulful Software, at least up to this point in time.

Our British manager, Terry, is a congenial and capable man in his early forties with a Japanese wife and three children. Terry's been in Japan for six or seven years now. Up to this point, his promotions have been largely symbolic, and while he continues to work diligently on learning the Japanese language, it's hard to imagine that he'd be allowed to fully participate in decision-making, even if he became fluent and stayed here for thirty years. Corporate Japan actually goes quite a distance towards accepting someone like Terry into the fold, but beyond a certain point, outsiders face insurmountable barriers. To draw a parallel, it would be as though the American law that prevents someone born outside the States from becoming president of the country, were to be applied to all corporations as well.

Terry occasionally expresses exasperation with the way he's compelled to operate. He has to work in tandem with a Japanese manager, who takes all of his recommendations back to a committee that makes the important decisions, or, as often as not, postpones making them. The toughest part of his job seems to be controlling his frustration at the powerlessness of his position.

In attempting to get action on one matter that affected all of the non-Japanese staff – trying to secure an increase in a two decades out-of-date housing allowance to reflect the Tokyo real estate price market – he was continually stonewalled.

Through Terry's monthly reports, we were provided with a case study of the famed Japanese intransigence. During nearly two years of meetings, Terry reported such feedback as, "They're looking into it," or "They're setting up a study on apartment prices now," or "They'll be getting back to us within two months."

For the longest time, none of us understood that we were supposed to be taking the hint. Japan, of course, is the 'Land of Indirect.' These comments were intended to tell us we should give up! Given how deeply ingrained *indirectness* is in the culture, many Japanese must surely think that Westerners are either pigheaded or completely daft or both. We just don't 'get it.'

In the international business world, such stalling strategies, as employed by Japanese government bureaucrats, are now legendary. As foreign governments and business people (such as Oregon apple growers) know all too well, such gambits have been used for years to put off opening markets for all manner of imported products. It's been instructive to get a small firsthand demonstration of these techniques in my own tiny company world.

Another colleague, a likable American who works in the advertising department, has been with Soulful Software for over 10 years. When Andy comes upstairs to see us, he often has a comical story to share about his dealings with his Japanese boss, but the gist of his stories always center on his being an outsider with second-class status in the company. As with Terry, he feels excluded from decision-making. His mock tirades are always very funny, but there's no doubting that he's serious in his complaints when he says he's treated like a lackey.

Andy's also married to a Japanese woman, has two children and looks to be here for the duration, playing second fiddle to his Japanese bosses and colleagues. But I suspect his sense of humour will get him through just fine.

Interestingly enough, Terry once confided to me that he's had more difficulty dealing with the culture shock of Brits and Americans working together on staff than with Westerners getting along with Japanese. Somehow, that didn't surprise me. The Japanese are so much less opinionated than us, or are more inclined to keep their views to themselves. In Japan, personal opinions get in the way of the *wa* – the much-valued harmony between people that must be preserved.

In my case, though I did not join Soulful Software with the intention of making a lifetime career of it, I've listened carefully to Terry and Andy talk about their many experiences in assessing my own situation. Suffice it to say that they've dispelled some of my illusions.

Nevertheless, working for Soulful Software has been a largely positive experience. I might well have stayed on another few years if not for a recent eye test, which revealed that more than two years of editing and rewriting under the glare of unsoftened fluorescent lights – ubiquitous in Japan in offices and on trains – have taken a significant toll on my eyes. Others I've spoken with in Tokyo have had a similar experience. Perhaps the scarcity of opportunities for gazing in the distance plays a role in this. Sitting in subway cars, and doing closeup work in closed-in office blocks all day long, your long-range vision probably begins to atrophy from lack of use.

So I'll soon be leaving my many warmhearted *salarymen* and *office lady* colleagues, moving on to another job setting, new challenges and less eyestrain. Working for a Japanese company has been a rare opportunity. Despite the occasional intercultural misunderstanding, I will leave with a lot of respect for the Japanese I've met through my work.

What a Difference a Suffix Makes

I was recently told a story whose origins I can't verify, but it was so believable that I don't hesitate to pass it along. At the very least, it's typical of the ways we *gaijin* make fools of ourselves in Japan, and how the Japanese never let on, allowing us to save face.

As the story goes, an American had been asked to give a lecture to a group of Japanese, on some topic that involved speaking about 'human beings.' In *Nihongo*, the suffix *jin* is generally used for expressions of nationality: *Nihon-jin* means Japanese, *Amerika-jin* means American and *Kanada-jin* means Canadian. The word for human being, however, is *ningen*.

Mixing up his suffixes, the speaker made a slight error in his Japanese, and repeated it throughout the lecture. He was intending to speak about the many things human beings around the world have in common, regardless of nationality or cultural background.

Instead of using the word *ningen*, however, he used the suffix *jin* and spoke repeatedly about *ninjin*, saying such things as, "All *ninjin* have the same aspirations, all *ninjin* want happiness for their children."

Unfortunately, *ninjin* is the Japanese word for carrot, so what the members of the Japanese audience were hearing was impassioned exhortations along the lines of, "All carrots need productive work, all carrots need safe homes for their families, it's time for carrots around the world to unite and realize how much they have in common!"

The lecture allegedly lasted 45 minutes, and as one would expect in Japan, the speaker was given no clue by anyone in the audience as to the mistake he was continually making. Nobody wanted to draw attention to his error for fear of embarrassing him. One hears many such stories in Japan, and they keep us laughing. For that reason alone, the good ones – fact or fantasy – are worth passing on.

Tokyo: Pros and Cons

As the novelty of being in Tokyo starts to wear off, you're faced with the bare bones of your life in this foreign land. Those bones had better be strong or you're likely to run into trouble in this city. You may start doing battle with it.

We're ever grateful that although Tokyo can be a frenetic place because of the sheer numbers of people rushing about, it's not, by and large, a threatening environment. Earthquakes aside, it's a safe and predictable place to live and work.

Even with all of the basics of your life in place, however, the ordeal of the morning and evening commute can start your mind going in a negative spiral. You can begin to feel like you're perpetually under pressure. This past month I've been taking a new route through gigantic Shinjuku Station and changing trains there. At one point, I have to do the sardine shuffle through an underground tunnel, inching along with wall-to-wall commuters all packed together, for about five minutes. It's just too intense, and I've begun exploring new commuting options.

Krista and I struggle with being here, as do many of the foreign nationals we meet. We often discuss short and long-term departure plans, be it for our next vacation or the prospect of leaving for good.

Sadly, the longer I'm here, the more often I meet foreign residents who really dislike their life in Tokyo, but they stay on because of work and money. Sometimes, you feel they should have left long ago, and that being negative is their coping strategy.

This can be especially unpleasant if you're working with people who are like this all the time. Unfortunately, it can also be quite contagious and I, too, fight the bug. If you succumb to focusing on the negatives about Tokyo, there's endless grist for the mill. Once you fall into the habit of looking at everything through a dark lense, simply living in this high-intensity city with its alien culture, will constantly oblige you in reinforcing your negative views. It can become a self-perpetuating cycle.

But when you focus on the positives, there's plenty going on in this city to reinforce that viewpoint as well. There's no point whitewashing the challenges of life here – Tokyo is a tough place to live. If you're going to survive in this urban pressure cooker, you need to make a pledge to yourself to keep the scales tilted towards the positive.

When I start losing perspective in Tokyo, I always come back to reminding myself of the worst sides of life in the other countries I've lived in – England, Iran and India in my case, in addition to my native Canada. Many comparisons serve to extol Tokyo – or make it look pretty good, all things considered.

When I'm in an upbeat mood about this city, I'll sometimes meet a North American with scathing things to say about life here. Oftentimes, their only frame of reference for Japan is Canada or the U.S. It sometimes occurs to me to suggest they catch the next plane to Calcutta, spend three weeks there, and then come back and have a second look at Tokyo.

I have a great fondness for India from the nine months I spent there studying Buddhism and Hinduism, and I treasure many memories from that time. But how can I ever forget the day in Calcutta when I had lunch opposite a man with no eyes – just hollowed-out sockets. He was sitting next to two boys who kept stealing his food and water. After that I wandered around and encountered maimed child beggars in rags, men with no legs propelling themselves around on makeshift skateboards asking for *baksheesh* (alms), and old women dying on filthy blankets next to train stations. In short, I saw human suffering on a scale I'd never dreamt of.

The fact is, like many foreign residents here, I still lose perspective all too often, despite having such comparisons to call to mind. The stress of Tokyo gets to you. Memories like this help to remind me to ease up on the complaining about life in Japan. In terms of hygiene, transport, delivery of goods and services, social organization and public safety, Tokyo - compared to Calcutta - is a little bit of heaven on earth. I've little doubt that the city counselors of Calcutta would trade their problems for Tokyo's any day.

When you look around the streets of Tokyo and really 'grok' that this city was flattened and left in ruins in 1945, you can't help but be astonished by what the Japanese have achieved.

"Yes, but what's the cost in human terms?" is the refrain we trot out in our expat discussions of Japanese society. And the question should be asked, especially because of the common Asian viewpoint that its successes have been the result of better social order. These questions will come up again in the years ahead, and a society's successes, however spectacular, should not be cause for glossing over its failings, for downplaying the sacrifices it has demanded of its people in achieving that success.

Tokyo was rebuilt by such sacrifice, by several generations of people like my colleagues at Soulful Software, who have ridden these horrendously crowded trains to work for the last half century. Person by person, they are the ones who reconstructed their devastated city from the ground up.

In my time here, I've learned a few things about what their sacrifice has entailed. When I think about Tokyo's pros and cons, the stories of these so-called *salarymen* and *office ladies* always come up. They are the ones riding the trains with you uncomplainingly everyday. You jostle with them, you stand next to them cheek to cheek without ever exchanging a word, and you observe their fortitude, tenacity and capacity to endure.

It's their story which is the real story of Tokyo. Depending on your point of view, it's a story of brave knights and courageous queens - or sacrificial pawns.

Kyoko and Miki: Two Stories of Japanese Women

During my time at Soulful Software, we've had three secretaries in our office, all delightful Japanese women. Through contact with them and a number of others within the company, I've come to have some sense of what it's like to be a young, modern Japanese woman working in a traditional Japanese company.

It's not difficult to summarize the biggest obstacle that appears to confront these women: Within corporate Japan, men matter most.

Some American women I know would state it in more emphatic terms: Within corporate Japan, only men really matter!

Historically speaking, however, it's not all that long ago that much the same could have been said throughout the Western world. In the '60s, my mother worked for the government in Canada, and there were two significant differences between her and the man sitting next to her doing the same job: He got twice her salary; and he could smoke and she couldn't - not that the second benefit was helping him any.

Four decades later, we are still a long way from achieving across-the-board equality for women in society and the workplace. But coming to Japan, you realize just how much things have changed for the better for women in Canada and the U.S., insofar as career opportunities and attainable social status in relation to men are concerned.

By contrast, the majority of Japanese women have comparatively fewer opportunities for career advancement. A university education may pave the way to a company position, but promotion is largely a male domain, though there are definite exceptions which prove the rule. Some women end up with important positions at universities and in the media, but across the vast sweep of the Japanese corporate system, patriarchal power remains pervasive.

After five to seven years in a dead-end career track, large numbers of Japanese women begin to look to marriage as the time-honored alternative to a lifetime of corporate servitude. Many confront a kind of 'late-twenties desperation' which takes unusual forms.

I got a firsthand taste of this recently. A woman at Soulful Software - whom I'd met briefly a few times before - was assigned to assist me for two entire days, during which the two of us conducted an English-software training seminar. Kyoko was there to help with translation and general organization. She was terrific - friendly, capable and efficient - and in that way typical. American firms dream of such predictable dedication from their employees.

Over the two days, we chatted during the breaks and got to know a bit about each other. I learned that she's 27 and very overworked. Soulful Software is placing more and more demands on her, taking up all of her time.

She did not know I'm seriously involved because I don't yet wear a ring. At one point on our second day together, I jokingly mentioned something my mother had said just before I left Canada to come to Japan. With the best of intentions, mum was hypothesizing about what I might do if things didn't work out between Krista and me. She trotted out a commonly-held stereotype about Asian women.

"Well, if you marry a Japanese woman, she'll massage your back every night."

On hearing me recount this story, Kyoko earnestly piped up, without a moment's hesitation, "I will."

There was no doubt that she meant it; she was totally sincere. I'd really only known her for 24 hours, but she's reached an age when Japanese men are beginning to pass her over, the proverbial slander being that women over 25 are "like stale Christmas cake," no good after the 25th of December. Still living at home, she can see the writing on the wall now. If she doesn't get married soon, she'll end up single for life, stuck in a low-status job because she has to make a living, run off her feet for Soulful Software.

She's entered a desperate phase, a time when some Japanese women begin thinking along the traditional lines espoused by their mothers, "When you're pushing 30, it's not *who* you marry that matters. Any man will do!"

There's still a dearth of choices for many young women like Kyoko in today's Japan. This society couldn't function without her, but traditional male attitudes continue to conspire to lock her into a life of second-tier status. You only have to watch the so-called *So desu* girls on T.V. news discussion programs to see a perfect illustration of this. Their role is entirely a supporting one; they are there to continually agree with the males on the show.

It wouldn't be fair to single out Japan in this. This country has plenty of company in its unequal treatment of women. In fact, Japanese women clearly fare better than their sisters in many other Asian and Middle-Eastern countries. Be that as it may, most American women I've spoken to have very few good things to say about how women are treated in Japan. For her part, Krista - coming from a very independently minded American and Swedish background - has disdain for the way Japanese women are treated and the obsequious way in which they seem compelled to act. But we share the view that the abuse of women here is a worldwide phenomenon - those Japanese men who treat women as less than equals have plenty of company.

But another Japanese woman I've gotten to know, Miki, trips me up with every generalization I'm tempted to make. She goes her own way, and she's not alone in being intrepid enough to shape her own destiny. I also met Miki at Soulful Software, where she worked as our part-time secretary during her last year of university.

When she finished her studies, Miki went alone to Mexico for about a month – so much for the stereotype of Japanese women being thoroughly meek and dependent. There, she took rolls and rolls of photographs before returning to start a full-time job with the American company Motorola.

Just 14 months later, she made the daring move of quitting that job, and heading off to Guatemala for a few months to hone her photographic skills and study Spanish. She got on well, though the Guatemalans insisted on calling her *Chinagirl*, even though she kept telling them she was from Japan. She then returned to Tokyo and surprised more than a few of us by easily finding a job working in television, albeit a part-time position. But that's exactly what she wanted.

The last I heard, she'd twice negotiated to take time off work – firstly to go to Cuba and later the Philippines – to do more photography. Recently, she held an exhibition of her Cuban photographs at a gallery in Tokyo.

Clearly, modern Japan is now flexible enough to allow for an adventurous and strong-willed woman like Miki to lead what is, by traditional standards, a very unorthodox life. I would add that she seems decidedly different from most of the Japanese woman I've had the chance to meet. She has an overt toughness to her, knows what she wants and is willing to sacrifice to get it.

Those qualities, coupled with a lot of courage, are undoubtedly the very least of what it takes to try to go your own way as a woman in this country, but where there is one, there must be many others. For all I know, Japan is now full of gutsy women like Miki. May she and other young women like her flourish in their independent quests.

Alive But Less Than Well

Lest my experience should fade from memory, leaving me to conclude that my depictions of the rigors of Japanese company life are an exaggeration, I'll be keeping that Gahan Wilson cartoon in my scrapbook. Better still, I'll tell the stories of five young Soulful Software *salarymen* who bring it to life.

First, there's Mr. Karikomi, a bright and personable man who's virtually fluent in English. He showed up in our office looking pretty shell-shocked the other day. His manager had kept him working all night, until 6:00 a.m. to be exact, but he'd been told to be at work by late in the morning just the same, allowing for about four hours of sleep.

I was surprised by his candor. Some of these young men are quite bold and outspoken, at least when confiding to third parties like me. As with other new phenomena in Japan, a term was coined years ago for company newcomers such as Karikomi-san (*-san* being a gender-neutral term of respect, like Mr. or Ms.). They were referred to as *Shinjuru* – a 'new species' of young people who didn't accept the traditional patterns of Japanese life. The phenomenon that it described seems only to be gaining steam – corporate newcomers have quite a different outlook. The 'strange' behavior of new recruits reflects their increasing reluctance to fall into line as their fathers once did.

"Do you get any overtime pay for that?" I asked.

"No, nothing," replied Karikomi-san. "No overtime pay and no extra time off. I get to have dinner with my manager."

He went on without being prompted. Karikomi-san was clearly frustrated and not trying to hide it.

"The younger guys are fed up." he said, "We don't have any time to talk or discuss anything. We're kept busy all the time."

This, from what one hears, is no accident. Longtime Japan residents tell me that management intentionally keeps young lifetime recruits on the run, more or less to break down their independent will. Early training has a clear goal: The young men must be re-educated – through total absorption in company life – to always put the company's needs first, and those of their own lives second.

Karikomi-san's complaints certainly seem valid from a Canadian or American point of view, but it would not help him to complain about the treatment he's receiving. He must learn to acquiesce, to give his all to the company and identify its destiny as his own. Such loyalty is all-important in Japan.

I've watched closely as another *salaryman* recruit, Mr. Kobayashi, has had to succumb in this way. I first met this young man nearly two years ago when he bounded into our office, newly hired by Soulful Software. At that time, he was 22 years old, straight out of university and full of pep, the experience of his four years of relative freedom fueling his sense of vitality. I remember our first encounter well. He was bubbling over with enthusiasm about windsurfing, which he intended to continue doing every weekend.

Unfortunately, Kobayashi-san was quite mistaken in imagining that would be possible. He soon realized there was no way he could continue windsurfing as he had before. His responsibilities at Soulful Software kept him working, or engaged in bonding with co-workers till late at night. Weekends were either completely taken up with company-related obligations, or he was too exhausted to do anything but sleep.

Over the two years I've known this young man, not yet 24 years old, I've watched him lose his generous smile, abandon his outgoing personality, and become more and more dejected. The last time I met him he looked tired, despondent and resigned. Seeing him in this condition reminded me of Krista's story about teaching a night course at a subsidiary of Soulful Software. For the first month or two, the section head had greeted her with some enthusiasm, but over time, that stopped happening. She said it was as though he could just no longer muster the energy for human interaction.

In the case of men like Kobayashi-san, I've little doubt that the prospect of going through his whole life with Soulful Software is depressing to him. By getting to know how these young men feel, I've been led to the conclusion that a major change in the lifetime employment system would be very good for Japan, because it would be good for its people. If they had greater freedom to change jobs, it would free up a lot of initiative and creative energy that is currently being stifled.

If Kobayashi-san is going to follow the path of the lifers who have gone before him, the way out of his dark cocoon is to wave a white flag, surrender to the company, and accept that they've basically captured him. At that point, he can at least set about bonding with the people he's going to be working with for decades to come, and enjoy their friendship.

At least three times a year, he'll have periods of time off during national holiday periods, and he may even be able to squeeze in a one-week vacation from time to time. Needless to say, he can probably forget about windsurfing throughout his life. Years from now, windsurfing will probably be a sport he does once a year, but still thinks of as his hobby. Or it'll be something he once did during his university years, much as one middle-aged *salaryman* told me that "music is for younger people."

He'll end up saying *shōgenai* (it can't be helped/there's nothing you can do about it), like most people do in Japan to explain their passive acceptance of their society's demands on their lives. My friend and colleague, George, a longtime American resident married to a lovely Japanese woman, once summed up the difference in attitude between Americans and Japanese in one succinct phrase: It's *Can do* versus *Shōgenai*.

Of course, in Canada, our refrain goes: "Why isn't the government doing something about this?"

Mr. Mitani, however, broke ranks, and did something quite unusual. In the Japan of 1990, a Labour Ministry survey reported that nearly 40% of salaried workers "hardly take" any of their annual paid vacation leave, 16 to 20 days being the standard paid vacation allotment in Japanese companies. This translated as "zero to three days off a year" since the next group – an additional 30% of workers – took "four to eight days off." That left only 30% of the full-time workforce taking more than eight days of the paid vacation they're entitled to. A report in 1993 showed virtually the same results, with "most people" still taking seven or fewer days vacation a year. It's a statistic that's not about to change quickly.

When it comes to getting married, many men at Soulful Software claim their five extra paid honeymoon days, and whisk their bride off to a well-earned week of sun in Hawaii or Australia. One man we work closely with chose to forego even this, however, confining his honeymoon with his bride to a weekend in nearby Hakone, an hour and a half from Tokyo. He returned to work on Monday without missing a day of work. We imagined he'd put company loyalty first, a highly respected statement to make in a Japanese corporation on an occasion as important as your wedding.

But Mitani-san, a wonderfully gentle man in his early thirties, confided to me that he was taking his lucky bride on an extended trip to Austria. Not only did he claim his five paid honeymoon days, he was tacking on an additional ten days of paid vacation leave, so he and his wife could get away for three full weeks and really enjoy themselves. Mitani-san was such a mild-mannered guy that I'd somehow never expected him to be so bold. He seems to be a man who's made his peace with himself and already knows the level of advancement in the company he'll be content with.

Then there's Mr. Yamamoto. He's one of several hundred of Soulful Software's newest recruits who recently gave us writing samples, since we need to assess their level of English to help them work with foreign clients and write reports.

Yamamoto-san, a 22-year-old who seems younger, has been on the job eight months now, and was asked to write about a picture he was shown. It was a photograph taken in the early morning rush hour in the Tokyo subway. It showed the crush of people and a guard struggling to muscle the last few bodies into the pile, so the doors could close and the train leave on time. In his essay, Yamamoto-san revealed in visceral terms just how much he "hates" the daily commute.

Yet his most revealing comment was this: "How do they feel at that time? Complaints, anger, sadness, etc. But I don't think they hate their work. Because they are so indifferent; at least they feel something at their office." [sic]

I think his comment explains how many Japanese come to terms with their lives. They throw themselves into their work, because they know their lives are going to be totally defined and dominated by it. Some, like Mitani-san, are finding ways of maintaining commitment to the company, while attending more to the needs of their wives and families.

Finally, there's Mr. Onuki, my fifth and final *salaryman* sketch. Onuki-san is a soft-spoken man in his thirties who toils away tirelessly in the accounts department. When I first met him, I didn't yet know that what people study at university in Japan often has no bearing whatsoever on what they end up doing in their companies.

In Onuki-san, I detected a sensitive spirit, one a bit too romantic to have chosen to be a number cruncher. I wondered sometimes what dreams he'd given up for his lifetime job at Soulful Software. Curious about his background, one day I asked him what his major had been at university.

Onuki-san looked up at me from behind his glasses, made eye contact, and gazed at me quietly for a very brief moment.

"Greek Tragedy," he replied softly, and returned to his work.

There are these classic moments in Tokyo you know you'll remember forever.

Lucky Westerners

Fortunately for me, I'm not locked into the lifetime employment system, nor do I run the risk of marginalizing myself by quitting my job. As *gaijin*, most of us are just passing through. Though our long-term security is often tenuous, we're in the enviable position of having more say about what happens next in our lives.

But a gradually increasing number of young *salarymen* are getting gutsy about job-hopping, and taking more control over their lives as well. I spoke a few weeks ago with Watanabe-san, a veteran of seven years with Soulful Software. I'd heard the surprising news that he'd just given in his two-months' notice.

Mr. Watanabe's English is excellent, and he's spent a lot of time traveling overseas for the company. Young men like him are in increasing demand by multinationals.

"Was it difficult to decide to quit?" I asked him, expecting a guarded response.

"Naw," he replied, with genuine cockiness, "I got a better job."

I was surprised at his self-assurance, but perhaps I shouldn't have been. Foreign media reports suggesting the imminent demise of the lifetime employment system seem exaggerated or premature. But headhunting has become a common practice in Tokyo. It helps those who really want to make a move to secure their new positions before jumping ship.

Watanabe-san's self-confidence and willingness to take risks in his own self-interest is a very healthy development, in my view. All of Japan will benefit when its people have more control over their own personal destiny.

Tokyo: Just How Safe is It?

You can get so caught up in the challenges of your working and commuting life in Tokyo that you begin to take some things, which made a very favorable first impression, completely for granted. But then a time comes when you're reminded of them again, as I was last night, strolling home through our neighborhood around midnight after visiting friends.

It was a beautiful night. Some stars were visible, and it was wonderfully quiet in Chofu. I felt completely safe and fearless walking home - and had I been a single woman, the situation might not have been much different. I know this from speaking with dozens of Western women here. They're careful, of course - we do hear stories of predatory male behavior of various kinds. Rumor has it that unreported rape is quite common. But even so, most Western women we know don't hesitate to walk home alone at night along a known route. After all - we all say - this is Japan.

American women living here sometimes speak about this with gratitude and amazement. It's a profound relief for those who come from large urban centers in the U.S., where they would never dream of walking home alone at night.

We wonder how a city of this size has maintained such comparatively safe conditions. I make a long list sometimes and speculate on the relative importance of each factor: education that stresses conformity; the community-based police forces with their tiny box-like *koban* (police stations); fear of reprisal and social shame; a low unemployment rate; close-knit family structures; collective memory of the time when stepping out of line meant losing your head to a Samurai sword; a social norm that keeps a tight lid on strong emotions; greater control over citizens' lives...

Is there one overriding factor? In her satirical send-up of the much maligned *salaryman*, an illustrated book called *The Way of the Urban Samurai*, the Japanese artist *Kasumi* (formerly married to a *salaryman* and now living in the U.S.) writes that, "Saving face is the reason that divorce and crime rates are lower in Japan than in most other countries."

Japanese know their own culture better than I ever will, so perhaps *face saving* is the linchpin. Whatever the explanation, this aspect of life makes a positive statement about this country. Satire aside, hard-line critics of Japan who downplay such positive features of Japanese life, or put them all down to repressive social engineering, are ignoring the big picture.

Umbrellas and bicycles often get 'borrowed' in Japan as though they were public property - sometimes drunk *salarymen* hop on the nearest bike to pedal home - but other types of theft and robbery are significantly less common than in North America. With the population of American prisons now approaching

2 million inmates, Japan – with just under half the population of the U.S. – has around 50,000. The relative safety here is no small achievement. Assaults of various kinds do occur – I've heard of a few happening with foreign friends – but a big-city American woman walking home alone in Tokyo will usually tell you she feels safer here.

That woman will probably go on an occasional tirade about the patriarchal corporate system or the lechery on the rail lines, with just cause. It's definitely true – perverts known as *chikan* stealthily go about the business of fondling female bodies on the jam-packed trains and in the department stores here. These creeps are very low profile – obscene but not heard, one might say. Japanese women are usually reluctant to accuse them, fearing the men will deny it. That's a scenario which would leave the accusing woman open to ridicule and loss of face, so most won't risk it. *Chikan* are a scourge for Japanese and non-Japanese women alike.

You hear many *chikan* stories when you live in Tokyo. When Krista is commuting, she's on '*chikan* alert' at all times – an additional source of stress in Tokyo for women. One day, talking about men on the trains, she said, "I get heavy vibes from most of them." Our American neighbor, Rebecca, also gets the heebie-jeebies during her commute. In a walk home from the station one night, she told me she gets "obsessed" about where she's going to position herself whenever she gets near a train.

"I think about it all the time," she added.

Fortunately, the authorities are finally taking some steps to respond to this covert social nightmare, by placing undercover *chikan* watchers on trains and catching a few red-handed. That should help – the risk of social exposure and accompanying loss of face probably being such a strong deterrent – though the problem goes beyond the confines of the trains. One man in Sendai grabbed Krista's breast as she passed him on her bicycle in the middle of the afternoon. Unfortunately for him, he picked the wrong woman. The next thing he knew, she had him up against the wall, clutching his shirt and tie at his throat and shouting at the guy, while a group of her female students stood by watching with astonishment.

But while railing against such blatant sexual abuse, my American women friends will still readily acknowledge the vastly reduced fear they experience when walking on the streets of Tokyo at night. Back home in cities like L.A. or Chicago, where the risks of being assaulted, raped or killed on a solo nighttime walk are dramatically higher, American women have had to learn to live with a steady diet of low-level apprehension and outright fear. I know that from Krista's experience. When we lived in Montreal, she was beaten up and robbed on her two-minute walk home from the subway station one night, and she needed stitches to close the gash in her face. She lives with that memory, but feels much safer in Tokyo.

My women friends in Canada used to attend an annual "Take back the night" march as a reaction to that fear and as a protest against the everpresent dangers facing them on the nighttime streets of their cities.

Most Japanese women in Tokyo, while they have their own battleground in dealing with *chikan*, have never even heard of such events. So far as walking on their city streets at night goes, may they never need to.

Reflections on 'Moving on'

Although many people have cautioned me that university students in Japan lack motivation, finding out firsthand about another aspect of Japanese life struck me as a good next move for a number of reasons.

I've sampled company life, and I've met the new recruits when they join companies like Soulful Software every April. My *gaijin* colleagues and I have met the young men in their newly purchased blue suits – relaxed, good-natured and awkward in their new roles, wearing their youthfulness on their sleeves. We've also met the exceedingly polite young women – cheerfully and optimistically embracing their working lives.

We've then witnessed their reactions to the pressures of company life. By comparison, the academic life these new corporate conscripts have had to leave behind sounds idyllic. I'm curious to know more.

My new university job gives me good cause to stay on longer in Japan. In addition to having more time off, and the chance to get away from the stress of Tokyo twice a year, I'll have a better salary as well. Besides, Krista's now working at a university, so we'll be better able to match up our time away from Japan. All told, it seemed like a logical move.

Having given my notice, I've found myself looking at my *salarymen* colleagues with very sympathetic eyes lately. I'm getting out and moving on to a very different job setting, something they can't so easily do.

I try to picture my younger co-workers toiling away with Soulful Software for another three decades. It's a sobering thought. I don't presume to have great insight into Japanese corporate life, but I've certainly seen enough to know that my colleagues' jobs will totally take over their lives, as they assume more and more responsibility in the company. The banality and intensity of the daily Tokyo grind is something they'll simply have to accept. It's not a prospect I could cope with serenely, I readily admit.

Of course, the daily commute is a big part of what makes the picture so daunting. Using a conservative estimate of an hour each way, my calculations tell me that someone working at a company in Tokyo, from age 21 to 55, spends a career total of approximately 17,850 hours (or 744 days) on jam-packed trains getting to and from work. That's approximately two full years of your life spent scrunched in a mob.

For even a moderately free spirit like myself, my company's promise of lifetime employment – spent in the confines of Tokyo – would feel like a curse as much as a blessing. For many Canadians and Americans more free-wheeling than I am, a lifetime spent working in a company in this city would be regarded as a complete impossibility, a kind of prison sentence.

Are we Westerners just selfishly individualistic? From a traditional Japanese point of view, definitely. But our societies never taught us that we'd have to accept such a life, and our deeply-rooted belief in personal freedom leads us to rebel against extreme restrictions and seek a better way.

I remember being told by an older Japanese colleague, a man I genuinely respected, that Japanese people thought of Canada's former prime minister, Pierre Trudeau, as being immature. On reflection, I decided that many Canadians undoubtedly felt the same way at times, at least in Trudeau's early days as P.M. But I also recognized that Trudeau's unique, flamboyant style must have been very off-putting for socially conformist Japanese. Their politicians would never act like that; they couldn't get away with it. Yet, Trudeau's personal style and wit are exactly what many Canadians appreciated most about him.

I've concluded that you simply have to be Japanese to understand how they cope with the sacrifices corporate life demands of them. For most Westerners I know, forfeiting one's personal dreams, ambitions and style to the extent required in Japan, would be regarded as an unacceptable surrender of life's possibilities.

Obviously, many Europeans and North Americans still choose to work at one job all their lives, but there are differences. They usually have many evenings and weekends to themselves. They have their vacations. And at all times, they have real personal choices available to them, one of which is the option to leave a full-time job and get another one with full social approval. Such acceptance has just begun to take hold in Japan, as circumstances force more and more people out of once-permanent positions.

In Japan, people work with a deeply ingrained attitude that you persevere, no matter what. Exemplifying this is the often-heard phrase *Gambatte Kudasai!* (Carry on!). Having worked relentlessly for years, many Japanese are habituated to the rigid schedule their society and company has always imposed on them.

When I first got to Tokyo, talk had just begun about companies giving their workers one or two Saturdays a month off, or releasing them from Saturdays altogether – a novelty for a country used to a six-day work week. I discovered that free or unstructured time was an unfamiliar concept for many Japanese.

The government actually released a song about it in the late '80s. It was intended to help workers who'd begun the shift from a six- to a five-day work week to adjust to the idea. The lyrics explained how they could use their newly acquired free time.

Krista once told me she thinks Japanese people might be better off not knowing how tough their lives are, when compared with much of the rest of the industrialized world. In other words, you don't miss freedoms you've never experienced.

Chatting one day with my co-worker, Mr. Hosono, after he got back from a business trip to Luxembourg, I wondered about this as well. Hosono-san is a very thoughtful and gracious man, and I respect his keen perception and openness. I asked him how things had gone.

He explained that one day, they'd been right in the middle of an afternoon meeting, when the chief negotiator for the European side had announced, "Well, it's 4:30, and we've had a productive session. Let's call it a day and reconvene tomorrow morning."

Within minutes, the place was deserted. Everyone had left and gone home to their families, or on to leisure activities. For the Japanese men, however, it was a definite case of culture shock, European-style. Hosono-san and his colleagues were astounded.

"We had no idea what to do," he confessed, most candidly. Accustomed to working on a regular basis until 10:00 p.m. or later, they were flabbergasted that working men were calling it quits for the day at 4:30 in the afternoon, with the sun still high in the sky! After floundering around for awhile, they eventually just headed back to their hotel rooms and got drunk, strangers in a foreign land with foreign ways.

Looking around at the faces here at Soulful Software, I know I won't forget them. My Japanese colleagues have taught me a great deal about perseverance. In fact, they've got 'hanging in there' down to a science. What they haven't had is a chance to learn how to hang a bit looser - without the addition of liquid fuel, that is - and how to achieve a healthier balance between work and leisure.

A Nation of Endangered Livers

After hours, Tokyo undergoes a transformation. The changeover takes place nightly in literally thousands of tiny local bars and more spacious *isakaya*. To my surprise, many North Americans I've talked to back home had no idea that Japan is a nation of drinkers.

The use and abuse of alcohol is so widespread in Japan that the recognition of alcohol addiction as a serious social problem would require a radical change in thinking. Beer is consumed like a soft drink. It's sold in big cans in vending machines to passersby of any age. You can also pick up a 'cup *saké*' if you like, and drink it as you walk down the street. The well-trodden path through a company dinner begins with a toast with beer, moves on to *saké* and eventually to whiskey – a rough mix for many a stomach.

Either as a follow-up to a company event, or just as an after-hours social gathering, millions of Japanese wind down in some kind of bar on Monday through Saturday nights. Try any Tokyo drinking establishment at 10:00 p.m. on a Monday evening – it's not an off-night. The place will be full.

Given that liquor provides a readily accessible escape valve in this pressure cooker society, Japan simply doesn't seem interested in looking at this as a social issue. So there is widespread denial of what appears to be rampant alcoholism, at least according to some definitions of the word.

As in France, the social acceptability of alcohol use in Japan creates an atmosphere that's totally supportive of everyday drinking. But considering the quantity of booze that's consumed in this nation, the absence of violent alcohol-induced behavior is striking. I suspect that the close-knit identity the Japanese people share with each other plays a major role in this. I have, at times, actually found myself envying the comfort and security they derive from their shared identity as a people.

But the downside of this social sanction of alcohol is that a lot of people drink themselves into ill health. I give private English lessons in my spare time to a pilot for a Japanese carrier. Ishi-san has been a domestic pilot for years, and now he's making the change from co-pilot to pilot on international flights. He needs to upgrade his English so he can communicate with his non-Japanese passengers. I've worked with him for a year and a half now. You couldn't meet a nicer guy, but for a 45-year-old man, he's in rough shape. The regular drinking routine he and his colleagues have maintained for years, during stopovers in L.A. and Paris, has finally taken its toll.

Japanese carriers have an exceptional safety record, and Ishi-san is probably a top-notch pilot. Nevertheless, because of his off-duty drinking, he's now been forced to take four months off work to take care of his beleaguered liver.

So far, curtailing his drinking as a response to his health problems does not seem to have occurred to my pilot friend. That surprised me at first, but there's a great deal of support for this kind of denial in Japan, both with alcohol abuse and cigarette use. Frequent drinking is the norm, and roughly 60% of adult males still smoke. As for related issues like 'passive smoking,' it's scarcely been acknowledged as an issue here – the air in small coffee shops in Tokyo is bad news.

As far as drinking goes, we all know that it provides a surefire way of inducing temporary anesthesia, guaranteeing a brief respite from the tough realities of life. I imagine that relinquishing that option is not an appealing prospect for many Japanese men and a good number of the women.

Said with a rhythm and a rhyme: the company life is much less glum when to its pains you are frequently numb.

Please Tell Me This Isn't Happening

There are some other sides to the drinking scene in Tokyo that everyone just learns to accept and tolerate – live and let live, Tokyo-style. The most conspicuous example of this is best illustrated by some unpleasant incidents that I hesitated to write about at first. But in hindsight, they're just funny, though they were hardly so at the time for the people involved, myself included. They're great reminders of how things that are initially bizarre and outrageous in Tokyo eventually become ordinary and commonplace.

As I've mentioned, one of my reasons for deciding to leave Soulful Software stems from the discovery that my eyesight has been getting much worse. I suspect that's because of the strain from all the editing work I've been doing, under the glare of harsh fluorescent lighting.

This being the case, I've taken to reading books on eye improvement, one of which recommended taking off your glasses when you don't need them. I recently started doing this just after leaving work at night.

I should point out that my eyes are bad enough that I wouldn't dream of trying to cross a street without having them on. But provided I'm attentive, I can take off my optical crutches once I've gotten down into the subway without suffering any consequences. Or so I thought.

On the night in question, I popped my glasses into my shirt pocket on my way down the stairs into Nihonbashi Station, purchased a ticket, went through the turnstiles, and took up a position on the platform to wait for the train.

Beyond the range of a few feet, everything was blurry – people's faces, advertisements on the subway walls – but I'm not so visually challenged that I'm in danger of walking off the platform into the path of the oncoming train. I soon heard its approaching roar. It rolled to a stop, the doors slid open and people piled out. Then in I went, Sony Walkman on, with Beethoven soothing my urban soul.

I stood for a moment, there being quite a few people standing, but then I noticed a vacant seat. That was surprising, but not totally uncommon for this time of night, a few hours after peak rush hour. Couples sometimes prefer to stand, rather than having one of them sit with the other leaning over to talk.

Pleased at my discovery, I made my way over to the vacant seat and plopped myself down. The first unusual thing I detected in response to doing this was a subtle movement of heads. Heads to my left, heads to my right, heads straight across from me – most of them turning just slightly, and all at once. With my glasses off, I couldn't make out faces, but there was no mistaking the movement of the blurry blobs, which I certainly knew to be the heads of Japanese people. I could also discern that they were turning for a glance in my direction.

"What is happening?" I thought. "What on earth has the foreigner done now?"

Anxiously, I fumbled in my shirt pocket and pulled out my trusty glasses to return the visual world to normal, with Beethoven's Seventh Symphony racing to a climax in my ears. It was one of those experiences when time stops, along with your heart, when you twig to the true horror of the moment.

As my eyes focused, I soon learned that there'd been a reason why this seat was vacant. As I glanced down, all the heads in my proximity – no longer blurry blobs, but now complete with Japanese eyes, mouths and faces – subtly moved in tandem with mine, and then quickly looked away. Mortified, I continued to gape at the source of their attention, paralyzed with revulsion and shock. My feet, I had discovered, ensconced within my black Reeboks, were planted right smack dab in the middle of a large, thick pile of fresh vomit.

"Oh God, this can't be happening," I thought, a wave of nausea assailing my stomach. For just an instant, I sat there like some immobile statue with feet of stone. Then I unfroze and lifted my upper body to a standing position, my shoes still rooted in the mound of regurgitated dinner barf, no doubt deposited there by some inebriated *salaryman* minutes before. Ever so slowly, I extricated my feet from their hideous moorings.

Fortunately, the Japanese are extremely considerate to people in such situations – they win first prize for that. Most of the time, when you're in a position where you feel unequivocably *hazukashii* (embarrassed), they'll carry on as if nothing strange is going on. I will never know if anybody actually vocalized a response or not, because I had my Walkman on the whole time and was in no mood to stand around on display long enough to take out my ear plugs. But even though they never looked at me again after that initial glance, I've little doubt that every person within range of the incident was simultaneously voicing the same collective inner response, something along the lines of, "Oh, how totally disgusting, the poor guy. But why didn't he see it?"

The train was now between stations, roaring along through the subway tunnel. Not knowing what else to do, I started walking ever so slowly, trying to make my way down to the other end of the car, away from the people who'd seen all of this. But I had to walk in slow motion to prevent the vomit on the bottom of my shoes from splashing onto my pants, or the clothes of all the people around me. Of course, I then discovered that I was leaving vomit footprints with every step. So everyone saw, even those further up who hadn't noticed before!

The nightmare ended at the next station. I deftly stepped out, wiped my shoes furiously on the train platform and quickly bounded back on the train in the next car up, anonymous once again. As the doors closed, I took perhaps the deepest sigh I've ever taken in Tokyo, and there have been many.

As the train again picked up speed, my stress dissolved into internal chuckling at what had just transpired. I shook my head in disbelief and pondered the question, "Whatever will be next in my life in this city?" Just for the record, I have now resumed wearing my glasses at all times in the Tokyo subway.

Variations on the Theme

Generally speaking, I find Tokyo to be an extremely clean city compared to others of this size I've visited or lived in. You see workmen diligently washing subway steps and garbage collectors picking up the tiniest scraps of paper. Certain Japanese customs, such as the dispensing of *oshibori* – steaming, hot towels to wash your hands before meals in restaurants – are wonderful and hygienic practices. I'd like to see this become an everyday custom around the world. Routinely ensuring that people clean their hands before eating would probably save untold billions in health-care costs.

But the good news comes with the bad, and an accurate portrait of life in Tokyo calls for both; fanciful descriptions belong in the tourist brochures. Still, I'm sensitive to the fact that my Japanese friends would like me to sweep the seamiest sides of Tokyo life right under the carpet and move on to the next chapter.

"Relax," I want to tell them, "I still love many things about your culture, and rest assured, my culture has sides that are every bit as seamy, an easy rival for anything I've seen here."

So, if you come to Tokyo, be prepared to keep one eye on the ground at night. You'll see the acidified remains of last week's carousing, staining the concrete around the base of the metal poles on the train platforms. If you stay around a while, you're bound to come across deposits of fresh vomit on those same platforms and city streets on any given evening, but you'll especially see it at certain times of the year such as *Bonenkai* – so-called 'forget-the-year' parties in December.

There must be a fair bit to forget, because at such times you'll see more than a few men passed out on train benches all over town. You'll also see lots of teenagers doing exactly what we did at their age in Canada – bonding and testing their limits in rite-of-passage drinking bouts. But they take good care of each other, these young people, the 'group' being all-important in Japan. I see comparatively few signs of the broken bottles, fist fights, and random acts of vandalism so common to the young drinking scene in Canada and the U.S.

Mind you, you have to keep your head up if you take the last train home late at night. Ask my pachinko-loving friend, Kathy, who lived through her own nightmare. On the evening in question, Kathy imagined she was immune to what was to befall her, because she was standing. Here in Tokyo, we all hear stories about the dangers of sitting on the late night trains. One American guy I spoke with recounted how he felt very pleased with himself one night for having secured a seat. He was just dozing off when the drunken gentleman holding on to the strap above him upchucked all over the head of the person seated next to him.

Now when he takes the last train home he stands up and remains conscious and vigilant, but even doing that didn't protect Kathy. An inebriated teenage lad barfed all over her, just as she was about to get off at her station. The doors opened and she staggered out onto the train platform, her long blonde hair and raincoat soaked in his vomit.

Kathy whipped off the coat and held it at arm's length with two fingers, momentarily shocked and not knowing what to do. All of this took place under the watchful eyes of hundreds of onlookers, packed onto the waiting train, with absolutely nothing better to do than scrutinize Kathy in the midst of her horror show.

The friends of this drunken teenager, horrified at what their buddy had done to a foreign woman, got off the train, guided her over to a sink on the platform, and helped her to wash the vomit out of her hair and raincoat – predictably darn good kids. Kathy told me you've never seen such a flurry of apologetic bowing in all your time in Tokyo.

Flashback – The Quest for Peanut Butter

In some ways, our first few days in a foreign country such as Japan are like a return to early childhood – the language is an unknown universe, and the most ordinary tasks are unmanageable. At times, we feel totally inept, lacking the skills needed for even the most basic acts of communication. Surely, this is a universal experience with travelers.

Our recent trip to the *Kansai* region – encompassing Osaka, Kyoto and Kobe – triggered memories of my first few weeks in Japan. Along came a memory that made me shake my head with embarrassment. I remember examining a jar of something that looked exactly like peanut butter in a corner grocery store, turning it over and over in my hands, pondering the unreadable *kanji* script and wondering how on earth to get confirmation of its contents.

I realized that by going up to the proprietor of the shop, I might simply succeed in making myself look ridiculous. At that early stage, I hadn't yet begun carrying an English-Japanese dictionary with me at all times. Besides, the shop owner might never even have heard of peanut butter anyway.

But my salivary glands got the better of me. The idea that this jar might actually contain something as familiar as peanut butter drove me on, as did my deluded sense that somehow or other, I'd be able to communicate. Jar in hand, I approached the counter tentatively, having decided to try charades with the poor man, who looked to be in his late sixties.

Knowing only how to say *Konichiwa* (Hello), I launched straight into miming a person spreading 'whatever it was in the jar' on an imaginary piece of bread with an 'air' knife. I also threw in a few selected words of English I thought he might know: "bread, peanuts!" Wide-eyed, the Japanese gentleman watched me with great curiosity and absolute incomprehension.

In the end, I abandoned any thought of communication and just bought the stuff. I went straight home, and made the mistake of forgetting that I hadn't been sure what it was. At the time, I was having trouble adjusting to Japanese food, and I desperately wanted this jar to contain peanut butter. Spreading a tantalizingly thick layer of the substance on a piece of bread, I took a large bite of the most revolting would-be condiment I've ever tasted. It turns out it was *miso* paste. Months later I met a Canadian woman who'd had exactly the same experience on her second day in Japan.

As I rerun the scene in that grocery store in my mind, I try to imagine myself as seen through the grocer's eyes – a kind of pre-verbal ape cavorting in front of his cash register, pointing at a jar of *miso* paste, making strange gestures in the air, and uttering the occasional foreign word.

Most of us in Japan will admit to having performed such a dance at least once, miming and gesturing intensely, and no doubt coming across as crazed lunatics to the totally mystified Japanese clerks we've confronted, usually to no avail. Trying to achieve the simplest task can turn into high drama, but in the early going in Japan, it's usually a playful scene.

The direct experience of this kind of culture shock is a valuable one. It sensitizes you to how non-English-speaking people feel when they come to your own country. In a shrinking world, with immigrants from the far corners of the globe showing up in your neighborhood, there's a great need for more young people to become multilingual.

I also learned, early on, that if I wanted peanut butter, I had to learn to ask for it in Japanese. I couldn't expect people to understand me if I didn't learn their language, however daunting the task. English is widely spoken in the world now, but there's no law that says everyone has to speak it. Living in

Japan, this lesson is constantly driven home to you. And if you refuse to learn it, you get free daily lessons in the virtues of humility.

Kyoto Revisited

Ah, Kyoto! Our recent visit there was a journey back into my innocent first encounters with this country. My body literally tingled with happiness at being there again, and it was great to share it with Krista, who'd lived in Sendai when I was in Kyoto. I'll always associate Kyoto with things I love most about Japan. In the literature on culture shock, you learn that the strongest shock actually occurs later, usually after an initial two- or three-month period of excitement and discovery. At first, there's a fascination with the totally new world - it's the infatuation phase of a newfound love.

In my infatuation period in Japan, I lived in a tiny cabin at the foot of a Japanese garden in Kyoto, Japan's historic former capital. It was perched beside the entrance gate to a private home, the latter being a beautiful and spacious house, situated on a hillside sprinkled with temples. Only on my return, however, some weeks ago, did I learn more of the history of my little abode from Kakuko, my former landlady. She's a lovely Japanese woman in her middle sixties who speaks excellent English, as kind and welcoming a person as you could have the good fortune to meet in any country. I was introduced to her through friends working in the Kyoto area, whom I knew through meditation circles. They knew about Kakuko's lodgings, because they've been passed on from friend to friend for years.

Kakuko's family home lies nestled at the end of a small unpaved laneway, halfway up a hill, in a splendid area of Kyoto called *Higashiyama-ku*. Her house and the one adjacent to it - both of which were owned by her family - were built in 1925, at almost exactly the same time as the enthronement of the former Emperor Hirohito, who died in January 1989.

The garden was created at the same time. To take care of it and also serve as gatekeepers, a couple were hired, and it was for them that the little doll-like cabin at the foot of the garden was built. Kakuko remembers this elderly couple from her earliest years.

On hearing this, I became more inquisitive about the gatekeeper's cabin, inside the minuscule quarters of which I had slept, written numerous letters, meditated, prepared and sipped Japanese tea and hot soup for a couple of months, feeling like a Zen monk. Living there had had its romantic side; it had been a spartan adventure dwelling in such a pristine Japanese setting, sleeping on *tatami* mats for the first time, and experiencing life in such tiny quarters. My cabin was an eight-foot square box with a six-foot ceiling, not even wide or long enough - if you were a gymnast - for a full forward roll in any direction. There was no shower or bath, so I headed down the hill to the local *sento* every night after returning from my day's work in Osaka, teaching at an English conversation school.

Now, I wanted to know more about this gatekeeper couple from Kakuko's childhood.

"How long did this couple live in the gatekeeper's house?" I queried.

"Oh, for nearly 20 years," came Kakuko's animated reply, "until the end of the war." She seemed delighted that someone would be so interested in the history of her home.

How incredible, I thought. What seems unimaginable to me had been everyday life for these people - a couple no less - living here for two decades. A two-month stay in a room this size had been easily bearable, but only because I knew it was temporary. I was flirting with the experience of living in such a lilliputian space. But 20 years?

Probing further, I discovered that after the war, the American occupation forces took over most of the homes in Kakuko's area of Kyoto. This lasted for nearly ten years, but Kakuko's father had persuaded them to allow everyone in his extended family to remain in one of their two family homes. So although the house adjacent was occupied by Americans, Kakuko's present home - and the gatekeeper's cabin at the foot of its garden - remained in the hands of the family. The ten or twelve members of the two families crowded together into one house to wait out the occupation.

It was around this time - her father's business having been destroyed by the war - that Kakuko's family began renting out the gatekeeper's cabin to foreigners. Later, after the second house had been returned to them, this practice was extended to rooms within the main houses, and so it has continued to this day.

During my few months with Kakuko's family, I briefly met her elderly father, Mr. Hiroo. From time to time, I'd see him strutting around the block in fine form, propelling himself along with his wooden cane like there was no tomorrow.

In fact, there was only a short tomorrow. In the year after I left Kyoto, his health began to fail. At practically the same time, the Emperor Hirohito (a man viewed by some as the peaceful and unifying symbol of the Japanese nation, and by others as a pardoned war criminal), fell ill and passed on, ending an era. Kakuko's father, a man whose lifespan had virtually paralleled that of the Emperor, followed within weeks.

So now Kakuko, who never married, lives on in this beautifully-situated traditional Japanese home, with her aging aunt inhabiting the companion house next door. The Japanese garden, with its narrow pathways winding between large boulders and over a tiny creek, remains lovely, but goes largely untended now for long stretches of time.

Foreign guests come and go. My giant, blond-haired American friend, Brian, so tall he towers over Kakuko and appeared to scare the wits out of her when she first set eyes on him, now lives on the second floor of her house. The rich, smooth, dark wood floors creak and moan as you climb up the steep stairs and along the broad landing to his comparatively spacious single-room apartment. Through the corridor-long window, nestled in the green hillside, you can just make out the gold spire of *Kiyomizu Temple*. I recall with a feeling of *natsukashii* that each day at precisely 6:00 a.m., the exquisite sound of its resonant gong would gently pull me out of the night and into the Kyoto morning, the gentlest alarm clock I've ever had.

Out beyond Brian's second-floor window, across the garden and next to the cedar wood gate, sits the gatekeeper's cabin. An Australian man is staying there now, experiencing, as I did, the incredible contrast between the confines of his new dwelling and the expansiveness of those in his homeland.

And yet, cramped though his abode may be, it's still located in historic Kyoto. This doll-like cabin is situated in as pretty a setting as I've ever seen in a Japanese city. Once you're out the door, you're within minutes of pleasant strolls through exquisite temple parks.

Through Kakuko's gracious hospitality, we've had a peek into a Japan that's been rapidly vanishing into the past over the last few decades. The homogenization of all of urban Japan proceeds apace. As many foreign tourists will tell you, one of the biggest disappointments you come up against is finding that most Japanese cities look disturbingly like the one you just left behind – you see the same tangle of neon signs, electric wires and copycat pachinko parlors wherever you go.

So on this return trip to Kyoto, I've realized that my short stay as Kakuko's guest, in my first months in Japan, was a very special time, despite my modest living quarters. We said a fond farewell to her, snapped a few pictures for posterity, and passed on through the cedar gate.

Glancing back at the gatekeeper's cabin one last time, Krista and I pondered the fact that 20 years living as a couple in that little doll-like cabin would have sent us both to the funny farm, or the divorce courts, or both. Yet, the two elderly people who did just that may have never even questioned it, lived there uncomplainingly and never thought it strange. Or maybe they did complain, but endured it stoically anyway, cramped together in that very small space.

Over half a century later, their story strikes me as remarkable. It prompts me to ponder the follies of the 'Me Generation,' our inability to compromise and reconcile our own needs with those of others, our refusal to hang on, instead of bailing out when the seas get rough. Perhaps we've suffered from a lack of perspective – our lives are too seldom nourished by a deep appreciation of our good fortune.

I leave Kyoto sensing I'll be back, feeling a connection with the city that's not yet fulfilled. If the wisdom of the Buddha is all true, we've lived many lives before this one. Perhaps one of mine was in Kyoto.

The Trouble with Tokyo

For Krista and I, coming from a lucky generation of Americans and Canadians raised on great expectations of freedom, returning later to Tokyo on the *shinkansen* is a strange homecoming. We blast across the southern part of the island of Honshu past rice fields, factories and Mount Fuji's snow-capped dome. We happily take in the beauty of Japan's open countryside. But as the concrete maze of Japan's largest city begins to slide by the window, our psyches collide head-on with its vast labyrinth of brown and beige high-rise apartments and office buildings.

Why, I agonize momentarily, did I ever leave Kyoto and choose the bleakness of Tokyo? I answer my own question: for the same reason millions of Japanese end up here when they'd much rather be elsewhere – most of the jobs are here.

My eyes fall on one narrow twelve-story block, with literally hundreds of identical red doors, lined up on balconies hanging in the afternoon sky. As we zoom on by, I notice that the other side of the building is an exact clone – hundreds more red doors! And behind all of those doors are hundreds of identical box-like apartments, not more than two or three times the size of Kakuko's gatekeeper's cabin.

I spend a moment feeling incredulous, reflecting on the fact that untold millions of Japanese throughout Tokyo live out much of their lives in apartments this size. They're so small that tens of millions of North Americans would balk at the idea of spending a year in one, let alone a lifetime.

I remind myself that although they're petite, these apartments are surely kept scrupulously clean, except perhaps for the bachelor pads. Behind each *genkan* – the little vestibule that serves as a psychic barrier to the outside world – lies the warmth of a Japanese home.

But as we re-enter Tokyo, the elevated view afforded by the *shinkansen* shows us a perspective we haven't had for some years. We are reminded again that with all Tokyo's money, and the opulence spawned by it in chic areas like Ginza, the average resident of this city must still contend with an acute scarcity of something Americans and Canadians have always enjoyed in abundance: miles and miles of space, wide-open spaces in which to move, play, breathe and live.

I share a memory with Krista, recalling our second visit to *The Cavern* in Roppongi to watch the Beatle look-a-likes, with friends visiting from the States. It was Christmas Eve, and we waited for three solid hours, packed into a narrow corridor. In the end, we never did get in. At such times, you're reminded that Tokyo just has too many people and too little space for them all.

You see evidence of the cost of space throughout Japan. Everywhere you go, you see miniature driving ranges dotting the landscape, small plots of land enclosed with a big net draped over them. It's the closest many Japanese get to a golf course for months or years at a time. I don't recall ever seeing a full-size 250-yard driving range here, a common sight back in Canada. It's little wonder that Japanese golfers thrill at the chance to play overseas.

Most of us are royally privileged in North America, even those of us from modest backgrounds. As my eyes take in the panoramic view of Tokyo's concrete sprawl, I fantasize: One day it will be mandatory for all middle-class Canadian and American high-school students to spend two weeks in Tokyo, living in one of these tiny high-rise boxes with the red doors. When they stand out on their balconies, suspended in the sky, they'll be surrounded on all sides by other concrete highrises, piled up for miles. They'll see, and they'll understand, and they'll appreciate. Then they'll go home and never complain again about life in North America. It'll become a graduation requirement – *Comparative Studies in the Quality of Life*.

I dream on. Our lives here drive me to such thoughts, in idle moments on the *shinkansen*. Once you've experienced years of Tokyo, space is just one more thing you can never again take for granted.

City of Phones

There are phones everywhere in Tokyo. When I first got here, they came in three colours: green, yellow and red. You've never seen so many phones in all your life. The Japanese love talking on them, and when cell phones came along, they caught on like a wildfire, taking some of the demand off the public phones.

But banks of 'green' phones are still everywhere, and you quickly get very used to there always being a phone nearby when you need one.

Japan was way ahead of North America in creating telephone cards, making the search for small change a thing of the past. A 1,000-yen card ($8 U.S.) is good for about a hundred three-minute local calls within the Tokyo area. The card keeps a record of the telephone time you've logged, and whenever you make a call, a number appears on a liquid crystal screen telling you how many units you have left.

This sure beats searching pockets for dimes and quarters, or running out of change. Armed with a phone card, you could call anywhere on the planet from a phone booth in Japan – from *green* phones with a *gold* face – long before phone cards began to catch on worldwide. Obviously, the phone companies love it – they get paid even before you've made your calls.

Japan spoils you with its telephone and phone card accessibility. On trips to Hong Kong, Seattle and Vancouver, I've been dismayed to discover how hard it is to find a phone in all three cities. In places where there would always be half a dozen in Tokyo, there were none, or only one. In Vancouver I wandered around for about 15 minutes, in the heart of downtown, searching for signs of telephone life. When I finally located a phone booth and started stuffing in nickels and dimes, the nickels kept bouncing back out with a will of their own. They whole thing seemed quite primitive, yet coin phones remain a standard feature of North American cities.

Of course, a big part of the reason for the preponderance of phones here is the huge population. With literally millions of people pouring through central train stations everyday, the authorities have, of necessity, filled entire rooms with banks of phones. One little hole-in-the-wall I discovered in *Shibuya Station* had 36 of them! It's a necessary part of life, in a city where many young people make routine calls to mum every day to say when they'll be home.

Before cell phones arrived, I learned the hard way that I ought to make use of such telephone rooms, rather than trying to make calls from train platforms. In most stations, trains come so frequently and are so noisy, that you just get your conversation started when the voice of the person you're speaking with is devoured in high-decibel screeching steel.

I once tried to play back the messages on my answering machine from a train platform pay phone. The playback of my first message coincided with the arrival of a screaming metal monster. But I realized that I had to wait out the inaudible messages anyway, until I heard the 'three beeps' signaling it was safe to hang up. Otherwise, I might have put the machine out of order for the rest of the day.

There I stood, late 20th-century urban man, in a desperate hurry to catch the newly arrived train, trying in vain to hear an anticipated message above the din, in hopes of learning that I didn't, in fact, need to be in such a desperate hurry. All the while, I was prevented from hanging up until an electrical device, producing three electronic beeps, freed me to leap on the waiting train.

The beeps finally sounded – ever so faintly – in my right ear. I slammed down the receiver and flew through the closing doors – on to my next meeting, urban absurdity in motion.

It's not just me, I've checked with my friends. With all its pressure and stress and running around, Tokyo can do this to you. The cell phone has come along just in time.

We Live in Tokyo – Why, oh Why?

It's time I admitted it – Tokyo is getting to us. It's more than just the stress of a huge urban center; there's the foreignness of the whole experience to compound the intensity.

I've found that living in Tokyo stirs up decades-old impressions you once formed about Japan in younger years, when it was just a bunch of exotic islands on a map you might visit one day. These dormant images sometimes pop out of nowhere and then collide head-on with the realities that confront you here. Nothing can illustrate this better than what happened to me one recent summer night on – no surprise – a Tokyo train.

But to tell the story, I must first go back a few decades in my personal past, to the place and time when one particular impression was first formed, when an image of *Japaneseness* was laid down in my mind.

It was during the summer of 1971, a time when my university friends and I spent hours hanging out in the evenings shooting the breeze, philosophizing and sharing pineapple and ham pizza at our local hangout, Pharoah's Pizza, near the University of Alberta campus in Edmonton.

On one such occasion – a long, hot, timeless evening in August, a night when every booth in the restaurant was buzzing with student chatter, I left our booth and went over to the jukebox. Perhaps because of what came after, I recall the moment clearly. An easy-listening tune was playing. It was the Carol King and James Taylor era – the calm after the sixties storm; it was also around the time that John Lennon had released his first solo album.

My eyes flickered eagerly over the 45 r.p.m. selections, searching for something new or a little out of the ordinary. I noticed that one of Lennon's tracks was among the choices. It may have been *Jealous Guy*, a song I dearly loved, but I don't remember for sure. I do, however, recall the little inner conversation I had with myself.

"Yeah, I love that song, but we've heard it enough. Besides, we've got the album at home. Wait a minute, what's this on the flip side?"

One word sat poised on the tiny jukebox label, ready to strike, waiting – I would soon discover – for victims like me. The one-word title of the track was *Why?*

Without hesitation, being a Lennon lover, I punched in my quarter and made three selections, one of which was *Why?*

I ambled on back to our booth and rejoined my friends and our happy conversation. The whole place was animated, alive with discussions and laughter and the alluring smells of mozzarella cheese and tomato sauce.

A few minutes later, the grenade exploded. What ensued was about seven minutes (it was one of those *Hey Jude* era extended singles), not of John Lennon but Yoko Ono, screaming *"Why?"* at her primal best, her lungs in overdrive. Convulsing vibrato and tremolo variations of, "Why, why, why" invaded and totally took over the restaurant. If you've ever heard this charming little number, you know that with its release, Yoko gave fresh meaning to the phrase 'blood-curdling.'

"Whaaaaiaiaiaiay? Whaaaaiaiaiaiy?"

After a minute and a half of this blistering assault on the restaurant's calm, all conversation had ceased. Everybody in the place was looking around to find the madman who'd voluntarily selected this monstrosity.

Three or four minutes into this plunge inside Yoko's psychic inferno, some of the customers started paying their bills and leaving, angst written all over their faces. Listening to this was just too disturbing.

The fever-pitched wailing continued unabated, a relentless assault on the ears, the mind and the heart. Only halfway through our pizza, we sat it out – amazed, distraught, and eventually perplexed – put to speculating what on earth Yoko Ono could possibly have gone through in life that brought her to an expression of such total anguish. Granted, she and John were doing primal scream therapy, we knew that, but was she expressing the collective torment of all humankind?

We didn't think about it for long. We were just glad it finally ended and I didn't get tarred and pizza-ed on 109th Street outside the restaurant. When it was over, we had a good laugh, picturing John recording a seven-minute response, "Becauauauauauauauase!" and left it at that. The incident slipped from my mind.

Over twenty years later, now in Japan, I found myself on another long and tedious train ride home, amidst the sweltering heat of Tokyo summer.

It was the regular summer commuter scene – our sweaty bodies all crammed together, the morose-looking salarymen in their sagging suits, the exhausted office women holding onto the overhead hand straps, the lucky ones seated, some asleep with mouths gaping, heads loose and bobbing up and down, left and right, on and off the shoulders of the passengers next to them – all of us blasting home along the rails in stony silence.

It sometimes feels to me like a muffled silence, this hush on the trains here. Sure, it's a silence augmented by the exhaustion of working in this heat; the summer humidity can be stifling in Tokyo. But in my gut, I feel something more in these train cars – a learned silence, a socially-imposed silence.

Am I projecting my own feelings, my own sense of oppression? Probably, but one senses long-suffering containment in these commuters – hopes and dreams reined in. And on that particular night it felt like a dark pall, spread over the hundreds of people packed together in my train car, like an all-encompassing cloak of resignation. It had never felt quite so oppressive before.

My mind started to race. I wanted to say something to someone, to make contact – to connect. Instead, the intensity of the moment triggered a memory of another evening on the trains, a moment in November 1989, when I'd happened upon an American friend on the nightly ride home to Chofu. What a night it had been. The Berlin Wall had come down, and the newspapers were alive with history in the making. And here, unexpectedly, into my silent world amidst the throng on the *Keio Line*, had come someone I could talk about it with. What an unexpected treat.

We had chatted excitedly, but not overly loudly, at least not by our reckoning.

"What an incredible time it is," we'd agreed, conferring on the details of the changes taking place in Europe, and what it all meant. On all sides of our lively exchange – surrounding it and rendering it conspicuous – were mute commuters, their silence masking unknown inner reactions to our loquaciousness. Then, just as the train doors had opened at our stop, a Japanese gentleman, looking to be in his sixties, lashed out at us: "Why do you talk so loudly?"

Shaken by his animosity, I'd attempted a response of some kind, but we were quickly swept out the door, along with the rest of those getting out at Chofu Station. We'd then shared a brief moment of anger at this man's seeming intolerance ("What's his problem?"), and said farewell.

Now, some years later, commuting on the same route home but in the blistering Tokyo summer, I relived the memory of that incident in the privacy of my thoughts. Evidently we'd broken some taboo, some unspoken social edict perhaps, requiring library-like muteness on public transport out of respect for other commuters. Maybe our spontaneous enthusiasm angered him, because to him, it mocked everyone else's restraint. Maybe our speaking in English had bothered him, or he'd just had a bad day and was dumping on us. Whatever the case, we foreigners had clearly touched a raw nerve.

As I relived that incident, the memory aligned itself with a small core of dark feelings stored within me, an accumulation of too many repressive and alienating hours spent on these rails. I felt like I was reaching some kind of explosive breaking point.

"What emotional torture this is," I thought, my mind struggling to maintain its balance, "for all of us on this train. How can these people be made to suffer like this for years on end?" I actually had to suppress a desire to scream, loud and long.

Then it happened. With the hot, night air whipping my face through the open window, and the silence of the compressed and perspiring throng of us punctuated only by the sounds of the train screeching along the steel rails, I suddenly became aware that in the back of my head, a voice was indeed screaming. But it wasn't mine. It was a woman's voice, and she was shrieking for all she was worth. It was the voice of Yoko Ono, screaming *"Why?"* with all her emotional might.

"Whaaaaiaiaiaiay?"

In a flash, I recalled the jukebox incident at Pharoah's Pizza. As I did, a window opened in my chest, and I drew in a deep gulp of fresh air. The turmoil in my mind started to settle down, as I began pondering the insight that a 20-year mystery might just have been solved.

"Of course, Yoko Ono is Japanese – or she was. Not only that, she's a woman, and a very creative one as well."

Thundering along the Keio Line, I was now jumping around like an excited monkey inside the isolation of my mind. I suddenly felt I understood Yoko's scream, her all-enveloping question. It was the anguished cry of a creative spirit, repressed and denied her own authentic voice, and demanding to know why.

Why? could hardly be called music. It was more like a monster that had to be exorcised, an explosion of absolute angst. But in the midst of my own personal cathartic moment – close to bursting from the psychic compression of Tokyo life – I felt I'd finally gotten a glimpse into where Yoko Ono's seeming craziness might have originated. She was purging herself, releasing her long-repressed anger at being kept down, as a woman and a human being, raging at social forces that conspire to prevent people from being true to themselves.

I pondered on, breathing slowly and deeply. The visceral release of this synchronistic moment, and the musings that followed, got me safely down the Keio Line without incident. Whatever the truth about Yoko's scream, thanks to the internal rescue provided by this memory, I hadn't flipped out, become the *henna gaijin* (crazy foreigner), and started screaming uncontrollably at my fellow passengers.

I reflected on the fact that it was Yoko Ono's character which had, years before, formed my first impression of Japanese women. Unhinged though she had seemed, her husband – the hero of my youth – had loved her dearly, so I'd always been sure she had wonderful qualities. When John sang, "Oh Yoko, my love will turn you on," I felt his adoration and the joy she brought him, deep in my heart.

The train finally slowed to a halt at Keio Tamagawa Station. When the doors opened, I quickly broke free from the grip of the silent crowd, burst out the train door and on down the stairs, three at a time. I headed straight for my neighborhood bar, *Heartbeats*, to get a stiff drink, seek out a friend, and talk through these pent-up feelings about Japanese society before I exploded. *Why?* – indeed.

One Way Out

Life in modern Tokyo can be extremely tough on its people. I remember a small observation I made years ago, on my first full working day with Soulful Software. Walking back to our section, I had to leave the main building and cross the street, in order to get to our office in the smaller annex where I work most of the time. The main edifice, a massive, block-long structure, is home to a number of companies, Soulful Software being just one of them.

Instead of taking the elevator, I decided to walk down from the third to the first floor. The stairs, I noted, were in short flights of about 15 steps each, and each flight turned at right angles to its predecessor. As you went down, they angled their way around a huge open square of empty space.

I walked down one short flight, and then stopped and glanced up and down the stairwell. Right up to the ninth floor, there was nothing but this wide, open shaft of space, about 10 feet across, that plunged straight on down to the bottom floor. I noticed that strong rope nets had been strung across this open space, on alternate landings, all the way up to the top.

Sometime later, in an idle moment, I asked Charlie - my section coordinator at the time - about this. A very friendly American from the Midwest, Charlie had been with Soulful Software for many years. In fact, he was somewhat of a celebrity in Japan in his early days, having been one of the first foreign employees to be hired by a Japanese company.

"Oh, the nets," he said with an uncomfortable laugh, "they had to put those in to keep people from jumping."

Yes, that fit. Japanese culture has a unique relationship with suicide. I already knew that, though I couldn't pretend to understand what lay behind it. Citizens who feel the urge to take an early trip to the Great Beyond appear to be aided by a historical and culturally skewed view that the taking of your own life has its place. In some circumstances it's perceived as a legitimate and honorable way out of a difficult situation.

That said, corporate management in our main building did the prudent thing, preferring that tormented souls who opt for a dramatic early exit do so somewhere other than the company stairwell.

The Hidden Powers of Japanese Women

It's a few weeks after my near freakout on the *Keio Line*, and my socio-claustrophobic crisis seems to have passed. By and large, objectivity has returned and I'm again coping quite well, distracting myself by reading on the trains, listening to my Walkman, and disappearing into my imagination.

But the events of that night did shake me up and start me thinking in new directions. Among other things, I've found myself reflecting more on the position of women in this society. I'm trying to get a better sense of the frustrations they feel, the compromises they have to make, their hidden realms of power, and the psychic price they pay for being female.

Although many young Japanese are assimilating Western ideas rapidly, the concept of the 'person' as an individual who chooses his or her own personal direction in life, strives to fulfill their potential and develop their own unique opinions and convictions, is largely an imported concept. It still flies in the face of traditional social restrictions emphasizing the importance of the 'group.'

In the case of Japanese women, these restrictions are double-damning, because women are still seen by most men as being subordinate. Chauvinism is not just rampant; it sometimes seems to be the only game in town for a great many men (as always, with notable exceptions). One of my former colleagues at Soulful Software, a genuinely nice man who'd only been married a year, casually said a telling thing about his wife one day.

"There's one adult and one child in my household," he quipped.

Basically, Japanese men are socialized to think this way. Meanwhile, women have been taught to act - at least some of the time - like the dependent children the men perceive them to be. Inherent in all hierarchical relationships in Japan is *amae* (a unique kind of dependence). According to the psychiatrist Dr. Takeo Doi, it's the basic Japanese trait. In *Pacific Destiny*, Robert Elegant defines it as, "vying for approval, that is, conforming to the wishes of others to win their approbation."

The senior person in a relationship is responsible for the junior, and the junior can count on the support of the senior, provided he or she conforms to their wishes. From the point of view of Western psychology, one could view it as a kind of nationwide and socially sanctioned codependence.

I vividly recall that my very first contacts with Soulful Software's *office ladies* left me laughing bemusedly and shaking my head with disbelief. Many were so incredibly deferential, but sweet as sugar. To begin with, I had to get used to their being dressed in identical uniforms and speaking with doll-like falsetto voices. Then there was the fact that they seemed to be forever apologizing.

Most seemed to apologize at the beginning of an encounter, throughout the discussion and again on leaving. At the time, not understanding anything about why they acted this way, I asked my more experienced colleague, Kieran, to explain it. He quickly caricatured this classic female presentation of self in Japan with the expression: "I'm sorry I exist!"

But this presentation is a performance, you eventually realize, one that young working women are pressured into conforming to, and are very adept at. Over time, as you come to understand more about how personal relations are conducted in Japan, you realize that ritual apologizing is a way of life for both sexes.

Everyone is forever intoning the words *sumimasen* ("Excuse me" or "Sorry"), *gomen nasai* ("I'm very sorry") and *Shitsurei shimashita* ("I'm so sorry to have bothered you"). People say these expressions routinely, just in case they might have interrupted, disturbed, or upset you in any conceivable way.

Sumimasen is a catch-all word that covers all the bases, so you won't inadvertently offend someone. I've actually grown very comfortable using it now. It can often be perfunctory, but it also makes it easy to express genuine sensitivity towards others, without feeling uncomfortable, and I really like that about Japan. Japanese can be remarkably sensitive and courteous, as when you're talking with someone who's about four feet away from you and another person walks between the two of you, bowing slightly and cutting the air with their hands, to apologize for coming between you.

These extremes of ritual-like decorum are more exaggerated with women, especially in corporate settings. Routinely squeezed into subservient roles, they're required to continually demonstrate deference as part of their jobs. That said, when the men get into bowing to superiors during farewells on train stations, they are easily a match for the studied obsequiousness of their female counterparts. It sometimes seems to me that most everyone in Japanese life is acting in a play half of the time.

If you go to a Tokyo disco after work, however, you'll see a radically different Japan. The deferential *office lady* will be busy transforming herself into a swinging, young Aphrodite full of energy and vitality, dancing her frustrations off, a quantum leap away from the socially restricted persona imposed upon her at the office.

Watching these women liberate themselves on the dance floor, I've sometimes wondered how they endure their office uniforms and carefully prescribed social mannerisms. The best explanation is that they've been prepared for it from an early age. Most young girls wear uniforms all the way through school, so the switch to company *office lady* garb is nothing new.

Nor is it a difficult adjustment for them to speak the required polite language forms to customers and superiors. Although language use is changing at the speed of light in Japan, *keigo* (deferential speech) is still widely used. To English speakers, it seems as if Japanese learn several languages.

Though the work of a great many *office ladies* is still just routine office work, some whom I've met have far more interesting jobs. Two women in their early thirties, Ayako and Sayuri, have been studying Business English privately with me for over a year now. Both trilingual, they speak English and Spanish well, and work for a Spanish shipping firm. Being employed by a non-Japanese company puts them in a somewhat different situation from most of their Japanese sisters, but many things remain the same, since the operation is in Japan.

From Ayako and Sayuri, I get the impression that the women in their office know more about what's going on than their male bosses, and I don't doubt it, knowing what good communicators they are. Yet, as women, they occupy the lowest positions in the company hierarchy, though that might also be the case if they worked in Spain. (As any informed feminist can tell me, the devaluation of women is a worldwide phenomenon; it's certainly not the monopoly of this country.) Yet, if they view their situation as demeaning, they certainly haven't let on. They appear to accept it gracefully and take it all in stride, with no evidence of cynicism. They're wonderfully cheerful women, and they talk humorously about the goings-on in their office. They seem to possess a broad acceptance of life, just as it is, that affords them a sense of contentment.

The fact remains that if a woman working for almost any company in Japan were to object to the treatment she receives – or to attempt to stand out from her blue-uniformed sisters by suggesting she's capable of much more than the tasks she's been assigned – she'd make nothing but trouble for herself. Belonging to the group requires accepting the behavior expected of you and the assigned social roles that come with your social station.

There appear to be millions of young Japanese women who do just that. They accept the uneven playing field, and then go on to stand up remarkably well, in the face of what American women here describe – virtually unanimously – as sexual discrimination and gender stigmatization. Both Krista and I have marveled at the extraordinarily human and helpful service we've received from numerous women working for various agencies in Tokyo. We wonder how many men here realize just how quickly the whole system would unravel without the consistent effort and diligence of the women of Japan.

In fact, the women have their own solidarity and hilarious inside-jokes about Japanese men, often voicing their view of them as helpless, overgrown boys. Wives have their own realm of power, not to be underestimated. In many Japanese families, it's the woman who rules the household and holds the purse strings.

So fortunately, there are happy survivors among the women we know, though the sacrifices the married ones have had to accept can be brutal. Not seeing her husband until midnight on a routine basis is just a part of life for our next-door neighbor in Chofu, as is starting a load of her family's washing, in the machine on the balcony next to ours, anywhere from 4:00 a.m. onwards. None of the apartments in our block have enough room inside for a washing machine, and she puts on a load every day when she first gets up.

But for unmarried company women like Ayako and Sayuri, two trips a year overseas are now a possibility, and they've taken full advantage of the chance to travel the world. It's something most males climbing the corporate ladder cannot do. For Japan's young women, who are waiting longer than ever to marry, the advantages of staying single are abundantly clear.

Married or single, Japanese women seem to possess an extraordinary capacity to accept their society's demands. Yet, there have to be many young creative spirits who are crushed under the weight of such conformity. We have no trouble at all understanding how the spirit of a gifted Japanese woman could be broken in this social climate.

Topping off the social stress, every day there's the relentless commute on the trains. We've lived that reality on a daily basis for some years now, and millions of Japanese women have lived it alongside us. When we factor in the stresses and disadvantages they face at work, the real mystery to us is that they don't all end up like Yoko Ono, at one point or another, screaming *Why?* at the top of their lungs on the *Keio Line*. They must have hidden powers we don't know about.

Wondering about Yoko

So what do I make of Yoko Ono's tirade, now that I've had more time to think about my near freakout? Obviously, her scream was inspired by the primal therapy she and John were doing with Dr. Arthur Janov, and there's no way of knowing the suppressed traumas that was bringing up for her. But Lennon and Ono's listening audience do know the many themes she and John were exploring at the time: Why war? Why hatred? Why fear and suffering? Why the universal repression of women? Feminism was definitely one of her themes.

We can get on our high horse in the West, and it's worth reminding ourselves that until modern times, Western societies treated women as abominably as anybody else. I remember being stunned to learn that Swiss women only got the vote in 1970. Obviously, major inequalities remain firmly entrenched to this day. So there's little cause for holier-than-thou in looking at the lives of Japanese or other Asian women.

But through living here, it's become clear to Krista and me that the progress women in our western societies have made – in struggling to achieve equality with men – has been quite remarkable. It's also made us realize just how far the majority of Japanese women have to go.

Whatever else led Yoko Ono to unleash *Why?* on the world from that recording studio, my own sense is that it had something to do with her being a Japanese woman. For one thing, I've never heard anyone else scream like that for seven minutes! I've since learned from an interview she gave to *People* magazine that she spent her early years in Japan and recalls feeling enormous pressure as a child. She described her experience by saying, "You can choose to live a dead life or an alive life, and I had to go against a lot in order to survive. I had to get out of that incredible, intimidating confinement."

So I've come to think of Yoko's scream as a proxy scream, for those of her modern sisters too timid or intimidated to speak up, for those who suffer in silence. It sends a message of fury to men who remain convinced that women are inherently inferior and not entitled to equal opportunities in life. The Japanese government's policy of *Kokusaika* – internationalization – has to include the genuine application of equal rights for women for it to be truly meaningful.

But many of the oppressive conditions in Japanese society are gender neutral. Our own sense is that many Japanese men want to preserve control over women partly out of frustration at their own feelings of powerlessness, though it's clearly the women who are in the weaker position, by far, professionally. Yet, a good case can be made that many married women with children eventually find themselves in an enviable position in Japan. Once their kids have reached school age, these mothers have some free time during the day, while their husbands toil away.

As for Yoko's traumatic scream, it reveals an awesome strength of feeling, the antithesis of the acquiescent Japanese woman in the Western imagination. When I first heard it on that jukebox in my distant past, I was completely ignorant of the social pressures Japanese people are subjected to. So I heard nothing but a lunatic, as did everyone else in the restaurant that night.

Now, after living in Tokyo for years, I'm more than willing to give you the benefit of the doubt, Yoko. You and John brought a lot of joy to millions of people, including me, and now I understand that you had plenty to scream about as well. But you've got to admit, you really knew how to wreck a good pizza.

The 6:25 Dog

During our first year in our new apartment in Chofu City, in western Tokyo, my day usually started at about 6:00 a.m. But I never needed to worry about shutting off the alarm and seriously oversleeping, courtesy of an animal we dubbed the *6:25 dog*.

Her enthusiastic barking resonated throughout the neighbourhood at precisely the same time every weekday morning, Saturdays included. It was as if she were sprung from a cage with a timer on it – a panting and exuberant wake-up call.

Over time, we pieced the parts of this puzzle together, with help from those mornings when duty called one, or both, of us up and out of the house earlier than usual, in time to actually see what was going on with this dog.

It turned out to be a game taught to her by her master, an older gray-haired gentleman, looking to be in his sixties. Riding a three-speed bicycle, he'd tear down the street adjacent to our apartment, his beloved dog bounding alongside and barking with zeal. At the T-intersection at the end of the strip, he went left, and she went right.

They then raced each other around opposite sides of the beautiful Japanese garden, *Hyakkaen*, that straddles our train station. They'd meet up again a few minutes later on the far side of the garden near the station's ticket machines, to continue their morning romp together. From all appearances – helped along by the companionship of his intelligent dog – our neighbour is relishing his retirement.

We didn't always view these episodes so positively, however. I remember being woken up at exactly 6:25 on a Saturday morning, after a late Friday night – on a day when we'd hoped to sleep in a bit – to hear Krista, bleary-eyed, murmur, "You know, in America, somebody would poison that dog."

For us, the *6:25 dog* became a kind of symbol, an exemplification of the stringent discipline and rigid adherence to routine which were surely a major factor contributing to Japan's rise from the ashes of the war. In the first place, she was the *6:25 dog*, not the 7:25 or the 8:25 dog. She was also a dog on a timer – her master's timer – precisely on time, to the minute, every single day.

The *6:25 dog* recalled for me one of my first memories of this country. I remember lying in bed one morning just after 6:00 a.m., in a *ryokan* (Japanese inn) in Kyoto, and hearing a kind of rhythmical rustling sound. Curious, I leapt out of bed and went to the window of my room, which overlooked a small and immaculately clean courtyard two floors below. There I saw a small, elderly Japanese woman bent over a grass broom, dutifully sweeping the ground in front of her tiny home. With the early morning sunlight splashing all around her, she was already hard at work.

Here in Chofu City, a similar drama is often played out as early as 5:00 a.m., in the small garden plot beneath our balcony. On days when I'm up that early, I can gaze down on a few elderly men and women, bent over their hoes in the first hour of light, quietly tilling the furrows of their vegetable patch. It's humbling to watch them, descendants of the *Old Japan* still working the fields as their ancestors did, but right here in Tokyo. Neither Krista nor I - nor the *6:25 dog* for that matter - are a match for their industriousness.

In fact, for unknown reasons, the ritual of the *6:25 dog* suddenly stopped one day, after being repeated six mornings a week for just over a year.

I hadn't realized how much I'd grown to accept and even appreciate her vocal and energetic embrace of the morning. On Saturdays I'd learned how to wake up momentarily at the sound of her bark, and then slip gently back to sleep. It didn't bother me anymore. After all, she was a joyful sentient being, not a power drill.

And though we aren't partial to overly rigid routines, such as those controlling the lives of millions in Tokyo, we found something nurturing and natural about this daily ritual and the rhythmic dependability of it. The dog obviously loved it too, which somehow affirmed its rightness.

What do you know? I actually miss the yelping of a stranger's dog at 6:25 in the morning. I can't speak for Krista, but I kind of hope to hear the joyful sound of her bark again some day soon.

Sunday Mornings in Chofu

Before I get lost in romanticism about our neighborhood 'wonder dog,' Krista has suggested I come back down to earth - to our futon, more precisely - and the auditory assault we face on Sunday mornings.

It's the only day of the week when we have the remotest chance of sleeping in. The '6:25 dog' always has, most of the neighbourhood does, and so do we - until approximately 8:00 a.m., that is. There's just no hope after that. You'd have to be stone deaf, or equipped with industrial airport-runway ear plugs, to sleep through the cacophony that quickly fills our neighbourhood.

On a typical Sunday morning, all hell breaks loose, in one form or another, at two or three minutes after eight. Virtually every Sunday at this time, a guy with a loudspeaker hooked up to his pickup truck cruises through the neighbourhood, blasting a static-filled recorded message that can be heard for miles. As any longtime resident of Tokyo will assure you, this is not an exaggeration.

Is he a lunatic? A political fanatic? No, not at all. He's just a local entrepreneur selling long, plastic poles, the better to hang up your laundry on your balcony - a standard apartment technique here.

By now, you'd think everyone in the area who wants one of his laundry poles would have bought one long ago, if only in hopes of banishing him to another neighborhood. But no, he keeps coming every Sunday morning, just after eight o'clock, his sales pitch detonating you out of your dreams.

As a rule, just as the laundry-pole man gets in the groove, the local high-school brass band starts rehearsing. Either it's an open-air rehearsal, or they have all the windows open in the gym across the way, because it sounds like it's all happening on our balcony. This is Sunday, keep in mind, the one day when most of Tokyo's working people do not have to haul themselves into work. We were recently awoken at 8:10 a.m. by a rousing rendition of the *Folies Bergeres*, played loud! The same piece was then repeated, over and over, for half an hour.

For a month of Sundays, they worked on their brass band version of *Obla di, Obla da, life goes on, bra!* It needed work – they were like the school band from hell. Perhaps I should have gone over to suggest they learn that other '60s song, "*They're coming to take me away, ha ha he he ...*" so they'd know the effect they were having on the local foreigners.

Even though it's not yet 8:30 on Sunday morning, a power drill operated by the local sheet metal merchant, who resides just below and beside us, usually joins the auditory free-for-all next. Needless to say, we are now up and making coffee, whether we like it or not.

When there's an election campaign going on, the laundry pole salesman has serious competition for airspace. Megaphone messages soon begin to boom, bounce and echo around the neighborhood in search of ears, often throughout the entire day.

In the midst of this barrage of noise, we endeavor to sit calmly in our little sanctuary, sipping our coffee, and reading the Sunday paper. There's absolutely nothing to be done about the assault on the eardrums here; the Japanese have yet to make a social issue of noise pollution. Given the social pressure to conform to verbal silence on the trains, it's puzzling that all forms of mechanical noise go uncontested.

People seem oblivious to most forms of noise. Bicycle brakes here deliver a high-pitched screeching sound which can actually be painful – nobody bats an eye. Standing on train platforms, I've sometimes had to cover my ears, so sharp is the sound of squealing train wheels. People seem not to notice. Long accustomed to an all-pervasive clamor, perhaps they're just numb to it. Or they notice, and dislike it as much as I do, but don't feel in a position to say anything.

In our neighborhood on Sunday mornings – and most other days as well – the noise is relentless. Eventually, you adopt a humorous attitude, or risk going bonkers. Putting your imagination to work helps a lot. Some Sunday mornings, I lie in bed picturing myself out on our third-floor balcony with my own megaphone. On the stage of my mind, I respond in kind to everything sent our way – a dueling megaphones fantasy.

An American woman we heard about did more than fantasize. She actually lost it one day, grabbing a megaphone out of the hands of a right-wing proselytizer and screaming back at him. She was quickly escorted away by mobsters, and later lost her visa. The story added to my conviction that a creative fantasy life is a useful tool for foreign residents in Japan – it can relieve stress to imagine what you'd like to do, but you have to leave it at that.

Still, most of us abandon all restraint occasionally. I now sometimes stay overnight at my new university dormitory, about an hour from central Tokyo. One Thursday night at midnight, power drills were still going strong, just below my window. Astonished by this and totally unable to sleep, I eventually yelled at the top of my lungs for them to stop. The next day I mentioned the incident to a friend and colleague, adding, "I think I'm losing it, Rich," to which he replied reassuringly, "Oh God, my wife screams at them all the time!"

In Tokyo, it's sometimes necessary to look for radical solutions. I used to rail against being awoken at 3:00 a.m. by the *bosozoku*, the packs of motorcycle rebels who race through Tokyo, revving their engines and claiming back some power for themselves. But one night I found myself reversing course and cheering them on in my semi-conscious state, "Go for it, you guys, rebel all you want!" Now they only ever wake me up momentarily; I smile and drift back to sleep.

As to how the Japanese deal with the screaming sounds of the *bosozoku*, when I've mentioned it to my university students, many appeared shocked, as though somehow I shouldn't have noticed such an embarrassing side to Japanese life! Yet, millions of people must be trying to sleep through it all, and the strategy of, "It's not happening" must have its limitations. Perhaps sleeping pill sales here are off the chart.

Of course, *shōgenai* is the Japanese response of last resort to intractable issues like noise pollution. It occurred to me once that the Beatles song *Let it Be* – still very popular in Japan – is probably interpreted through its lens, meaning Japanese people understand it their own way: "There will be an answer – *Shōgenai.*"

Meanwhile, on Sunday mornings in Chofu, life goes on for the members of the high-school brass band playing *Obla di, Obla da*. Though they may be a bit short on musicality at this point, these young people certainly have to be credited with diligence. I suppose their early practice time is, in part, just a reflection of the traditional early start to the Asian day.

No doubt they're also conforming to their very driven society, caught up in its noisy and unrelenting momentum seven days a week. I just hope these kids are having some fun while they're at it, like the song suggests.

Female Turf

After living in Chofu for a couple of years, I've finally found out what our neighborhood looks like on a weekday. To my surprise, it's not the same place I'm familiar with from walks to the grocery store with Krista on Sundays.

This discovery came about courtesy of my new university job, which allows me the luxury of a day off during the week, an impossibility when I was working for Soulful Software. I count my blessings.

On my first free weekday morning in Tokyo, I decided to celebrate my newfound freedom by heading down to the post office and having a look around the local shops. In explorer mode, I enthusiastically bounded out the door to find out what was going on.

'What was going on' stared back at me with a combination of disbelief, suspicion and disapproval. It came in the form of local mothers, grandmothers and toddlers, checking me out with varying degrees of shock – 'a male and a foreigner too, wandering about on a weekday – what gives?' I quickly realized that I was the only non-working man on the loose for miles. I felt like an intruder, a male who'd inadvertently stumbled into a private inner sanctum for women and children only.

"This is our territory," their stares seemed to be saying. "Members of your gender don't belong here on a Thursday morning."

I did run across one male, my local noodle-shop delivery boy – hard at work – but even he looked at me quizzically, wondering what I was up to. He'd never seen me on the streets, except on the weekend, either.

The experience confirmed for me that the traditional demarcation line dividing Japanese men and women into separate realms and roles is sharply drawn. It also reminded me that when it comes to understanding Japanese society, your wisest move is always to assume you're still more ignorant than you think you are.

I hadn't anticipated this reaction at all, and I quickly picked up that being friendly and respectful wasn't going to win the day. I was obviously some kind of derelict, one who lacked the proper understanding of duty. Most of these women, I suspected, were thinking, "What's with him, doesn't he work?"

On my first Thursday morning visit to my female hairdresser, I soon got confirmation that that's exactly what they were thinking.

"What do you *do!?*" she asked incredulously, not the way you'd normally inquire into someone's line of work. She was intensely curious to know my schedule, to know how on earth I managed to be free on a weekday. I actually caught myself feeling guilty as I explained that I had Thursday mornings off. I found myself trying to justify my situation to her, emphasizing that I only had the morning off. Other Westerners tell me they've had similar feelings of guilt when telling their Japanese friends they're taking a three-week vacation, something most Japanese can never do.

Many of my former colleagues at Soulful Software probably go years without ever experiencing this Monday-to-Friday side of their own neighborhoods. It's conceivable that a Japanese company man could spend his entire working life without having any real sense of what his wife's everyday experience is. Perhaps many have little interest; it's not their domain.

My last visit to family members in Victoria, B.C. highlighted these contrasts in lifestyle still further. I went for a walk on a local public beach on a Tuesday morning, and saw people who would be considered odd and unusual sights most anywhere in Tokyo on a weekday: a man in his thirties playing 'fetch the stick' with his Labrador retriever; a couple in their late twenties strolling hand-in-hand and barefoot, the water lapping at their feet; a father walking alone with his two young children, playing at writing names in the sand with a stick.

Granted, Tokyo is an incomparably bigger city than Victoria, B.C. But these would be very uncommon sights anywhere I've been in Japan on a weekday, this being a country where most everyone's life is more highly regulated, in conformity with the traditional workweek.

Of course, some of those strolling in Victoria might have been unemployed against their will, and there's no joy in that. But others no doubt do shift work, have part-time schedules, or they're self-employed with flexible hours. There's much greater variety in work schedules in North America, and most of us can make arrangements to free up a few hours spontaneously, from time to time.

Whatever their reasons for being on the beach that morning, these people were in a position to be outside enjoying it, and that was very pleasant to see. As in Tokyo, there were women with children. But the men walking with women, and especially the men playing with their kids – taking in a sunny day at a relaxed and leisurely pace – were a welcome sight for eyes like mine, acculturated as they now are to the pace and routines of Tokyo life.

Krista and I very much respect the hard work the Japanese are famous for, but when that dedication to work requires being locked into a rigid schedule that separates the sexes, our loyalties become clear. Long live the odd and unusual.

Has Fellini Taken Over my Mind?

Our neighborhood in Chofu is quite low-key, but occasionally it has unusual happenings. For example, our apartment is located within a few blocks of a bicycle-racing stadium, and from time to time this leads to some wild afternoons.

Compared with neighborhoods near major train arteries, Keio Tamagawa is comparatively uncrowded, and weeks go by with no action in the adjacent arena to alter this. Seen from our balcony, the velodrome looks like a Roman Coliseum with its wall of empty seats hanging in the sky above the Tama River.

Then one day, without warning, our neighborhood transforms. The whole area will be suddenly overrun with hundreds of rough-looking, unshaven men, sitting on their haunches in the streets munching *yakitori* chicken on sticks, guzzling beer and poring over racing forms. This will then go on for four or five days in a row, giving our amiable *yakitori*-chicken man a chance to rake in some money, along with all the local proprietors.

During these times, the sounds from the race track boom throughout the neighborhood, echoing up and down the Tama River for miles. For each stage of the proceedings in the velodrome, there's a specific melody or sound signal (one of them resembles a British police car siren). One jingle tells everybody it's time to place bets; another one lets them know betting will soon stop. One more tells everyone the riders are on the track; yet another signals that they're at the post.

The most unusual-sounding segment is a computer-melody version of that lively Russian tune, *The Song of the Volga Boatmen*. Since there are nine races on the card, we hear it nine times throughout the day when we're home on a Saturday. Fortunately, I like the melody – I remind myself of that during the latter part of the afternoon when an entire day of this racket has taken its toll on our patience.

In our first months in Chofu, we often made the mistake of going to catch the train just as the whole mob was getting out of the velodrome at the end of the racing day. Not only was our little station suddenly swamped with hordes of slovenly dressed men, but some were quite drunk – singing, bellowing and staggering along in the middle of the afternoon.

Then one day, another feature was added to the bedlam. The first time it occurred, I couldn't believe what I was witnessing. The contrast with the demeanor of the normally subdued people of Tokyo was so extreme as to seem Felliniesque.

Not only had the repressed urges of the velodrome patrons been unleashed, but one fellow, who didn't seem to fit in with this crowd at all, was bounding up and down on the train platform. He was acting as if he thought he was on a pogo stick, and he was doing this dangerously close to the three-foot drop down to the tracks. This man was also making incomprehensible squeals and seemed to have come completely unhinged. A dozen other people around him were in a similar condition, yelling in a way Japanese rarely do – all of this, in the midst of the mobocracy already prevailing among the inebriated gamblers. For a few short moments, I was completely stunned. I'd never seen such a crazy scene in all my time in Tokyo.

"This is Japan?" I thought.

Much more than I realized, I'd gotten accustomed to standing on our local train platform without hearing a peep out of anyone, everyone minding their own business and looking straight ahead, with what someone aptly described to me as 'not-knowing face.' It's the expressionless mask you get so used to seeing in Tokyo. I suspect it derives from *samurai* days when you could lose your head with one wrong look, or perhaps from the pre-war period when citizens could be charged with 'dangerous thoughts' offenses.

As I made my way through this riotous scene, I noticed that 'normal citizens' (standing quietly among the huge crowd queuing on the train platform) were all in fine form, expertly pretending to *not-know* anything out of the ordinary was going on. Meanwhile, the platform was packed, a few of the intoxicated revelers were howling to themselves, and these other folks seemed ready to bound off the platform right in front of the next train. To me, it felt like absolute bedlam.

After a few more seconds of disbelief, the penny dropped, or as the Japanese say in such moments of realization, *Yappari*! These people were mentally disadvantaged, and I've since learned that somewhere in our neighborhood, there's a home where they live. Occasionally, twenty or thirty of the residents will descend on Keio Tamagawa Station together, seemingly without a guardian. This is what had happened on race day, and though it was quite frightening to watch them in the midst of that crowd, they did seem to manage all right in the end.

As for the velodrome regulars, it should be noted that in spite of their numbers – and the fact that unrestricted drinking goes on right in the street – I've never seen any fighting, and things appear to be kept from getting out-of-hand by a conspicuous police presence. Besides, the Japanese of Tokyo are more used to crowds than they are to empty places.

Speaking of crowds, on some Sundays our neighborhood is flooded with a quite different species – groups of radiantly beautiful women in exquisite *kimono* visiting *Hyakkaen*, the Japanese garden near the station. They come *en masse* to see the seasonal flowers.

I keep wondering if it isn't all going to happen at once one day – rough-

and-ready gamblers knocking back beer and chewing *yakitori*, mingling with highly refined and immaculately dressed *geisha*-like females: culture clash, Japanese-style. Something tells me the people who run the garden have got the velodrome's calendar, and schedule their events accordingly.

Not-knowing Face

We recently had another brush with the Japanese capacity for non-disclosure that we've taken to calling 'not-knowing face.' Actually, that unreadable countenance, from which we surely get our stereotype in the West of the 'inscrutable Oriental,' is known as *muyojyo* (expressionless face), and the word *mushi* means to 'see without seeing' or ignore. Our latest experience of it came courtesy of Halloween night.

Krista and I had been invited to a costume party at my university. This meant riding for nearly an hour on the Odakyu Line with the after-work crowd. Although I was reluctant at first, we talked ourselves into wearing our costumes on the way there and left the house in a party mood. Krista was dressed as a mime artist with a striped shirt and suspenders, her face painted white and her lips ruby red; I was looking clownish with a half mask - phoney black glasses that came with a sheath of orange hair - and a shocking-yellow tie.

We must have looked unimaginably weird to most of the Japanese on that train. Halloween, until quite recently, was not very well known here, though young people have all heard about it now since the shooting of a Japanese student in the U.S. on Halloween night. Still, it's a strange foreign event, especially for older Japanese, and they provided us with another classic demonstration of their expertise at handling the unknown - by simply pretending it's not there.

The mask of 'not-knowing face' was quickly donned by most everyone, and it reigned supreme, carefully guarding inner reactions. Even those boarding the train, suddenly exposed to our bizarre costumes, were almost all able to totally hide their surprise. There were a few exceptions, especially among young teenage girls, who would turn away and then giggle surreptitiously with each other, with hands guarding their mouths.

Generally, however, people gave no outward sign whatsoever of seeing anything out of the ordinary, and throughout the entire trip, nobody asked us any questions, turned to have a direct look, or shared a smile or a laugh.

Of course, most of the commuters probably wanted nothing more than to get home, and were just too exhausted to bother with these ridiculous foreigners, who were doing something inexplicably weird. As for my own inner reactions during the trip, I imagined that the Japanese around us might feel very uncomfortable, even though they did nothing to suggest that. This fed on my own personal discomfort, and I'm not about to do this again next year.

But once we got to the party, where everyone was expecting weirdness, the many Japanese who were there got just as involved as the Westerners did in the fun of masquerade. Most Japanese love a party, and they seem to really enjoy the idea of a theme party such as Halloween. When they know what to expect from such an event, they have a great time and are a lot of fun to be with. Cultural differences completely vanish in the spirit of the moment.

For the Japanese, there's a greater sense of time and place, and an appropriate social pattern for most types of behavior. As a cultural outsider here, you learn as you go. Now we know that getting on a train in costume is just not something most Japanese would ever dream of doing.

Living in Tokyo, we've found out that every Halloween there's a spontaneous gathering at a designated station on the *Yamanote Line*. Hundreds of foreigners and an increasing number of Japanese - most dressed in costumes - meet there. Then they get on the last few cars of the train together and do most of the 53-minute loop around central Tokyo in a spirit of revelry, protected by a sense of safety in numbers. It's a test of cultural limits that steps well over the line of acceptable behavior.

So what's a *gaijin* in Tokyo to do? You can adopt an approach of across-the-board cultural sensitivity and live strictly according to Japanese norms. Or you can be yourself, at least some of the time, and behave in ways that might be normal back home, but which the Japanese regard as inappropriate.

If you choose the latter - as Krista and I did on Halloween - you may simply get a total non-reaction. You may experience a kind of chill and find yourself feeling as if you don't really exist. As *gaijin*, we already stand out in Japan, so standing out even more is not necessarily difficult. You just have to be prepared to stand alone.

Convenience-Store Protocol

It bears repeating that North Americans living in Japan often fall into believing that Japan is very Westernized. After all, on the surface, a lot of things - like convenience stores - are very similar. But I've learned the hard way that if you don't continue to question your own assumptions of familiarity, you may put yourself on a collision course with your own expectations of what Japan *should* be like.

One of my steepest learning curves has involved deciphering the Japanese concepts of *tatemae* and *honne*. At first, I concluded that *tatemae* (meaning appearances, the way one is expected to communicate in social situations) and *honne* (one's real feelings) reflect a much sharper delineation between the two worlds of public and private than we uphold in American culture. In other words, Japanese say much less of what they really feel to anyone but intimates.

Later on, I began thinking that Westerners are not really all that different; we're certainly familiar with distorted public presentations by government and corporations, what with the 'collateral damage' of war and the nebulous 'restructuring' of companies, not to mention the dissembling of real estate agents and lawyers. In our personal relations, perhaps we just pretend to be straightforward all the time, but also practice *tatemae* and *honne* as the Japanese do. They withhold and they know they're withholding; we withhold and pretend we're not.

Without a doubt, these cultural differences can be unsettling and confusing to Anglo-Americans, raised to believe that it's good to be 'up-front and personal' as much of the time as possible. I found myself shaking my head with amusement one day as I sang along absentmindedly to a Moody Blues song, with a chorus that goes: "Say what you mean, mean what you say." It dawned on me that I'd always assumed such a sentiment was universal. Not so – honesty lauded as praiseworthy by a British rock band would often be viewed as foolhardy self-exposure in Japan. Japanese people tend to reveal next to nothing about their personal lives compared to 'tell-all' Americans; they routinely dissemble to keep secrets or avoid loss of face.

Assisting in this is the fact that communicating in an indirect manner is second-nature in Japan. I was once told a story by a salesman at Soulful Software. He explained that in Osaka, after he'd demonstrated the products he had to sell, prospective clients would usually say, "Well, why don't you come back tomorrow?" Translation? Sorry, we're not interested, goodbye.

It's not surprising that many Westerners end up concluding that people aren't being straight with you. You have to learn how to decipher the code. From a Japanese perspective, a person's real thoughts and feelings may have no part to play in a given social interaction, and this is completely acceptable.

As with many social phenomena here, I often sense it's more a difference of degree than of kind, but the intensity of Western reactions to these 'perceived' differences speaks volumes. One day at work, an exasperated American colleague of mine blurted out, "In Japan, *tatemae* is a religion!"

Actually, my colleague is known around the office for his overreactions, but we all understood the source of his frustration. As foreign residents in Japan, we often fail to understand the hidden sides of this culture we're immersed in, but we're compelled to try to make sense of it anyway on a daily basis.

One handy example of 'public face' is provided by the employees in our local convenience store, a 24-hour outlet on the main floor of our apartment building, similar to thousands of others in Tokyo.

Krista and I have gone into our local store virtually every day for the past two years to pick up milk or juice. Invariably, the store's employees deliver the exact same verbal routine - in Japanese, of course - to us or anybody else: "Please come in. That's such and such a price. Thank you very much."

The words are repeated in a parrot-like fashion. The language forms are exceedingly polite, and they serve to fill the need for a polite presentation to the public. But they are spoken so mechanically as to be meaningless, and they have a hollow ring to them.

Yet, they're the only words our local convenience-store workers will ever say to us. They evade interaction on any other level. When we've asked human interest questions, such as, "Are you a university student?" or "Do you like your job?" we always get a flat-affect response or a startled *Eh?* (Japanese for 'What?'), suggesting either that the question is incomprehensible or that it's taken them completely by surprise. If we're genuinely friendly and smile when we leave, they seldom respond naturally to an attempt at warmth. They may give a perfunctory little tilt of the head, but that's it.

We tried, early on, to establish a rapport with people working in the store, being outgoing by nature and knowing we'd be seeing them almost every day for a number of years. But after a while, we just gave up.

Trying to make sense of this, we concluded that being human is not part of their job description. We now suspect they may even be trained to act this way, in assembly-line fashion. Working at a convenience store, you come to work and 'put on your face.' In fact, they may actually prefer to operate on automatic pilot, avoiding all real interaction and leaving their personalities on ice. It takes less energy than being a person.

For comic relief on an especially bad day, we've made jokes about hanging a sign in the window: 'Help wanted. Zombies only need apply!'

But this behavior may be especially shocking because it's in such sharp contrast with that of employees in many stores outside of the 'chain store' category. In these other shops - our local family-run dry cleaner, for example - proprietors are extremely pleasant, lighthearted and sometimes chatty. On occasion, we share a laugh and a story and have wonderful interactions. Even when some are just going through the motions required of *tatemae*, it's done with real panache. Sweet old grandmothers in 'mom and pop' shops will deliver spirited versions of the ten-syllable *arigato gozaimashita* (thank you very much) again and again as you leave the store. If they can't win you over, *you've* become the zombie.

In part, this may just boil down to a universal business phenomenon: The independent small shop owners have a personal stake in their ventures, while chain stores homogenize us all. But I suspect another force is at work as well in the case of the aging grandmothers. They grew up in an era when the polite language forms, which they still use religiously, were linked in a meaningful way to the cultural traditions of deference and respect from which they sprang. If they're really just going through the motions when they say *arigato gozaimashita*, you'd never know it. In other words, I feel genuinely thanked for being their esteemed and much-valued customer.

For most of the young generation staffing convenience stores, the link between form and substance has clearly been lost. As employees, they're required to pay lip service to these forms, in deference to custom and convention. But their automaton-like delivery of them is a statement of how emotionally barren modern Japanese life in Tokyo can be at times, for the students themselves and all of us participating in it, Japanese and *gaijin* both. No doubt, they 'take off their face' when they get off work.

All of that said, my magnanimous American friend, Randall, has used his golden charm and smile to win over most everyone at his convenience store. They smile when he comes in, and he usually gets them laughing. Granted, he lives in Kamakura, a much less intense place than Tokyo, and he admits to less success in breaking through protocol in Tokyo stores. Still, Randall reminds me that it can be done, that *tatemae* is not as thick a wall as it sometimes appears.

Living with a Smile Deficit

Soon after I arrived in Tokyo, I met Ayako and Sayuri (my private students) through my American boss, who had taught them for many years. Ayako later told me that the first few times we'd met, she was surprised by how often I smiled.

"Canadians and Americans all smile so much," she observed, with some incredulity. Ayako, herself, has a beautiful smile and twinkling eyes.

I rather wistfully recall that comment, some four years of Tokyo life later, now that my face has adapted to its new surroundings. I now smile much less and frown more, like most of the people I see around me every day on the streets and trains. I wonder sometimes if my 'zygomaticus major muscles' (otherwise known as *smiling*) will atrophy from disuse in Tokyo.

I've learned something about 'smiles' from living in Japan, a less smiley culture. This wasn't so apparent back when I took them for granted, but now I realize that smiles are interactive events; they require feedback. You can't just walk around smiling to yourself, unless you're happily going crazy or content with being eccentric. Generally speaking, you have to have someone to smile at, to exchange and share it with.

Tokyo can be challenging for Westerners more accustomed to making eye contact, smiling and hugging than the Japanese. If you're a person who loves engaging in facial dialogues, your countenance may slowly freeze up here without your even noticing it happening. However big its surplus in the area of international trade, daytime Tokyo definitely has a smile deficit, and the mirror of other people's faces is usually going to be a dour expression.

Of course, if you're Mel Gibson and you show up for a few days, you'll be the subject of adoration and smiles galore. As Ayako made clear to me with her comment, many Japanese would love to smile more and to have more reason to do so. During holiday periods such as the Golden Week vacation in early May, there's a sudden explosion of smiling in Tokyo as millions get a chance to relax. It's a treat to be around then.

The fact that Japanese are much less comfortable with strangers than North Americans is one reason for the smile deficit. In Tokyo, most everyone's encapsulated in their own private world while they're in transit. People are less open to spontaneous acts of communication, including smiles and conversation with people they don't know.

I was on the Yamanote Line once with a Japanese acquaintance. A guy got on who appeared to be an African-American, which turned out to be the case. We exchanged greetings and had a short conversation along the standard *gaijin* lines: "How long have you been here? Oh, four years. Holding up okay? Yeah, but I'm leaving next year."

A few stops later, we said goodbye, and he got off. My Japanese companion then turned to me and said, "Who was that?"

"I don't know," I replied, "I just met him."

"What?" she said incredulously. "You don't know him?"

Another time, I befriended an uncommonly open and congenial Japanese man in his sixties, Makoto-san, at my local indoor swimming pool. Later, while I was using the blood pressure machine near the front desk, a Japanese woman about Makoto's age wandered up, said she'd noticed us chatting and asked me how I knew the man.

"We just started talking in the pool," I explained. This clearly surprised her. I suspect she liked him and was looking for her own opening.

Of course, friends walking and chatting do smile and laugh with each other in a completely normal manner in Japan. I don't want to paint a false picture of a social deep-freeze. There's plenty of cheerfulness to be found in Tokyo, though the world 'outside the group' is of much less importance. Still, when I first got here, fresh and fascinated, I could more easily nudge a smile out of strangers I ran across in public. It's gotten harder for me to do that the longer I've stayed, likewise for the many unsmiling foreigners we see walking around Tokyo. And though the language barrier is obviously an important factor in limiting contact, even fluency won't break down the cultural barriers between you and those you've never been introduced to.

In North America, we're much more willing to be outgoing with total strangers. Chatting with someone at a bus stop or in a coffee shop is an everyday event, whereas in Tokyo, people aren't expecting to make spontaneous connections with strangers. If you need directions, of course, someone will surely help you, and when I go jogging at 6:00 a.m., I do run across some early birds like myself who'll exchange a friendly greeting with me. It's a real pleasure when that happens.

But if you just want to strike up a conversation in a coffee shop, a minimal response or non-engagement will often be the response in Tokyo. So after being here a while, I found myself conforming to being much less outgoing with strangers. Gradually, I become less able to spontaneously reach out.

I eventually learned to accept that Japanese people feel comfortable in relationships that are well defined, such as those between co-workers, teacher/student, clerk/customer or friend/friend. Outside of such pre-set relationships, the discomfort level rises sharply and efforts to make contact are much harder, unless you add alcohol and a bar setting, which can change things considerably.

Despite knowing this, neither Krista nor I have adjusted well to shutting down our instinct to offer a spirited 'Good morning' and a smile to a passerby in our local neighborhood, as we would back in the States or Canada. I guess it goes against our natures to avoid eye contact and ignore our fellow humans. When I mentioned this to one longtime American resident, he said, "You need a Japanese mask."

To get an emotional lift, I occasionally find myself walking around with one eye open for Japanese people who are smiling and laughing with each other, so I can vicariously soak up some of their good energy. Being in a foreign culture, you have to do without the network of support you would naturally have in your own country. We realize that's an ever-present source of stress.

Despite Tokyo's limited supply of spontaneous interactions, I remain thankful that the absence of smiles here doesn't lead to much overt hostility, especially considering the huge number of people moving around this urban landscape every day. The fact that people remain as stoic and considerate of others as they do, within an environment this intense, is one of the seven wonders of Tokyo. People are forever going through the routines of bowing and apologizing, accompanied by the mandatory *sumimasen*. As a non-Japanese, you sometimes feel this is overdone, as when someone gently bumps you on the train and obviously couldn't help it. Still, it's very respectful behavior just the same and a way of establishing contact.

But it's hardly a big love-in. Tokyo hasn't escaped its own forms of rudeness, self-interest and aggressive behavior. Young people – exhausted themselves – rarely stand up for the elderly or for pregnant women on the trains, leading to the phenomenon of the *obatarian* – women, middle-aged or older, who 'bull' their way into getting a seat. In a society where people are strongly conditioned not to express negative emotions, the rudeness which does occur often takes the form of passive aggression – you can't be sure if the shove or snub you received was intentional or not. Krista finds this especially difficult to cope with.

Nevertheless, I've gotten used to relying on the fact that when I can manage to sustain a good mood and show consideration – in spite of subway chaos and urban angst – much of the time it will be reciprocated. In getting around Tokyo, I know that if I show respect and humility to the Japanese, they'll show me the same respect with a high degree of consistency.

From time to time, you'll have an encounter that really calls for an apology and it's not forthcoming, often because you're a foreigner and the fear of confrontation is doubly unnerving. As I walked up the stairs in Shinjuku Station one day, I failed to notice that the young man in front of me was swinging his closed umbrella, and the tip suddenly slammed into one of the lenses of my glasses. I was lucky; thanks to *Zeiss* – the German lens maker – it didn't shatter. As for the response of the young man, when he turned and saw who it was he'd hit, he panicked, bounding up the stairs two at a time without saying a word, to quickly lose himself in the crowd. I somehow wasn't surprised when I heard that 'hit and run' is quite common on the roads here.

Living in Tokyo, you have to accept the fact that you can't hope to mingle with millions of people every day without having frequent impersonal bumps and collisions of this kind. It can be exhausting having to make twenty little swerves and detours a minute, just to walk in a straight line through a train station.

Obviously, dropping your smile and putting on a mask to blast around with your co-commuters is a necessary urban survival strategy, but though some might feel that Tokyo is really no different from places like Chicago or Toronto, that hasn't been our experience. Even in large and busy American cities, total strangers more often share a quick smile or exchange a few words about something they both see happening.

In frenetic and more restrained Tokyo, such contact is much harder to come by. For North Americans like ourselves, who keep trying to replicate the norms of our own cultures, it can be a losing proposition. Sometimes it can seem as if people are sealed into themselves psychologically, or if they're with a group, they're sealed into that group and only prepared to relate to those within it. We struggle with this cultural difference.

It's my problem, I recognize, wishing them to be otherwise. There's no reason on earth why the Japanese should be other than the way they want to be. Still, there are times on the streets of Tokyo when I'd bay at the moon for a spontaneous smile and a generous comment like, "Hey, great weather isn't it?"

– directed my way for no other reason than that I'm somebody's fellow human being.

Through being in Japan, I've come to recognize that smiling in North America – when it's phoney or artificial – is one of our forms of *tatemae*. But responding to a genuine smile is one of life's great little pleasures for me. I trust that when we return home, we'll find that smiling is a recoverable skill.

The Upside of Orderliness

In Japan, even as I do battle with cultural differences, I keep noticing that the Japanese do a great many things well. Only a Westerner with a heavy axe to grind about this country could fail to acknowledge them.

When roadwork is being done, the care that's taken to ensure safety is very impressive. By contrast, such operations in many places in North America – let alone other Asian cities – are strictly second-rate or worse.

Before workers dig up a sidewalk or a street in Tokyo, they carefully arrange the pedestrian detour. It's a marvel to behold. A protected corridor walkway, with metal fencing, is set up as a temporary path. All along it on both sides, there are flashing lights to clearly mark the route, but the precautions don't stop there. At night, there'll be a courteous fellow with a flashlight directing you through. Invariably, he apologizes for the inconvenience! Even in the daytime, there's usually a man at either end, making sure you pass through safely. Citizens in Canada and the U.S. can only dream of such consideration on the part of construction workers.

It's obvious that each detail of the operation has been thought through, and is carried out in strict compliance with code. Such careful planning is one of Japan's greatest strengths. In North American cities, setting up a pedestrian detour is not something that's given a lot of thought; half the time, workers just seem to wing it.

I'm convinced that this meticulous and disciplined concern for every single detail of an operation, lies behind Japan's extraordinary success in so many fields. It helps explain why Honda and Toyota make consistently great cars. Like millions of other North Americans and most Japanese, I've learned that I can depend on their quality.

Likewise, it's no accident that Yamaha pianos are such superb instruments, the only kind I ever care to own. I like them so much I went to visit their grand piano factory in Hamamatsu, 135 kilometers outside of Tokyo. Just as I'd expected, the whole operation was one of calm orderliness. My guide walked me through the factory and carefully explained each step. The pianos were slowly moved along through the assembly process on an automated railway line. At each stage, technicians, carpenters and tuners worked diligently –

with scarcely a glance at visitors like me – each attending to one task, as the pianos-to-be passed in front of them.

They were helped along by robots, doing such things as popping in the piano pins and playing each key 300 times to stabilize the action before the retuning process. The whole factory had an atmosphere of sublime order, calm dedication and focus. Given the repetitive nature of many of their tasks, the workers appeared to me to have the patience of saints. After watching them work, I have a renewed appreciation for my piano.

Living in Japan has given me a new standard of comparison for things I'd seldom questioned before. On trips to North America, I'll now notice that a sidewalk is being dug up, but there's no pedestrian corridor. Everyone is obliged to walk right on the road – exposed to the traffic – around the outside of a makeshift ribbon border. There are boards piled up inside the ribboned-off area and stuff is strewn about, evidence of a haphazard system of doing things.

After a wind storm in B.C., I read a story about a piece of loose metal flying off a roof and injuring a passerby. I think of the summer typhoons in Tokyo, and how incredibly careful everyone is about securing potentially dangerous objects.

Walking along a Canadian street next to a high-rise construction site, a thick piece of reebar – for holding concrete together – bounced on the road not six feet away from me. I looked up to see a guy on the fourth floor looking down at me sheepishly.

"Wouldn't happen in Japan," I thought to myself.

I remember an evening many years ago in Montreal when we were driving along a side street. Suddenly, without warning, we plunged four inches down into a section of road that had been cut away. The workmen had forgotten to put up a flashing light to warn drivers the road was under repair. At the time, I'd thought, "Oh well, this is just the way the world is now."

Not so. Growing up in Canada, we were taught that we lived in the best of the First World nations. Supposedly, that meant we knew how to do 'everything' better than anybody else. After living in Japan, I now know that's just not the case.

A Mania for Control

All of that said, there are definite downsides to Japan's love of planning and organizing everything so carefully. The general feeling you get is that the authorities would pretty much like to control, not just things like road maintenance techniques, but everything they can get their hands on. The government and media do their best to convince the populace that nothing has been left to chance – 'risk' has been eliminated.

This authoritative penchant for total supervision helps explain why so much of life feels 'controlled' in Japan. Yet, the means by which this control is established and maintained are mysterious, according to some who've seriously studied it. This was the subject of Dutch journalist Karel van Wolferen's in-depth examination of Japanese social structure, *The Enigma of Japanese Power*. Overt techniques of repression, practiced in any number of regimes around the world, would never wash here. Instead, the *System* – as van Wolferen referred to it – operates much more covertly, casting a net wide enough to extensively regulate all aspects of behavior, without there being any clear idea of how this is being done.

There are obvious advantages to maintaining such tight control; the safety of Tokyo's streets is a reflection of it. To many Japanese, America's drive-by shootings are symptoms of a society wildly out of control. But when it comes to what I would call the dance of life, there's a significant tradeoff. Working in Japan, you often rub up against a tighter mindset, a pervasive sense that everything in life is controllable, even the weather. It's subject to rules like everything else.

When we first got here, we learned that there were announcements in the media about the official start and end of *rainy season* in June and July, a seasonal occurrence less predictable than it's made out to be. Sure, it will rain a lot and get pretty miserable at times. But this year there were seven or eight sunny days in a row following the official proclamation that rainy season had begun. Yet, far from being taken as evidence of the unpredictability of nature, a development of this kind often seems to be interpreted as an aberration in an otherwise rule-bound universe.

During this sunny reprieve, I made a comment about the lovely weather to one Japanese colleague, but quickly found that for him, rainy season mindset had already kicked in. His attitude seemed to be that if it weren't raining today, it would be soon – probably tomorrow – so what was the point of getting enamored of this fluky, sunny weather, because it wouldn't last. Perhaps I've simply come up against an example of the famed Japanese pessimism.

Krista once commented that – regardless of the season – she's always being told that, "This year, the weather is strange." It seems as if people around the world are saying similar things, more and more, because of changing climates. But in Japan, the feeling you get is that Mother Nature is actually under the control of some government bureaucracy, but these days, things are a little peculiar. Of late, I've taken to strolling down by the Tama River and delighting in the wind's freedom to circle the globe exactly as it will, clear evidence that something in Japan is not subject to government control!

Krista and I sometimes think that being pessimistic, and accepting powerlessness, is how the working masses cope with life here. Like Americans, Japanese people have a shared social reality, and move within it from the security of one socially-defined experience to the next. But Japanese seem much more wary of *catching the joy as it flies*, at least during the course of a working day.

This helps explain why many Americans experience life here as being quite bland; there's a sameness to day-to-day existence that can be enervating. I chatted with one Japanese woman at a party who'd spent a few years in America. Comparing the social ambience of her own country with the enthusiasm for life that she'd discovered in the U.S., she commented, "Japan is warm water."

On a day when Japan's lassitude is stirring up all your resistance to being here, you look around, and people corroborate your view by seeming emotionally flat and lacking in vitality. And though I remain aware that the absence of my own cultural support system serves to exaggerate my own experience – meaning that things seem much worse than they may actually be for most Japanese people – we sense that there's a despondency here that's quite pervasive.

A study that I read an article about seemed to support our feelings. Young people at universities in 14 countries were asked about their student experience. One question asked them to describe their day-to-day lives as students. They had two possible responses: (a) every day is a new adventure, or (b) every day is more or less the same as the one before. In 13 countries, a majority selected choice 'a'. Only in Japan did a clear majority of students describe one day as being more or less the same as the next.

You have to factor in the Japanese love of predictability and stability when you hear of a study like this, but it does help to explain why many Westerners get bored with Japan. Millions of Japanese are probably just as bored. They also seek escape from their routines, heading to the bars every night of the week to lubricate their feelings. In Tokyo, the social forces permeating Japanese society during the daytime do a bang-up job of inhibiting us all. It's not hard to imagine what Jim Morrison would have been singing if he'd lived in Japan. He'd have reached for that old Weill-Brecht number he sang so well, "For if we don't find the next whiskey bar, I tell you we must die …"

Speech Contests

Moving from a company job to teaching at a *daigaku* (university) has added entirely new dimensions to my understanding of Japan. I'll call my new employer *Shōrai-dai University* for all the same reasons I used the name *Soulful Software* – they're treating me well, and I've no wish to ruffle feathers. As I look back over my first year at my new job, one event that occurred early on at Shōrai-dai really stands out.

Soon after starting my first semester, I was approached by a few exceedingly polite and friendly members of the *English Speaking Society*, a student club, and asked if I'd volunteer to judge their speech contest. I was enthusiastic about helping, but quite unprepared for what was to follow.

I anticipated that the students would be giving prepared speeches on topics of their own choosing, though I felt sure they'd have them memorized, given that having a simple conversation – let alone speaking English extemporaneously – is difficult for most Japanese university students. This is because they've generally been taught how to read and write English in junior- and senior-high school, but given little or no practice at speaking it, at least until recently.

It turns out I was quite right about the memorization, but I couldn't have been more wrong about the content. I soon learned that all of the participating students had memorized, word for word, one of the following four historic speeches: Lincoln's Gettysburg Address; John F. Kennedy's Inaugural Speech; Martin Luther King's famous oration – "I Have a Dream"; or Charlie Chaplin's monologue about freedom in *The Great Dictator*.

Thus was I introduced to the notion of 'Speech Contests' in Japanese universities. From Jonathan Rauch, I've since learned that Japanese society did not even have the concept of 'giving a speech' until the idea was introduced by the West, but the members of the *English Speaking Society* are now true devotees.

Listening to student after student present one of these famous oratories, with an audience of hundreds politely applauding, was sometimes a twilight-zone experience. Determined to be completely professional about it, I found there were moments when I actually had to bite hard on the inside of my cheeks to keep from exploding into sympathetic laughter, as yet another young, earnest Japanese man gesticulated wildly – on suddenly remembering that 'gesture' is one of the judging criteria – all the while intoning, "I have a dreeeeeam today!"

These young men and women had obviously spared no energy in preparing for this contest. Imagining myself going through the same process of learning, memorizing and delivering a famous Japanese monologue, I got a sense of just how much work they'd put into it.

I also began to appreciate the problem they face. Having not been given the chance to learn to speak English in school, many find themselves equipped with a large 'passive knowledge' of the language – meaning vocabulary and grammar – that doesn't necessarily come to their aid when they're called upon to speak spontaneously.

Famous speeches serve to bridge this gap. Students who might be quite unable to engage in the simplest English conversation, were able to do a very commendable job of bringing John F. Kennedy to life. A few students added a twist, such as the young fellow who played background music as he spoke. I noted with interest that most of the young women chose Charlie Chaplin.

Occasionally, students would forget their lines, and I would wait patiently, sometimes for up to a full minute or two, until they remembered what came next. Eventually, they were able to carry on and finish the speech.

From a cultural point of view, it became obvious from the choice of speeches just how much influence U.S. society has had on the Japanese mind. But the clincher was my discovery that this identical format has been followed by members of the *English Speaking Society* for decades, not only at Shōrai-dai University, but at similar societies at universities throughout Japan. It never varies from year to year, and each new crop of students follows right in the steps of its predecessors, with those a year or two ahead guiding the way.

It never ceases to amaze me that, as fervently as Americans insist on novelty and the chance to put their own unique stamp on their experience, the Japanese prefer the tried-and-true to the untested. Given a choice, most will gravitate towards well-established patterns every time.

Off to Work We Go

When you have a bit of time off during the week in Japan, you can be hard-pressed to find company in your leisure. You feel like a bit of a freak, and you really *grok* that this is a country that lives to work and shares the same schedule.

Experiments with flextime have been introduced at some companies, but daytime work schedules still tend to be fixed. It's probably a reflection of the Japanese preference for group solidarity and structured time. More than any other city I've lived in, when Tokyo is working, the whole city is on the job – in lockstep.

Of course, people do take breaks and go to coffee shops, but generally it's with their co-workers, since everyone's locked into their schedule. The pachinko parlors are havens for those who may be unemployed or working odd hours, but the daytime ambience is a radical departure from Vancouver, Toronto or

New York, where tens of thousands of people have flexible hours and some segment of the population is idle at any given time.

In Tokyo, the social atmospheres of day and night are more divided. The whole city waits for the late evening hours to relax, be personable and let its collective hair down. Only committed workaholics pass up opportunities to socialize. One Aussie guy I met told me he admires the Japanese for their hard work, but he has a boss whom he described as being "24-hours-a-day-on-line." He said the guy is rapidly disappearing into his computer and losing touch with the people around him. But such antisocial behavior is not the norm.

In fact, it's an open question whether most Japanese actually work harder than Americans. According to my Canadian friend Brian, Canadians and Americans work more steadily while they're on the job and then go home. At his small Tokyo publishing company, his Japanese co-workers alternately work hard, then sit around reading magazines and doing very little, sometimes for hours. This goes on throughout the day and right on through the evening. One is tempted to coin a saying: Americans work harder; it's just that Japanese are always at work.

But whether people are actually working or they're simply 'at the office,' Tokyo, on a business day, appears to be a place where virtually everyone is on the job. Most are going about their affairs with a great sense of purpose.

When Japanese tourists visit North American cities, they pick up on the different social flavor right way. On my recent trip to Canada, I happened to wander into just the right barbershop to get more insight into this. In fact, once I started working on a book about Japan, the stories began popping up in the most unexpected places – hairdressers, in particular, are great sources of information.

Once a year, it turns out, this particular hairstylist gets a visit from a Japanese millionaire, a woman who loves visiting B.C. and always drops in to have her hair done.

"Every year, she says the same thing," the stylist told me. "She comes in after looking around Victoria and says, 'I can't believe this place, nobody here works!'"

After you've lived in Tokyo for awhile, it's a cinch to see how she gets that impression. Granted, Victoria is a small place, but seen through Japanese eyes, most North American cities come across as places where all manner of people have nothing more to do than chat, sip coffee, read newspapers to pass the time, or lie in the parks on sunny days like beached whales.

Even those who are 'on the job' often appear to be having a really good time of it. I watched one encounter in Canada that I would never even have noticed before living in Japan. A postal truck pulled up alongside a milk delivery van; they'd been passing in opposite directions and stopped to have a gab. I listened from a parked car for a full 15 minutes, as these two guys chatted about how good fly-fishing used to be years ago at a local lake. As the minutes ticked by, I shook my head in disbelief, reflecting on how unlikely such a laid-back conversation would be on a city street in Japan on a weekday morning.

In Tokyo, routines and schedules are more rigorously adhered to. Punctuality is all-important, and the pace of everyday life attests to its supremacy.

It's the first thing you notice when you come back across the Pacific for a visit – everything seems to slow right down in many American and Canadian cities. Just off the plane, you observe that some people are ambling along in what seems, after the pace of Tokyo, like slow motion.

"Hey, maybe they're just relaxed," I find myself thinking. "Maybe this is normal, and I've just forgotten what that's like."

Returning to Narita, picking up your luggage from the carousel, you can already feel Tokyo's throbbing energy taking hold of you again. I acknowledge that a part of me must love it, because I keep coming back.

In Tokyo's enormous Shinjuku Station, people are constantly on the move, at a pace that communicates hurry, time pressure and duties. Yet, despite the speed and the stress, a sense of social order is always there, guiding and shaping everyone's movements. At the famous Shibuya Crossing, hundreds of people skillfully weave around and between each other at a fast clip.

The movie *Baraka* focuses on this intersection, using speeded-up footage. It looks totally frenetic, but what's most astonishing is that despite its intensity, Tokyo is anything but chaotic. The city runs like clockwork, to a great extent because its people live and work with relentless dedication and follow the rules they're asked to obey with a high degree of compliance. What a great society! So why do we always keep coming to the conclusion that something very fundamental is missing here?

Delhi Flashback

I have a distant memory of a young man in his early twenties who approached me in Delhi in the '70s. On finding out I was from Canada, he immediately said, "I want to stay in your mommy's basement."

"Ah, excuse me?" I replied cautiously, not sure what I was dealing with.

"Please understand," he explained, "I want to stay with your mommy so I can study in Canada."

I politely wished him well, saying that I didn't think my *mommy* was all that keen about having him live in her basement, at which point I hopped in a rickshaw and headed across town. The driver sped about 5 kilometers through the wild streets of Delhi with characteristic abandon. Arriving at my destination, I jumped out to pay the fare just as another rickshaw pulled up behind us.

The same young fellow leapt out, already in full verbal stride. "No, no, no, no, no," he intoned excitedly, "please understand. I will *pay* your mommy to live in her basement!"

Living in Japan, I chuckle at this memory. I recall how exasperating it seemed at the time. But I recognize how that little encounter contains a missing piece of the puzzle as to why our Tokyo life feels less than satisfying. As a place to work, I would never trade the safety and cleanliness of Japan for the chaos of India, despite my respect for India's spiritual and artistic traditions. Nor do I forget how India wears you down because somebody is always hassling you for one reason or another, whereas the Japanese leave you alone. Yet I pine for such encounters here - unexpected happenings, serendipitous moments, meetings with 'characters.' It seems the longer you stay in Japan, the harder they are to come by.

Most of the time in Tokyo, nothing out of order seems to be happening, as though life here is on auto-pilot. In fact, perhaps the harshest criticism I hear from Westerners is that this astonishing country is boring. *Shinkansen* trains blast across these islands all day long, come to a stop not a second late, and with such precision that their doors are always perfectly aligned with marks drawn on the station platform. Amazing! Yet, an uncomfortably high percentage of your conversations feel like tape recordings; you've had them many times before. Off-the-cuff remarks and unexpected encounters are like precious gems; you treasure them because they're so rare.

At Christmas time, it's always Beethoven's Ninth - nobody seems to think of trying something different for a change. Western teachers strive to make their classes interesting, but their students consistently fail to surprise. Many seem bored or tired, like they're just going through the motions long required of them.

Are Krista and I just locked into culture shock, endlessly comparing? Is Tokyo driving us nuts? Is the writing on the wall? Is it time to leave Japan?

The Cost of Social Order

Even the bag people (yes, Tokyo has plenty of them) often sit around in orderly rows here in subway stations, like Shinjuku and Ohtemachi, their worldly possessions neatly piled against a pillar, reading newspapers that require the knowledge of at least 2,000 complex *kanji* characters. Meticulous, law-abiding and literate bums who never stoop to panhandling - what else would you expect in the Japan we've come to know?

At lunchtime, restaurants fill up and empty out in record time. By 1:15, most are deserted, since just about everyone's on the same schedule. If you could adopt a routine that goes totally against the grain in this city, you could eat in solitude in restaurants, wander around in deserted parks throughout the work week, and wonder where all the millions of people are.

Since such an option is an impossibility for most of us – even if it were desirable – the approach longtime residents usually take is to join in. We merge with the workaday hordes and fill up any leisure time that's out of sync with everyone else with – what else? – more work. I should be thankful; it's one of the features of life here that got me into writing. Personally, I've found it hard to slow down when nobody else is.

Despite the treadmill quality of Japanese life, there's obviously something comforting and secure about having plenty of work and a safe and predictable routine. This can keep you 'hanging in there' in Tokyo even when your instincts tell you to move on. In actual fact, some Westerners come to Japan for a couple of years, have a tremendous time, and leave feeling great about this country, or they bail out at the first sign that they've had enough. Many spend a lot of time in the *isakaya* – Japanese pubs – with Japanese friends who are at their best in such settings: They're relaxed, open and friendly. If you really like drinking when you socialize, there's a good chance you'll have a fabulous time with the Japanese.

But for those who stay on for five or more years, there tends to be a breaking point when the differences in culture 'get to you.' It usually takes familiar forms.

My friend and colleague Marianne, who's watched dozens of her American compatriots come and go over the past decade and a half, told me one evening over dinner that on leaving Tokyo, most everyone she's known has said something along the lines of: "Life here is just too predictable, like it's been rehearsed. Even the spontaneity seems planned!"

To some considerable extent, this is just an expression of cultural bias. Interacting among themselves, the Japanese people can be as spontaneous as people anywhere, and if you get lucky and receive an invitation to an exclusive *Ginza* jazz club, as I did, you'll hear terrific, extemporaneous improvisation.

But we are 'out of the loop' of the intimate connection Japanese people share with each other. It's a consequence of forever being the *outsider*, adrift in a kind of social anomie, disconnected from our own society's psychic energy and social anchoring, all the while continually trying to adjust to Japan's greater subverting of individual identity.

It's also a reflection of our resistance to living and working in a more structured and ritualized way, one in which 'form' is routinely valued over 'content.' My favorite example of this is seeing Japanese girls take photos of each other out on the dance floor, while the Westerners around them are boogying away like there's no tomorrow. It took me a long time to accept that in their own way, these girls are also expressing themselves in a way that's natural for them. And of course, some Japanese girls can boogy with the best of us.

As for the more ritualized patterns of social interaction, such as those with waitresses and cashiers who have been discouraged from stepping outside of a scripted routine with customers, this lack of spontaneity can definitely begin to grate. It often seems painfully restricted to Westerners, while not being at all unnatural to Japanese. Yet even here, there are more and more pleasing exceptions to be found, as Japan goes through rapid social change while you watch it happen. There's a wonderful bar in Yokohama called *Samadhi*, staffed by laid-back and super-friendly young people. If you speak Japanese, your conversations with them will flow as they would anywhere. You have to deliberately seek these places out in Japan, and it's so refreshing when you find one.

In all fairness, it must be pointed out that we often have our own scripted styles in similar circumstances, even though they're meant to seem light and breezy.

A story a British guy told at a party in Tokyo drove this home to me. He was in a restaurant in Hawaii, and the waiter introduced himself by saying: "Hi, I'm Bob, and I'll be your waiter for this evening." The Brit, Colin, perceived this as being 'American false friendliness' and responded, "Right, I'm Colin, and I'll be your customer for tonight."

The Japanese may well argue that they avoid this kind of nonsense by establishing clearer boundaries around what goes on in 'functional' relationships, such as that between waiter and customer. I've grown to really appreciate the fact that in Japan, your waiter will seldom interrupt your conversation with continual comments such as, "How's everything here?" or "Can I get you some dessert?" There's a far greater sensitivity to your personal, private space, an awareness that you didn't come to the restaurant to talk to the waiter. Yet much of the time, when you really need something, you barely have to turn your head and look up, and your needs will be sensed, in spite of the fact that nobody is expecting a tip. Advantage Japan.

When relationships are more than just functional, the Japanese – like people anywhere – interact with each other in natural and spontaneous ways, as surely as the sun rises every morning. But these conversations will reflect their cultural preferences, meaning there may be more pauses. That can be uncomfortable until you get used to it, at which time it can start to seem very pleasant.

There's also likely to be more attention given to non-verbal communication – and much more reading between the lines – than we're used to, not to mention the Japanese reticence about being free-and-easy with strangers. I was once told a story about two Japanese neighbors, who stood on the same train platform every morning for three years, without ever saying a word to each other. People beyond your family, your work, or your school 'circle' are just not so casually engaged in Japan.

When it comes to interacting in English, many times a Japanese person, who acts in a completely natural manner with other Japanese, will seem frozen once they start to communicate in English. Fear of making mistakes and sounding inappropriate can be especially paralyzing for many Japanese people.

Coming to terms with the ways of a foreign culture this different from your own is not easy. On our good days in Tokyo, we take life in stride, get a real thrill out of being here, and find much to be grateful for. On our bad days, we have the sense that something is definitely amiss in this society, that natural human impulses have been systematically stymied.

Some Westerners actually notice they're having trouble making decisions because in Japanese life, so many more are made for you by various authorities, and much less is left to the discretion of the individual. The 'world outside Japan' can start to seem daunting, after you've lived on a steady diet of Japanese apprehension about 'dangerous foreign countries.'

It's an ongoing challenge to maintain balance and perspective, to keep remembering that you're walking blind through a culture you only partly understand. I think Krista and I both fully acknowledge that there's much we don't understand about how the Japanese people think and feel and why they live as they do. Japan is anything but a quick study.

Ultimately, many American foreign residents find they simply have to leave. Life in even a small urban center in the tougher American social climate will definitely present more threats to life and limb than Tokyo does, but it's home, and a far greater percentage of daily interactions will make sense again. Strangers are going to chat and share an observation with you more readily. Spontaneous moments are going to happen all the time. Your workplace has the potential to be more laid-back, because American society has condoned a more sociable working environment. In more conservative Japan, extremes of protocol, and norms of indirect speech, are much more likely to rule.

Perhaps most significantly, you'll no longer be the *gaijin*, an outside person looking in, and feeling partly out of touch at all times with what's going on around you.

I've learned to respect many things about Japan and its people. I'm quite sure we have as much to learn from the Japanese as they do from us. From Japanese families whom I've had the pleasure to get to know, I've learned a lot about holding together, thinking of others, and sacrificing for the betterment of everyone. After living in Japan, a philosophy of 'every man (or woman) for himself' seems sadly misguided.

And what can Japanese learn from us Westerners? Looking at life in Japan the only way I can, from my own Canadian perspective, knowing the impulses and longings of my own heart and spirit, one thing stands out. I appreciate the remarkable social order and safe conditions of life in Tokyo very much, yet find myself most bemoaning the absence of one intangible I used to take for granted: The appeal of the optimism and ubiquitous spontaneity at the heart of American life has never been so clear.

author's collection

頑張り

4

UP AGAINST THE SOCIAL CONTRACT

Appreciating the Japanese People

There's an abundance of goodness in the Japanese people. Japan gets a lot of bad press around the world, and not nearly enough appreciation for the many good qualities of its people. For many *gaijin*, part of the problem seems to be the difficulties involved in gaining access to that goodness.

Out in public, on the crowded streets of Tokyo, maintaining a sense of humility works in your favor, because it's a quality people recognize and respect, and they'll sometimes respond in kind – even in Tokyo, where people routinely adopt a big-city surface coldness. For Westerners, learning to bow ever so slightly in your daily encounters is also essential, just as learning to shake hands is necessary for Asian people coming to the West. I've found that it makes a tremendous difference; it's a clear demonstration of your willingness to be culturally sensitive.

Obviously, keeping an even disposition also helps a lot. There's an amusing phrase in Japanese I like a lot – *ishin denshin* – which loosely means 'knowing how other people are feeling without the exchange of words,' a kind of psychic or telepathic knowing. When I first heard of this, I was skeptical – the Japanese believe their non-verbal communication skills are far superior to ours. But I've come to believe that perhaps they actually became especially good at this over the centuries out of necessity, living in a culture where people had to hide much of what they knew, in order to save their skin. When I first arrived in Tokyo, people often wandered up to me and asked if I needed help. After a while, that stopped happening; people knew I wasn't a newcomer anymore. In Japan, there's a greater attunement to unspoken signals.

Living in the urban pressure cooker of Tokyo, however, a few too many uncomfortable incidents can really shake you up. It takes a lot of patience to stay calm and non-judgmental here, and not lose sight of the good will in the people around you. Many Japanese do seem to know when you're in a bad way, and they steer clear of you, which can leave you feeling even more alienated. If you don't watch it, you can easily get into a vicious circle.

When I think of the mountains of criticism of Japan – often emanating from U.S. media sources – which have been a regular feature of the English newspapers in Japan for years on end, it's no surprise that so many 'foreigners' acquire a jaundiced perspective.

At one point, I actually decided to stop reading Karel van Wolferen's intense assessment of this society, *The Enigma of Japanese Power*, while traveling on the trains. His argument about the absolute control wielded over the Japanese people, by the 'enigmatic' collusion of government bureaucracy and corporate Japan, was striking many chords. It was also stirring up strong feelings I couldn't really deal with, while coping with the pressures of the commute. It was like watching an in-flight news broadcast about a plane crash.

Defusing such stress can be a major challenge. I've been extremely fortunate to have wonderful Japanese friends like the Tagawas. Mika is a colleague who's lived in the States, and every Thanksgiving she and her husband Kazuo invite a whole crew of us, Westerners and Japanese alike, to their lovely home on the Izu Peninsula, on the outskirts of Tokyo, for the whole day. With their gracious generosity and lighthearted manner, they supply us with an annual reminder of the sweet kindness of the Japanese people, a welcome antidote to the litany of negatives one is exposed to, just through being here.

Not everyone is so lucky. Not a few longtime foreign residents become unable, or unwilling to see what's good here anymore. Some end up ragging on and on about Japan on a daily basis, and that negativity can be very seductive. Regrettably, 'what's wrong with Japan' becomes an all-too-familiar lunchtime topic of conversation. I briefly met one young American woman on a train, who'd only been here only a short time. She made the comment, "Everyone I've met who's been here more than five years is bitter and twisted."

It's bad news when this perpetual culture shock sets in, because the goodness of the people can get completely overlooked in denunciations of the 'System.' My optimistic friend, Randall, who spent a year in Vietnam in the late sixties, consistently maintains a positive outlook on Japan. He believes that Americans who have trouble here create their own little self-fulfilling eddies of discontent. He counters their negative viewpoints with his inimitable flair: "Tokyo is a fine city, filled with Japanese being Japanese!"

And why should they be otherwise? Many non-Japanese who come to live in Tokyo need constant reminders that the intense pressures of being thought of as an 'outsider' demand a healthy counterbalance – a continual supply of positive input. That can be hard to come by, but *gaijin* in Japan fare much better if they have someone in their lives with a very balanced perspective. You need someone around you like Randall, who never ceases to see the Japanese simply as ordinary people like yourselves, doing their best to cope with the exhausting demands of this city and society, much like us.

These days, what's helped me enormously is to view the people separately from the exacting system of social control which enmeshes us all. It keeps me from sending them into the black hole in my psyche labeled 'System Abort.'

One Japanese acquaintance made a real difference by pointing out something that hadn't occurred to me.

"A third or more of the Japanese in Tokyo feel like outsiders, just as you do," he told me. "They come from somewhere else in Japan, and seldom feel completely at home with Japanese born in Tokyo. They're like you, they're here because this is where the jobs are."

Tokyo, the enormous magnet, pulls us all in like so many iron filings. Then it lines us up and plays with us, as we move around in its force field.

The Japanese-style Welcome

Just as with my entry into Soulful Software, I was welcomed – during my first weeks at Shōrai-dai – with a dinner party that had ceremony, human warmth, and unlimited food and drink. It's a simple fact: The Japanese are exceptional hosts! They're also especially welcoming when marking your entry into their group.

I'll retain a lifelong sense of gratitude for this and for the opportunities I've been given in Tokyo. Thousands of us, from countries like Canada and the U.S., have been blessed with full-time work in Japan, courtesy of companies like Soulful Software and institutions like Shōrai-dai University.

It's always necessary at these gatherings to give a formal introduction of yourself and to say a few words of greeting, preferably in *Nihongo*. As my new boss, Tanaka-san, said to me with a smile, "We Japanese seem to love these kinds of ceremonies."

There's no disputing that. Most of us at Shōrai-dai work part time at other Japanese universities, and they all have annual dinner parties. The hospitality they extend to us is invariably gracious.

In addition to giving us a hearty welcome, many companies and institutions that foreigners work for in Japan provide special daily support to their foreign staff. This is not always the case, unfortunately, but I've been very lucky. Shōrai-dai provides subsidized housing to its foreign staff and assigns one English-speaking person to deal with all the problems that come up. As far back as anyone can remember, the person in this role has always been a woman. It's by no means an easy job, dealing with the demands and complaints of foreign English-speaking staff all day long, and Michiko-san does a masterful job of handling us.

Another English-speaking woman in our department, Mariko-san, deals with the endless paper chase of our work-related matters. I have endless praise for these women. They do a continual cross-cultural tightrope walk and work tirelessly on our behalf.

On a recent Sunday afternoon, our boss, Tanaka-san, invited the foreign staff into his home. I learned that he's done this for years at the beginning of the academic year. He and his wife freely shared their time, served lunch to us, and made us feel very comfortable and included. Foreign press reports often convey the impression that the Japanese are always standoffish with foreigners and keep us at arm's length at all times. Such reports routinely fail to acknowledge a wonderfully warm side to Japanese people that I've been privileged to get to know.

As for Shōrai-dai's offer of housing, though most of the foreign teachers live near the campus, I chose to stay in Chofu and commute. I knew it would be a long trip – nearly two hours all told – but it made sense given our situation. The main Shōrai-dai campus is located well over an hour from central Tokyo. That commute is manageable for me, but it would be a nightmare for Krista if she had to make her way from there back into Tokyo every morning.

So I continue to be a train-dweller, but at least now I head away from central Tokyo every morning instead of straight into town. Surprisingly, it's as crowded as ever (because Greater Tokyo is so enormous), but the change in jobs has been a boon in many ways. Instead of skyscrapers, I actually see mountains by the time I get to my destination. My spirit never fails to lift at the sight of them, and they feel just as welcoming as my new colleagues.

Japanese Generosity

Ten-thousand yen is 'the' good round number in Japan. It often seems to be a kind of watershed price, guaranteed to make the best impression. 'Less' might risk seeming cheap, so this helps to account for gifts such as the 10,000-yen boxed cantaloupe.

For Westerners, gift giving, as it's played out in modern Japan, can be unsettling. It can seem very manipulative. It's hard to avoid the impression that it turns the natural act of giving into a sterile commercial contest, though the practice of always paying back and not being in debt to others probably stems, historically, from Japanese Buddhism.

Still, I'll never accede to the idea that the act of giving for its own sake, as a simple expression of genuine affection, is little known here. There's definitely two sides to it. Japanese people have given much of themselves to Krista and me, and we've no doubt that it's often been from the heart. Whatever the variety of motives for their giving, I now have the general impression that the Japanese can be very generous people. Compared with them, many Westerners in Japan seem quite tight with money, though that's partly a reflection of how expensive things are here.

Even as expressions of *giri* – reciprocity as an obligation one can't escape – many gestures Japanese people make to thank you are remarkable. One young woman we knew told us she was going to England, so I gave her my uncle and aunt's address in Brighton. She met up with them for just a couple of hours, and my uncle drove her around the Sussex countryside. Later, he wrote to say they'd received a huge tin of biscuits, mailed to them from Japan on her return.

In terms of how Japanese people give and receive among themselves, it's easy to conclude that *giri* plays the central role in a great many interactions. Both at O-*Chugen* in summer and O-*Seibo* in winter (gift-giving seasons), Japanese give gifts to those above them in social status, and especially to those who have served or assisted them in some way in the recent past. They give gifts to their dentist, for example, as well as their boss and their teacher.

On an abstract level, there's something very pleasing to me about this kind of reciprocation, this consistent acknowledgement of the things people do for you. Nevertheless, the way '*giri* gift giving' is played out in modern Japan often feels uncomfortably symbiotic – I'll scratch your back, because I know you'll scratch mine in due time.

In fact, much as Ruth Benedict pointed out in *The Chrysanthemum and the Sword* – written late in the war years to aid U.S. intelligence on Japan – it's still conducted in a very business-like manner: "These debts are regarded as having to be repaid with mathematical equivalence to the favor received and there are time limits."

During gift-giving seasons, it's mostly overburdened Japanese women who are obliged to fulfill this duty. You can see them lining up in upscale stores like *Takashimaya* or *Mitsukoshi Departo* (Department Store) next to piles of specially boxed merchandise. They fill out forms with a store clerk, pointing to various items, priced to show the relative status of the gifts.

"This one goes to this address, and this one goes here," they say hurriedly, making sure not to miss anyone important. Conveniently, the store then takes excellent care of sending everything off. Japanese retailers are incredibly reliable at delivering goods promptly and efficiently, in spite of Tokyo's size and population.

To Westerners, the mandatory and perfunctory nature of this ritual can appear to undercut the whole purpose of giving, at least as we like to believe we practice it. We prefer to think of our giving as the performing of generous or spontaneous acts of sharing with no thought of return. We don't want to see ourselves as engaging in measured and calculated exchanges.

So Krista and I both had the same reaction to this mandatory gift-giving ritual. We could do without it, because it feels contrived. But I now know that many Japanese feel much the same way. As one Japanese woman put it to me, "If you want to continue being part of the neighborhood, you do it."

But gift giving here has prompted me to take a closer look at how Westerners *actually* give and receive, as opposed to how we believe we approach it. We like to see ourselves in a good light, as everyone does. In certain circumstances, however, the Japanese may actually be more honest about the whole thing.

In giving gifts, we often say we don't expect anything in return, but most of the time we do. Then we complain when a reciprocal gift or favor is not forthcoming as we'd hoped.

By contrast, the Japanese also expect something in return, but that's clearly understood by everyone. They expect it, and they get it! They know they'll have to give when it's their turn next. Probably the simplest example of this is when Japanese go away on trips. However short the trip, there's no confusion about whether or not to buy gifts for co-workers, family members and friends. It's mandatory.

They're *obliged* to bring back gifts from wherever they've been. It's called *omiage*, and when you're going on a trip, people will tell you straight out – albeit playfully and with a smile – "Remember my *omiage*." And yes, they mean it. It's very much as if they're saying, "Hey, you're getting a chance to go away and we aren't. Even up the score."

In Japan, enjoyment has to be spread around and shared – an interesting social value. In fact, many Japanese seem to get a lot of pleasure out of giving *omiage* gifts; it certainly feels that way when they give them to me.

On the train platforms of major stations throughout Tokyo, you come upon small mountains of *omiage*, wrapped and ready – gifts to go. Japanese returning to the hinterland after a trip to Tokyo have no trouble finding that last-minute gift for Aunt Yukiko.

The obligation to buy *omiage* is so strong that Tokyo actually has *omiage* stores, specifically targeting the domestic traveler who forgot to buy his *omiage* gifts, or ran out of time. These stores are stocked with representative gifts and regionally distinctive wrapping paper from all parts of Japan. They serve as lifesavers, more specifically face-savers. Nobody need ever know that you actually forgot about them and bought their *omiage* in Tokyo, after getting back to town.

As for gifts like the boxed cantaloupe, it's kind of a catch-all gift, perfect for the hurried and harassed executive, or the wife of an upwardly-mobile businessman. Hustling down the street, late for that hospital visit with the general manager, they know they have to bring an appropriately priced gift. To fail to do so would be an inexcusable *faux pas*. Enter the exorbitantly priced cantaloupe, perched on its bed of shredded paper on its sidewalk stall. It's ready to go and guaranteed to cut the mustard, at the watershed price of *ichiman-en* (10,000 yen).

It sometimes seems that a nation such as Japan, in which gift giving is extremely important and a majority of people seek to be like everyone else, is a manufacturer's dream. Once you get a product that most everyone agrees they need to buy – a particular *giri* gift, for example – it's as if a subliminal nationwide consensus is reached. From that point on, the only problem for the producer is keeping up with demand.

Although it can be difficult to understand the motives behind giving gifts in this country, I salute my Japanese *tomodachi* (friends) for their heartfelt generosity. Beneath the commercial face of Japan, allied as it is with the requirements of social duty, lies a very thoughtful and caring attitude towards 'significant others' in your circle. No one could ever convince me otherwise.

Incident in Kudanshita Station

There was an incident that happened one morning at Kudanshita Station a few years ago, back when I was still working for Soulful Software. The images return to me from time to time, and now find their way onto paper. I suppose it's easier to write about now that I'm no longer a *salaryman*.

I always had to transfer trains at Kudanshita, and that morning, as always, I was waiting in a queue – amidst the frenzied dashing around on the platform – for the next train on the Tozai Line. They come every three minutes during rush hour, so it wasn't to be a long wait.

Kudanshita Station was unique, I'd discovered, because it offered the commuter something different from most other underground subway stations in Tokyo. Someone working there had chosen to play an unusual recording over the loudspeakers in the morning. Unlike other stations, where the commuter can usually expect silence, or a round of the station signature tune every time a train pulls in (Vivaldi's Four Seasons is used at one station), Kudanshita (which means 'nine steps down') graces you with the sound of hundreds of birds, chirping away in a virtual forest, as you wait for your train to pull in.

The first time I heard it, I was reminded of my years in Montreal listening to National Public Radio wafting up from Vermont. They introduced their 7:00 a.m. program in the same way, and I used to lie in bed and wake up slowly to the sounds of a forest full of song, savoring a few sublime moments before jumping back into the urban steeplechase.

This bird song had quite a different effect on me in a Tokyo subway station. In an underground cavern of concrete and steel tunnels, it underscored just how far away we all were from the natural world of trees, birds, flowers and mountains, up above the subway tunnel and way beyond Tokyo.

But I appreciated this small touch. It was calming and provided a gentle illusion of the presence of nature. And on the morning of the 'incident,' the presence of bird song made what happened all the more poignant.

I hadn't been waiting long when my train thundered in, filling the tunnel with metallic screeching as it braked to a stop. Thirty or forty mechanical sliding doors – three in each car – snapped open, and the tidal wave of commuters getting off at this station flooded out to the exits. I lingered, as always, until most of those on the platform had gotten on. Getting on last was my survival strategy at Kudanshita; other stations required different approaches. Here, being right next to a door (instead of further in towards the center of the car) made the most sense, since I'd be getting off at the third stop. You can get trapped in the middle of a subway car in Tokyo's rush hour, unable to get off in time.

The last to get on, I leaned all my weight against the passengers nearest the entrance, so as to create enough space for the doors to slide shut, with me squeezed inside. Strangely, they remained open. A few more seconds passed, and then I began to hear some commotion from several train doors up. I poked my head out and glanced to the left, in the direction of the voices.

A young blue-suited man was lying on his back, about a foot from the first sliding door one car up, perhaps 30 feet from where I stood watching. He was writhing in what seemed to be great pain, his torso convulsing up and down, his legs bent at the knees. It might have been an involuntary spasm, or a reaction to pain; it was impossible to tell.

A semi-circle of concerned people had formed around the man. They stood watching, while those of us inside the train remained motionless. No one knew what to do, or they knew it wasn't their responsibility to take action.

"My God," I thought, "maybe he's having a heart attack." I also realized it might be an epileptic fit, or any number of things I knew nothing about.

We all continued to watch, in stunned silence – like frozen mutes. Suddenly three words popped into my mind, learned in a first-aid training session I'd taken years before in Montreal: I know CPR!

With the poor man still writhing, I engaged in a furious inner monologue playing on fast forward.

"The training was only valid for one year – it's expired. I can't go out there; I don't speak Japanese well enough to properly explain what I'm doing. Besides, most Japanese haven't even heard of CPR (cardiopulmonary resuscitation) being performed by ordinary citizens. Even if they had, what good is an expired CPR card? I'd probably get arrested for interfering. Damn, there must be somebody among the hundreds on this train who knows something about emergency care!"

A full two minutes went by. The half-circle of onlookers surrounding the struggling man stared at him in a mesmerized state, and helplessness prevailed. Nobody did anything, though my inner monologue raced on. All the while, the birds continued singing in their virtual forest – an otherworldly backdrop to this tense urban drama.

I decided that even if my CPR training were up to date, it would have been crazy for me to take action. In Japan, even ambulance paramedics are pretty much limited to administering oxygen and artificial respiration. The idea of ordinary citizens – let alone a *gaijin* – taking action in situations such as this one is unheard of. Japanese people are taught to leave all such emergencies to the doctors. I'd only have put myself in jeopardy by trying to help.

Still, it was hard to stand there and do nothing. I realized that if my CPR training had been up to date, it might have been more difficult to justify my decision not to get involved.

By this time, the birdsong tape had been turned off. A full three minutes had passed, and now the man's body writhed upwards one last time, seemed to hang a moment in mid-air, and then dropped to the concrete, motionless. I have no idea if he'd had an epileptic fit and it was finally over, if he'd lost consciousness, or if the poor man had actually died.

The whole train load of us watched this scene, transfixed, enduring our own private experiences in the face of his suffering. Another 30 seconds passed, and then there was the sound of hard shoes running on concrete, echoing through the tunnel.

"Finally," I thought, "a doctor's arrived."

It was not to be. I looked towards the sound of the footfalls to see what looked like the station master sprinting along the platform towards the supine young man. Tokyo train stations can be large and sprawling, and I suspect he'd come from some distance away. Reaching the circle of onlookers, he stood and gazed down with them at the motionless form for just a moment. Like the rest of us, this was not his domain.

Deciding first to get the backed-up rush-hour train system moving again, the station master motioned for the small crowd of onlookers to move away from the train. Some got on; others moved back to the wall. Signaling to the conductor with his upraised arm, he blew hard on his shrill whistle. It pierced the silence like a dagger, and the mechanical doors rumbled shut.

With that, we slowly pulled away in our sleek, steel snake, the prostrate man lying right next to its metallic skin as we passed, the small head of his unmoving body less than a foot away on the concrete platform. We quickly picked up speed, and he disappeared from view.

I'll never know what happened to that anonymous young man. Maybe paramedics arrived soon and he survived, or perhaps he actually passed away that morning, watched over by helpless strangers. But images of his ordeal are recorded indelibly in my mind, as are the feelings that accompanied my own inaction and the paralysis of all of us watching that day.

I don't pass through Kudanshita much anymore, being a former *salaryman* now. When I do, I always listen for the sound of birds, singing away in their virtual forest.

The Purposes of Higher Education

I've waited until my second year of teaching before doing much writing about my new life, working within the Japanese university system. First impressions are often misleading when you're an outsider trying to make sense of a society as complex as Japan's. Your impressions undergo constant metamorphosis, so I've taken notes and waited for a clearer picture to form.

As a full-time teacher at Shōrai-dai, with experience as a part-timer at two others, I've now discovered - as have my colleagues - that much remains the same wherever you teach. Japan's top-down style of control brings its standardization to education along with everything else. There can, however, be dramatic differences in the ability level of the students from one institution to the next, because Japan's universities are all meticulously graded from the best on down to the humblest. As would be the case elsewhere, the caliber of students in a university ranked seventh in the country is usually head-and-shoulders above those in one ranked 139th. The surprise is that so much remains very much the same, wherever you teach.

Some of the students at the best of the three universities I've worked at are exceptionally bright and polite young people, and it's a great pleasure to work with them. Classes of *kikokushijo* (returnees), students who have lived abroad for long enough to become virtually fluent in English, are impressive groups. If Japanese society will allow it, many of them may become the leaders of a far more international Japan some fifteen or twenty years down the road.

Putting these young people in the same class and calling them *returnees* seems strange, at first. But after a while you realize it's a sensible solution for a group of students whose life experience is so radically different from that of their peers.

Actually, a few of the students in my returnee classes have never been out of Japan, but they've been put into the class because their English is excellent. They always feel insecure next to students who have spent five years in Iowa or seven years in Zurich, but most manage to fit in. Including these *non-returnee* students is a smart idea – *returnees* face a tremendous challenge dealing with reverse culture shock and the uncomfortable feeling of 'being different' now that they've returned to Japan. They need to mix with their 'non-returnee' peers.

Japanese universities with significant numbers of returnees are struggling to adjust to the presence of these young people in their institutions, and some are doing an excellent job of reintegrating them. The opportunity to teach them has been very enjoyable.

At Shōrai-dai, most of the students I teach are also well-mannered young people, but working with them has been much more challenging. I keenly recall my first few classes just over a year ago. Shōrai-dai is a less prestigious, middle-of-the-road institution, and the classes are often huge. The freshmen English 'discussion' classes generally consist of somewhere between 40 and 50 students, almost none of whom have overseas experience.

My initial feeling was a kind of shock! I walked in to see a subdued group of 45 students staring at me with what seemed like hypnotic focus. Sitting on benches in straight rows looking quite somber, these first-year students were eerily quiet and expressionless. A few were still wearing the school uniforms they'd been obliged to wear throughout high school. My first impression was that they all looked incredibly sad.

During the first few classes, I asked them to bring in photos so I could make up a seating chart. As foreign teachers, we all discovered that in order to put names to faces (especially given that Japanese names like Atsushi Watanabe, Yukiko Ito and Hiroyuki Ikeda were completely new to us), photos were essential if we were to get to know our hundreds of students.

Most brought in leftover black-and-white high-school photographs of themselves in school uniform, always with the same unsmiling faces. Some told me that students are actually told *not* to smile in such official photo sessions.

"Now there's a contrast with America," I thought.

Suddenly, I had yet another explanation for the 'smile deficit' in Tokyo. I was reminded of my experience of getting a passport photo done in a professional photographic studio here, and being told I *couldn't* smile! Such photos are still considered serious business in Japan, much like group shots were in my grandfather's day. The photographer pointed to an official government 'face-sampler' sheet on the wall of his studio in which a smiling face was listed as unacceptable. Again and again, I patiently explained that Canadians *are* permitted to smile for their passport photos, but he simply couldn't get his mind around this. Begrudgingly, he went ahead and photographed me smiling against all odds, and I now have a passport photo in which it appears that I'm baring my teeth in self-defense.

On a number of occasions, I've visited principals in their offices in Japanese schools. Invariably, I've found myself surrounded by the framed photographs of severe-looking men, former principals going back decades. There's almost never a smile to be found among them. That's because in Japan, a person with such an important position who smiles for an official photograph is suspected of not being a 'serious person.'

In my university classes, however, it became clear within weeks that most of these young people do have smiles, as well as distinctive, lively and expressive personalities all their own. At least, this is the case when they're speaking their own language on their own social territory - in the university cafeteria, for example, or at the local pool hall.

It was a relief to discover this, because it wasn't immediately apparent at all. In my classes, I found their often sullen faces to be profoundly disconcerting. Eventually I was able to recognize that most Japanese young people are capable of displaying the same healthy range of emotions as young people anywhere, but only outside of the classroom.

Part of the classroom puzzle was this: When it came to studying, most of these university students had a problem. They'd just spent the last 12 to 15 years (with many of them getting started at age three) gearing up for the all-important university entrance exams. Their preparation had involved the development of exceptional mathematical skills, as well as the memorization of reams of facts, absorbed not only during school hours, but in after-hours *juku* - or cram schools. This often went on till 7:00 p.m., for years on end, and included the summer months as well.

Now, at long last, here they were - at the finish line. They were like marathon runners, and the race was over. They'd placed as well as they could place. Now, after the initial excitement at finding themselves in this new world - the winner's circle - they did what many marathoners do after a race: they collapsed. Japan must hold the record for the greatest number of 'burned-out students under 20' in the world.

Their school years had also involved six years of English study using the antiquated grammar-translation method, one which permitted them to exhaustively study English grammar without – in the majority of cases – learning to confidently utter much more than a simple greeting. It was now our job to engage them in conversation and discussion.

Only one thing seemed sure: We were not about to lose our jobs because our students got so good at what we were assigned to teach them that we were no longer needed. My colleague Jan told me one day about a student she met on campus, who rapidly said in passing, "Hello, how are you? Fine thanks and you?" before Jan could say a word. We amuse ourselves with such stories. I remember to imagine how my fractured *Nihongo* sounds to Japanese ears.

Having finally made it into a university, most Japanese students have precious little incentive to carry on studying seriously. Their status in society has largely been determined by the ranking of the university that's accepted them. The company that hires them four years down the road, on hearing what university they went to, will feel they know a great deal about their prospective candidate just from that information alone, so systematic and hierarchical is the pecking order in the Japanese university system. A graduate of *Waseda* – a highly ranked university – will be a credit to the company, regardless of what he or she did, or didn't do, during their university years.

Traditionally, one other thing prospective employers have wanted to know, is whether or not a student joined a club while attending university, since this information will ostensibly help to pick out the team players. Students know this and feel pressure to join a club, even though they may not want to.

As for grading, university marks are often not taken anywhere as seriously as they are in the West. At many of the institutions we work at, my colleagues and I have been discouraged from failing students if they come to class at least two-thirds of the time, regardless of whether they actually do anything or not. The fact that these students passed the entrance exam, and were accepted into the university, seems to justify their being given a passing grade in our English classes.

In part, this is because the university business is very competitive in Japan. If you run a private university here, attracting new students every year to write your entrance exam is essential for survival, since private educational institutions earn a lot of money from each candidate who writes their exam. To attract prospective students, you need a good reputation. That includes being an institution where young people can rest assured they'll be able to ease up on the pressure for a few years, in addition to actually learning something. After all, the traditional thinking has been that the company will train them later anyway.

Thus, university life in Japan is widely understood to be a kind of free space, a four-year hiatus between so-called *examination hell* and the corporate grind. Students know all of this – it's how their system works. Basically, they feel entitled to take it easy now, and how can you blame them? This is how things have been set up.

All of this was borne out fairly quickly for me, as was the fact that for most of my first-year students at middle- and lower-status universities, a love of learning for its own sake is simply not on their radar screens just now. Fortunately, my part-time job at one higher-status university provides a welcome contrast with this – some of the students there, especially the young women, are very dedicated students.

At middle- to low-end universities, however, many of our male students demonstrate a consistently lackadaisical attitude. Others make an even clearer statement: they come to class and promptly go to sleep.

Some of these students work all night in part-time jobs in convenience stores; others appear to be catching up on sleep foregone during the last 12 years. Whatever the explanation for their fatigue, they're about as interested in what their university teachers have to tell them as they are in going through *examination hell* again just for old time's sake. Teaching them is a tough assignment, and perhaps that's why they pay us well – so we won't complain, or hop on the next plane home.

Speaking of sleep, according to a question I perused during proctoring, Japanese people need less of it than Europeans. I triple checked: That was the correct answer to a multiple-choice question on a university entrance exam. One has to assume it's taken to be a fact. A nation habituated to chronic sleep deprivation has convinced itself that this is a unique national characteristic.

It's an example of the kind of myth that many Japanese appear to believe about themselves. Another myth that you hear repeatedly from students is that 'only Japan' has four seasons. Ah, Vivaldi was Japanese?

We Canadians have our own myths, of course. We love our reputation as a peaceful, friendly bunch who believe in fairness. But a good case can be made that we're also professional complainers. Whether it be Quebec's future, our government's failings, or our geographical plight – being forced to share the continent with the aggressive Superpower to the south of us – we often deal with the vicissitudes of life by whining about them.

As for Japan, when you reflect on Japanese history, its myths should really come as no surprise. There's actually a whole school of thought called *nihonjinron* ("theorizing on the Japanese") dedicated to the idea of Japanese uniqueness. It's my guess that at least some of these attitudes have their roots in Japan's 250 years of isolation, prior to 1868. After all, Japan was a society that completely walled itself off from the outside world, with its foreign devils and perils.

But who knows, maybe the Europeans do sleep more now – the vacation-hungry louts! Ah, but if the correct answer had been that Japanese students put in more time sleeping on commuter trains, and in university classrooms, than the students of any other nation on earth, that would definitely not have been a myth!

Paradise Lost (and Regained)

I paid a visit to our old neighborhood in Setagaya yesterday, mainly to shop at the import grocery store. We needed a few items like American oat bran cereal and Canadian maple syrup that you can't get at most food outlets in Tokyo. Only a select few stores have them.

I'd been back to the area a few times before to visit friends, but as most of them have moved on now, the store is about the only reason I ever go there. This import shop was a favourite of ours in our first year in Tokyo, partly because they played Beethoven as background music. That had been an unexpected treat, and I'd been pleased enough to write about it.

I felt a sharp pang of dismay to discover that things had changed dramatically. Some possible explanations scurried through my head as I stood in the check-out line. Did somebody get to the manager since our last visit? Maybe he – one assumes a store manager is a male in Japan – had no idea how much his choice of music pleased his *gaijin* clientele – we ought to have told him. Or perhaps he hadn't even been playing classical music out of conviction, as we'd imagined, and now he'd been wrestled to the ground by some salesman hawking this generic background anesthetic.

Perhaps he was a music lover, but he'd been transferred; I preferred to believe that. Now a new manager was seeking the lowest common denominator of 'atmosphere' like everyone else in town.

I'd entered the store hopefully, wondering what they'd be playing today. In Japan, small things like this can take on a lot more significance than they ever would back home, and my ears reached out expectantly. In response, they were assailed by harmonies that would have made Beethoven roll over: Hawaiian muzak.

Help! I hurriedly picked up what I needed, endured the check-out line and fled the store, now just any other place to buy consumer goods. There was nothing to do but chalk up another casualty in the culture wars, another victory for mediocrity.

Realizing I needed to use a washroom in a hurry, I dashed up the stairs of a McDonald's across the street and made my way into the men's room. Horrors – the diligent salesman had combed the whole area: more Hawaiian Muzak!

I thought of the film *The Unbearable Lightness of Being*, the scene where Sabina is subjected to neutered music in a classy restaurant. She rails against the "uglification of the world," lamenting that, "Everywhere music's turning into noise."

It seemed synchronistic that later in the day, I came across a book review in one of the Tokyo English papers. It seems I have some company in making a big deal out of this. Someone's written a guide book to 700 restaurants and stores in London, England that do not play muzak. The backlash has begun - paradise will slowly be regained for those who want it.

As for Tokyo, I have less hope in the short term. What I'd believed to be a conscious decision to opt for culture may well have been just a fluke, I now see, an aberration that's been smoothed out. Of all the world's great cities, Tokyo was perhaps the most likely to opt for city-wide muzak, simply because so many things here are standardized, therefore easier to control. How did I ever imagine that bona fide Beethoven would survive here?

Soothed by the knowledge that music lovers are fighting back, I turned up *The Pastorale* in the privacy of our living room last night. Then I sat back, closed my eyes and began planning our next trip to London.

Fast-food Flashback

I have this clear recollection of sitting in a Mr. Donuts coffee shop somewhere in Japan on an autumn afternoon. It was in the late '80s during my first few weeks here. It could have been anywhere because at the time, I was racing around the country from one end to the other on a Japan Rail Pass. I remember that the shop had only three or four tables, and I was the sole customer for the whole time I was there.

I could hardly speak any Japanese at the time, and chose Mr. Donuts because I could just point to what I wanted. I got my order and went to sit down, drink my coffee and munch on my Venetian Creme donut. Suddenly, all seven of the sweet, young uniformed waitresses with nothing else to do were swarming all over me, filling up the sugar dispenser, rewiping the table, trying to find ways to serve their only customer. It felt like the seven dwarves in reverse - Prince Foreigner and the Seven Maidens. I cannot tell a lie; I loved every minute of it.

The days when Japan had money to burn on excess employees are now long gone. It was an amazing blip in time, an afternoon stopover in fast-food paradise. America's donut shops are destined to forever pale by comparison.

Mass Teaching for the Masses

During my first year with Shōrai-dai University, I was assigned to teach one morning a week at one of its affiliated junior high schools. I learned I'd be teaching four 50-minute classes to students in grades seven, eight and nine. I hadn't anticipated this at all, but I welcomed the opportunity to see one more side of Japanese life.

Schools from kindergarten right on up to the university level are sometimes linked in what's called the *escalator system*. If your child can get on the bottom rung with a particular institutional chain, the passage to the top should be much less traumatic. This is because the transitions from elementary to junior high school, and on into high school and university, will be pretty much assured, providing the child stays within that particular institutional system and accepts the ranking it confers.

My university is part of an escalator system, so most of the junior-high-school children I taught will eventually enroll in one of its universities. They'll be spared the experience of a do-or-die *examination hell*, though some will lack motivation as a result. Others will aim higher and write the entrance exams of more prestigious institutions, knowing they can always fall back on their escalator school if they fail. So the competition for such schools, among parents seeking guarantees for their children, starts very early.

I enjoyed my Friday mornings teaching four classes of 45 uniformed children – aged 12, 13 and 14 – for one year. Generally, the students were extremely well-behaved. Their demeanor reminded me of the situation in Canada a few decades ago, when I was in their position. The grade-seven kids were very innocent and cooperative, while some of the grade nines were starting to rebel and show a definite lack of interest.

The classes were enormous by Canadian standards, but I never had a problem holding the floor. Respect for the *sensei* (teacher) is still much stronger than it is in Canada or the U.S., though I did observe how difficult it was for one female teacher to get any respect from some of the grade-nine boys.

Serious discipline problems are occurring much more often now in many Japanese schools. But compared with students this age back home, my experience – and that of many other foreign teachers I've spoken with – is that Japanese students, who prove challenging in other ways, are still much easier to manage.

Still, in a year of Friday mornings, I was able to glean that Japanese school teachers have one tough job. They work a punishing schedule. They're also required to be far more responsible for the well-being of their students in after-school hours than is the case with their North American counterparts. I have a lot of admiration for the dedication of the teachers I worked with.

Teaching classes of 45 students and encouraging them to speak English was not a simple task for a variety of reasons – class size being one; Japan's grammar-based approach to learning a foreign language being another. Fortunately, efforts are being made to incorporate more speaking into the junior-high-school years, largely through the help of foreign teachers like me. Many others have been hired through the JET program (an organization that's brought many foreign English teachers to Japan).

But so long as the entrance exams do not require English speaking skills, the focus – especially in high school – will still be on preparing these young people to answer 'testable' grammar-based questions. Although they may not be able to talk to you about it, your average Japanese knows a lot more about English grammar than most native speakers.

Grammar, like everything else on the curriculum, is taught using the Confucian model of pedagogy – the teacher knows and imparts the knowledge; the students listen and absorb it.

Of the many incidents I could write about to illustrate this learning style, one stands out from all the others. I choose it because it illustrates a central feature of Japanese education, and seems to hold up a mirror to the workings of society at large. I also select it because many Canadian and American parents and educators have become fed up with the failings in our system, and envy the successes of the Asian model, without really knowing much about what that model entails.

On the day in question, I was teaching 12-year-olds about Canada through a game I'd made up called Canada Bingo. They were very attentive and eager to learn how to play! They'd have done anything I asked them, provided – I was to learn – that I explained everything perfectly clearly.

Each of the 45 students had a bingo sheet with 25 blank squares. I'd decided to let them put an X in the center of the sheet themselves, rather than filling it in for them. Bingo players know that this space is a free spot, which every player covers from the beginning of a game. I had no idea how many of the children would be familiar with bingo, but I assumed they'd pick it up quickly.

I hadn't imagined the difficulties that would be involved in getting these children to put a simple X in the center of a bingo sheet. Throughout the four classes of that morning, I kept refining my explanation and demonstration of what they should do because of the problem I encountered. I discovered that if there was even a trace of doubt in their minds as to the correct procedure, many students simply would not act.

By the fourth class, I was sure I had it down. Holding up my copy of the bingo sheet on a clipboard for all to see, I drew a big, black X in the center box with a felt pen and asked them, in Japanese, to do the same. Many did, but about a third of the class did not put pen to paper.

I was eventually left to conclude that even though I'd drawn my X in the center box and told them to do the same, there was still plenty of room for doubt in some of their minds. I imagined they had thoughts like these: Could they choose any box, or only the center one? I'd pointed to the center box and had said 'here,' but maybe other boxes were okay too. If so, which box should they choose? Did they have to use a pen like mine? Or was pencil okay?

My assumption is that without 100% certainty of what was wanted, the students had been trained to wait to hear more from the teacher, rather than taking the risk of getting it wrong. Making a mistake was clearly a big deal! Many of the students simply waited. Eventually, I had to go around and actually put the pencil in the box for some of them. But the upside of this has to be acknowledged: Not one of those 180 students put an X in the wrong box. Providing I was able to clearly explain what I wanted, the students would do it without question, and do it correctly.

This incident and others like it began to convince me that Japanese children are taught above all to follow rules, and to follow them well. It's impressed upon them from an early age that they should never act until they're absolutely sure what they're supposed to do. If there's any doubt in their minds, they know they aren't expected to guess, or to try to figure things out on their own. They also know that their best move is to just stop and wait for further instructions.

Speaking with Japanese people has provided confirmation of this. My friend Maggie's Japanese friend, Masaya - a very congenial man in his mid-twenties - told me one day that because Japanese people are raised on rules, most feel very comfortable and secure with them. He believes most people are happier to follow rules than to decide things for themselves, since they haven't been taught much about acting independently.

Lending more credibility to this view was one amazing Japanese fellow in his early forties whom my colleague, Ken, and I met and chatted with a few times. He'd been a student radical in the late '60s and was eventually expelled from university. He then went to the U.S. where he remembers spending his first two or three months wandering around asking people, "Excuse me, what am I supposed to be doing here?" He finally figured out that nobody was going to tell him, that in America he had a lot of choices available to him, and it was up to him to decide.

This, he recalls, was a new concept to him. Granted, this happened decades ago, but this was the experience of someone who grew up in the '50s and '60s in Japan. He'd been taught very little about making decisions or thinking for himself.

A Japanese woman in her thirties whom Maggie teaches at a private language school remembers being told a morality tale by her grade-four teacher. Hanae told us the whole story. A baseball team is competing for the championship, and it's a critical juncture late in the game. The next batter comes to the plate, having received instructions from the coach to bunt. The score is 2-1 for the opposing team, and there's a man on first. Ignoring the coach's instructions, the batter swings away, hits a home run, winning the game and the championship for his team! The next day, the player is dropped from the team.

Having told the story, the teacher then asked the children who was right – the coach or the player? Hanae recalls that they all knew enough to say nothing. By grade four, they understood that it was not a real question with a variety of possible answers. They knew they would soon be told the one correct answer.

"The coach was right," said the teacher, after a short pause. "The player was wrong to disobey orders from his coach."

Such insights, provided by Japanese people themselves, and coupled with experiences like the bingo game glitch, shed light on the disciplined, meticulous behavior we see all around us in Japan. I'd barely set foot on these shores before hearing a fellow tourist in Hiroshima trot out the stereotyped view that the Japanese are phenomenal imitators, but poor innovators. That assessment seemed shallow to me then, and it still seems so now. Many Japanese have been phenomenal innovators. Creating great corporations like Sony, or developing top-of-the-line products like Toyota cars, surely counts as innovation. As we all know, Japan single-handedly transformed the car industry by introducing unrivaled quality standards in automobile manufacturing.

Still, five years into our Japanese experience, I now believe that the controlled behavior we see around us every day is a reflection of an education system that teaches people to act much more deferentially towards authority. This consensual willingness to live by the rules has a very positive side, but there's clearly a major tradeoff.

Many companies in the West would pay plenty to find 180 workers who've been taught to do exactly as they're told, and who seldom make a mistake. But one also wants to know what those same children will do as adults fifteen years from now if they're asked to innovate, to come up with some kind of new design out of their own imagination. Will they wait for further instructions?

One teacher I met insists that if he gives his students permission to be creative, they eventually respond. But he has to work hard at it for a few weeks before they'll strike out on their own.

With certain groups of my own students, I've found much the same. Working with visual and non-verbal exercises such as collages, some demonstrate plenty of creativity and sensitivity. But at one university I was told not to use collages, despite the fact that most students were very motivated by them, and enjoyed explaining them to me. It was considered to be too unorthodox a method.

With a strong foundation of discipline already in place, many Japanese students reveal a natural capacity to build on that, and then go on to express themselves in unique ways. I often wonder what the educational authorities are so afraid of.

The Game of *Wakaranai*

Perhaps because of the indirectness required by Japanese culture, most people are very skilled at bluffing. It can take you some time to figure this out and before you do, you often doubt yourself. It helps enormously when you're 100% certain as to what's going on.

I remember getting on a *shinkansen* bound for Kobe one morning with a ticket for a reserved seat, for which I'd paid an extra 500 yen ($4). A young Japanese man, probably about 20, was sitting in my spot by the window though the aisle seat next to him was vacant.

I checked and double-checked my ticket. Yes, he was definitely in my seat. If he'd been friendly, I might not have cared, but it quickly became obvious that he had an attitude. It was also clear that he intended to stay where he was, either because it was a window seat, or because he was all settled in now for the three-hour journey and didn't want to bother getting up. Or because he thought he could bluff the *gaijin*.

The young man played at pretending he didn't understand my Japanese and couldn't figure out what on earth I was getting at. When I showed him the seat number on my ticket, he repeated "*Eh?*" (What?) and "*Wakaranai*" (I don't understand) over and over, something Japanese students often do with foreign teachers. It's a tactic that can drive you quietly mad.

Occasionally, he glanced at the empty seat, hoping I would take the hint. By this time, however, I had taken a dislike to the guy and was determined to quietly wait him out and claim my rightful seat. I just stood there looking at him and waited patiently, having learned long ago that getting angry is the very last resort for waging this kind of mental battle in Japan.

It actually took a full five minutes before he gave in. When he finally broke and hauled himself up, the young man's exasperation gave the whole game away. Of course, he'd lost all face and that didn't help, so he went to another car and I didn't see him again. It's an uncomfortable memory of a side of Japan most foreign residents could do without.

For the Love of Shopping

Ah, a delightful sighting in the subway tunnels! Few would dispute that these are bleak, uninteresting places, especially during evening rush hour, but people are lined up in neat, orderly rows – tired, stoic and unsmiling though they may be. It's a civilized approach to minimizing chaos that I've come to appreciate more and more about Tokyo, but you'd be hard-pressed to have a 'Eureka' experience in these concrete tubes.

After spending years in Tokyo's underground, you've long since read all the subway signs and accepted you'll never be able to read parts of them. You've listened an uncountable number of times to identical voice messages. A super-polite Japanese male or female voice heralds the arrival of each and every train the same way: *Mamanaku, densha ga mairimas* (a train is coming soon). Inside the train cars, another voice reminds you: *O Wasuremono no naiyouni go chui kudasai.* (Don't forget your belongings!)

Your best defense against tedium and torpor involves some form of escape. Most *gaijin* keep their mind engaged in some other dimension with a newspaper, novel or Walkman, but it's helpful if you can manage to keep alert to what's around you. The feeling we often have in Tokyo is that there's a sameness to everyday life, so it doesn't take much of an event to give you a chuckle.

That was certainly the case today. As I perused my evening paper in the queue, who should meander into the space next to me on the platform but a walking philosophical statement.

This was not an 'event' of any kind – nothing actually happened. A pleasant-looking middle-aged woman simply ambled up with a cloth bag over her shoulder, filled with consumer goods. But in the interior of a long, drab tunnel where scarcely anything out of the ordinary happens 97% of the time, it was a moment to savor.

The bright red letters on my fellow commuter's bag spoke out like a Tokyo Credo held close to the heart, succinctly capturing the primal urge underlying Japan's rise to a lofty peak in the boom years. Written large in flawless English – that being an event in itself – her credo proudly proclaimed: *I Shop Therefore I Am.*

My anonymous co-commuter may not know Descartes from Billy the Kid, but she looked positively chipper. From our earliest days here, we recognized that this is a country of dedicated shoppers. In good economic times and bad, shopping is surely right up there next to sleeping as the favourite national pastime on weekends.

Actually, anyone who taught English here in the bubble years knows that if you asked female students the question, "What are you doing this weekend?"

the most frequent response by far was the one-word answer: *Shoppingu* (I'm going shopping). Even a dampened economy has not changed this all that much.

My colleague Jan decided to get her freshman students at an all-women's university to choose discussion topics at the beginning of term: Shopping not only topped the list, it was the runaway favorite. In fact, she told me they didn't seem especially interested in much else.

As for the young men in my university classes, when I ask them, "What are you doing this weekend?" their answer is almost always "no plan" or "sleeping." On one Friday in a class of 40 students, one too many of these lads gave this response, and before I knew what I was doing I had leapt up on the desk with both feet and roared, "When I was your age, we had *fantastic* weekends!"

The following Friday, at the end of the class, one of these same young men approached me timidly and said with all sincerity, "Mr. Mack, have a *fantasutiku weekendo*." Success! Somewhere out there are 40 Japanese who will always understand the word 'fantastic.'

Of course, to some extent, standard answers like "no plan" and "shopping" are just 'language class responses' – the easiest way to get the teacher out of your face. Learning French in Canada, we, too, had our 'pat' answers. But in Japan – public face being all-important – even the standard answers need to give the correct impression. When I first started teaching at universities in the early '90s and asked students, "What's your favorite movie?" – young women in class after class kept answering, "*Roman Holiday*."

"Ah, as in Audrey Hepburn," I would say, puzzled, since this was a movie made in the 1950s. Yes, that was the one. I finally concluded that this was as politically correct a public statement as a young Japanese women could make about herself. The public spin seemed to be: I'm a good girl, and the idea of being a princess sounds wonderful, but I only take 'safe risks.'

As for questions about weekend plans, the truth about the standard answer *shoppingu* is not in doubt. The proof is in the stores on Saturdays and Sundays; namely, hordes of shopping-crazed females.

Many working women have no choice but to do their shopping on the weekends. Like people everywhere, they're too busy during the week, and most Tokyo department stores close by 7:00 p.m. In Japan, the 24-hour convenience stores have become a necessity for millions of us, flying through the workweek by the seat of our pants.

But on weekends, the real no-nonsense shopping begins. The food sections of many Japanese department stores are in the basement, and they can be frenzied madhouses on a Sunday, best avoided if you dislike mob scenes. Market-style hawkers call out from all sides, and I have to admit that it has its appeal. Despite the crowds, I've grown to like Asian-style markets.

During bonus week in early July and December, Tokyo is suddenly awash with cash. Hundreds of billions of dollars are plunked down into the hands of consumers at the same time. The 'bonus system' serves as a built-in twice-a-year guarantee of consumer spending. Companies and governments hold on to part of the workforce's salary for six months, and then give it out in one sizable chunk. Just before people get their bonuses, advertisers unleash an information blizzard to whet appetites.

Soulful Software had its own store in the basement of its main office building. Like clockwork, we got its advertising flyer about 72 hours before Bonus Day. Many of the prices were bargains, so once it arrived and the money was in our company-bank accounts, lots of people just headed downstairs to the company store to do their shopping in-house. This way, the company managed to instantly recycle some of this bonus money. They paid it out in the morning, and a portion of it came right back in over the lunch hour – very clever.

Speaking of bank accounts, when I first came to Japan in the '80s, savings accounts in Japanese banks were dishing out a whopping 0.75% interest, and that has scarcely changed over the years. Meanwhile, Soulful Software's company bank was offering a whopping 6.5% to its employees! Obviously, a lot of the money paid out as salaries was going right back where it came from – into the company's coffers, where it could be used for further research and development. It struck me that the whole system was a brilliantly organized closed circuit. To top it off, many employees had opted for 1% of their monthly salary to go into company stock.

As for the bonus system, I don't pretend to understand the intricacies of the Japanese economy, but even an economic layman can see the upside of this biannual infusion of cash into the hands of consumers, coinciding – as it does – with the two gift-giving seasons.

You can find fault with the bonus system – some commentators refer to it as withheld pay. They point out that companies collect interest on this money, and use the bonus system to protect themselves against sudden resignations. For example, you don't just quit your job suddenly in Japan if you ever want to see your bonus money. You wait until after bonus day to announce your departure. Years ago, it was reported in the newspaper that even the former Prime Minister Takeshita waited to resign until just after he got his summer bonus – a sizable amount in his case.

But all the Japanese people I've spoken with seem to like the bonus system. Many see it as enforced savings, a form of fiscal discipline. Many husbands and wives make some kind of arrangement, where the wife handles the monthly salary, for example, and the husband gets the bonus.

In spite of initial reservations, we've grown used to it ourselves, because it's a tidy sum of money you can count on twice a year. Given Murphy's Law of spending, we might not save any of our bonus income if there were no bonus system and our monthly checks were just proportionately larger.

For Japan itself, no matter how bad things get here economically, at least twice a year there's a surge in consumer spending, because people have cash in their hands and gift-giving obligations to meet. You can hardly pretend you don't have the money, since everybody knows you just got your bonus, the same as they did.

After bonus day, which conveniently falls on a Friday, shopping binges continue on into the weekend and into the week after. Yet in spite of all this, some bonus money gets tucked away for a rainy day. Polls consistently show that the Japanese are great savers, saving upwards of 15% of their income while Canadians and Americans save a mere 1% to minus 2% of theirs (i.e. living on credit). Japan consistently accounts for about one-third of the world's savings.

At Soulful Software, many people routinely ate *bentō* (box lunches) prepared at home, or purchased at the company canteen. The Japanese do a terrific job of combining generosity and frugality. It's one reason I remain cautiously optimistic about this country's long-term future, despite Japan's economic problems.

The love of shopping and the urge to save for the uncertainties of the future are a powerful combination, but at some point in the '90s, Japanese women started holding on to more of their money. What a change! We recall that when we first got here, we heard that one reason people bought new consumer goods - and trashed last year's television set in the *gomi* (garbage) - was to help the nation's G.D.P. That thinking is long gone. (In the late '90s, the government actually started issuing consumer coupons, offering $250 worth of free merchandise to encourage consumption.)

We're fairly typical, I suspect. We spend a small fortune here on living expenses, with restaurants being our Achilles' heel. But like the Japanese, we also stash away part of our salaries and bonuses for the future.

Besides, we have our own Weekend Credo: *We seek solitude on Sundays; therefore we survive, and also save our yen.*

Mirrors: Handle with Care

Obon is an annual mid-August event, the Buddhist Festival of the Dead, when the ghosts of ancestors return to have a reunion with the living. It's one of three times a year when huge numbers of Japanese people have some time off, time to dance the *Bon odori* and get together as family. Many companies or businesses close for a few days or even a week or two, and millions of Tokyo residents go back to their hometowns or villages where they grew up. Throughout Japan, 50 to 75 million people are on the move for *Obon*.

But Tokyo is also home for millions of people, and cities such as Tokyo's Setagaya-ku district hold festivals in parks at this time of the year. Yesterday, a Sunday, was the last of a three-day festival held the week before the *Obon* exodus. Another Canadian and a Japanese friend and I wandered around in the late afternoon and early evening. We sampled the hundreds of booths selling plants, wind-chimes and all kinds of exotic food from around the country.

At one point, we took in a terrific hands-on workshop for children where they were constructing wooden dolls. Further along, we watched as a long, thick stick was placed in the unsure hands of a smiling but blindfolded six-year-old girl. She was then spun around three times and sent staggering dizzily off towards a distant watermelon, coached by a helpful gallery: "Left. Go left. No, too far! Come forward, okay, you're there. Now, slice it in two!" Cheers and laughter all round.

Dozens of red, yellow and purple lanterns swung gently in the evening breeze as night fell. On a portable stage in the center of a track-and-field circuit, a Japanese Dixieland band did a fine job of playing some swing; then a female singer came on and did a credible version of *New York, New York*.

The crowd, though much more subdued than an American audience, was appreciative and clapped warmly. I looked around me. An elderly man grinned broadly for a few seconds at a young child in a woman's arms, perhaps his grandson. The thirtyish couple beside us were quietly enjoying the music, the woman tapping her foot. In the middle of one rollicking number, I traded smiles with her, both of us acknowledging the shared pleasure of the moment.

As my friends and I wandered back through the rows of booths after the concert, I noted the calm atmosphere, the groups of vendors sitting around sharing a hearty laugh and the relaxed faces. Another young couple passed by us. The man, casually dressed in slacks and a T-shirt, and carrying what was surely their young son in his arms, had a wonderfully serene expression on his face – a proud father, no doubt. His wife was equally at ease.

Perhaps he was a company man who normally keeps a tight schedule, though there were no clues to confirm that. Some of the other men strolling around were dressed – as always – in their suits, ties and starched-white shirts, performing their *family service*, as many would refer to it. Yet they, too, exuded contentment just the same, strolling alongside their smiling wives. Clearly, this was a very happy time for everyone.

I suddenly found myself inwardly confronted with all of the media generalizations about *salarymen*, *office ladies* and deprived housewives, because the truth was right there in my face - those generalizations just didn't fit this picture.

There's no way to convey an accurate and balanced view of Tokyo life without including descriptions of scenes from events like the *Obon* Festival in August. These are scenes of relaxed and carefree families, having a fine day out on a Sunday just as people do around the world. Perhaps it's time to abandon altogether these overused terms *salaryman* and *office lady* - to reject them for the shallow stereotypes they are.

My inner pendulum swung wildly last night as a few of my long-held Western perceptions fell into question. Yes, Japanese company men work arduously under conditions considered oppressive by most Western standards. Yes, most of their wives are limited professionally and toil away as mothers and housewives. Yet just because Westerners would chafe at the extremes of the lives they lead, that tells us little about how the Japanese feel. Perhaps the majority of men and women in Japan gracefully accept the conditions of their lives. Last night, I acknowledged that may well be the case.

Many millions of Japanese men may feel that by working like the devil, they prove they're still warriors in this modern age. Being the bread-winner is still an honorable role here, and they do have these brief but wonderful periods of relaxation with family.

Millions of their Japanese wives may well be quite content to live as mothers and housewives. They are *uchi-no* (of the inside), and many wield plenty of power there. They're quite happy to let their husbands be *soto-no* (of the outside), doing battle with the world. Undoubtedly, many Japanese females view American women - frantically juggling careers and motherhood - as unfortunate in the extreme.

I remember one American guy I chatted with briefly, who told me he thought Japan operated like a kind of one-way mirror for Westerners. We look at Japanese society, and we see ourselves, by seeing what's *not* reflected there. That brings up all manner of reactions.

As I look in the mirror of last night's festival, I see the Japanese of Tokyo, satisfied and contented on an August night. I'm the one who isn't really satisfied on this night. I'm the one who hasn't wanted to believe that people could ever be so content, amidst the challenging constraints of life in this society. And I'm the one who may have been mistaken.

Such is the pendulum-swinging experience of Japanese society for outsiders like myself. I sometimes feel that as much as I'm actually seeing Japan, I'm seeing myself in the mirror it presents to me. There, I see my own critical eye and restless heart reflected large. During the festival of *Obon*, I've seen Japanese at peace with themselves and their lives. I've also seen myself struggling with life, with my relationship, and with the trials of being the uprooted *gaijin* in a foreign land.

Out-of-town Visitors Shed New Light

Visitors from out of town supply us with much-needed perspective. It's needed, because the longer you live here, the more fixed your perceptions become of the actual conditions in which you're living. You stop being able to see it as it is.

Our friend Brian, whom I knew from my time living in the gatekeeper's cabin in Kyoto, passed through town a month ago on his way to China, because his flight was leaving from Tokyo. He stayed overnight, and we gave him the spare key so he could lock up after he left in the morning. Both Krista and I had to leave the apartment by 7:00 a.m., whereas Brian intended to head off at about 8:15. He'd be back in Tokyo in a month, he told us, and he'd like to stay another night with us then.

A month passed, Brian returned from China, and we met him in downtown Tokyo to get the train home together.

"A month in China! He'll have so much to tell us," we thought expectantly, intending to visit China ourselves soon.

Yet the first topic he raised had nothing to do with China. Brian, who it's perhaps useful to note is about 190 cm (6 feet 3 inches) tall, started right in about Tokyo. He ranted and raved about the rush-hour train he'd caught a month before, at 8:30 in the morning, after leaving our Chofu apartment.

"People go through that every day?" he asked. "Is that what it's normally like? I thought I was going to actually break bones. There were people pushing on my back, I almost got forced right down on top of the seated passengers. There was pressure from all sides, my knees were buckling, I mean we're talking about actual pain here!" he laughed.

"Welcome to Tokyo, Brian," we chuckled. "By the way, how was China?"

It had completely slipped our minds to prepare a newcomer for this ordeal, so habituated had we become to dealing with it ourselves on a daily basis. I suppose we'd both just assumed that since Brian lives in Kyoto, he knew about Japan. I'd forgotten that there's no comparison between the two cities.

"Thanks for telling us," I said, "we won't forget to issue a warning the next time we have visitors."

The incident reminded me of how amazingly adaptable we humans can be – how we can grow accustomed to tolerating a situation that initially seemed totally abnormal. Perhaps when we return to North America, it's going to seem largely uninhabited.

Dial for Soba

Living in Tokyo has been made much easier because of one member of our Chofu community whom we've grown to love: our *soba* delivery man. After three or four hours at the word processor, I'm often ravenous, but reluctant to break the flow by going out to get something to eat. Being more and more health conscious these days, we try to keep pizza orders to a minimum.

Help came along in the form of 'The Soba Solution.' One short phone call to our local *soba* (meaning 'buckwheat noodle') shop, and a healthy and appetizing lunch is soon on the way. It bounces along on the back of a motor scooter equipped with a shock-resistant contraption permitting the transport of *soba* noodle soup!

Just a ten-minute walk from our home in Chofu, this family-run *soba* shop is another example of Japan at its best. It's become our second kitchen. The Japanese have the world's longevity record – roughly 75 years for men and 80 for women – and something has to account for it, especially since this is a nation of smokers and drinkers.

I've decided that it's probably the *soba*, the *miso* soup, *shitake* mushrooms, tofu and seaweed, and the daily intake of green tea. I read one story about a Japanese man who lived to be 121. He attributed his long life to his daily cup of saké (rice wine), but I suspect his diet had a lot to do with it as well. Likewise for two wonderful centenarians, twin sisters, who became T.V. celebrities here. Kin-san and Gin-san made it past 100 in robust good health and great spirits.

When Krista and I are not ordering in, the *soba* shop has become our regular haunt. We sometimes get off the train and meet there for dinner. It closes three times a year for at least a week, so the family can take much-deserved breaks. We miss it then, but we're happy that they take real vacations. It's one big advantage to owning your own business here and being out of the clutches of the companies – you can keep your own schedule.

As for the fine service, it's something that you experience again and again in Tokyo, and life is made much easier because of it. I get the same friendly, reliable service at my local dry cleaner. I can drop off my shirts at 7:00 a.m. on the way to work, and pick them up in the evening if I'm home before 8:00 p.m. As a busy foreign resident, I don't take any of this for granted now.

As for today's lunch, 'The Soba Solution,' is only a phone call away. It's nutritious and delicious, and allows me to keep working without interruption. *Domo arigato* (thank you), Japan.

Workaholics Anonymous

Over time, like most everyone we know, Krista and I have both taken on more and more work. Basically, we've become workaholics living on fast forward like most of the Japanese – as well as the other *gaijin* we see around us in Tokyo. Our apartment has become a launching pad, and we blast off at 6:30 or 7:00 in the morning and return late at night. We're both working six days a week now. In fact, we hardly see each other these days except on weekends and late at night, much like many Japanese couples.

There's a kind of snowball effect that happens in Tokyo. Everyone's incredibly busy, so you follow their lead and get busy too. After a while, you're totally caught up in the momentum of the city.

These days, I get no end of offers for part-time jobs of various kinds: speech writing, narration work, writing and rewriting assignments. It's such a contrast with the situation we faced in North America before we came here, that we feel we should take advantage of the opportunity to build up a nest egg. Besides, Tokyo is all about work. Outside of the 'after hours' scene, there's nothing much else to do. It's too stressful a place to relax, so you just keep going.

But uncomfortable things begin to happen to your psyche when you're steeling yourself for these trains six days a week, and working dawn to dusk. You go through periods when you feel exhausted on all levels, but your schedule obliges you to carry on. All the while, you're doing battle with invisible cultural barriers that keep coming at you. Still, your rising bank balance tells you it's all worthwhile.

You talk to your foreign friends, and it's often the same with them if they've been here more than a few years, but especially if they have jobs that entail lengthy commutes everyday. You hear of someone who's leaving Japan, and something inside you stirs and aches. You catch yourself gazing out a train window into gray drizzle, daydreaming for a few moments about other times and better places, but the momentum propels you forward.

One day, it came to me that Japan is like a 24-hour express train. If you want to leave, you're going to have to hurl yourself down the embankment because the country will never stop long enough to let you off.

At some point, it begins to dawn on you that you're actually just acculturating. You're becoming like the harried Japanese of Tokyo for whom the most socially acceptable response to the question, "How are you?" is "Ah, *isogashii des*" (I'm very busy), a typical response to which is, "*Gambatte kudasai!*" (Hang in there). You've learned that you fit in best by doing as they do – working like a beaver at all times to demonstrate that you're a fully contributing member of society.

In Japan, above all else, you want to avoid been thought of as lazy. So now you, too, are working to live, and living to work. *Shōgenai* – the money and the opportunities are good, and work is the only game in town.

Saved by Hosono-san

To relieve the stress of life, once or twice a month for most of our years here in Tokyo, Krista and I have both paid a visit to a man named Hosono-san in Shibuya. More than once, he's rescued us from the brink of exhaustion and sent us back out to rejoin the crush of humanity, rejuvenated and ready to carry on.

One time, I remember rushing through Shibuya Station like a man possessed, not wanting to be late for my appointment with *relief*.

Hosono-san, a diminutive man with indefatigable energy, is a practitioner of *shiatsu* massage. It's one of the many extraordinary healing arts and practices the Japanese have offered the world. Another that comes to mind is the fabulous ritual my hairdresser follows. She always indulges her customers in a soothing shoulder, neck and head massage after she's finished cutting their hair. We absolutely must import this practice.

At the *shiatsu* clinic, some Japanese lie on tables with burning incense pyramids placed at various points on their naked bodies. The technique is called *moxabustion*, and I plan to give it a miss.

But I'm sold on *shiatsu* treatments, as well as Hosono-san's skill. He works like a Trojan to de-stress his clients, though we've noticed that he wanders off to the back of the clinic between patients to have a smoke. We wish he'd take better care of his own health.

Another anomaly is that the clinic has bright fluorescent lights that seem incongruous alongside the natural treatments being offered. One trusts that the day will come when Japan will allign the wisdom of its ancient healing arts with a holistic view of health. Centuries ago, it probably embraced such an approach naturally.

Oddly enough, when I tell my Japanese university students about the wonders of *shiatsu*, they recoil in feigned horror. Such things are for old people, they insist, checking me out for signs of gray hair.

"Hey, you don't get it," I tell them. "Living in Tokyo, it's *shiatsu* that's kept me from getting old before my time."

Flashback: Sunnyside Hotel

In December 1987, I took the *shinkansen* from Kyoto to Tokyo for my life-changing job interview with Soulful Software. As the train pulled into Tokyo Station, I remember feeling distinctly ambivalent. Did I really want this job badly enough to leave my little garden cabin in Kyoto and move to the *Big Mikan* (or the *Big Orange*, as we sometimes call Tokyo)?

Later that day, I accepted the job, and Soulful Software kindly put me up in a business hotel, *The Sunnyside*. I hardly slept at all that night, feeling confined in my little concrete box of a room. Its single window looked out onto a noisy, bleak-looking parking lot. I remember tossing and turning, thinking I'd made a terrible mistake. I decided the name of the hotel was a misnomer – it should be called *The Sunset*.

It was one of those nights when Bruce Cockburn's song swirled around in my head. The story of his insomnia in this city offered me some solace: "Oh, Tokyo, I never can sleep in your arms. Mind ... keeps on ... ringing like a fire alarm."

The next morning, I got lost in some underground subway station near *Kayabachō*, one where various subway lines intersect, and complicated U-turn arrows point around corners and up staircases. I couldn't figure out where I needed to go. I remember the moment well. On all sides, there was cacophonous noise and hordes of people going every which way. I looked around and got my very first taste of the feeling that people in Tokyo were stone-faced and zombie-like.

"What have I gotten myself into?" I thought, feeling more and more distraught as the full implications of my decision to move to this monster city began to sink in.

Just then I spotted a young, carefree-looking guy sporting a Walkman. I went straight up to him and asked for help, and in that instant, something quite wonderful happened. With a sense of ease and calmness but scarcely a word, he guided me through the maze and right to my train platform. Then he graciously bowed to me to say goodbye.

I suddenly felt enormously relieved and connected, aware now that this city was inhabited by humans after all, not androids. It was at that very moment that I knew I'd be all right in Tokyo. I recognized that despite external appearances to the contrary, many of this city's people must be kindhearted and friendly, and I could survive here. And that has turned out to be the case.

This Too is Tokyo

Picture the scene: A huge and colorful house, looking a lot like a French chateau, is fronted by a massive lawn and garden, like you'd find on an estate. The entire landscape is pink.

In the pale-blue sky, leaping over the house in cow-jumping-over-the-moon fashion, are four members of the natural kingdom – more or less. Within the bodies of each of these playful creatures is an interior outline of his or her body-shape made up of stars, as though they represented constellations like Orion, or Cassiopeia the Queen.

Leading the troupe is a dolphin; she's already made the jump over the chateau and is plummeting towards the pink lawn. Following close behind is a strange-looking pony, which you realize on closer inspection is actually a rocking horse. Flying behind that dominant figure of the nursery is a white goose, winging her merry way over the chateau. Pulling up the rear is the oddest of the lot, a very well-fed guinea pig with a splash of spilled gravy for hair.

Wait, there's more. Now imagine the front portion of the lawn, at a point perhaps 50 meters from the chateau itself. Standing at the foot of this vast stretch of pink grass, beneath the storybook sky filled with leaping beasts, and in front of this magnificent mansion which is clearly theirs, stands a very happy and fanciful couple. The good, pink earth around them is covered in multicolored heart-shaped leaves. He's wearing a tuxedo, and she's dressed in a gown and veil; he is obviously the prince, and she's the princess. Both of them also happen to be rabbits – with long, slender ears.

Up above the chateau and in the far right corner of the sky, a snippet of reality intrudes. There, in a circular insert, we see a photo of a Japanese woman with a white wedding veil and dress, wearing a pearl necklace.

Hallucinations from too many years in Tokyo? No, I'm just sandwiched into the home-bound train, and there was no time to get my newspaper folded. Mesmerized by this advertisement for a packaged wedding ceremony, I decided to study every detail and see what I could recall on getting home. Many are the uses of the captive modern mind.

Wedding Bell Daydreams

The graphics in the Tokyo subway ads are excellent. In a society where you have to be more careful what you say, the 'visual' gets more attention than the 'verbal.' This probably helps to account for the Japanese brilliance with computer and video animation. It also ensures that lots of thought goes into the 'colours' of product labels, since the choice of 'purple' over 'red' may result in millions of dollars in extra sales.

I spend a lot of time face to face with these ads, and I can't help but notice them. The wedding ads are among the best. For one thing, they provide some comic relief, showing provocative scenes and offering up fractured English. One that was on display for years came with the caption, *How to Wedding.* [sic]

They also stir up a whirlwind of speculation in my train-bound mind. Is this just the Japanese male advertiser's view of the 21-year-old Japanese female heart and mind? Or is a fantasy like this genuinely appealing to Japanese women? Is it also appealing to men? And what's with the rabbit bride and groom? It's not the 'year of the rabbit'; are bunnies in vogue this year anyway?

In Tokyo, many couples contemplating marriage do hire an agency. Staging a wedding is a lot like planning a seven-day trip to Hawaii – you get a package deal. Some packages include absolutely everything, including the honeymoon in Honolulu. Once you choose an agent, they plan and execute everything down to the last detail, for ten to twenty thousand dollars or much more.

What fascinates me the most about the whole wedding process in Japan is right there, up on the walls of the trains on the Keio Line. I imagine showing that advertisement to young people back home. Would they hire this agency to run their wedding reception? I don't think so. Yet, unusual wedding ads are commonplace in the subway cars in Tokyo. Marriage is big business here; so is escape fantasy, and that probably explains a lot.

The world-renowned *Love Hotels*, with their 101 bedroom themes – ranging from spaceships to 1950s Chevrolets to castle motifs and cowboy/cowgirl ranch settings – are a great example of how the Japanese find an outlet in fantasy. And why not? In a country this crowded and socially demanding, hotel rooms that offer a two-hour departure from reality should come as no surprise.

As for these wedding advertisements, newly married couples usually end up in tiny apartments for years. In lieu of having actual soil for lawns, Tokyo is fertile ground for fantasy diversion.

Yet what kind of woman responds to an ad like this, I wonder? When you live in Japan, you often find yourself in conversations with fellow expats when such topics come up. Many Western women in Japan view Japanese women as passive and naive, incapable of independent thought or action and lacking strengths they value in themselves. They often devalue the traditional feminine qualities many Japanese women seem happy to embrace.

In fact, the core issue is probably this: They find it impossible to imagine themselves in the position a Japanese woman occupies socially and professionally. In other words, it's not 'Japanese women' they reject; it's the roles Japanese society forces upon them that Western women abhor.

As always in Japan, appearances can be very deceptive. From encounters with Japanese female acquaintances and the Japanese wives of foreign friends, I know there's a great deal more thoughtfulness and tenacity lurking beneath the surface of their minds than first meets the eye.

What can be confusing is that many Japanese women seem to hang on tenaciously to symbols of girlhood, such as stuffed animals and an Anne-of-Green-Gables innocence. (This is a popular book here, and Canada's Prince Edward Island is a Japanese travel destination as a result.) So perhaps they are vulnerable to a mythical wedding ad, where a Versailles-style palace is watched over by the animals of the nursery.

But tens of millions of Japanese women have been doing a lot of thinking lately. They've figured out that they're far better off working as long as they can, vacationing in Europe twice a year, and postponing the drudgery of married life. Japan's birth rate keeps falling as a result; it's now below 1.5 children per woman.

Among my university students, a consensus seems to have been reached that marrying in your late twenties is socially acceptable now, and it's rapidly becoming the preferred choice. The sky-high cost of living in Japan has been another factor in the decision to delay marriage and parenting.

Single women working in companies or department stores often live at home with their families, given the smaller size of their incomes relative to men. Most companies prefer – and some even require – that women live at home until they're married. So marriage to a man with a good salary remains the only way out of the family nest for many young women, especially those with limited education. It's still the most acceptable way to grow beyond 'girlhood.'

It sometimes seems as if there's a dearth of 'women' in Japan, because men are too threatened by the concept. So there are young girls, and women acting like older girls, and then there are wives and mothers.

So despite the changes Japanese women are going through, marriage – for millions – is still the "ultimate," as one women put it to me. The thought of ending up as a lifetime commuter and *office lady* who's still living at home, must be a nightmare prospect for countless women in their late twenties, who fear they've waited too long.

All of these single women riding the Tokyo trains face daily bombardment with wedding ads. For those who are beginning to worry that they'll be passed over and end up trapped, these fantasy ads probably hold a certain kind of power. Their creators no doubt hope that they'll stir up wedding-bell daydreaming on the long journey home.

For a woman whose biological clock is ticking loudly, these ads may even be quite unnerving. There is, however, something that can be done. In Japan, both women and men often end up contacting one of the many agencies specializing in *omiai* (meetings leading to arranged marriages). It's still surprisingly common here.

Of course, if a Japanese couple have already become engaged, and they're just shopping around for a wedding package, the French chateau, with its pink lawn and leaping dolphin, is a psychedelic eye-catcher they're not going to miss on the long commute home. It sure caught my eye.

A Room Without a View

On the topic of escape fantasy, one cannot reflect on life in Tokyo for long without mentioning the ubiquitous *manga*, the often pornographic cartoon stories the size of small phone books. These are lugged around and read everywhere by men of all ages in this city, and by women too, with their own usually tamer versions.

People read *manga* obsessively on the trains. They rush to pick up the latest issue from atop a six-foot pile of them in Shibuya or Ueno Stations. It's fantasy diversion for the journey home. While I disappear into my newspaper or novel, many commuters vanish into a cartoon world, at least partly made up of sadistic sex and violence.

If you stop off at a *ramen* noodle shop, there'll be a ledge beneath the counter stacked with used *manga*. Now there are even *manga cafés* sprouting up around Tokyo. It's a kind of counterpart to pachinko, a place to park your mind for awhile. George Orwell would surely have been fascinated by some aspects of this society; *manga* is one of them. I sometimes think it's an expression of truncated childhoods, cut off early by the long years of study, preparing for *examination hell*.

At it's worst, *manga* can be pretty awful stuff, not that it's any worse than material you can easily find in America and Europe. That said, scenes of bondage involving Japanese and Caucasian women, often tied up with ropes and gagged with tape, are not uncommon. One can only speculate about the effects *manga* has on the minds of young men in their evolving views of women, relationships and sex. I've read a few stories of Japanese mothers who are extremely concerned about this.

Krista and I have often speculated on the links between the reading of *manga* and the phenomenon of *chikan* (molesters) on the trains. *Chikan* are surely a minority of disturbed Japanese men, but they've made a bad name for their fellow males. There are enough men with loose hands running around to cause many foreign women to paint all Japanese men with the same brush. Krista has now reached the point where she says, "I only trust Japanese men I've been introduced to, and I've okayed. Anonymous men on the trains are all suspect until proven otherwise – a steady diet of *manga* since childhood has perverted a lot of minds."

Our British neighbor, Anna, recently told us about an encounter she had in a crowded train car on the Keio Line, when it was stopped at a station with the doors open. A Japanese man was rubbing himself up against her and wouldn't stop, so she took his glasses off, dropped them on the floor and stepped on them. Then she ran out of the train, astonished at herself for what she'd done in her own defense.

My insightful educator friend, George, took a walk on the bright side one day. He made the observation that *manga* – more than any other single factor – probably accounts for the high literacy rate in Japan. I hadn't thought of that, and had to admit that he might be right. I used to work with functionally illiterate people in Canada, and learned that roughly 30% of Canadians and Americans fall into this category. Japan doesn't appear to have such a problem, and this is a country of voracious daily *manga* readers. But isn't this a high price to pay for literacy?

Scenes of sexual violence in *manga* are also typical of business-hotel video fare throughout the country. When I worked for Soulful Software, my colleague Kieran and I sometimes went on business trips within Japan, and we watched one of these once in our hotel room in Kobe. I recall one scene of a schoolgirl in uniform walking home alone at night. She was suddenly attacked by a guy who leapt out of the bushes. In another scene, a woman was grabbed by a man in an underground parking lot and dragged into his car.

Being a newcomer to Japan at the time I watched these, I was saddened and finally puzzled to see that this hasn't been controlled, when so much else in Japan has. I now take the view that the shadow side of the human psyche has to come out somewhere, and in Japan, this is one of its outlets.

The mountains of porn in curtained-off areas of video shops here certainly have their counterpart in the U.S. and elsewhere. We're hardly in a position to scream with righteous indignation, as if we've got the issue of hard-core pornography under control.

But the exploitation of women does show up in a variety of unique forms here – the porno-magazine and porno-video vending machines down the street from our apartment, for example. There's also the piles of nude-photo cards and booklets that are placed in phone booths, advertising young women for hire, not to mention the incredibly provocative flyers that show up in our mailbox, easily racy enough to get people arrested back home.

Of course, the whole world heard the incredible stories about high-school girls selling their used panties, because they fetch such a high price. As usual, our media took the ball and ran with that story. Sure, it happened, but do we ever hear about the millions of Japanese girls who'd never dream of doing such a thing? Perhaps it's our media that are the sickest perpetrators of all, highlighting the worst and overlooking the best in people.

But there's no disputing that Japan – like many countries – is now awash in pornography. That is, unless you're the Customs official at Narita Airport whom my friend Kieran ran into. Without even knowing what it contained, he confiscated Kieran's American-made video with the comment, "We have no pornography in Japan." Right, and we have none in Canada either.

It was, however, the beautiful movie *A Room With a View* that left us shaking our heads about the absurd inconsistencies of Japanese censorship. Having already seen it in Canada, but being struck by the similarities between Japanese and turn-of-the-century British formality, we decided to rent the video and watch it again here in Japan.

To our astonishment, the wonderfully playful scene where the men are romping around the lake in the buff – and run into their fully-clothed women friends – was almost completely cut from the film. On comparing later, I found that 140 seconds of the scene had been zapped.

"Of course," I realized, "it's a Japanese censor's nightmare!"

When we first came to Japan, pubic hair was still totally off-limits here in every medium. Fuzz balls that follow the erogenous zones of the actors are still added to deal with explicit scenes in movies, although in the early '90s, an explosive proliferation of sexually explicit magazines put an end to pubic-hair censorship in the print media.

So chasing these guys' erogenous zones with fuzz balls, as they jumped in and out of the water and ran around the lake, no doubt proved to be impossible, since there was continual movement and bouncing private parts.

However, we suspect that the joyful and spontaneous nature of that male horseplay must also have been threatening. Homosexual fears may have entered into the decision to censor this, but the mood of the scene is lighthearted and fun-loving – naked men just having fun together in a lake. We're left to assume that this is a state of affairs that endangers the moral fiber of the nation.

Modern 'Comfort Women'

One summer night, I was wandering through *Roppongi* – the entertainment district popular with foreigners – and I met a Thai woman at a vending machine, an unusual encounter in Tokyo. She headed up some nearby stairs into a so-called *Snaku* (Snack Bar), and I followed her out of curiosity, deciding to stick my head in the door and see what it was. On the inside was a single room that looked exactly like an ordinary *karaoke* bar, so I wandered in to discover it was staffed by a Japanese *mama-san* (female manager) and three or four Thai girls – all with Japanese names – right in the heart of Tokyo.

The woman I'd followed was using the Japanese name *Sachiko*, and I decided to stay awhile to chat with her and find out more about what was going on. I had a few beers and sang some songs, and the Japanese *mama-san* was very pleasant with me, but her presence made it difficult to ask Sachiko questions – such as how long she'd been in Japan.

After awhile, the *mama-san* began asking me questions, and it was soon clear that these girls were for hire. The *mama-san* eventually figured out that I wasn't interested in being Sachiko's customer, at which point she became very hostile and demanded 10,000 yen!

I was taken aback by her sudden explosion and paid without resistance. I did so to avoid a scene, and because I knew by then that the place was probably run by the *yakuza*. If she was this aggressive, I certainly didn't want to mess with them. From then on, I was completely ignored, which was just fine by me.

I was about to leave when a middle-aged Japanese man wandered in. I decided to stay a while longer, so I could watch as he was put through the same paces. I'd certainly paid enough to take up space and observe. Before long, there was a negotiating session, and he settled on paying the *mama-san* 45,000 yen to take one of the other Thai girls away for the evening. At that point, I went over to Sachiko, who was now in the kitchen, said goodbye and left.

I later learned a bit more about the sex trade in Japan, from a report by an investigative journalist. In a small town north of Tokyo, one Japanese man got his legs broken for his attempts to expose a similar scene in the local *snaku* there. The *yakuza* don't take kindly to having their turf disturbed. In the same story, I read that one group of Thai girls allegedly killed their *mama-san* in order to escape captivity and get back to Thailand. They ended up in a Japanese jail.

That night, I suspect I saw a side of Tokyo that is now – in various forms – a side of San Francisco, Amsterdam, Bangkok, Vancouver and Istanbul as well. In its treatment of vulnerable women, the world's oldest profession may also hold the dark distinction of being the cruelest.

Escape from Tokyo

Foreign residents of Tokyo have their own forms of escape. One of the most popular is side trips to Hong Kong, Seoul, Bali, the beaches of Thailand and other exotic destinations in Southeast Asia. During my third year in Tokyo, I once went to Seoul for 24 hours for a short break. It was one of those 'use-it-or-lose-it' situations, my ticket being a round trip from the U.S. to South Korea with a stopover in Tokyo.

I'd 'stopped over' for just under twelve months, but had been too busy to take advantage of the side trip to Seoul. But rather than forego it altogether before the expiry date, I hopped on a plane on a Wednesday night and returned the next evening. It was a great little adventure, and I noted that the length of the flight was about the same as my daily commute.

Watching the sunset on the journey back, I saw the top of Mount Fuji poking through what looked like a floor of clouds, and found myself writing a poem on the airplane dinner napkin. Released from Tokyo for just a day, I felt as though a hypnotic spell had been broken - a case of 'worknosis' perhaps. Back in Tokyo, this good feeling remained for about three weeks.

Such sojourns are illuminating for what they reveal to you about your life in Tokyo, because the social climates of Asian cities and societies can be so radically different. Compared to other places, the sameness and predictability of Tokyo can be very reassuring; it can also drive you wild.

Predictability, however, is a desirable thing in Japan, and most Japanese appear not to react against it the way many Westerners do. Generally speaking, the unexpected is less sought after; a plan with no surprises is much more to be preferred.

Perhaps this preference for the predictable is hardly surprising of a people so recently clobbered by war and always vulnerable to earthquakes. I get the impression that the Japanese are terrified of chaos. I once asked a class of my first-year university students to write about their greatest fears for the future. One male student wrote that "something unexpected might happen."

As a longtime foreign resident, you start to yearn for the unexpected in Tokyo, but most of the time you just carry on yearning. Then you call your travel agent.

We recently took a trip to Hong Kong, my third since coming to Japan. It's always an exhilarating feeling to take the five-minute ride on the Star Ferry to Kowloon for the equivalent of 15 cents, and to feel the ocean breeze on your face, right in the heart of the city. Of course, when you're on vacation, you've left your work schedule behind, and you're predisposed to feeling good.

But being freed from the social constraints of Tokyo is what feels best of all. For an Anglo-Canadian like myself, Hong Kong - with its British legacy and widely-spoken English - is culturally familiar and closer in spirit than Tokyo can ever be. That, in itself, helps to explain the ambivalence many Westerners have about Japan. We want to talk more to people we meet, and we want to feel free and easy about doing so.

In Hong Kong, we're immediately reminded that Japan is a more standardized and regulated society than we're used to. We feel an immediate sense of expansion, sensing that there's more psychic breathing space.

But then your trip comes to an end, and it's time to go home - to Japan, that is, where you only partially fit in, and where you'll always be an outsider to most Japanese. With a sigh, you acknowledge that the good money you're making – and Japan's close proximity to other Asian destinations – is what makes all these side trips possible anyway.

So you tell yourself to quit complaining. You say a prayer of gratitude for your job and your Japanese friends and colleagues, bite the bullet and fly back to Narita. Then you gear yourself up to renew your ambivalent relationship with the Land of the Rising Sun.

Tokyo Still Winning

Once I return to Tokyo from a trip overseas, I'm often surprised – given that it was such a relief to get away – to find that it feels fine to be back. Perhaps I shouldn't be. After all, this is now very familiar territory, and the last time I came through Customs and presented my *Alien Registration Card*, the Customs officer was genuinely friendly. As he stamped my passport, he smiled and said, "Welcome back." I don't suppose he realized how good it felt to hear that, to feel so included in the Japanese life that has become such a part of me.

If my life in Tokyo were unceasingly traumatic, I'd have left by now. The same is true for many of my foreign friends, who speak about their experience of this city as being that of a love/hate relationship.

On a recent trip to the U.S., I was asked if I liked living in Tokyo. I found myself comparing it to a close, high-scoring basketball game. After a moment of thought, I decided that *Liking* wins out over *Not liking*.

Liking 96, *not liking* 93 – exciting game!

If I were still a *salaryman* in the company trenches, that score would probably be different. But though I continue to ride the rails almost as much as ever, working at Shōrai-dai has freed me from the company grind. I'm nothing but grateful for the extra time off that comes with my university schedule, despite the fact that my work is somewhat less interesting. In many ways, my foreign colleagues and I are the most fortunate of *gaijin*.

Despite its crowds, pollution and social conundrums, I now consider myself to be lucky to have wound up working in Tokyo. But I've met foreign residents on all points of the spectrum during my time here – some get along fine, and others complain about Tokyo (and Japan) from morning to night.

Many foreigners have rotten experiences that color their whole view of Japanese society some shade of gray. Perhaps they've felt manipulated and deceived at work; they've been promised – but later denied – some guarantee in their contract. Or they've been blocked from renting an apartment, simply because they're a *gaijin*. Or they've managed to rent a place, but later they've lost a huge damage deposit for no good reason.

If they're females, they may have been groped by *chikan*, as Krista has. It can be hard to bounce back and regain your objectivity about Japan, after a few of these kinds of things have happened to you. It's much more difficult than it would be in your own culture, where you have more outlets for expressing your feelings and getting help in your distress.

In an especially charged moment, my American friend, Carla, once really let fly. She told me that she wanders around Tokyo feeling like a "flat-affect robot." She added that she hasn't met a single Westerner who doesn't consider Tokyo to be "oppressive, repressive and depressive!"

Such incredible reactions! The intensity of this city and society has likewise plunged me into some wild frames of mind. At times, I move between exhilaration and despondency. I've found Tokyo to be a place of tremendous mood swings for many Westerners, and I now look upon outbursts like Carla's as being a kind of *gaijin license*. I think of them as being similar to the license given to *salarymen* to lambaste their boss during a drinking session, with no repercussions the following day.

Tokyo-bashing for resident foreigners serves much the same essential function; it's a much-needed release valve. Most of us feel a recurring need to let off steam with other foreigners, because expressing such negative emotions is unacceptable with most Japanese. It's deemed selfish to complain about the suffering you're enduring.

Surely that only compounds the intensity of the feelings this city – and Japan itself – brings up for many foreigners. American women often seem to have a particularly hard time of it, especially if they're on their own here.

My Japanese colleague, Maki, who spent a year in the States, told me one day that Japan, unlike the U.S., is "not an information society." In so many areas of life, it can be harder to find out what you want to know, or to learn more about a predicament you're facing.

But even she reacted to the incessant complaining by the *gaijin* on staff one day with the comment, "If you don't like it here, you can leave. No one's making you stay."

Maki had a good point; many Westerners get into overkill about Japan. But what she perhaps failed to recognize is that '*gaijin* complaining' is often an end in itself. It's just an emotional release. In a similar vein, when Japanese *salarymen* complain about their bosses during drinking sessions, it doesn't mean they want to quit their jobs.

Yet despite Carla's feelings about the oppressiveness of Tokyo, many Westerners do adjust well to life here. Some love it and thrive on its energy. As for those living in smaller cities and rural areas throughout Japan, I met one Canadian who'd lived for 20 years in more-manageable Hiroshima, and then returned to Canada. When I asked him how he felt about Japan, his comment had a Zen-like simplicity: "Wonderful country, nice people."

It bears repeating that foreigners lucky enough to have good Japanese friends usually have a much less rocky experience. It helps enormously to know Japanese people who don't have an us-and-them view of Japanese versus 'foreigners.' My new friends Sachiko and Fumihito have warmly welcomed me into their home and their hearts.

Foreign residents with young children find that the Japanese respond openly and readily to kids, in ways that are often heartwarming. Nothing serves as a bridge between cultures better than children. In small *ramen* noodle shops, the *mama-san* will rush over and swoop up your one-year-old, spiriting the child off to the kitchen with cries of glee!

You hear many stories of wonderfully kind gestures, but especially from people who live away from the center of this overcrowded city. My colleague Chris and his wife, Liz – who live more than an hour outside of Tokyo – told me that the grandmother living next door to them knitted sweaters for all three of their children.

The Japanese girlfriend of an American acquaintance of mine invited me to stay with her family, two hours out of Tokyo, anytime I wished. She also told me they don't like – and never use – the word *gaijin* in her family. In Japan, the wisest decision you can possibly make is to choose to focus on these positive stories and downplay the rest.

Personally speaking, Randall's positive attitude about Japan provides a very steadying influence. He takes full advantage of the many cultural experiences available in Tokyo and in nearby Kamakura, where he's based. I'm indebted to him for his upbeat attitude. Again and again, he's prompted me to see Japan with fresh eyes, and to practice Zen and the Art of Living in tumultuous Tokyo.

Making the Best of It

It's unfortunate that it's incredibly costly to take trips around Japan, because there are whole other dimensions to Japanese life outside of Tokyo. All foreign residents of this city could benefit from ongoing exposure to other parts of the country.

In fact, hiking in the beautiful Japan Alps around Matsumoto and Kamikochi is accessible and inspiring. Short homestays with a family in Kyoto and elsewhere are easy to arrange, whereby anyone with the will to do so, can discover for themselves how gracious and openhearted the Japanese people can be at their best.

Tokyo and its people are fighting the big-city battle at all times. Once you, too, are caught up in its demands, you can easily stop developing your sense of Japan as a whole. Living in this urban hothouse, one can't appreciate the lives of Japanese in rural *Gifu* any better than living in New York enables you to understand Montana ranchers.

Still, most foreign residents say they prefer to leave the country when they get the chance. For one thing, it's actually cheaper to go to Bali or Thailand from Tokyo than it is to travel to interesting places within Japan, such as Kyushu or Hokkaido.

Then there's the stress of Tokyo, as well as the sense many *gaijin* have that Japan is too standardized. People fear it'll be too much the same, wherever they go. By the time they get a break, most want a definite change of pace during their vacation.

So many of us end up thinking of Tokyo as a kind of 'work camp.' It's quite bearable, providing you can get away every three or four months. Under those circumstances, it remains a surprisingly liveable city. During major holiday periods like O *Shogatsu* (New Years), when millions leave town, Tokyo suddenly becomes a great place to be. For four or five days, the streets feel half empty.

In an article published in *Shared Vision* magazine, Canada's foremost environmentalist, Dr. David Suzuki, referred to this city as a "nightmare." He then described "streets crammed with people and motor vehicles; visible air that catches the throat; rivers of sludge in cement canyons beside the roads."

It's not difficult to understand his point of view, given the haphazard manner in which Tokyo was rebuilt after the war, and the pollution at its worst. On a bad day, trapped by its horrendous crowds and congestion, I sometimes feel overwhelmed. That said, I think Dr. Suzuki makes things sound much worse than they are.

The longer you stay on here, the more Tokyo reveals its delightful secrets to you. There are the carp in the Kandagawa River, flowing through the center of town. There's the beautiful park surrounding the *Meiji Shrine* near Harajuku. Then there's the close-knit sense of community in the multitude of small towns and villages, which together make up the megalopolis called Tokyo. Without a doubt, there are many cities on this planet with far more appalling conditions than this one.

Rick Kennedy's book *Little Adventures in Tokyo* gives residents the inside scoop on discovering the best this city has to offer. Accompanied by another Canadian friend, I took his recommended walk through 'Old Tokyo,' near *Sendagi*, and we had a magical day. We stopped in for steaming bowls of *soba* that cost only 300 yen, and we felt like we'd stepped into a small village, right in the heart of this vast metropolis. It's true that what's left of 'Old Tokyo' is imperiled on all sides, but the area still has the unmistakable feel of small-town neighborliness to it.

Staying for a few nights with Randall's son, Jason, during the *Golden*

Week holiday, I learned of a red cobblestone street, with a tree-lined island down the middle of it. It literally goes on for miles, snaking its way across town. The city engineers have done a great job of putting this together, especially given the constraints they had to work with.

Starting out near Toritsu Daigaku Station, I took a late evening stroll around 10:00 p.m. and walked briskly for 40 minutes in one direction, encountering only a few vehicles – just local traffic. The route took me over plenty of cross streets, but I seldom had to stop for long to let cars pass. Granted, this was Golden Week. But right here in the heart of Tokyo, this well-designed artery was serving the needs of both pedestrians and nighttime strollers. It was quiet, green and peaceful.

With all due respect, I wonder if Dr. Suzuki – in his visits to Japan – has had the pleasure of such a stroll. I think I could convince him that even in the midst of the Tokyo nightmare, there are some pleasant dreams to be had.

Living in this incredible city is much too stimulating an experience to sideline yourself with a jaded attitude. If you're going to choose to be here, you might as well make the best of it. In my case, I continue to work for Tokyo, and Tokyo continues to work for me.

How Do These Things Happen Here?

I took notes in April 1991 on a metamorphosis I watched unfolding before my eyes. It was my fourth year in Tokyo, and I can now look back and recognize that during the spring of that year, a new phenomenon – catching on like spontaneous combustion – happened all at once across this city.

Everywhere you went that spring – in parks, on the streets and even on the trains – young couples were doing the previously unthinkable: They were touching! They were holding hands, putting their arms around each other and hugging – expressing affection in public and taking delight in doing so.

It was like the whole thing had come right out of the blue, as if some kind of cathartic social consensus had been reached by osmosis. Everyone suddenly understood that touching in public was now okay.

From my first day in this country in the autumn of '87, right through to the spring of '91, a young couple touching or holding hands in public was an uncommon sight. Guidebooks on Japan, and videos preparing Americans to accept homestay students counselled people to be aware of this feature of Japanese society: People did not touch or express affection openly in public.

Then, as if through a collective and simultaneous response to some invisible cue – it all changed, and quite dramatically too.

It's perhaps the single most refreshing change that's come about since I arrived in Tokyo. Instead of always being separate and self-contained – and acknowledging each other only by bowing – millions of young Japanese are now routinely bridging the physical, and probably the emotional gap between themselves. Even some older Japanese are getting in on it. The touching taboo has clearly been abandoned. Tokyo will never be quite the same.

How did this all come about, I wonder, in the spring of 1991? Perhaps a program on television addressed the issue over the winter. Or maybe it was something more esoteric, a consensus reached in Japan's collective unconscious. You probably have to be Japanese to understand. But I think I've learned something about the Japanese comfort zone when it comes to social change: They'd really prefer to all make the change at the same time.

Michella – Yet Another Perspective

During my years in Japan, I've had the same experience again and again, like a recurring dream. Just about the time I start feeling that Tokyo is beyond the pale, and that Japanese society is impossible for a non-Japanese to come to terms with, something positive happens to shake me out of that viewpoint.

Let me introduce Michella. I met her a few weeks ago on the Chuo Line, on my way to my Saturday job near Ochanomizu Station. We quickly struck up a conversation. That's a very pleasant treat, because it's something I just can't do easily with anyone but *gaijin* on the trains. The fact that Japanese are much less comfortable chatting with strangers is something I'm finally learning to accept.

When I spoke to Michella, she responded with enthusiasm and without hesitation. She was from Germany and was only visiting Tokyo, for the second time, it turned out. She also had a great story to tell me, and one thing came across very clearly. Michella loves Japan!

I listened intently as she told me that last year, in Germany, she'd inexplicably begun to lose her sight. It got worse and worse until one day, she woke up completely blind. Her German doctors told her there was nothing they could do for her, that a cure had not yet been discovered for her condition.

Beside herself with despair, Michella spoke with a Japanese friend, a nurse who worked at *Ochanomizu Byōin* (hospital) in downtown Tokyo. Michella knew her through their mutual interest in working with race-car drivers on the international circuit.

"Why don't you come to Tokyo?" her friend suggested. "Perhaps they can do something for you at my hospital. Besides, what have you got to lose? Your own doctors in Germany have said they can't help you."

Now completely unable to see, Michella came to Tokyo on faith. The hospital agreed to pay her expenses, in exchange for being able to conduct some experimental research on her eyes, as well as document her case.

This is a story with a wonderful ending. Eight months later, her Japanese doctors had restored 80% of her sight, and Michella went home to Germany, elated and eternally grateful to Japan.

Michella had returned to Tokyo just to say thanks. She wanted to thank her doctors, her nurses, the rest of the hospital staff, the other patients she'd met and friends she'd made during her hospital stay in Japan. She told me they'd all been so wonderfully supportive of her throughout her ordeal.

Michella also told me that on her return to Germany, her German doctors had asked her to arrange an exchange. They wanted to learn the technique that had restored her sight from their Japanese counterparts.

My heart lifted on that day. It had been weighed down with personal concerns, with the painful knowledge that Krista and I were separating. We'd been drifting apart for months, and now all the cards were in the air. Tokyo had taken a huge toll on our relationship. Krista had 'reached the wall' with Japan and was now going back to America on her own. I was choosing to stay on, even though I was in turmoil.

But Michella's story cheered me immensely. It seemed timely, and I took heart. My problems suddenly seemed much less significant. I invited Michella to Krista's thirtieth birthday and *Sayonara* party, and we parted at Ochanomizu Station. Michella went off to see her Japanese friends, and I headed off down the street to work, with a newfound spring in my step. I sensed that my vision of this country had shifted yet again – this time for good.

Eventually you have to make up your mind how you feel about this city, this society and its people. You have to decide what you would say to someone who'd never been here, but who asked you not to mince words about how you feel about Japan.

On the day I met Michella, a bottom line about life in this tumultuous city began to shape itself very clearly in my mind. For one thing, in order to keep living here, I needed to slow down and lighten up! For another, I now knew that Tokyo – even with its Orwellian-like ambience and all the stresses, controls and anomalies of the social system that created it – is, above all else, home to millions of people, the great majority of whom are decent, dedicated and well-intentioned human beings worthy of the world's respect.

∞

author's collection

5

COMING TO TERMS WITH JAPAN

Japanecdotes

If you're going to stay in Tokyo for five or ten years and survive psychically, there are two qualities you've got to cultivate. Firstly, you have to keep your sense of humor – not to laugh derisively but to appreciate the funny side of the little predicaments, cultural anomalies and maddening moments that never cease cropping up here. Secondly, you need a genuine sense of pathos, because I think an honest response to Japan calls for that as well.

I can look back now and see that I lost both for quite awhile, and I paid dearly for it with my own misery. But I didn't go down for the count, and I've survived to again enjoy a healthy perspective on my adopted country. The truth is, you need an eye and an ear test if you can't see and hear things that bring a chuckle in Japan. Either that, or you're succumbing to the pressure, and it's time to get out before you crash and burn. For a Westerner, what Allen Klein calls Vitamin H (for humor) is all around you for the taking in

Tokyo, as are those moments that bring a tear to your eye. A sampling of both is in order.

I had a haircut and a shave once in a barbershop I was trying for the first time. I was relaxing with my eyes closed when I suddenly realized the fellow was shaving my forehead – with the best of intentions, no doubt.

For years, my travel agent in this city has been A.H.P., which stands for *Aquarian House Projects*. Despite its bizarre name, it's the best agency I've found; maybe they'll book me into a New Age Condominium on my next trip home.

Then there was that student of mine who returned from a short trip to the U.S. and proclaimed with delight, "You know, they have McDonald's there, too!" Well, how would he know? In Japan, it's called *Ma-ku-do-na-ru-do*. Besides, many Americans undoubtedly don't know that *karaoke* – invented in Japan and meaning 'empty orchestra' – is a Japanese word that's pronounced *kah-rah-o-kay* in Japanese.

At closing time in stores all over Japan, *Auld Lang Sang* is played as a gentle reminder to customers that it's time to leave. It plays over and over again until the store has cleared out. My friend Maggie's Japanese friend insisted that it was an old Japanese folk song. The discussion ended with his comment, "Well, all Japanese think so."

I met a middle-aged man on the Odakyu Line one Saturday morning with whom I somehow struck up a conversation in Japanese. He didn't speak any English, he told me. Instead, he was off to his *Esperanto* class, the 'world' language he'd been studying seriously for six years. I mentioned that he was the first person I'd ever met who was studying Esperanto, but that didn't seem to register. He earnestly sought to convince me that it was the hope of the future, and gave me a brochure. "Come join us," he said. I didn't have the heart to point out that the spread of English appears to have turned Esperanto into a linguistic relic, despite its inspired beginnings.

A friend told me about an expat who went scuba diving in some coastal area of Japan. He'd already expressed exasperation about all the regulations governing Japanese society. Diving in, he discovered there were arrows underwater, all along the embankment, pointing *This way, this way*. On surfacing, he went to his travel agent and booked a flight to Thailand.

So-called 'Japanese English' keeps getting ever more bizarre the longer I'm here, partly because it's almost starting to seem intelligible. Not long ago, I spotted a newspaper delivery boy near my home. He was packing papers onto his motorcycle, which allowed me enough time to read and write down the small treatise on the back of his T-shirt. (I confess, I've never been able to stop myself from reading this stuff.) Here it is, verbatim: *Free Dope, fucking in the streets, possible utopia exists almost instantaneously.*

I recently bought a car, and every working day I drive through the 'gates' at

Shōrai-dai university. Without fail, the uniformed guard gives me a smart salute, and I wave back. From time to time – this formality being something you'd never see at a university in Canada – the little ritual will poke my funny bone, and I'll play with imagining I'm the ambassador to Swaziland.

At Shōrai-dai, we attend the same three or four ceremonies every year, with thousands of us packed into the main auditorium. There's one main event for the incoming students, and another to send the graduates on their way. The basic format never varies, right down to the musical selections. We all sing the university song together, and at some point the orchestra starts up with Elgar's *Pomp and Circumstance*. It's music I've always loved, though hearing it in this context, it feels like something out of The Twilight Zone – I have to pinch myself and remember that this is Japan.

The speeches all plod along with mind-numbing solemnity. Many of the students chat among themselves. A few are catching forty winks. My colleagues and I pass the time together way up on the upper walkway, trading one-liners and marveling that the speakers can drone on for so long without even attempting a joke. We speculate that in the West, they'd be booed off the stage! In Japan, however, such ceremonies are serious affairs. But the music's good, and the grandiose feel of the ceremony is so unique that we have a fine time.

I'll be on a train on the *Chuo Line* speeding through the heart of Tokyo. I absently gaze out the window, and my eyes fall on a dinky little pond with thirty people sitting side by side fishing. It's like a mirage as we fly by; I blink, and it's gone.

I'm on another train with a colleague from France. We're speaking English, but suddenly we switch to French. All around us, it's as though people have been listening to a radio station, and they've suddenly lost the frequency. Eyebrows go up, heads twitch, and there's a few coughs and shuffling of bodies. 'English listening practice, anyone?'

I call up the *Japan Hotline*, a service run by the local phone company (N.T.T.) to help foreigners cope. The women who answer these phones are always helpful, courteous and usually very efficient. They handle all manner of requests, so I call them because I need advice on locating a carrot cake for a birthday party. I'd looked everywhere in Tokyo without success. They ask me to call them back in 15 minutes, at which time they excitedly give me the name and address of a bakery in Chofu. Taking their recommendation, I make my way there the next day. Up on the tenth floor of a department store in a glass case, I come upon your basic pound cake with one tiny, sugar carrot sitting on top!

My British neighbor, Mike, told me of a restaurant he and his wife, Anna, often go to. As they walk in the door, they catch the young staff playing *jun ken po* (paper, rock, scissors) to see who gets stuck with the frightening experience of serving the *gaijin*.

You gaze out the window of a high-rise in Tokyo. There's a minuscule driving range on the roof of the next building over. The distance from the tee to a large net is about 20 feet, and some fellow is swinging away like he's training for the Olympics.

You go to see a doctor. A man in the waiting room stands up and starts playing 'air golf,' perfecting his swing while he waits for his appointment.

You go to an Italian restaurant with friends. The decor is like the inside of a Bavarian castle. You listen to Swiss yodeling music as you enjoy your American pizza.

For decades, the song *My Way* was one of the most popular songs in Japan among *salarymen*. Clearly, there's something I'm not understanding.

Correcting an essay by a male university student on whether or not Japan should open its doors to foreign workers, I read: "If foreign workers are allowed into Japan, occasionally there will be an accident, and a non-working Japanese will be born."

We danced the night away recently in a Tokyo nightclub. At 6:30 in the morning, my Canadian friend Brian and I were standing in front of the *Roppongi* McDonald's, tired and bedraggled, watching the human parade. A Japanese man in his sixties or seventies, wearing a straw hat and round-shaped spectacles, strutted by with a cane. Looking up at Brian as he passed, he paused momentarily and exclaimed, "It's General MacArthur!" Two seconds later, he'd passed behind a pillar and was gone.

I go to a public swimming pool after work, and soon learn that it's rush hour in the pool as well. It's so crowded that after each lap of 25 meters, you have to wait in a two- or three-minute U-shaped lineup behind 15 other swimmers before you can swim back to the other end. It's a similar situation at both ends of the pool. I see two men up to their necks in water, bowing politely to each other to determine who will go ahead in the line.

I go to a private sports club in the late afternoon, again to have a swim. There's a class in progress on one side of the pool. About 40 middle-aged Japanese women are doing water aerobics to loud rap music, shimmying in a long chain from one end of the pool to the other, grooving to M.C. Hammer. They see me walk in, the only male in the pool – and a *gaijin* as well – and dissolve into joyful, embarrassed laughter, but they carry right on shimmying. I smile with a little embarrassment of my own but appreciate the moment. Where else but in Japan would this happen to me?

I remember going swimming in a pool in *Setagaya* very early on in my time here; the pool was exactly three meters long. Of course, I did laps. Later in the evening, I was out in the parking lot getting my bicycle. A mother with two kids smiled, and then motioned for me to follow her.

"Why not, this is Tokyo?" I thought. I ended up in her kitchen sipping coffee and eating cake, perhaps the first man to set foot in the place before midnight in years. Looking back on that experience, I acknowledge, "Well, *some* Japanese certainly communicate with strangers. What do I know?"

I could hardly speak any Japanese back then, so the four of us - mother, son, daughter and I - just sat around smiling and giggling with each other. Then she gave me a copy of her absent husband's company calendar. We all waved goodbye at the front door as though we'd known each other for years.

Striking a Balance

Keeping a sense of humor in Japan is a balancing act, because the Japanese generally come across as being hypersensitive to how 'foreigners' feel about their country. In some ways, it reflects the same cultural pride that Canadians and New Zealanders often exhibit when our larger neighbors - the Americans and the Aussies - tease and taunt us. With Japanese people, you learn to be especially mindful of what you say, since innocuous stories can be easily misconstrued.

I remember telling a Japanese acquaintance a Brazilian joke I'd heard at a conference in Kobe. It went this way: God had created this wonderful place, Brazil, in six days. Everything was so gorgeous - beautiful mountains and rivers and plains. Overcome with delight at the perfection of the place, God finally decided it was too perfect, and that there should also be something *imperfect* in Brazil. So God created Brazilians!

My Japanese acquaintance did not laugh. She said it wasn't funny, and refused to believe that Brazilians would ever tell such a joke about themselves. The upshot, of course, was that Japanese would never do so either - only outsiders would tell such a terrible joke. According to her, it was racist, and nothing could persuade her otherwise. But from what I've learned about Japanese humor, I knew her reaction was a kind of self-righteous smokescreen.

When I first arrived in Japan, television producers were having no trouble making fun of other cultures, and quite brazenly. At that time, there was a popular T.V. program here called *Naruhodo the World*. The word *naruhodo* means to 'really understand' something, but the Japanese film crews, who went around the world to do documentary pieces, often came up short on empathy towards their subjects. They sometimes looked at foreign customs in an unmistakably condescending way.

Then one day, to our great surprise, they showed a short piece as a *Naruhodo* on Japan. It all took place in a typically tiny Japanese apartment, packed with stuff. I remember one hilarious moment with a miniature chin-up bar, and the whole scene made Japanese life look very peculiar. To the show's great credit, no one stopped it from being aired, and though the host seemed quite uncomfortable, the audience had a great laugh.

Obviously, somebody on the scene was trying to balance the score. I'm very glad I learned early on that Japanese people can make fun of themselves, along with everybody else. I remember another film called *Bakayaro* about an overworked Japanese *salaryman* struggling to learn English. It was wonderfully self-effacing.

In fact, Japanese have an outrageously good time making fools of themselves on television, and get an enormous kick out of doing so. Luckily for them, they can still set up candid-camera-style antics, without fear that someone will initiate a lawsuit.

Yet, while the Japanese can be acutely sensitive to foreign commentary of any kind – critical or comical – regarding Japan, they often seem innocently oblivious to ways in which their own actions tread on foreign toes. One American friend of mine goes on occasional tirades. He points out that we're obliged to respect Japan's cultural icons at all times, while they get to do what they like with ours. "If we used their Emperor in our advertising, there'd be a huge outcry. But they put the Statue of Liberty on top of love hotels all across the country and think nothing of it!"

You've got to laugh. Humor is the essential antidote to taking the politics of life too seriously here. After reading one too many rabidly critical letters to the editor by my fellow Westerners, I eventually stopped taking most of them seriously. I began to acknowledge that while it's necessary to let off the steam of culture shock from time to time, the Japanese are never going to change to suit us. And frankly, why should they – anymore than we should change for them?

Expats who have married a Japanese, settled down and lived here for twenty years, are in quite a different position. Such people have made a long-time commitment to this country that entitles them to push for changes, such as having the right to vote or run for political office.

Such transplanted expats aside, it's still obviously up to the Japanese – not angst-ridden foreigners who have only been here a few years – to change their society in ways that suit them. As for those aspects of their lives which most Japanese are content with, Ruth Benedict said it well, years ago, in *The Chrysanthemum and the Sword*: "I do not know why believing in the brotherhood of man should mean that one cannot say that the Japanese have their own version of the conduct of life and that Americans have theirs."

Learning from the Japanese

From the perspective of many foreign residents, Japanese people are generally over-schooled and over-controlled. Diversity, flow and expressiveness are not buzzwords here. To go with the flow would more likely mean to fall in line with the group, yet this conformity is clearly the source of much of Japan's strength.

Early on in my time here, a story came out that illustrated how dramatic the requirements of conformity can be. It was about a 16-year-old girl with red hair, whose private all-girls high school had forced her to dye her hair black. This was so it would be the same colour as her classmates – almost all Japanese having black hair, or so goes the party line. There are actually many shades of it.

The school had a prohibition against bleached, dyed or permed hair, and school authorities refused to believe the girl's hair was naturally red. She had to dye her hair black for nearly a year, until her mother finally made a formal complaint. At that point, school officials announced that high-school students with hair which is not naturally black, must get a letter from their junior high school to prove it!

Japan, of course, is famous worldwide for mandating what many in the West perceive to be excessive conformity. Though many things have loosened up considerably in the years I've been here, strict school regulations are not about to be jettisoned wholesale in favor of a liberal approach. It can seem harsh, yet within the confines of this stringent discipline, young people here learn thousands of *kanji* characters and end up able to read and write one of the world's most complex languages. Enviably, they also consistently outperform their American and Canadian counterparts in tests of math skills.

One educational study I read showed that American students, compared to students from five other countries – including Japan and South Korea – were poorest in math. Yet on a questionnaire administered after the test, the young Americans said they thought they would be the best.

Against the backdrop of such delusionary bravado, Americans are dealing with the virtual collapse of discipline in many of their public schools. There are the high-school graduates who can't read, not to mention the metal detectors and the gun-toting mass murderers. So it's hardly sensible to just discount the Japanese educational system as being too rigid. They're obviously doing some things right. In fact, for a time the West was obsessed with discovering the Asian 'secret.' Surely we have something to learn from the Japanese approach to education.

The main problem is that even if we wanted to adopt an Asian model of education – or parts of it – the shoe doesn't fit. The higher math scores in Japan and Korea are products of the systems and cultural mindsets that generated them, and those are hardly transferable. The scale of socially imposed conformity in place in Japan is unworkable in America, because students could never be made to toe such a line.

In fact, a growing minority of Japanese students are rebelling against it, and in low-prestige schools that friends of mine have worked in, at least some of the kids are now out of control. Having already blown their chances at success by ending up in a dead-end school, with no chance of getting into university, the students feel they have nothing much to lose.

But prestigious high schools are still successfully enforcing the conformity of old. Many North American teachers would love to teach such students, disciplined and attentive as they are. After a few false starts at difficult schools, one Canadian friend of mine got a job at a private, all-girls high school, and she described her students to me as "well-behaved dolls" (in the most positive sense of the word).

Still, there's usually a price to be paid. The threat of failing the much-dreaded university entrance exams hangs over the heads of these young people at all times, like the sword of Damacles. Many undergo an extremely stressful ordeal for years, preparing for *examination hell.*

Japan has a long history of schooling its young people in a quite militaristic fashion. Some schools have gates that are shut at precisely the same time every morning, barring entry to latecomers. In one famous case in the early '90s, a young girl died tragically because of an overzealous teacher who shut the gate just as she entered.

One Japanese woman in her thirties, whom I met through Maggie, told me she remembers lining up with hundreds of her classmates in the school courtyard in the heat of summer, to listen to the principal speak. Hanae recalls that over the course of his speech, three female students actually fainted from heat exhaustion.

Teachers quickly ran to their aid, but the principal carried on and finished his speech. Meanwhile, the other students did not flinch. From previous training, they knew it was not their place to do anything but carry on listening. That was in the 1970s, and I doubt that such a thing could happen now, not without immediate media attention exposing it. As with education in the West, Japan's schools have also become more humane.

Yet Japan still takes discipline to extremes. One of my university students explained to me that at her all-girls school, they weren't allowed to stop anywhere on the way home – at a record store, for example. This was against school rules. Still, she hastily assured me that many things about her school had been good, not wanting me to get a totally negative impression.

In children's playgrounds throughout Tokyo, there are enormous clocks on the tops of poles, right next to the swings and slides. The clock faces are often as big as 18 inches in diameter – you can read the time a block away. From their earliest years, young children get the message that being on time is critically important.

As for the physical disciplining of children in schools, it still goes on, and my presence in the classroom didn't serve as a deterrent. In one class I observed, a male high-school teacher whacked a boy over the head with a thick rolled-up magazine, something I used to see in school in Canada as a kid in the sixties. The student just looked up and smirked sheepishly. It would never occur to him to complain to his father and mother; that would only get him in more trouble. The *sensei* has more authority and gets much more respect – or is more feared – than most teachers in North America.

In fact, many parents in Canada and the U.S. are so fed up with what's going on in our schools, that they would even support the idea of a return to disciplinary measures – such as giving the strap on the hands. But fear of lawsuits makes such a thing impossible. In lieu of that, increasing numbers are sending their children to private schools that have reputations for enforcing disciplined learning and providing for more than a mediocre education.

When they see what's going on in U.S. schools, Japanese parents feel reassured. Despite the extreme pressure their children face in school, at least young people are safer in Japan. Incidents of violence – even horrible acts of murder – definitely occur in Japanese schools, but the 1996 statistics on handgun-related deaths make quite a statement. In the U.S., 4,643 children and teenagers died as a result of a handgun shooting of some kind. In Canada, the total was 106, in Britain 30, and in Japan – with half the population of the U.S. – only 15 children met such a fate. Statistics, as they say, don't lie.

The University Playground

One great Western misperception about the Japanese education system is that student attitude and performance are consistently exemplary. Nothing could be further from the truth. What goes on in high schools and universities is like night and day.

As a university teacher, I get to meet the winners and the wounded at the end of the line, once *examination hell* is over. Fortunately, a good number of the students have survived their ordeal by fire, but some of these young people have been pretty much burned-out by the rigors of their high-school experience.

The fact that many freshman students are very afraid of doing or saying the wrong thing – lest they incur the disapproval or wrath of the *sensei* – is not at all surprising to me now. Deference to the teacher is deeply ingrained in this culture. There's definitely a very positive side to this respect for the *sensei*, and for older people in general. My best Japanese students are consistently attentive and well-behaved, and even those who are not interested seldom interrupt the class with jokes or attention-seeking distractions.

But what's disturbing is to see how emotionally numb some of these young people seem to be, though this especially applies to the males. My colleague, Ken, once described the young men in his freshman English class by saying: "These guys haven't just given up on English, they've given up on life."

It can definitely seem that way. Most of us teaching for a number of years at universities in Japan experience moments of great angst. We look around our classes at the astonishing lack of vitality in many of our students, and we shake our heads in disbelief. We conclude that something is unquestionably amiss. An education system that routinely produces so many 19-year-olds in this passive and apathetic condition has a problem that's not being addressed.

I'm sure now that some of this is fallout from living in Tokyo. On quite a few occasions, I've noticed that a particular student in a new class has a noticeably bright and alert face, coupled with a buoyant spirit. Later, I've found out they're from some remote place like Hokkaido, or rural Gifu, or Sado Island. Perhaps a childhood spent in Tokyo is, in itself, enough to smother many a sunny disposition.

The young women will often claim to be shy, but a Japanese friend insists that "shyness is learned once we get to school." Doubtless, a good number *are* genuinely shy, but I sense that shyness is a coping strategy for many students. It's a psychological hiding place, adopted to deal with the demands of school settings. Actually, it's a cinch to confirm this by watching 'shy' students walking, talking and laughing together outside the classroom – shyness is no longer in the picture!

Other factors, like the pressure to conform, strongly affect student behavior in Japan. *Ijime* (bullying or teasing) is a major issue in grade schools; kids get bullied or ridiculed for being different from others.

One first-year university student of mine talked excitedly with me on the first day of the term about her experience in England. Her English was good, and she spoke in a very natural way. Then within a few weeks, she started stammering and pretending to be hopeless at English. Peer pressure not to be better than the others was too strong for her to handle, since she was the only one in the class with overseas experience.

This is why classes made up almost entirely of *returnees* are so necessary in Japan. Universities that have large numbers of such students are able to address their needs by grouping them together.

But the strongest influence on these young people stems directly from the way the system is set up. Most high-school students have plenty of motivation.

Their time is totally given over to preparing for the crucial entrance exams, so they can get into a good university. But within a month of experiencing the initial excitement of university life, their incentive evaporates like dew on a summer morning. That's because they feel there's nothing more for them to shoot for.

University students all know that the pressure's off for four years. Now, they want to enjoy themselves for once. I know stories of young people who went to *juku* (or cram school) summer camp for ten days, studied from early in the morning till 10:00 pm. at night, and never went near the lake!

Now that's all over, and they're finally free to kick back. So how do you inspire and motivate young people under such conditions? Suffice it to say, it can be quite a challenge. But knowing from firsthand experience the hard work that awaits them at companies like Soulful Software, I've slowly learned to go easy on them.

At the worst of times – as you near the end of the semester in the baking heat of July and most of your students seem utterly uninterested – the whole thing can seem absurd. In fact, articles examining the absurdities inherent in the system and calling for drastic educational reform appear in the newspapers on a regular basis. I showed one such opinion-piece to a very internationally-minded Japanese colleague, and asked for her view. "Oh, she laughed, "people have been writing that same article for 20 years, but nothing ever changes."

Yet, rather than throw the proverbial baby out with the bath water, I try to remain open-minded and continue to ask myself if there are sides to Japanese educational life I prefer to our own. The truth is that I've found much to admire in my university students. Many have wonderfully good natures, and they seem a lot less prone to many negative qualities – such as sarcasm and mean-spiritedness – than young people in the West. They often appear to share something quite special with each other, a kind of group kinship. At all times, they seem to maintain an awareness of the supremacy of the group's needs. It's a radically different focus from "taking care of Number One."

Maintaining lifelong connections with fellow students – as well as teachers – is very common in Japan. The social cohesion and mutual concern that students have for each other's well-being often strikes me as remarkable, and I'm now convinced that this is one of the keys to this country's strength.

But at the university level, comparing Japanese 'academic' life with the three Canadian universities I've studied at, I haven't personally come across anything especially innovative in higher education here. You often get the sense that university life in Japan is partially a charade, and everyone understands this. Classes are not to be taken so seriously – the real training has always happened later when companies get hold of their recruits. Yet, paradoxically, administrators and professors still approach their roles with the utmost seriousness.

Many Japanese professors I've observed typically lecture in traditional style, while the students who have bothered to show up listen passively, take notes or snooze. However, there are inspiring teachers and innovative textbook writers in Japan. I respect their efforts to improve the lives of their students as I respect my own. Judging from comments some of my students make, I believe we do make a significant difference in their lives, in spite of the limitations of the system.

For those students who are eager to benefit from their university studies, the system can be inflexible and unresponsive to their needs. Once they enter a program, for example, changing their major is just about impossible. My students were astonished and envious to hear that in Canada, I was able to change my major in my second year.

In Japan, university hierarchies still pay scant attention to youthful brilliance – you have to wait your turn. One Swiss friend of mine put in nearly three years in a doctoral program at top-ranking *Todai* (Tokyo University), but he finally gave up in despair before attaining his degree. There was simply no place for his ideas above those of his advisors.

Experiencing life 'on the ground' in Japan, I've found it very helpful to have my own views corroborated by other Japan watchers. Many have a broader view, better connections and much more expertise than I have. Jonathan Rauch, pointing out how comparatively few Nobel Prizes have gone to Japanese, formed the impression that Japan is "a story of wasted intellectual resources. Japan has all that is necessary to make a magnificent contribution to the world's stock of knowledge, but it is failing to do so."

Japan does seem to do an excellent job at getting its children off to a great start. I've heard mostly good reports about *hoikuen* (daycare), kindergarten and primary school education. These have come both from written accounts and from teachers and friends whose children are attending school here. One Canadian teacher friend told me that the Japanese mothers all sobbed at their child's 'graduation' from kindergarten. At the *hoikuen* I visited, I met darling children. They were clearly much loved, well disciplined and happy. Japan seems especially sensitive to the needs of young children. An annual event called *shichi-go-san* (for children aged 3, 5 and 7) is a joyful celebration of childhood. Wonderful animation films such as *Kiki's Delivery Service* and *Totoro* – my personal favorites – offer a refreshing contrast to America's violent fare.

In terms of academic progress, a typical grade three child in Japan is clearly ahead of his or her counterpart in the U.S. in subjects like math. Most of my friends seem content to have their children in school here until the sixth grade. But at that point, most say they'll leave Japan for their children's sake.

From the junior-high level onwards, the pressure begins and builds. In classes of 45, the role of the learner becomes primarily that of sponge. Students soak up fact-based information and absorb mathematical and scientific calculations that might show up on the university entrance exams down the road. Everything is geared to the exams. In the final stretch in the last year of high school, it's commonly said that if a student is sleeping more than four hours a night, they're not going to make it.

Students pour all their energy into cramming information into their brains, simply for the sake of passing these crucial exams. As they do, the spirit and curiosity of millions of these young people get dulled.

It occurred to me one day that this is probably the Japanese way of harnessing the energy of puberty. At the cost of a truncated childhood, Japanese teenagers achieve tremendous focus through having this one target to aim for. The Japanese system errs on the side of an excess of structure and discipline, with too little allowance for originality and spontaneity. By contrast, problem schools in North America err in the other direction: tolerance of free expression to the point of 'anything goes,' and too little discipline to support and shape it.

Yet from living in Japan, I've come to believe that the emphasis on the development of individual expression in Canada and the U.S. is our greatest strength. I've never met a Canadian or American who said that junior- and senior-high schools here offer a solution to our educational problems. The math test scores do prove that plenty of excellent teaching is taking place in Japan, but that's only part of what an education is about.

High-school students in the U.S. and Canada are more likely to be encouraged to develop their own unique personalities and talents. In Japan, this is simply not emphasized. One Japanese high-school girl I knew did a one-year homestay in the U.S. When the year was over, she didn't want to return to Japan. Her explanation was succinct: "I know who I am now."

On the other hand – what with the chaos in so many North American schools – there's one practice in grade schools here that every Canadian and American I've ever mentioned it to has greeted with a resounding, "Yes, that sounds all right!" That's the fact that in most Japanese schools, the kids do half an hour of cleaning up every day or two, usually after lunch. It's considered a part of their education. They're taught to sweep the classrooms, mop the hallways and staircases, clean the washrooms and tidy up the teachers' room, while the teachers supervise. Add me to the list of those who think this is a fine way to teach young people that we're responsible for cleaning up our own mess!

Fettucine Format

My new friend, Shiraz, was only in Japan for one year, but after living for more than half a decade in Tokyo, I found his stories to be very refreshing, not to mention hilarious.

Shiraz worked for an architectural firm doing design work, but he was really only here in passing. During the course of his year in Tokyo, he learned that he'd been accepted to do graduate work at Harvard, starting in September. But staying true to himself, he wrote to the admissions board and asked for a one-year deferment of his acceptance, a request rarely granted.

Shiraz explained that he wouldn't be able to live with himself if he didn't follow through on his plan to research his roots in India, where his grandparents had been born prior to their move to Uganda. He himself had been born in Canada, and grew up there and in the U.S.

His plan was to save enough money here in Tokyo to allow him to set out across China and down into India. In its wisdom, the admissions board of Harvard University accepted his request and granted him his one-year deferment. Shiraz recently set off in search of his ancestry.

During his last three months in Japan, however, Shiraz and I got together for dinner once a week. He was great company and good conversation for me, what with my living alone again after years with Krista. Knowing that I was writing about my experiences in Tokyo, Shiraz was always eager to share his own.

"Put this in your book," he told me one night at Arun's Curry and Music Bar. It's our favorite meeting spot, run by our Bangladeshi friend, Arun, who's married to a Japanese woman. "If you asked me for one story that typifies Japan for me, this is it!"

The situation he then proceeded to describe is one of a hundred variations on a theme that are part and parcel of Japanese life for *gaijin*. Shiraz explained that he'd gone to an Italian-style restaurant with a Japanese friend. Looking at the menu, he decided he wanted to order the fettucine with cream sauce. But when he noticed that ham - which he doesn't eat - was one of the ingredients, he had his friend request that the ham be left out.

"It's impossible," came the reply, translated by his Japanese companion, "that's how it comes."

With his friend serving as interpreter, Shiraz persisted for awhile, trying to persuade the proprietor to comply with his request.

"Surely it can't be that difficult to just leave the ham out when you make it. I can't eat ham," he said.

But the proprietor was adamant. "That's the way it comes," he insisted. "Sorry, but there's no changing it."

Finally concluding that accommodating his wishes must be more difficult than it seemed – that the fettucine was probably pre-mixed with the ham – Shiraz succumbed to his friend's suggestion. He would order the fettucine, then pick the ham out himself before eating it.

With that compromise, they placed their order and waited for their meal. When it arrived ten minutes later, Shiraz could only shake his head in disbelief. There was the fettucine and cream sauce, with the ham all sprinkled *on top*, quite separate from the fettucine and garnished with a sprig of parsley!

Why the proprietor could not simply have left the ham off, since it was just plopped on top anyway, is a question you stop asking after you've been in Japan awhile – unless you want to wend your way to the funny farm. Sooner or later, you realize that once an employee has been trained to do something in a certain way, the fact that making a change would be easy is not the issue at all. In Japan, you don't just go around bending the rules with impunity. If anything is inviolable in this country, it's the little rules everybody abides by.

Shiraz's story reminded me of the time I arrived at a restaurant in the Sendai railway station at 10:01 in the morning – my watch accurate to the minute – looking for breakfast. The sign advertised breakfast as being from 7:00 to 10:00 a.m.

This being way back in my first year here, I thought, "Oh, one minute late, that shouldn't be a problem. I'm sure I can persuade them."

You can be very wrong in Japan when you make such assumptions. Though I could hardly understand any Japanese at all at the time, I'd already learned to recognize that much sucking in of breath, and multiple use of the catch-all word *chotto* – as performed by the super-polite young coffee-shop attendant – meant something like the following:

"Terribly sorry sir, breakfast was finished several trillion eternities ago. No way could we serve you breakfast."

Of course, I've since learned that this religious adherence to schedule does have an upside to it. If you arrive at 7:01 a.m. – one minute after 'opening' – it'll seem like they've been at it for hours. Seldom are the times when you'll have to wait in Japan while a dawdling employee gets it together.

In fact, once you begin to speak the language, by invoking *gaijin* ignorance you can occasionally move boulders from in front of the mouths of caves. I once ended up in a *Jonathan* 24-hour restaurant at 10:20 a.m., ravenous for breakfast. I decided to do my level best to get the 10:00 a.m. rule bent. I launched into a rambling apology to the manager in my most polite Japanese. ("I'm so very sorry to disturb you in this way. Please forgive me because I was quite unaware. If it would be at all possible to make an exception just this once, I would be most grateful and would be sure to never let it happen again.") Presto! He relented, and I learned that there is a way to ingratiate your way into eggs and toast beyond the breakfast deadline. For the Japanese, an attitude of contrition is much harder to say 'no' to than a demanding tone.

Shiraz had more stories to tell. He never went into too much detail about his design work with me. But he did talk about his work environment and recounted one experience he kept having throughout his year with his company. It went like this: He'd finish a design, then seek some feedback on it from a Japanese colleague. The dialogue that invariably ensued took roughly the following form:

"Hey, what do you think of this?"
"Hmm, maybe O.K."
"Oh, come on, tell me how you feel about it."
"Hmm, it's not my field."
"Yeah, but at least tell me if you like it."
"I don't know if I like it. Maybe you should ask the boss. This isn't my job."

Sometimes, Shiraz and I used this as a running joke for commenting on the food at Arun's.

"What do you think of dinner?"
"Hmm, maybe O.K. How about you?"
"Hmm, not my field, ask the cook."

Shiraz told me he probably heard *tabun daijōbu* (maybe O.K.) about thirty times a day, until he just stopped asking what his colleagues thought.

The impression he was left with is that in Japan's hierarchical society, what the boss thinks is not just important, it's 'all-important.' What you – as a subordinate – think, doesn't really matter. So if you're a junior in the company, and you don't know what your boss thinks about something, you hold your tongue. The risk of getting caught holding a contrary viewpoint holds few benefits.

This is quite baffling to Westerners raised to trust their own individual value judgments. But once you understand the protocol of hierarchy, life in mainstream Japan gets much easier. Most of the time, the restaurant proprietor will not leave out the ham, because that scenario wasn't part of his training, and the boss never told him he could do that.

Once you've realized this, you start to walk around with your antennae up. The minute you feel some resistance, you recognize that you may be encountering the weight of the entire system, as embodied in the mindset of one humble employee.

After a few traumatic experiences, you start to understand what you're up against if you put up a fight. Unless you thrive on futile conflict, you learn to back down right there. You either eat the ham, or you take it as it comes, and pick out the ham later. And at 10:01 a.m., you try the ingratiating bit, but if that doesn't quickly work its magic, you give up and eat an early lunch.

The alternative can be nasty. I worked with one British guy who insisted he'd been told that he could get his money back on a train ticket (though with all the nuances of *Nihongo*, he may have misunderstood). At the time Gordon made the inquiry, the train had not yet left, but the clerk said he was not in a position to give refunds. Nevertheless, Gordon felt he'd been reassured that he could get a refund later, after the fact.

When 'later' came, he was refused, but Gordon was one of the more stubborn foreign residents I've met in my time here. He told me he spent five hours battling away to get his money back! After four hours, the beleaguered and infuriated official tried to give him 80%, but he held out for the whole amount, which took another hour to get.

Surprisingly, in encounters with government and corporate bureaucracy in Japan, you find that exceptions to rigid rules can be made. This happens when you are the lucky recipient of a *case-by-case* judgment, the built-in loophole in the rule book through which officials are permitted to allow some people to pass. Japanese officialdom can be remarkably flexible when you least expect it. But this is much less likely to happen when you lose your cool, and there may be unpleasant consequences if you do.

The great strength of Japan's rule-bound universe would seem to be the tremendous control that can be maintained over human behavior and, therefore, over how society is organized. During one discussion, an American university colleague of mine, a man who's been here nearly 20 years, gave this succinct assessment:

"The fact is, it works," he said.

Most Westerners react less favorably to the rigidity we come up against. We grumble about it, and we're initially mystified at the willingness of the vast majority of the Japanese people to always toe the line.

Modern Western societies are hardly immune to the kind of inflexibility Shiraz met up with in ordering his fettucine. Jack Nicholson's character in the famous restaurant scene in *Five Easy Pieces* comes to mind. Furious that the waitress will not make a simple change to the menu format, he sweeps everything off the table.

What a contrast with the acquiescence of Japan! I can imagine many Japanese being mystified by Nicholson's behavior and thinking, "Why does he choose to rock the boat and make his life more difficult?"

All of which brings up Shiraz's third and final comment on his one year here – on the issue of criticism.

"Don't forget to mention," he said on his last night in Tokyo, "that this is a country in which the slightest disapproval of anything Japanese – even a mere suggestion that something might perhaps be improved – is taken as a direct criticism of 125 million people."

It can certainly seem that way to a newcomer. I now know that it's not at all so black and white, but this was Shiraz's conclusion after one year of working in a company here. It's worth noting, because it's a common impression that many Westerners take away with them. Had I left after one year, I think I would have felt the same.

Shiraz recounted a few more stories that revealed his exasperation with Japan. The funniest was about the morning he came into the office after enduring a horrendous train ride to work, and started talking about it. He wondered out loud how the crowds on the Tokyo trains might be reduced.

"Hey, you could build double-decker trains, or institute flex-time to spread out the rush hour," he volunteered.

Shiraz imagined that this was surely one situation that only a masochist would defend. Ah, wrong again! His colleagues took his comments as a direct criticism of how the trains are run in Japan.

As my Jewish friends would say, *Oi vey*.

Shiraz and I agreed on one point about those Japanese who are culturally defensive in this way. In spite of the fact that his colleagues – whom I met at his farewell party – are agreeable and likable people, it's not really possible to have a meaningful dialogue with people for whom social criticism is totally out of bounds. But you can still have a very pleasant time with them at a party.

This hypersensitivity has been noted ever since foreign residents started coming to these shores, and it's still very much in evidence today. Working with hundreds of students who continually ask me what I think about Japan, I now believe it's a learned response, passed down through the education system and the culture. It sometimes seems as if everyone's monitoring your reactions to Japan, and placing you in one of two simplistic categories: those who are with us, and those who are against us. The fact that even those *gaijin* who seem to fit in the first category will 'think what they like' must be disquieting for some.

I finally began answering the frequently asked question, "Do you like Japan?" by saying, "Well, if you'd asked me what I think about the United States, China, France, India, Japan or my own country, Canada, I'd say pretty much the same thing. There are some things I like very much, and other things I have a problem with."

It's interesting to observe the reaction when I respond this way. It seems to do an end run around the deeply ingrained notion that the only answers are 'yes' or 'no', especially when it comes to Japan. Japanese students do not appear to get much training in learning to tolerate and examine differences of opinion.

When my students fish for advice in dealing with the West and Western people, I always tell them it's just not a realistic expectation that everything said about Japan will be nice. I encourage them to just ignore the off-the-wall attacks, but to try to learn from well-intentioned criticism and not to take it personally. I get the feeling that these are approaches to dealing with criticism that they haven't been exposed to before.

I go on to say that powerful countries are always under scrutiny. America, for example, gets continually bashed from all sides. As the second largest economy in the world, Japan is now destined to be examined extensively. Like every other society on the face of the globe, it has its flaws, and foreigners are going to talk about them.

I also remind my students to take pride in their remarkable and ancient culture, and to remember that the world loves many things Japanese. In America, sushi is now traditional culinary fare.

I suggest they learn from those of their countrymen who know how to poke fun at themselves. I remind them that most Westerners view the ability to do so as a sign of strength. By way of illustration, I relate what a very witty and wonderful 65-year-old Japanese professor said to me one day at our university.

"There's one thing the Japanese do better than anyone else in the world," he declared. "They make people nervous!"

I felt as comfortable with a Japanese man on that day as I ever have. Self-deprecating humour is not so common among individual Japanese, but every now and again, someone will really surprise you.

Shiraz and I shook hands and wished each other well. I asked him if he'd enjoyed his time in Tokyo.

"Yeah, it's been great," he said.

Was he happy to be leaving Japan now after his year here?

"Hmm, maybe O.K.," he replied.

"We Japanese"

In Japan's highly conformist society, people grow up learning to adhere to convergent views. This is surely true everywhere to some extent, but Japan takes it further than I've ever seen before. The concept of members of the same society entertaining a variety of widely divergent perspectives is not easily understood by most young Japanese. Presented with one American viewpoint, many quickly jump to the conclusion that it holds true for all Americans.

Visiting in a junior-high-school class, I was asked the question, "Why do Americans like guns?" (American/Canadian was taken to be the same.) I got the impression that young Japanese imagine American cities and schools to be scenes of daily shoot-outs, with every child for himself and every man and woman with a gun!

Another example of this came from a colleague of mine. Frances invited a young American man into her university class one day to speak with her Japanese students in English.

He himself was a student and was taking a semester at our university on an exchange program. When he was asked if he was learning Japanese, he said, "No," explaining that he doubted he'd ever use the language once he got home to the States.

An American listening to this might conclude that it was a shortsighted view on his part, given the golden opportunity to get a head start on this important Asian language. But the listener would certainly understand that the student's decision represented nothing more than his own personal viewpoint.

When the American student had finished talking and left the classroom, a male Japanese student immediately asked my colleague, "Why don't Americans want to learn Japanese?"

Frances patiently explained that Americans do not all share his viewpoint, that many Americans *do* want to learn Japanese and other foreign languages. But in a culture where people quite commonly explain their belief systems to you by starting with the phrase, *Ware-ware Nihon-jin* ("We Japanese..."), the Japanese student may well have assumed the American student to be saying, "*We Americans* don't want to learn to speak Japanese."

There's no saying how well he was able to understand my colleague's explanation that diversity of opinion is about as basic to America as rice is to Japan. Perhaps he'll need to meet a living, breathing, Japanese-speaking American to figure that out.

The Many Faces of Conformity

Some years before he became Russian president, Boris Yeltsin paid a visit to Japan, and at one point he toured a car-factory assembly line. He spent a few hours looking around, and after the tour was over was asked if he had any questions.

"Only one," he was reported as saying. "What makes them work like that?"

I can't imagine he got a straight answer. Perhaps the best one would have been, "It never occurs to them not to."

In other words, it has a lot to do with Japan's much-talked-about conformity. Grade-school students are sometimes called upon to perform mechanical and repetitive verbal tasks that appear to be meaningless. One purpose of this is probably to teach obedience and submission to authority. But learning to endure these repetitive tasks has another function – it prepares students for more of the same once they enter the workforce.

During my first month in Japan, I watched a young teenage boy standing outside his school in a small city called Uji, near Kyoto, where friends of mine were living. He was wearing the Prussian-soldier-style school uniform that many schoolboys still wear. He was also repeating *Ohaiyo gozaimasu* (Good morning) hundreds of times to his fellow students as groups of them passed by him on their way into the school.

I watched and listened to this young boy, perhaps 15 years old, for a long time. The boy's fellow students all just ignored him, but I could see that he was taking great care to say one *Ohaiyo gozaimasu* for each student who passed him by. This meant that when a group of 10 students showed up at the same time, he sounded a bit like a parrot gone berserk. Maybe the whole exercise was a form of punishment, like writing "I will not talk in class" 500 times. Or perhaps it was a form of obedience training, designed to teach humility, and it was something everyone had to do on a rotational basis.

In any event, I forgot about the incident until one morning months later in a Tokyo train station. There, I was exposed to exactly the same performance, this time done by a young ticket-taker delivering one *Ohaiyo gozaimasu* to every commuter who passed through his gate, exactly as the student had done in Uji. Over time, I began noticing how common this ritual patter is.

All of this training has helped to produce Japan's civilian army of diligent, reliable workers, who follow orders well and work with great dedication to their jobs. One teacher friend of mine delights in the fact that his students "will do whatever I ask them to do!"

This obedience has been an essential component of Japan's rise to economic power. But this reliance on outside direction and mechanical repetition has also led to what some Western experts have referred to as Japan's 'creativity problem.'

In teaching at the university level, foreign teachers working with Japanese students routinely encounter students who seem unable to speak hypothetically, employ predictive skills, make inferences, or formulate and support opinions. Legion are the teachers, myself included, who have been driven to the heights of exasperation trying to get our students to say what they think about anything.

In my first weeks teaching freshman university classes here, I knew next to nothing about how to work with 45 expressionless young people who seemed to have zippers on their mouths – the young women clustered together on one side, the young men on the other. They were all sitting expectantly on long, unmovable benches, waiting for me to teleport them to English fluency.

I had taught many groups of loquacious Europeans and Central Americans in Canada - there was no problem getting them to talk. But deadpan silence was something I'd never encountered before. I remember asking one young man a question and deciding I would just patiently wait until he responded and occasionally repeat the question to encourage him. Surely, I imagined, he'd eventually come up with a response of some kind, even a simple "I don't know."

After 10 minutes of 'you could hear a pin drop,' I surrendered that traumatizing technique forever. Dozens of experiments later, I had them working in groups of four, doing things like memorizing small scripts, a rote-learning task they had done before and were very comfortable with.

I've spoken with numerous teachers who have had such experiences teaching Japanese students, both in Japan and overseas. One university teacher I met at a party interpreted his experience this way: "I'd always assumed that having a 'critical faculty' was a given. But after teaching in Japan, I know otherwise. It's a learned skill, and not one they learn well."

For what it's worth, I learned from Karel van Wolferen that *Nihonjinron* (a fringe - but widely known - school of thought promulgated entirely by Japanese) takes the view that Japanese people, "unlike Westerners," are "not logical" - meaning they think differently.

For a number of reasons, you have to assess all of this pretty cautiously. For one thing, these students are working in a difficult second language, and one that's used in radically different ways and for different purposes than their native tongue. For most Japanese, English can be a frighteningly *direct* language compared to their own. They also run into trouble when they try to translate directly from their native *Nihongo*, a language that often drops the subject, and always puts verbs at the end of the sentence.

Secondly, cultural factors are hard at work, restricting what Japanese people are willing to say. Expressing personal opinions and emotions is way down the list of valued skills in Japan; avoiding conflict and seeking agreement are far more important. It's not axiomatic that your students don't possess a given skill, simply because their culture has never encouraged them to use it.

Thirdly, as many commentators on Japan have pointed out, these students have been educated with a Confucian model of learning: The teacher expounds, and the students absorb. Whatever subjects they've been exposed to in their school years, the majority tend to know extremely well. But they haven't been encouraged to ask questions and develop their own viewpoints to anywhere the same extent as Canadian or American students. Yet this hardly proves that they don't have any. Assuming that silence reflects ignorance is a mistake I've made many times. It may simply reflect extreme caution, learned inhibition, or fear.

Lastly, it's a truism that many Japanese students appear to temporarily park their brains and their motivation during their university years. Later, once they begin their working lives, they wholeheartedly dedicate themselves to developing whatever skills their jobs call for. At that point, you'd be hard-pressed to find people more dedicated to learning their jobs and fulfilling their duties.

Yet many teachers I've spoken with have come to the conclusion that at the very least, teaching thinking skills has not been the educational priority here. Teaching young people *what* to think - in order to be in tune with other Japanese - has been emphasized much more than teaching them *how* to think creatively or express their own viewpoint.

I used Ron Fricke's *Baraka* - a film without words - in some of my classes, to stimulate discussion. Using footage from 24 countries in six continents, *Baraka* slowly unveils the incredible beauty and range of cultural diversity to be found on planet earth. It also reveals much about humankind's horrific capacity for destructiveness and exploitation. But all of this is presented without a word, though culturally appropriate background music is used to create atmosphere.

The film made a huge impact in my classes. But when I invited students to write and interpret it for themselves, a good number seemed to be at a complete loss. I got the feeling that they'd seldom been given such an open-ended task in all their years at school, and many students asked me, "What is the message of this movie?" Clearly, they wanted to be told 'the answer.'

I once asked one group of 30 pre-med students to think of some possible medical breakthroughs in the future. Ten minutes later, eliciting individual responses, I discovered that everyone in the class had the same answer - "a cure for AIDS." Needless to say, it was not a case of synchronicity; someone had come up with the idea and everyone else just followed suit.

It always has to be kept in mind that the Japanese frequently use their spoken language to express things indirectly. It's a cultural norm to conceal as much as to reveal. A trivial and humorous example of this that everyone learns when they first get to Japan, is the traditional way a man used to ask a woman if she would spend the night with him. He would casually say, "Shall we have breakfast together tomorrow?"

In Japan, culture and language influence each other constantly and in surprising ways. When I was learning how to work with Japanese students, I would ask a class of thirty to get into groups of four. Nobody would move! At first, I wrongly assumed that they hadn't understood me, and I'd tell them again. Only when I'd finally learned to give the instructions and then sit back and watch how they dealt with it, did I begin to learn something about how the culture operates.

No individual person would step forward and take on the role of organizing everyone, nor would they start looking around to find partners for themselves. Having understood the instructions, the students would simply wait in silence for about 30 seconds. Then, as though in response to some silent signal they all heard, everyone would suddenly start turning their heads at the same time, usually choosing the people nearest them. Great care was taken to make sure everyone was included in a group.

I learned over time that they love random selection, which explains the huge popularity of *jun ken po* (paper, rock, scissors) as a means of choosing who'll go first, or who will be in which group. It's not just a game for kids in Japan; university students use it all the time.

I once witnessed a very sweet Japanese moment on the steps leading up to Kamakura's *Hachiman-gu Shrine*. In the moonlight, a young couple were patiently making their way up its dozens of steep steps by playing *paper, rock, scissors* all the way up. With each round, the winner moved up three steps. The young lovers, totally taken with each other and their game, played round after round. She kept winning, and the gap between them kept widening. It was very touching to watch – it soon became 'long distance' *jun ken po*.

In my classes, I eventually began choosing groups by shuffling a deck of cards, and then passing them out. Everyone who got an Ace would get together, as well as the Kings and the Queens, and so on. It worked like a charm, because everyone loved the element of serendipity. They seemed very comfortable with having the decision placed in the hands of chance.

Obviously, the fact that Japan has become the second largest economy in the world is ample evidence that there's tremendous strength in such cohesion and group-mindedness. But what about the ability to think independently and form individual judgments?

It's the conclusion of many of us teaching here that there have been other priorities, such as the importance of obedience, punctuality and precision. The exact use of language – learning how to carefully write thousands of *kanji* characters – is a cultural imperative. When you're learning to speak Japanese, you discover that even a little bit of sloppiness, or a minor deviation from the expected language pattern, will throw many people off. You've got to get it right, because guessing what you might mean does not come easily for the Japanese.

This can be exasperating when you first start using *Nihongo* with waiters in restaurants. In the early going, breakdowns in communication are a dime a dozen, because people in the service industries want to be absolutely sure they've got your order right. This is a complete contrast with Thailand, where waiters prefer to ask only once, and then bring you what they thought you ordered!

I still remember my very first Japanese class at Soulful Software. Our *sensei* was teaching us *Ohaiyo gozaimas* (Good morning), and she went over and over the pronunciation for 20 minutes. It seemed ridiculous at the time, but I now realize that she knew something I didn't – you either get your pronunciation right in Japan, or nobody will understand you.

Over time, you discover the merits of being extremely brief and saying only what you need to. It took me six months to be able to consistently order coffee without having to repeat myself two or three times. I eventually realized that the only people trying to construct a sentence, or bothering to say *kudasai* (please) when ordering, were me and the other foreigners struggling to learn *Nihongo*. Japanese men routinely say *kohi* (coffee) and nothing more. They can seem rude when they're overseas and neglect to say 'please.' But in Tokyo, *café au lait* is simply *O-re*. The fast lane here includes becoming a minimalist in your speech.

You also learn to be very patient when misunderstandings occur, and to take time to work it out. Things then start to get easier, even when they're challenging. Nowadays, most of the interactions I have with people in the service industries are extremely pleasant, but I've had to memorize the quick verbal formulas. I've also learned to relax when communication breaks down.

All of this said, many of my Japanese friends not only speak English much better than I speak Japanese, but they're sharp as whips. Obviously, this country didn't get to where it is without managing to produce its fair share of brilliant and multi-talented people. When Mark Twain quipped that he "never let having to go to school get in the way of his getting an education," he was also speaking for the many talented Japanese who have had to do much the same. And lest I forget, I did not have a pleasant time in high school in my own country; we had lots of complaints about the style of schooling we were subjected to.

I now have confirmation – through the behavior of my university students – of something I first suspected with Soulful Software's *salarymen*. The minute they step inside a classroom – or any environment where authority rules – out comes this seeming lifelessness, absorbed through thousands of hours of passive learning in their school years.

But stepping outside and going across the street to the local pool hall, these young people quickly leave the educational mindset behind, and they display a completely natural range of expressiveness. In fact, they have a harmonious way of relating with each other that North American young people could learn plenty from.

Western young people have their own forms of conformity, some of which are every bit as tyrannical as what young Japanese face. It now seems to me that Western youth face strong pressure to 'act out,' to conform to the imperative of expressing themselves in a 'unique' way.

In Japan, the requirements of the group routinely trump the imperatives of individual expression. Yet my Japanese friends, students and acquaintances, though consistently mindful of the needs of the group, are individuals in every sense of the word. If my book serves only to debunk some of the negative stereotypes that abound about Japanese people, and to present a more balanced picture than we often get in our media, I'll feel it was well worth writing.

But what about rules like the ban on red hair? Isn't that an outrageous symbol of the repression of diversity?

Sure, that's the most obvious way to look at it. But recently I saw even that in another light. Authorities in a conformist and group-oriented society such as Japan's find themselves in quite a dilemma. Young people here are especially prone to fads. For example, I brought a brown tartan scarf back with me from Montreal after one trip home. Then I watched as a bizarre thing happened. The identical pattern and colour of scarf started to become popular here in Japan, and before the winter ended, it seemed as if every second schoolgirl in the country was wearing my scarf. Eventually I stopped wearing it, because it was just me and the schoolgirls!

The Japanese school authorities must live in constant trepidation, ever on the lookout for evidence of this conformist impulse run amok. Given the speed of modern communication, when a fad catches on, every school child in the country knows about it in the blink of an eye.

Millions of these girls have donned the same thick, white socks during after-school hours for most of the '90s, rebelling in unison against school dress codes. You can see them changing from approved socks to illegal socks on train platforms - a more benign form of protest would be hard to find.

So the potential is always there. I could imagine some school administrator waking up during the night in a cold sweat, having dreamt that every schoolgirl in the country has transformed herself overnight into a redhead.

Piccadilly Trumped

I should have known I'd be a sucker for Tokyo. When I was 10 years old, my mother took us to visit England and Northern Ireland for six weeks. It was her first time back to the 'Old Country' after emigrating to Canada 15 years earlier to marry my father, and the trip changed my life forever. It converted me into a lover of travel. Even after all these years, I remember it as though it were yesterday. The magic of London captivated me.

I can still recall the first moment I set eyes on Piccadilly Circus. I just stood there with my mouth open at all the glittering lights and neon advertisements. It was amazing to my 10-year-old mind that such a place existed. It had been here all along, on the same planet I'd been walking on, and I hadn't known!

Now, all these years later, I sometimes feel much the same astonishment looking at Tokyo's version of Piccadilly Circus: *Shibuya Crossing*. When I have the time, I just stand back for a few minutes and let my eyes drink in the armies of people flooding across its four-way crosswalk. I often think of Ron Fricke's film *Baraka*, with the whole scene on fast forward looking like humanity on the run, in too great a hurry.

Yet, when I watch the three enormous screens that overlook Shibuya Crossing, high up on the walls surrounding the intersection, I sometimes take delight at the sight of the larger-than-life techno-humans dancing above our heads. These images of youthful vitality celebrate our capacity to project ourselves around the world and across cultures, at the speed of light. I saw and heard Enya up there once, singing *Anywhere Is*, and everything about Tokyo and my life here seemed just fine in that moment – "I might be just beginning, I might be near the end."

At Christmas time, I took comfort, one December evening, in the familiarity of Shibuya's Yuletide decorations. I stood to the side for a moment and took it all in – the giant Santa Claus in his enormous sleigh with his whole troop of reindeer, all hanging on a wall of Christmas lights overlooking *Hachiko Square*.

A few memories of Christmas in Canada drifted through my contented mind. I found I wasn't bothered at all by the commercialism of these Christmas lights, ablaze in a primarily non-Christian land where some people hold weddings in fake chapels. We're just *their* version of 'exotic,' I suddenly realized. And after all, Christ's message was about showing tolerance and loving one another. That night, I let Shibuya be exactly what it wanted to be, and I found myself still marveling that such a place even exists.

On the Issue of Race

Japan is described by many foreign and some Japanese commentators as being a nation obsessed with race. In his book *Looking at the Sun: The Rise of the New East Asian Economic and Political System*, James Fallows discusses a government poll of foreigners that we all read about here. It revealed that the most irritating thing for foreigners in Japan was "the constant reminders of the perceived racial gap between *ware ware Nihonjin* ("we Japanese") and everyone else."

It can be exasperating; I wouldn't pretend otherwise. There's no disputing that there's institutionalized discrimination here. In their remarkable book *The Japan We Never Knew*, David Suzuki and Keibu Oiwa carefully document such discrimination against Koreans in Japan, and the *Ainu* people of Hokkaido. They also examine prejudice against the two to three million *Burakumin*, Japan's version of India's untouchables. They discuss these issues in detail and with much sensitivity.

In addition, they relate similar examples of institutionalized discrimination and practices of assimilation in Canadian and American history. Yes, Japan has a long history of discrimination, and so do we.

In my daily life in Japan, reminders that I'm not Japanese are everywhere I look. An us-and-them viewpoint seems to be part of the fabric of the country, and this leads to many racial issues that make it into the news. The unfortunate thing is that this side of the equation gets almost all of the coverage.

Shintaro Ishihara's infamous and widely read book *The Japan That Can Say No: Why Japan Will Be First Among Equals* added fuel to this fire with a chapter entitled *Racial Prejudice: The Root Cause of Japan-Bashing*. Personally, I found parts of his book to be very stimulating reading, especially since such candor can be hard to come by in Japan. He takes aim at his own country as easily as he does America, and I appreciated that.

But on the topic of racism, Ishihara-san – who became mayor of Tokyo in the late 1990s – sounded like an extremist. While granting that "discrimination is still widespread in Japan," he wildly generalized about America, saying that "Japanese should not forget that Caucasians are prejudiced against Orientals."

There are certainly plenty of white supremacists, outspoken or clandestine. Their attitudes are indefensible and often despicable, and I don't pretend to be in a position to insist that such racism is not widespread. Reporting on police brutality in America, *Amnesty International* has described it as being "persistent and widespread, especially against members of racial and ethnic minorities."

But reading Mr. Ishihara's warning to his fellow Japanese, I felt disappointed and saddened. Such a blanket statement only perpetuates fear and suspicion, and it discounts the attitudes of millions of Caucasians for whom it's obviously false. Speaking for many people, Canada's former prime minister Pierre Trudeau once remarked, "I always believed in the superiority of a multinational society."

Living in more homogeneous Japan, it has struck me that many Japanese must believe quite the opposite. Refreshing indeed are the views of Takeyo Abe, the Japanese Literary Activist of *Burakumin* background whom David Suzuki and Keibo Oiwa interviewed for their book. She gives voice to a much needed spirit of optimism on racial issues.

Speaking of intermarriage with *Burakumin*, Abe expressed her belief that "When human beings encounter and feel one another's human warmth, they will overcome their prejudices."

When it comes to their attitudes towards Caucasians, each Japanese has his or her own experience, of course, and can speak for themselves. I know only my own experience with the Japanese during my time in their country. Despite incidents of racial slurs and prejudice, I've been provided with ample evidence of racial tolerance by countless ordinary Japanese. These are people who have consistently treated me with respect and good will, both in brief, everyday encounters and through deeper friendships. They may or may not fall into the majority, but these people transcend a racist way of thinking, and I'm convinced there are millions of Japanese much like them.

One of my university students invited me to stay with her extended family in the countryside outside Gifu, with three generations living under one roof. They welcomed me into their home and hearts in the most wonderfully gracious manner. I stayed with them over two nights and three days, and they made me feel right at home. From the grandparents on down, they were about as liberal-minded as you can get. I was very moved by their kindness and generosity, and I left Gifu feeling affection and respect for them all.

Such people may have little power to change a system with entrenched patterns of discrimination, but they've made all the difference in my perceptions of Japan. The latest verbal gaffe by some elderly and racist politician always makes it into the news. Needless to say, we know that members of the Ku Klux Klan do not speak for all Americans. Given 10,000 acts of kindness and one of intolerance, we all know which one we'll be reading about in the mainstream press.

Discrimination versus Tolerance

Unaddressed racial issues are a central feature of Japanese life. Though few Japanese ever talk about such things, it's a simple fact that second- and third-generation Koreans in Japan are still struggling to be recognized as equals. They've long faced discrimination. Many bitter feelings between Korea and Japan remain to be resolved after Japan's 35 years of occupation, and the bringing of several million Koreans to Japan as slave labor.

Some Bangladeshi, Indian and Filipino people I've spoken with have talked about feeling condescended to by the Japanese. I don't pretend to know what it's like for the Asian people I've met to do the jobs they do; some work as maids, others as rug salesmen or construction workers. I've only heard their stories. Many came to do jobs most Japanese now refuse to do, work that is *kiken, kitsui and kitanai* (dangerous, strenuous, dirty).

Yet, other than those in the sex trade, most who have recently arrived are hardly here against their will, any more than I am. We've all come because Japan offered us something our own countries didn't. As for foreigners from other Asian countries, of interest to me was the discovery that many Japanese people do not even consider themselves to be *Asians*. In their own minds, the Japanese more commonly think of themselves as standing apart from Asia, not to mention the rest of the world. The sense of *Japaneseness* is definitely the great binding force.

Whereas American or Canadian passport holders are citizens of a country, regardless of racial ancestry, Japanese passport holders are almost exclusively members of the Japanese race, though there are exceptions. I do know one American married to a Japanese who's managed to secure citizenship, so it can be done, but it's rare. The fact that someone born in America is automatically an American citizen is an alien notion in Japan. This country is still doing its best to preserve its much-valued homogeneity.

So there's no getting around the fact that many 'non-Japanese' have a rough time in Tokyo because of their racial background. Trying to rent an apartment can be very frustrating; you almost always have to ask a Japanese friend to serve as your *hoshōnin* (guarantor). Most Japanese view and treat *foreigners* quite differently from themselves – they have a tight cultural and linguistic identity, and they believe that we just don't fit in. Every now and again, I still see signs in Tokyo that say, "No foreigners" or "Japanese only."

I remember answering our home phone in my first year here in Tokyo. I soon realized that the man had the wrong number, and I did my best to explain that to him in my fledgling Japanese. His reply was, "*Gaijin dame*" (Foreigners no good!). Then he hung up.

Experiences like this can have a chilling effect on you, especially in the early going. There's simply no denying that Japan has an issue with xenophobia. But over time, I learned that it's a big mistake to make a federal case out of these incidents and focus all your energy on them. For one thing, you encounter such characters everywhere you go in the world. In my own case, the experience I had on the phone has never been repeated.

As a *gaijin*, it's helpful to keep reminding yourself that most Japanese people shy away from contact with strangers of any kind - Japanese or otherwise. If you're upset about needing a *hoshōnin* to rent an apartment, you've got plenty of company with single Japanese women. Most of them also need a guarantor.

If you're not Japanese, people's avoidance of you may simply mean that they don't know you and they feel no social connection with you. This can be misconstrued as a racial issue when it's nothing of the kind. Most Japanese react much the same way to other Japanese whom they have no social connection with.

My American friend, April, wailed to me on the phone one night. She'd seen a drunk Japanese *salaryman* fall down on the steps in Kawasaki Station and just lie there. Nobody stopped to help; they just walked around him - shades of New York City at its worst. Generally speaking, Japanese feel great responsibility for those with whom they share *giri* relationships. But people outside their work, family or friendship 'circles' are not their concern.

Some Japanese who have emigrated to Canada and the U.S. speak and write about their initial astonishment at being aided by complete strangers. They say it would seldom have happened to them in Japan. Linguistics Professor Hiroko Noro, who came to Canada from Japan in 1982 and now works at the University of Victoria in B.C., remembers her early experiences at the University of Toronto this way: "Several classmates also offered support by lending their notes and editing my papers. I found their compassion for a stranger pretty amazing and unlike anything I'd ever experienced before."

Ironically, many foreigners in Japan *do* get helped in this way. On my way to a party in Tokyo, I once asked a Japanese construction worker for directions. I showed him my map, and he was kind enough to walk half a block to be sure I knew where to go. Arriving at the party, I told the story to a Japanese woman, saying how much I liked this side of Japan. "Well," she replied somewhat resentfully, "he wouldn't have helped a Japanese person like that."

Interestingly, the Western experience of the Japanese is often completely different from their experience of themselves. Maggie's student, Hanae, once told us, "We found out from Westerners that we're 'kind.' We never thought of ourselves that way."

When it comes to interracial relations with the Japanese, I have a clear sense that what a great many Japanese people most look for in non-Japanese is amicability and trustworthiness. If they can really be assured that you are friendly and can be trusted, your racial background will not usually stand in the way. When it comes to *foreigners*, Japanese people seem to need a lot of reassurance that we're not dishonest, dangerous or emotionally volatile.

The discriminatory barriers against foreigners that are entrenched in the system here obviously get foreign press attention, and so they should. But so should the attitudes of individual Japanese who have few or no racist sentiments.

Where's the press coverage for the Japanese people I'm continually meeting who bend over backwards to help foreigners, and who have no use for Japan's traditional xenophobia? Where are the banner headlines for those who call me over to join them for a drink in the park during *Hanami*?

When there's a problem, it often has to do with language more than anything else. When I traveled around India, I was able to communicate with people - in English - from the day I arrived. By contrast, *Nihongo* is a formidable and ever-present barrier in Japan. It confronts you everywhere you turn.

I met one Canadian woman briefly in *Kinokuniya* (an import grocery store) who'd been in Japan seven months. She'd come here to explore her roots. Her grandparents, both Japanese, had emigrated to Canada, where her Japanese-Canadian parents were both born. Being *sansei* (third generation overseas), she spoke very little Japanese.

When I asked her how she was doing, she told me she felt excluded and uncomfortable in Japan, and looked forward to going home at the end of the year. Although she has Japanese ancestry, going back centuries, she had no doubt about her identity now. She's Canadian, and now knows from experience that few people in Japan consider her to be Japanese.

In total contrast with this, my colleague Lisa - who has an American father and a Japanese mother - is right at home in Japan. But Lisa is perfectly fluent in the language. She once told me that she has her mother to thank for that. Her father only spoke English, but her mother insisted on speaking Japanese to her when she was a child. She resented it at the time, but as a result of this - and her culturally appropriate behavior - Lisa has no problem fitting into Japanese life. Hearing her story and others like it, I've come to believe that language, attitude and social manner are the crucial factors in overcoming cultural and racial barriers in Japan.

I tell my Japanese students that in increasingly multicultural Canada, you risk seriously offending someone by asking them where they're from. With nothing to go on but their racial features, you've got no way of knowing how long a person has lived in a city like Toronto or Vancouver. Someone may look like they're from China, Japan or India, but they may well be third-generation Canadian.

I go on to encourage them not to make assumptions about how long a foreign resident has been in Tokyo. I teach them to ask the question, "How long have you been in Japan?" instead of "Where are you from?" As I explain this, they always listen intently. It's just a way of thinking they've never been exposed to before.

Many in the younger generation are opening up in ways their parents and grandparents couldn't have imagined. They're hungry for contact with people from outside Japan. They respond readily to gestures of good will from foreigners, regardless of the origin of the person expressing them. Millions have now traveled overseas, and they've returned with an expanded view of themselves as people, and as Japanese. It may take a few decades, but the changing attitudes of these young people will eventually impact official Japan in a big way.

As a white North American, I recognize that I'm generally given more favorable treatment in Japan than black Americans, or people from Asian countries such as India. A Japanese friend affirmed the same thing one day, telling me she thought Japanese society is guilty of reverse discrimination – preferential treatment for whites. I think Japan's defeat and occupation by American forces after World War II predisposed this country to such a bias, ambivalent as that deference often is.

But many Japanese demonstrate great breadth of spirit. I have an Indian friend and colleague who tells me his students have consistently approached him with warmth and kindness. My Bangladeshi friend, Arun, and his Japanese wife received many gifts of flowers from well-wishers when they opened their new restaurant. To say that all Japanese are racists is as nonsensical as saying the same thing about all Americans. It's harmful and wrong.

Needed: Respect and Tolerance All Round

Living in Japan throughout the period when this country became powerful enough economically to be constantly in the news, it was impossible not to notice that issues of Japan's institutionalized racist policies suddenly became headliners. Clearly, these issues became important in the Western press because Japan was now an economic threat, not because mainstream America had suddenly grown concerned over Japan's treatment of the *Burakumin*.

Every possible negative point of view about Japan was trotted out, and people I knew who were living in the U.S. told me that anti-Japanese sentiment was strong and unrelenting. Japanese children in schools in the States and elsewhere get called 'Jappie' at such times, and many get beaten up.

It was an intense time to be in Japan. Books with titles like *The Coming War with Japan* were selling well. During the early '90s, I remember sitting in my living room in Tokyo and watching a CBS news clip. 10 or 12 American midwest good-old boys were dropping a 10-ton concrete ball on a Japanese car with the rising sun painted on its flank. Someone was gleefully burning a Japanese flag.

They were venting their anger at the unfairness in Japanese trading practices. No doubt they were emboldened by American media reports, which revealed the ways corporate Japan strictly limits the import of foreign cars, while enjoying open season in America.

I remember having very mixed feelings as I watched. On the one hand, I empathized with these guys, and I felt I understood their anger. I knew the statistics: In 1990, Japanese car manufacturers sold 7.8 million cars to their domestic market in Japan. At the same time, Japan imported a mere 220,000 cars from all other countries combined, amounting to a mere 3% of domestic sales.

Meanwhile, in the same year, Japan exported 5.7 million cars worldwide, enough to secure an incredible 30% of the U.S. market. Despite endless discussions and agreements in the years since then, American negotiators have been only marginally successful at righting this imbalance in the 'car wars,' the prime cause of Japan's trade surplus with the U.S. In the words of Asian expert Robert Elegant, the Japanese "are ruthless in commerce."

But as I sat watching, I also wondered how my Japanese neighbors - above, below and on either side of me in our four-story *manshon* (apartment block) - were feeling as they watched this symbolic attack and the burning of their flag by Americans. It was undoubtedly on Japanese television news - they never miss a story like this. Did they feel that 'all Americans' hate them? I wondered about that for a long time.

It must have struck at least some Japanese as sour grapes. After all, wasn't it the Americans with their consumer reports who'd kept telling Japan how great its cars were? Their message was loud and clear: Japan's cars were better. Given such rave reviews for their own products, why on earth would people from a recently humiliated nation as proud as Japan - hungry to finally come out on top of the invincible Americans - have gone out and bought the very cars that Americans themselves were passing over in favor of Japan's Toyotas and Hondas?

Double-damning was the fact that U.S. car makers had been ultra-slow to make cars suited to the Japanese market. I knew from living in Tokyo that most American cars were much too big for Japan's narrow streets, and the steering wheels were on the wrong side. How many people in America even knew that the Japanese drive on the left?

Then there was the incredible irony of one tidbit of information I'd come across. Way back in 1960, the U.S. had grown concerned about the imbalance in trade with Japan in automobiles. But it was America that had the huge trade surplus then. It was so unbalanced that the U.S. government took steps to restrict the sale of American cars to Japan. This was done to allow the Japanese to get their own industry on its feet. Now here were the same Americans, 30 years later, at the mercy of a vehicular King Kong they'd helped to create.

As we sat in Japan watching all of this go down, 'polls' we read about in the newspaper began to seem absurd. First, there'd be a media storm about Japan being an unfair trader. Then polls were conducted in the U.S., asking the question, "Was Japan an unfair trader?" Why yes, Americans thought so. Yet one poll also revealed that 40% of Americans believed the U.S. was running a trade surplus with Japan. Ignorance appeared to be in the driver's seat.

As for the car-bashing Americans, I wondered how those same mid-west protesters would feel if they saw the reverse scenario being played out on their own television sets: a protest where Japanese men were destroying an American-made product, while the stars and stripes burned in the wind.

I imagined they'd have felt much as they did in 1979, when Iranian students burned the American flag as they took over the U.S. Embassy in Teheran. In other words – angry and violated.

I assumed that as the good-old boys burned the Japanese flag, they didn't stop to think that the message received by your average Japanese – sitting in his or her living room halfway across the global village – might be a message of racial hatred. I also wondered if scenes like this helped explain Shintaro Ishihara's comment that "Caucasians are prejudiced against Orientals."

Having lived in Iran for most of 1978 – in the days leading up to its revolution – I knew I needed to give some thought to how my Japanese neighbors were responding to this. Although most Iranians had been very warm and friendly, I remembered receiving a note under our door one day, one widely distributed to foreigners that said, "Yankee go home. Now you know why we hate you." Later, the bread kiosk across the street from our house was set on fire, and eventually we had to flee the country. Three weeks later, the British Council – where I'd worked – was burned to the ground.

Did I need to be concerned for my safety here in Japan, because news items like this were now being aired on television? No, I soon concluded. Even as a white guy living in Tokyo, ever conspicuous amidst the sea of Japanese faces all around me everyday, I knew I could go downstairs later that day and pick up some milk in the convenience store. I didn't have to fear that someone would attack me because of what they'd seen on television. Most people would totally ignore me, and that was sometimes unpleasant. But I could feel quite confident that they wouldn't pose a threat to my safety, and that struck me as pretty remarkable.

There had only been a handful of occasions in all my years in Japan when I'd felt really threatened in a manner that had racial overtones. I suspected it was more than I could say if I were a Japanese living in the States and the scenario were reversed. I doubt if I'd have been nearly as confident about my safety.

This is not to say that Japan is free of racially motivated violence and verbal slurs. Like America and most every country in the world, Japan has complex and ever-changing racial issues, and some Japanese say quite appalling things about the foreigners in their midst. Oddly, through teaching young Japanese, I've learned that most grow up believing there is no racism in Japan. They think of racism as a 'foreign' issue faced only by other countries with multi-racial populations.

If young Japanese are to recognize the many forms racism can take – and the racial issues that exist within their own country – they need much more exposure to this topic. Most have been shielded from examining such problems. If Japan's birth rate keeps dropping as its population ages, this country is almost certainly going to need more immigrants to bolster its workforce in the years ahead. Educating the young to be tolerant of racial diversity will help to avoid problems later.

In my own experience living and working in Japan, I recognize that many institutions are taking significant steps towards accommodating the needs of 'foreigners.' My local prefectural government now publishes brochures in four languages to help foreign residents get the help they need. Another local government responded to the diverse range of non-Japanese-speaking residents living in its jurisdiction by setting up a multilingual 911-style exchange to deal with emergencies. I suspect it's quite frustrating to the Japanese that they adopt these measures and then get so little credit for them in the Western press. I, for one, applaud such efforts.

Shōrai-dai University used to have a six-year limit on foreign teachers, but that was finally changed. Some foreign teachers have now been allowed to stay on staff indefinitely. Meanwhile, the university has begun hiring teachers from a greater variety of racial backgrounds and treating them equally.

It took a long time for change to come about, but to the administration's credit, it eventually did. Shōrai-dai comes out looking good on this issue. Many other universities in Japan still retain strict limits on 'foreigners,' restricting us to arrangements such as one-year contracts, renewable three times, or keeping us on part-time contracts with no benefits.

Small cities like Utsunomiya and Hamamatsu, both within an hour and a half of Tokyo by *shinkansen*, have a bit of a multicultural flavor to them now.

This is because thousands of Brazilians and Peruvians with Japanese parents or grandparents were encouraged to come or return to Japan, to fill a labor shortage.

On my trip to Hamamatsu to visit the Yamaha piano factory, I was surprised at how much their presence has influenced the city. The Japanese give these 'foreign-Japanese' specific designations such as *issei* – the generation that emigrated – and *nisei* – the second generation overseas but the first one born in the foreign country. These extroverted Brazilians with Japanese ancestry are now settling in, and they have their own newspaper and radio station in Hamamatsu. Even in homogeneous Japan – despite the resistance of those who would prefer to keep all foreigners out – small but significant changes in the direction of greater social diversity are slowly occurring.

With my Japanese friends and acquaintances, I seldom feel racial overtones or barriers. The issue just doesn't come up, and dozens of my friends have married across cultures. It's certainly true that some Japanese parents disown daughters who decide to marry non-Japanese partners, but others simply accept it. This mixed response to intermarriage is hardly unique to Japan.

Children of mixed marriages sometimes have a difficult time coping with taunts from other children. They may get bullied because they speak English so well, or they get called *hafu* (half Japanese) in the playground. Again, such harassment is obviously not restricted to Japan. With help from their parents, most of the children I know from racially mixed backgrounds seem to be doing quite well, especially in Tokyo, where they usually have friends with similar backgrounds. Awareness of the need for acceptance of racial differences is growing, and I believe things are slowly getting better in Japan, not worse.

Increasingly, intermarriage is simply a fact of life. According to information in *The Japan We Never Knew*, over 80% of Koreans in Japan now marry a Japanese. In a similar vein, I recently heard that over 50% of Asian-Americans now marry a partner with a non-Asian background.

As I've wandered around Japan, again and again I've come upon a little sign on people's houses that reads *May Peace Prevail on Earth*. I never did find out which organization was behind it, but the sentiment was clear. I trust that there are large numbers of Japanese who wish for nothing so much as to respect and show tolerance towards others, and to live in peace.

Our survival as a species may turn out to depend on the 21st century becoming the one in which humankind finally embraces a universal spirit, transcends identity based on race, and agrees to work together as one. That's a very tall order, but we probably don't have a prayer without it. And what a welcome contrast it would make with the racial horrors of the 20th century.

Join the Party

Being single for the first time in years, I welcome the camaraderie of my Japanese colleagues at official functions like the one I recently attended. A few of us teach classes of medical students, so Shōrai-dai's medical department invited us to their annual dinner for the second year in a row. "*Tanoshimini*," I said enthusiastically (I look forward to it).

It was an evening of great fun, and we 'foreigners' all felt comfortable, and included in every way. The fact that we weren't Japanese was quite irrelevant. Within the womb of a company or institutional 'circle,' I have always been treated magnificently in Japan.

But part of the price of feeling totally part of the group does come in a glass. I've gone back and forth with the pressure to drink here many times, but now I usually just surrender and join the party. More than any other country I've lived in, alcohol is the means by which Japanese open up with each other.

I actually heard of a Christian missionary who came here to spread the Good Word, and ended up opening a bar. He concluded that this was the best way to make progress talking about the ways of the spirit in Japan!

As always, we opened the ceremonies with a *Kampai* (Cheers!) – a toast with beer. The food was incredible, all catered for us in a luxurious private restaurant. Oh, we of great good fortune! We sat on *tatami* mats, leaned back on fold-up chairs, and listened to short speeches. The first few were somewhat formal, but even they were sprinkled with humor. This was a gathering of intimate colleagues who knew each other well.

We soon got into the *saké*, and eventually moved on to the whiskey. Everyone was pouring for each other with great good cheer. Before long, the jokes and the laughter were ongoing. It occurred to me that imagining Japan without alcohol is a bit like contemplating Hawaii without surf. In the *Land of Wa*, this is the wave everyone rides on.

I confess that the rest of the evening begins to fade in memory. But I do remember the head of the department falling over backwards on his fold-up chair, and all of us howling with laughter. The next thing I knew, he was crawling around on all fours. Of course, he was entertaining us with a masterful show of his not being above such a performance, in spite of being the director.

This is how Japan lets its collective hair down. All that takes place in drunken revelry is fair, and promptly forgotten. I could have stood up and laughed like a wild hyena, and nobody would have held it against me the next day. It's a culturally sanctioned release valve, and it's hard to imagine what straitlaced daytime Japan would do without it.

When the party wound down, I was sent home in a taxi all the way to

Chofu, a $100 fare, paid for by Shōrai-dai. The outskirts of Tokyo whirled by me as I tried to guide the poor driver, now miles from his local turf. At times he knew less well than I did where we were going.

Once I was sure he knew the way, I sat quietly in the back seat. I watched the moonlight reflecting off the waters of the Tama River, and experienced a sweet moment of contented appreciation. With "the Johnny Walker wisdom running high" – as Leonard Cohen once put it so beautifully – I felt perfectly fine about Japan. I might be becoming a lush, but at least I was making my peace with my Japanese hosts.

Maintaining Perspective

I've long since concluded that many Americans, Canadians, Germans and other foreigners spend much of their time in Tokyo in a state of continual culture shock. For some, it's simply a case of oil and water – there's no reconciling the differences, and living here is like receiving daily electric culture-shock treatments. If some entrepreneur could produce 'cultural perspective' in the form of a pill, there would definitely be a market for it.

As my friends will attest, there have certainly been times when I've needed such a prescription. I'm no stranger to the emotional discussions about Japan that go on endlessly between Westerners here. Innumerable hot topics – such as the required conformity in schools, and Japan's amnesia about its military past – can lead to intense talk.

Enter my American friend and mentor, Randall, to the rescue once again. Every *gaijin* in Japan should be so lucky as to have such a friend, someone who consistently brings another way of looking at things to these heated discussions. Randall has a knack for revealing the imbalance in emotionally charged and polarized positions. The Japanese government should hire the guy as a cross-cultural consultant.

I remember one of our hot discussions well. It was memorable for what we all learned from it. A group of us were gathered for an evening in Randall's apartment in Kamakura, and Maggie was on a roll about *ijime* (student bullying) in schools, a perennial topic here.

Another teenage boy had been bullied to death, and we all agreed that it was one of the ghastly side-effects of Japan's extreme emphasis on conformity. Young Japanese school kids are sometimes tormented, or even killed by their peers, because they stand out in some way.

But Maggie then began doing what many of us do on occasion in Japan. She 'snowballed' the issue, got caught up in the emotion and started getting carried away. On the night in question, I was right in there with her. Before long, she was decrying the horrors of group tyranny in Japan, and making the case that what goes on here is without parallel anywhere else in the world.

"They actually murdered him," Maggie said at one point. "They rolled him up in a gymnasium mat and killed him. It's unbelievable."

To which Randall, her fellow American, calmly replied with a big grin, "This, from a citizen of the country that produced Jeffrey Dahlmer?"

There was a pause, and then we all burst into laughter. America could match Japan horror for horror, that was easy to see. We all relaxed after that, and started enjoying our evening together in magical Kamakura.

The Gaijin's Lament

It seems like it's stating the obvious, but what's most helpful in your daily life in Japan is just to remember to be human. After years here, you notice that some foreign residents never run out of anger at being called *gaijin* by school children. But it's usually a complete overreaction, because there's rarely anything malicious about it. It's quite innocent, and if you play with these kids, they'll often play back.

As Westerners, we undoubtedly look hilarious to Japanese children, but most of the time they're just trying to make a connection, as kids do. The ways those of us living here in Japan choose to respond to them makes a difference. More than anything they'll learn elsewhere, our reactions probably determine whether they'll like 'foreigners' or not.

Occasionally, when kids whisper *gaijin* to each other as I pass by, I'll whisper *Nihonjin* (Japanese) with the same conspiratorial secretiveness. They always get the joke and laugh immediately. I'll then point to myself and say *Kanada-jin* (Canadian). I wink, and we all go away happy with each other. When all is said and done, perhaps this is how the world actually changes for the better – one encounter at a time.

I still clearly remember being on a local train in the Japanese countryside in my very first month in Japan, way back in the autumn of 1987. Five young boys about eight years old were sitting on the other side of the carriage from me, trying to muster the courage to say something. Four of them were pressuring their buddy – the one with the best English – to speak up. He finally managed to come out with a perfectly spoken question, "Where are you from?"

"Canada," I replied, and without missing a beat, all five of them chimed in unison, "Ben Johnson!"

This, of course, was before Ben's sad demise at the Seoul Olympics, back when he was the fastest man in the world. He was also – way out in the Japanese countryside – a true hero to these five boys. The fact that he was a *gaijin*, and a black man as well, didn't matter a fig.

Equal Time for our Cultural Horrors

In Japan, 'newspaper reality' can take on too great an importance for foreign residents. Seeking to fill our cultural vacuum, we end up focusing on all of Japan's sore points, and forget to examine our own. I sometimes think we'd all be better off doing as Randall does – ignoring the English newspapers here entirely. After all, the trigger point for Maggie's exasperation about *ijime* (bullying) was something we'd all read about a few days before.

When I read yet another article about Japan being an ethnocentric nation, in complete denial of its military past, I get upset. But then I remember my dear friend Ayako. She visited Malaysia, then came back to Japan and started studying Malay. When I asked her why, she explained that she felt guilty about what Japan had done to the people of Malaysia during the war, and this was her way of atoning.

The journalist Ian Buruma writes about such gestures in his exploration of the post-war psychological burden borne by Germans and Japanese, *The Wages of Guilt*. He talks about the many Japanese "whose efforts to make public the 'sins' of their country are definitely meant as gestures of atonement. That is why they travel to China and Southeast Asia to apologize to former victims."

Individual Japanese who courageously speak up, or who take a private stand of conscience, demonstrate moral courage and sensitivity in the face of institutionalized denial. The various factions of the Japanese government never seem able to agree on how to deal with Japan's wartime actions. But the deliberate actions of conscious individuals like Ayako are more worthy of media attention than the ongoing obfuscation of the government.

Ayako once explained to me that most Japanese know what their military forces did to the people of other Asian nations during the war years, but they don't learn it in school. Japan's march into China in 1931, and the Nanking Massacre of 1937, are only touched upon in school textbooks. Students receive a very cursory presentation of this whole period; the only serious study point is on what was done to Japan in 1945.

After the war, students were basically taught to wear the cloak of victimhood – with Hiroshima as its symbol – a not surprising development given the horrors of the atom bomb. Yet as Ayako has shown me, there's much more awareness among ordinary Japanese than one might think, especially considering the censorship of textbooks.

In polls conducted in 1994 and 1996, 56% and 61% of Japanese used the word 'despise' to describe how they imagine Asian countries feel about Japan. There seems to be a keen awareness that Japan has acted in ways that have brought tremendous resentment.

The approach of the Education Ministry has been changing only glacially slowly. This has led sensitive people like Ayako to assuage their yearning for understanding and resolution in private and personal ways. But the fact that many Japanese take such actions is something that receives too little attention. Japanese tourists pour through the war museum on Sentosa Island in Singapore, so they can learn about their own wartime history.

One can find no greater example of a hero in Japan than the historian Ienaga Saburo, who has been fighting censorship of history textbooks almost single-handedly since the early 1960s. I am in awe of the courage of this man, as well as the small group of Japanese who have supported him through his long solitary quest. He has sought relentlessly to open this country up to teaching its children the truth about the actions of Japan's wartime military forces.

Recent English language publications, such as Iris Chang's painstakingly researched book *The Rape of Nanking*, are providing more widely disseminated documentation than was available before. Drawing parallels between Japanese wartime atrocities, the Holocaust in Germany and slavery in America, Chang has this to say, "Japanese culture will not move forward until it too admits not only to the world but to itself how improper were its actions of just over half a century ago."

I seldom find it appropriate to speak about the war in my university classes. But when the topic comes up in a reading we're doing, I've developed a short little talk that I'm certain my students have never heard before. I tell them that they're not personally responsible for atrocities committed against Chinese in Nanking, any more than I'm to blame for similar horrors committed against Native Americans before I was born.

Yet, I explain, we bear responsibility that comes with inheritance. I suggest that we're all obliged to become aware of our own country's transgressions. We have to acknowledge that these things happened, and experience genuine sorrow for the suffering that was caused. Then we need to do what we can to make amends, and most importantly, to vow that it must never happen again.

In the classroom, I occasionally run into flat-out denial that events like *Nanking* ever happened. But sometimes I pick up a palpable feeling of relief as I say these things. The heavy burden of guilt, silence and denial has been passed on to these young people, because so many of their leaders and elders have avoided coming to terms with the emotions generated by the war themselves.

Though I've felt too constrained to do so, I've always wanted to tell these young Japanese that if confronted overseas, they could simply say, "Yeah, our military messed up, and nobody wanted to talk about it, or admit that we started it. A lot of the soldiers were turned into monsters by the training they had to undergo."

I've no idea how a Chinese might respond to such candor from a young Japanese. But I suspect most Americans would react to that kind of honesty by saying, "Well, we screwed up in Vietnam too." And that would be quite enough said.

But such an admission requires breaking ranks with Japanese consensus reality, and there is strong social pressure not to do that.

My own sense is that despite the censorship in Japan, a great many Japanese are much like Ayako. They've thought deeply about the atrocities of the war and how Japan came to be ripped apart because of it. How could they not? Their country was decimated. On March 10, 1945, the fire-bombing of Tokyo took approximately 80,000 lives in less than three hours. The horror of it is unimaginable to me.

The ceremonies held every year at Hiroshima and Nagasaki are annual remembrances of the atomic bombings that came later that year. Those who lost family members in these bombings have obviously not forgotten.

I remember a moment I spent with one lovely student, whose father was in the war. She was a very thoughtful high-school girl. She played the violin, and I taught her English in the evenings at a private university, while I was still working at Soulful Software. In a subdued voice, on the train home from our class one night, she carefully explained to me how much her father disliked the *Banzai* chant to the Emperor. He hated all the associations it had with Japan's militaristic past.

These one-on-one encounters are much more important to me now than anything I might read in the press. Continually finding fault with this country becomes a habitual activity for many foreign residents with cultural cabin fever. I know about that, because I've been there myself.

In fact, I now understand how personal upheavals - which happen while you're living here - can get projected onto Japan. You can end up blaming this country for everything under the sun, when the real problem is something in your personal life. At least some of my confusion, anger and heartache at my breakup with Krista got directed that way. For the longest time, my inability to forgive her for what happened between us, came out as griping about Japan.

Such projection can be hard to avoid, because even as you're undergoing your inner ordeal, you're still having to endure the claustrophobic traumas of the daily commute. It's all happening in a city that seems even more alien and unmanageable because of your inner turmoil.

Most Westerners - on an almost daily basis - are reading negative articles in the newspapers about official Japan's endless stonewalling. And as a teacher, you go to work and see forms of this denial played out in the psychological makeup of your students.

But sorting out your own projections, and adopting a balanced viewpoint, eventually becomes an absolute imperative. Taking Japan to task for its social and historical nightmares is absolutely fair, provided we're prepared to examine our own culture's flaws with equal vigor. After all, most of our own atrocities – such as those committed against native Americans – were hidden for decades, and remained so until quite recently.

As I've learned to consistently look at both sides of every cultural equation, some topics, like *ijime*, lose their charge. The illusion of their being Japan-specific dissolves. It quickly becomes clear that bullying is a universal and age-old problem, hardly unique to this country.

A major challenge for foreign residents is to remain aware that we're living in a kind of bubble here. Incidents similar to the ones we're constantly reading about in the Japanese press are also happening in North America and Europe. But we're not hearing much about them. Most of the news we get is about Japan.

When you're living in Tokyo, thinking this way has an immediate pay-off – it lowers your stress level dramatically. More and more often, I find myself remembering to just live and let live.

Courting in the Dark

Being single now in Japan, and immersed in an ocean of Japanese women, the odds of my eventually turning a serious gaze towards them increased dramatically. It did, however, take most of a year for this to happen. At that point, I was to discover that a lot of what I thought I knew about women had to go out the window.

I could have guessed, given that so much else about Japanese culture is enigmatic. And being a single guy for the first time in years, I was already in unfamiliar territory, much more that I realized.

One of my first attempts to arrange a date here was a classic case of cross-cultural groping in the dark. Over a period of many months, I'd had three or four very pleasant interactions with one of the secretaries at Shōrai-dai, Ichikawa-san (Miss Ichikawa). A few times, she'd graciously written out an explanation of some *kanji* I was learning. I found myself attracted to her and one day, I spontaneously asked her if she'd like to join me for dinner on Friday night.

"Oh, I'm sorry, I'm busy that night," she said, offering no alternative date. But that hint went right over my head, and I plunged on, suggesting next Friday night.

"That would be fine," she said somewhat hesitantly, and we arranged a meeting place.

I looked forward to the date, and a week later went to the prearranged spot. She soon came running up breathlessly and exclaimed, "I'm so sorry, my mother's in the hospital with a cold. I can't meet you tonight."

"Gosh, I'm sorry to hear that," I replied. "I hope she gets better soon. Perhaps another time," I added, though I did have a funny feeling about the whole thing and wasn't sure I'd ask again.

A few days later, I learned just how little I knew about the dating code in Japan. Lisa approached me at work with her characteristic good humor, gently chiding me on my ignorance. The secretary in question, an acquaintance of hers, had come to her mid-week.

She'd been quite confused, explaining that I'd asked her out, and that she'd tried to put me off by saying she was busy. But when I'd asked a second time, she felt she had to accept my invitation so that I wouldn't lose face. After all, in the social hierarchy, I was her superior.

It wasn't that she didn't like me, but she already had a Japanese boyfriend. When she'd told him, he'd calmly suggested that she go ahead with the plan. But being a cautious woman, she didn't want to take a chance that something might develop between us. So she'd decided to use the most commonly used Japanese camouflage – the 'cold.'

If everybody who told you they have a cold in Japan actually did, you'd have to conclude that the whole country is perpetually in bed drinking fluids and taking aspirins. It's the catch-all face-saving way out of many situations. My students use it on me all the time.

I wanted to say, "I knew that." But the addition of the word 'hospital' had thrown me. I couldn't believe someone would actually make up such a thing.

No, Lisa assured me, laughing uproariously, Ichikawa-san's mother wasn't in hospital, nor did she have a cold!

Suddenly, I understood just how insulated I'd been in my *gaijin-couple-cocoon* with Krista, right here in the middle of Japanese society. If I really wanted to go out with Japanese females, perhaps dating women I worked with was not a good idea. And I was also going to have to learn a whole new way of communicating. Was there somewhere I could take lessons?

How May I Praise You?

In Japan, it can seem impossible to give anyone a bit of praise or encouragement. Many young Japanese go overseas for a month to study, and when they come back their English has noticeably improved. But if you point this out, they'll often say, "*Ie, ie, ie*" (No, no, no!), while waving their hand from side to side to discount your admiration. For public display, they're announcing, "Don't single me out for praise. I'm just like everyone else."

I spoke to one Canadian woman who got really fed up with this. She was becoming friends with a Japanese woman whose husband was a doctor, and one day at an appropriate moment in the conversation, she offered the supportive comment, "I'm sure he's a very good doctor."

"*Ie, ie, ie*," came the immediate reply.

"I felt like saying, 'Fine, he's a terrible doctor'," she told me, "I'll never recommend him to anybody!"

In getting such responses from Japanese, Westerners sometimes repeat their praise, suspecting there's been a miscommunication. This usually only leads to a doubling in the intensity of the hand waving.

I met another woman in Canada who told me a great story about this. Her daughter was teaching in Yokohama, and on a trip to Japan to visit her, the two of them went to see an artist who did watercolors.

Carol thought they were superb. She approached the artist and said, "I think your watercolors are terrific!"

The artist, a Japanese woman, quickly replied, "Oh, but not as good as yours!"

Mystified, Carol responded, "Well, I don't paint. But I can tell that yours are really well done."

"Oh, but they're not as good as yours," the artist repeated with equal conviction, deflecting the praise again.

Another common response to being praised in Japan is to humorously accuse the one extolling your virtues of engaging in flattery, with an ulterior motive. You do this by saying *goma suri* (meaning 'the grinding of the sesame seeds') while placing two fists in the air - one above the other - and making a turning motion with the upper fist. Obviously, there's plenty of room for false humility in a social environment where everyone is busy deflecting praise.

It can all be quite maddening, that is until you figure out that this is nothing more than cultural protocol. The 'correct' way to receive praise from someone in Japan is to downplay it, as though you're negating it.

But it's a mistake to conclude that you might as well quit offering praise. You just have to be prepared that when you do, you can expect it to be discounted - at least on the surface. Nevertheless, it's much appreciated, though it's helpful if you can be subtle and discreet about it. Japanese are human beings first and foremost, and who among us doesn't like being acknowledged for our abilities?

When it comes to Japanese people praising foreigners, it's sometimes done to get a 'take' on our level of humility. These days, I'm studying *Nihongo* harder than ever, and I'm now quite fascinated by the picture images you find in *kanji* characters. But it still feels a lot like *judo* did in high school - remembering the *kanji* has my brain in a hammerlock.

I confess that I still sometimes resort to using *rōmaji* - the Japanese language as written in the Roman alphabet. So when someone tells me my Japanese is *jozu* (good), I'm right in there with the best of them, "*Ie, ie, ie.*" At least in my case, I know I'm telling the truth.

Bound by the Rules

If America is ruled by legalism, one way to look at Japan is to see it as a country ruled by perfectionism. I get some mileage out of this. It helps me to deal with the psychic collisions I keep having with rules that rankle, but which everyone is compelled to abide by.

Tokyo, of course, has its good and sensible rules, without which a crowded metropolis teeming with this many people could never function as smoothly as it does. Strict rules of conduct - for crowd control, and rapid and organized movement of commuters and goods - are understood by Japanese people to be vital for everyone's survival.

But in certain social arenas where you might expect a break, there's no escaping the rules of conduct, and some of them would try the patience of a saint. Take, for example, my local public swimming pool.

It's a hot and sunny summer Saturday, and I wander off to the pool near my apartment. It's crowded, of course, but thanks to government support, the price is 100 yen. That's about a buck - a small miracle in Tokyo. So I get changed, put on my swimsuit and head into the water to have a dip. I know enough from swimming at my sports club to have a swim cap on. Even men must wear one here, to cover our locks.

After a few minutes, I've cooled off. So I put down my towel, stretch out in the sun and heave a big sigh, ready to relax. But it's a blisteringly hot day, so I pull out some sunscreen. In a flash, one of the many attendants is at my side, bowing and smiling and informing me of a pool rule - suntan lotion is not allowed.

"Oh," I murmur, glancing up at the hole in the ozone layer. There's no soap or shampoo allowed in the showers, and now no sunscreen out in the

Japanese sun. What to do? He wanders off, and I soon decide I'd better put on my T-shirt, so as not to get fried.

Within a minute, he's back. Shirts are also not okay, he regrets to tell me. I do promise I'm not making this up.

Soon after that, I leave for the day, but I come back the following Saturday. By then, I've figured out that anyone who uses sunscreen puts it on at home – or furtively, in the locker room.

On this day, I've brought a magazine and a Walkman to entertain myself. I soon discover that there are rules against both, and the chain necklace I'm wearing must also come off.

This time – on the verge of losing it – I point out to the attendant that somebody on the other side of the pool is also listening to a Walkman. Alerted to this additional infringement of the rules, he forgets about me and dashes off to intercept this other transgressor.

I also discover that every two hours, the pool is closed down for half an hour. This happens four times a day, all summer long. If you intend to spend the whole day at the pool with your kids, it can be done. But every two hours, you'll have to get dressed, go outside, wait half an hour in the lineup, and go through the whole procedure again.

I suspect it's designed this way to discourage people from staying all day. In a crowded city like Tokyo, that might prevent others from getting a turn. That's fair enough.

In Japan, you learn – again and again – not to bother asking 'Why?' too often. I've heard quite a few stories of foreigners who have almost had to be carried out of this country in straitjackets. If you intend to stay a long while, you've simply got to come to terms with the futility of resistance.

I take one final swim in the government-subsidized pool, and vow to stick to my indoor sports club from now on. After all, what did I expect for 100 yen?

I later spoke with my new Japanese friend, Masaya. He shared some more of his theories about life in modern Japan with me. He reminded me again that most Japanese feel comfortable with rule-bound situations, because that's what they're used to. They feel a need to know what they're supposed to be doing at all times, just as they did in their school years, when they were trained to follow orders with meticulous care.

According to Masaya, everyone's thinking in Japan is highly conditioned by one feature of *examination hell* – the high-school rite of passage. Throughout this period of intensive training, everyone studies with one assumption uppermost in mind. This assumption is so deeply ingrained that it unconsciously guides the rest of their lives. It goes like this: For every question, there's only one answer. It's the right answer; the others are wrong.

A fellow Canadian I met, who was teaching in a high school, had this to say: "There are so few things they can do, that most just decide it's safer to do nothing. They resign themselves to a totally passive attitude."

Within society at large, the end result appears to be this: Most people adopt the view that in any given situation, there's only one correct and acceptable way of doing things. The others are wrong. You can fight the rules against sunscreen and T-shirts all you want, but most of the time, you won't win. *Shōgenai* – them's the rules.

The Upside of the Rules

Singapore has gained a worldwide reputation for being the 'rule' capital of the world. My high-spirited American friend, Donna, spent four years at loggerheads with the rules in Japan. She then moved south to the notoriously overregulated city state. After a few years there, she assured me that Japan looked good by comparison. Singapore was scrupulously clean, had a great medical system and was a good place to do business. But it was too focused on 'money' and seriously lacking in soul.

She felt even more constrained in Singapore, but had fewer emotional outlets. Much of modern Japan lives and dies by its rules. But at least it has its out-of-bounds areas where the rules fall away – such as the all-night dance bar where Donna met Toky, her Peruvian husband.

The strict rules of Japan's social chess board are about as clear-cut as the rules of chess itself. In order to play and win, you have to learn the rules. In one area of life, there's a lot of latitude. In another, there's absolutely none.

It's also unfair to enjoy the fruits of the system's efficiency without acknowledging that the way it's set up has contributed to that efficiency. The undeniable truth is that a great many things in Japan work incredibly well.

Take, for example, the Japanese *takubin* delivery service. You can drop off a package at most convenience stores and later in the day, someone will pick it up, then truck or fly it to its destination in record time. I once received a large package at 9:20 a.m. that had been deposited at a 7/11 store 55 kilometers away the previous afternoon.

Why is it so efficient? Well, to get the ball rolling, you have to fill out a form in 'heptagoplicate' (seven copies) for each package you send. I remember when 'triplicate' first came out in North America, and we thought life was getting crazy then. Once you've filled the forms in, the convenience store attendant carefully weighs and measures your package with a tape measure and dutifully records the details. If there are no problems, you'll be through the procedure in about 10 or 15 minutes, and your packages will be on their way.

This is what happens most of the time. It's a great service. If they have time, the store attendants will even help you to write out the address in *kanji*. As long as you don't try to do anything that goes against the grain, all goes well.

Occasionally, there's a glitch, and when that happens, it's you against the almighty rules, and good luck to you! After all, they are what keep the whole operation flowing smoothly. I once got through the paper trail, only to learn that the length and height and width of my package added up to exactly 121 cm. The problem was that the dimensions of a package cannot exceed 120 cm.

I then had to try to convince the university student doing this part-time job to let it pass just this one time. I suggested to him that one centimeter over the limit was not going to bring on the end of the world. I also promised that I would never let it happen again.

He was not persuaded by any of this. But I was determined that I was not going to repack everything in a new box, all for the sake of a baby-fingernail-width of space.

Finally, after about 10 minutes of fruitless cajolery, I took another tack. I suggested that, if asked, he could say that the *gaijin* didn't understand the rules, and it was impossible to explain them to him. With that, he finally relented. He seemed relieved to have a rationale that allowed him to get rid of me. But this was obviously a major infringement of the rules, and he was uncomfortable breaking them.

This is vintage Japan at its most controlling. As a good citizen, I ought to have gone back home and unpacked the box. Then I should have scoured the neighbourhood to find another one a teensy bit smaller, repacked and retaped the whole thing, and come back two hours later.

The problem confronting my convenience store clerk was that in my formative years in Canada, I was taught something he's never heard of – to 'question authority' when it's being unreasonably inflexible. Surprisingly, in that instance, I succeeded in getting the rule bent. But I doubt if most Japanese would have had the same success, if they'd even bothered to try.

Yet the rigmarole of this one encounter aside, as long as you don't throw a spanner in the works as I did, the procedure normally goes like clockwork. I gratefully acknowledge that here, in this densely populated city, I've never lost a single package with Japan's *takubin* service. Nor have I even encountered a delay in delivery. The packages are always delivered, safe and sound, the next day within the Tokyo area, or within two days most anywhere else in the country. You can count on it; the efficiency is extraordinary.

By contrast, the very first time I sent a parcel through a courier service in the U.S., I couldn't help but notice how lax the system was in comparison with Japan's. And what do you know – the parcel got lost. It was sent to the wrong address, and it took days and many phone calls to track it down.

The Japanese have ample cause to feel somewhat smug about the upside of their rule-bound systems. In my experience, small mistakes and screw-ups are much more common now in North America than they are in Japan.

As for the postal service, in what other country in the world can you find a list of undelivered letters addressed to foreigners in the daily newspapers? Mail service here is superb, with six-day delivery. New Year's cards called *nengajo* (Japan's equivalent of Christmas cards) are carefully sorted and stored by post office workers. Those mailed before the deadline – usually December 20 – are then all delivered on exactly the same day – January 1.

I once sent a registered letter to my mother in Canada. As always, the letter was out of this country and on its way within a day or two. But when it arrived in Canada, it got lost in a drugstore post office for 10 days. Such things seldom happen in Japan, even though some business practices can seem antiquated. In the central post office near Tokyo Station, you can still watch postal workers rubberstamping piles of forms, one after another, the old-fashioned way. Yet, in all my years in the Land of the Rising Sun, I know of only one letter that's gone astray. Mail sent from the States and Canada with half of my Japanese address missing has still reached me.

Aspects of this highly regulated efficiency are all-pervasive in Tokyo, and you find examples of it sprinkled throughout your life. My current morning newspaper *The Daily Yomiuri* is normally delivered by a young fellow on a motor scooter at around 4:30 or 5:00 in the morning. He bounds up the stairs to the third floor and sticks it in the letter slot in my door.

But every now and again – as would happen anywhere – there's a mix-up, perhaps when someone else substitutes and takes his route. One morning, after a few hours of writing, I took a break to read the newspaper. I went to pull it out of the letter slot at 11:10 a.m., only to discover it hadn't been delivered that day. So I called downtown to let them know.

Twenty minutes later, at precisely 11:30, a dapper-looking gentleman in a suit showed up at the door with the newspaper, apologizing and bowing profusely. Keep in mind that this is in Tokyo, a huge sprawling maze of streets and trains going on for miles, and I live in the suburbs. If this does not impress, I'd like to be where you're living.

It's clearly more than unrelated good luck and circumstance that my *soba-*shop delivery boy is so punctual; that the women at my travel agency respond to my inquiries at lightning speed with a detailed fax; that on occasions when a train is in the station but not ready for boarding, people all wait patiently in line on the platform until the conductor announces they can get on.

Similarly, it's no coincidence that the convenience store beneath my apartment – completely gutted one day – has been remodeled and reopened for business within two weeks, while the delivery of my new computer shelf, or washing machine, arrives exactly when they say it will, from right across the city.

They even let you specify 'morning' or 'afternoon' delivery, a request you can't easily get honored back in Canada anymore.

There's a phenomenal work and service ethic in place in Japan. It's predicated on serving the customer carefully and without error, but always according to the manual. This combination of social discipline and allegiance to procedure produces a society in which little mistakes happen much less often.

You seldom receive the wrong change in Japan – they almost always count it twice or even three times. I rarely come across an error in dealings with banks, companies and stores. By contrast, when I return to North America, these are surprisingly frequent occurrences. I've yet to rent a video which isn't rewound in Japan; either the last customer or the store clerk has made sure of that.

Constraining as they can be at times, there's definitely an upside to the rules that make this country run. Obviously, there are links between them and the impressive efficiency that results. My Western education taught me to bristle at rules that seem excessive or ridiculous, but I also learned to give credit where credit is due.

What Matters Most

In Japan, what matters most is how things are done. In other words, 'form' trumps 'content.' In many instances, one could say that The Form *is* the Meaning, much as The Medium is the Message. You see this all around you in myriad ways. At the worst of times, it can be mind-numbing. On a good day, you remember just to laugh, and go with the Japanese flow.

Every year, our university chairman selects somebody to be the 'non-Japanese' representative at the monthly departmental meetings of Japanese faculty. This past year, it was my turn. Though my ability in Japanese is steadily improving, it's still woefully inadequate for understanding the jargon of a meeting held at native-speaker speed, or for reading the agenda, a thick booklet of pages passed out to everyone.

That was not a problem, however. I was not required to understand anything or to report back to my English-speaking colleagues. It's simply on the books that a 'foreign body' must be present at these meetings.

So once a month for a year, it was my job just to be there, along with about 50 Japanese – mostly male. I used the time to mark student papers and study *kanji*. Half a dozen of the men simply dozed off.

Though I needn't have done so, from time to time my own duplicity led me to cast looks of feigned comprehension at our director. My sense of *tatemae* told me I had to keep up the pretense that I was at least paying attention.

He's a very friendly man whose eloquent tongue knows no fatigue. Though there were a few questions, and some points to be made from faculty members after he'd finished, it was, by and large, just a long-winded 'read-out' of administrative decisions already made.

As Asia expert Robert Elegant puts it in *Pacific Destiny*, "Japan's consensus is not formed by free interchange of ideas. A *directed* consensus, it is formed by a very small group of the elite."

The whole process feels like a 'form' that must be filled: monthly faculty meetings. Discussion is minimal, because the content of the meeting has all been taken care of. Administrative officials have dealt with that long before the meeting takes place.

Yet, the Japanese seem to be addicted to meetings. They love getting together to listen to someone read an important document, outlining plans made by absent administrators.

In the view of some of my Japanese friends, organizations here do not rely on 'geniuses' or 'guiding lights' at the helm. Social order depends on everyone pulling his weight in the same direction. Members of the same institutional group trust the wisdom of their mentors above them, while guiding the neophytes below. This is the *sempai/kohei* (senior/junior) relationship - touched on by Sean Connery in the film *Rising Sun*. Most important is the feeling of mutual obligation. Everyone must show their willingness to work together co-operatively.

Sometimes it seems that the primary purpose of these meetings is simply to reinforce the unstated premise of Japanese society, "We're all in this together."

Our department also holds regular meetings for all the non-Japanese on staff, which Japanese faculty members can also attend. These meetings are similar in the sense that the agenda is basically read out to us, exactly as it's written on the paper. The *gaijin* ask a greater number of questions, but requests for changes to a plan are almost invariably met with polite resistance, or put off till later. Basically, *administrative guidance* rules life in Japan; you can't mess with decisions that have already been made.

So how do Westerners deal with a situation in which so much of life is about following prescribed and empty routines, with just going through the motions? I've taught myself to rely on these answers - you lean heavily on your ability to improvise, and you get a lot of help from your friends. Opportunities to practice ceaselessly arise.

I recently wandered through Omiya Station in the days leading up to December 25, a time when much of Tokyo is adorned with lavish Christmas decorations. I later called up my American frien Keith, a wizened longtime Tokyo resident. I wanted to talk about the incomprehensible thing I'd seen in the center of the station.

"There was this enormous stuffed dog," I told him. "It was about 30 feet high, and surrounded by all this Christmas stuff. How on earth did somebody get the idea that a dog has something to do with Christmas?"

"Ah, the Holy Dog – how quickly we forget!" replied Keith, without missing a beat. In a flash, he reminded me of how survivors deal with the circus-like nature of Japan. Foolish me – I'd forgotten Rule Number 1 yet again: Stop looking for content and meaning, when 'form' is pretty much all there is. Try filling it in with your own meaning, and remember – the absurd is best wedded to the absurd.

Nights in the Singles' Jungle

Japan is often touted as a kind of paradise for single Western men. Clearly, there are plenty of women and lots of eye candy around, but it's hardly an idyllic and problem-free utopia. My journey – from the breakdown of my relationship with Krista, through to "What now?" and on to the question, "Maybe a Japanese girl" – has been a crash course in courting techniques. Other guys I know have been quick studies, but for me, it's been a steep cross-cultural learning curve.

For one thing, an unmarried man in his late thirties or forties is called a *Peter Pan* in Japan. It did seem as if there were *Tinker Bells* everywhere I looked, but I had no idea what the rules were for someone in my situation. Perhaps I've gotten too used to rules.

I met one Japanese woman named Izumi in a great little conversation bar called *Mickey House*. It's a tiny space on the fourth floor of an office building, in an area of Tokyo called *Takadanobaba*. Run by a lighthearted Japanese couple, it's a good place to meet people. English speakers pay 350 yen for endless coffee and tea, while Japanese pay 1,500 yen, so they can practice their English in a casual setting.

I spoke with Izumi for a couple of hours, at which point she suddenly turned to me and said, "Hey, why don't we live together?"

That was the end of any remaining assumptions I had about Japanese women being shy, less than forthcoming, or always prepared to wait for the man to make the decisions. Izumi knew exactly what she wanted, and I guess I'd passed the interview.

I mentioned something about taking a bit of time to get to know each other. We then met one more time a few weeks later, after which I returned to Canada to attend to family matters. When I got back, I learned from her employer that she'd quit her job and left no forwarding address. Izumi was long gone – on a new manhunt, no doubt.

My good friend, Ayako, started teaching *salsa* dancing, so I took classes from her every Sunday for ten weeks. Then I decided to hit the town and test my style. At a Latin bar near Ebisu called *Bodegitas*, I asked a Japanese woman to dance. Still rooted to her chair, she asked me where I was from.

"Canada," I replied. She laughed and said, "You can't dance salsa!"

Suffice it to say that the aftermath of my breakup with Krista was a challenging, topsy-turvy time. With the Western females I tried to get something happening with, one or the other of us always struck out.

At one point, Maggie set up a 'blind brunch' for me and an American friend of hers. My blind date then showed up late, briefly said hello and immediately got into an intense conversation with someone else for the rest of the meal. Perhaps she felt as uncomfortable as I did about the whole thing. Later, Maggie called to tell me how upset she was with her friend.

"It's no problem," I said, "it's obviously not meant to be."

So I was surprised when the woman in question called me a few days later to apologize. She asked if we could try again. I reluctantly agreed, and on our next rendezvous, she was 45 minutes late! As this had been a pattern of Krista's, I took it as a sign. It was time to give American women a rest, and to figure out how to date their Japanese sisters.

I eventually started dating a Japanese woman named Makiko. I met her one night at Arun's bar, where I was studying Japanese on my own. When I asked her for a little help, she responded readily. Before long, we were seeing a lot of each other.

It was a new and sometimes uncomfortable experience being 'checked out' in public everywhere we went. I wondered how many Japanese people disapproved of such cross-cultural liaisons. At times, I felt more conspicuous than ever.

But Makiko had a gentle disposition, and I was soon very glad we'd met. Although we only saw each other for six months, I'll always be grateful to her and remember her fondly, and I'm sure she'll do the same with me. If she hadn't come along when she did, I suspect I might have stayed bitter at Krista for much longer and sunk into a real funk. Instead, through knowing Makiko, a new world opened up for me. I suddenly had the beginnings of a much better understanding of Japanese women.

In *gaijin* circles in Japan, one prevalent view among Western men is that Western women are jealous and angry. That's because 'their guys' are choosing to get involved with Japanese women. Some clearly have the perception that all of us take advantage of Japanese women, as though they can't take care of themselves.

One night, I started talking to a Japanese girl in a frantic bar called *Deja Vu* in *Roppongi*. I'd barely said a word to her when a British woman, on some kind of vigilante crusade, came over and shook her finger at me. She stopped just long enough to shout, "You leave her alone!" Then she stormed off across the bar, no doubt on the lookout for other cross-cultural encounters she didn't approve of.

It's exasperating to some Western women that given a choice, a Western man would choose a Japanese woman. Stereotypical rationalizations abound to explain it away. The most common is that such guys are all looking for a traditional woman they can dominate. Another is that they don't have any other choice: They're social misfits who couldn't attract a Western woman to save their life.

And what about the part Japanese women play in starting relationships with foreign men? On another night, I met a much saner British woman in a calmer bar called *What the Dickens*. She quietly shared her views with me.

"Japanese women are ruthless at getting what they want," she said. "They don't care if they get in-between a Western guy and his wife. I've known quite a few couples that have broken up here because the man fell for a Japanese girl."

That had not been the case with Krista and me, but I had also heard such stories. In the bars of Tokyo, foreigners compare notes. Theories, impressions and generalizations abound, and everyone has their own viewpoint.

In the meantime, my *Nihongo* is improving. At times, I feel like I've been given a whole new lease on life in Japan. After Krista and I separated, I no longer had an American partner to constantly bounce ideas off. I began to realize how stale some of my viewpoints had become. For years, we had mutually reinforced, on a daily basis, our Anglo-American attitudes and biases. I now recognize how that prevented me from reaching a better understanding of the Japanese people.

My longtime Japanese friends have been consistently supportive of me during the years I've been here. I've grown to value many things about them, and I appreciate their generosity and goodwill more than ever. Going through my personal trauma of separation in their midst confirmed all of this in a powerful way.

At one point along the line, I actually called Ayako one night and suggested we start dating.

"Well," she replied, "if you'd asked me a few years ago, I'd have definitely said yes. But we Japanese have a window on these things. It's only open for a while, and then it closes."

So my stumbling about in the singles' jungle continues. Meanwhile, Ayako and I remain very good friends.

My writing has been another essential friend – the unfolding saga of an often-baffled Westerner's encounter with Tokyo and the Japanese people. Mine is certainly not the story of someone who peeled away all the mysteries of 'being Japanese,' if such a thing is even possible. But seeing Japan through the eyes of the Japanese women I'm getting to know, I definitely feel like I'm rediscovering the country. That's bringing small revelations, one after another.

I now recognize that I won't ever fully understand what it's like to be Japanese. I'll never have the perspective that comes from having been brought up here, just as a Japanese can't ever know the same about my culture. As a Westerner in Japan, it's wise to acknowledge that you're learning and guessing about a lot of things, and you always will be.

Anyone for a Night in a Capsule?

Ever since I arrived in Tokyo, I've heard about these strange tubular places where you can stay if you get caught out late at night. They're called *capseru hoteru* - capsule hotels. They're unique, quite unlike *love hotels*, or any other accommodation on earth, for that matter. But just how unique I could never have imagined, not without checking in and spending the night.

I don't know why, but I was always curious about these places. Years went by, and the time never came when I needed to stay in one. Nobody else I knew had ever done so either. Then one Saturday night, I just got tired of waiting for a reason. I decided it was time to do some investigative sleep research.

I went downtown, visited some friends for dinner and watched an N.H.L. playoff game on video - *Hockey Night in Tokyo* - sent from fellow hockey devotees in Canada to Brian, our local hockey guru. When the party broke up, I said good night to everyone, and caught the train to Shibuya, with the intention of finding and checking into the local *capseru*.

My fascination with these places had always stemmed from the images that sprang to mind when I heard that word: capsule.

"What exactly are we talking about here?" I wondered.

I would visualize myself curled up inside a gigantic *Contact C* capsule, or a John Glenn early-astronaut space capsule, or a 'human' time capsule. The word has so many splendid visual associations.

I continued to wonder what these places actually look like. I'd heard that they're frequented by drunk *salarymen* who miss their last train home (trains in Tokyo stop running around midnight or 1:00 a.m.). They're a great help to sober *salarymen* as well, who have worked too late to even bother going home. Traveling salesmen also use them, and so do students who can't afford a regular hotel.

Inquiring at the Shibuya police box as to the whereabouts of the nearest *capseru hoteru*, I was pointed in the direction of *Dogenzaka*, an area that includes Love Hotel Hill, where hundreds of love hotels are all packed together. After about a five-minute walk, I glanced up to catch a glimpse of one English word written in blazing neon: CAPSULE. It was way up on top of what turned out to be a 10-story building, still another few blocks away.

Once up close, I discovered that the building itself looked a lot like a capsule, elongated and standing on its head. It was tubular in shape, rising like a thumb into the evening sky from a small patch of land, the optimal money-making design in land-starved Tokyo.

Wandering up a circular staircase to the second floor, I came upon a set of automatic sliding-glass doors. Once through them, I found myself in what is undoubtedly an excellent candidate for 'smallest hotel lobby category' in the *Guiness Book of Records*. There was a tiny *genkan* where you took off your shoes, then one step up, a little front desk, behind which a young man and a woman were knocking elbows. Except for a minuscule alcove on the left, with a pay phone in it, that was it for the lobby.

Inside of two minutes, they'd processed my American Express card – 3,950 yen (or about $35 U.S.) – and given me my room key. Off I went to find Capsule 406.

It occurred to me that most of us – on checking into a hotel – probably have much the same thought once we get our key: "Hmm, I wonder what the room's like?"

What a bizarre feeling it was to be thinking, "I wonder what my capsule is like?" I felt like I was in a sci-fi flick in the year 2116.

Up I went in the elevator to find out. The doors to the fourth floor opened to reveal another small alcove. It had a table and two chairs, and a wall of lockers. They were much smaller than even the tiniest-sized lockers in the train stations. Inside locker 406, I found a face towel, a toothbrush with a tiny tube of toothpaste, and a *yukata* (cotton robe).

"Not a bad start," I mused.

Then I headed down a narrow corridor, both sides of which I could just about touch with my elbows. There was a room on the left with a couple of toilets, three urinals and one shower. On the right, there was another alcove. It had six sinks equipped with aftershave and hair tonic. A machine on the wall dispensed razors for 300 yen.

I continued down the corridor a few steps, not really having any idea what to expect next. All of a sudden, there they were – the *capseru* themselves – big gaping holes in the walls with thick, black rubber trim. There were ten on one side of the corridor and six on the other, uppers and lowers. But wait, here was another corridor branching to the left, with 12 more capsules tucked away down there. That made 28 in all, in a floor space not bigger than one or two rooms in a typical American hotel!

My first impression was that the outside of the capsules looked like those heavy-duty wall-mounted washing machines in laundromats, but with about twice the diameter. My second thought was that the whole place looked like a beehive, complete with drone cells lined up, side by side.

I checked the numbers underneath the capsules and found 406. There it was, right at the junction of the corridors, an upper berth – my home for this night in Tokyo. I peered inside.

Now it looked like a mine shaft, or a blocked-off tunnel in the wall. The capsule extended exactly six feet in from the corridor. It was windowless and doorless, with a pull-down curtain at the entrance. You could secure some measure of privacy and discourage intruders, but the key – it turned out – was only for the locker.

This being Japan, everything looked spanking clean, but an odor of sweat was clearly detectable. Perhaps it was coming from the fellow in the capsule below mine, who had his curtain down. Maybe it was a more permanent feature of the hotel; I couldn't tell for sure.

Grasping some metal handrails like those at the sides of swimming pools, and then climbing a ladder made of three steps built right into the wall, I pulled myself up and launched my body into chute 406. I was ready for takeoff, or a claustrophobic fit.

A thin mattress with a sheet on it took up all the space on the bottom of the capsule. Stretching out with my head touching the wall at the head of the mattress, I had about 15 cm. (six inches) to spare at the entrance. Any guy over six feet in height would have had to bend his knees all night long.

The capsule was 75 cm. (two and a half feet) across and 90 cm. (three feet) high. I could sit up with about 10 cm. (four inches) to spare between my head and the ceiling, but your average American male would not be so lucky. Lying prone would be the only comfortable position.

I pulled down the screen and secured it with the two metal hooks. Clearly, anybody who really wanted to, could get in. I lay there awhile watching my chest rise and fall, and looked around. The walls on all three sides were lined with soft material covered in vinyl.

"Hmm, a tiny padded cell," I thought. "It's come to this." At least you couldn't accidentally bash your head on a hard surface during the night.

I checked the rest of my surroundings. A minuscule pay T.V. hung from the ceiling on the right side, halfway down the capsule – meaning about two feet from my face. To my right, there was a kind of control panel with dials for a radio, the T.V. and an alarm clock. There was a phone receiver for emergency calls to the front desk, a dimmer for the light, a switch for a fan and a tiny shelf.

As it was already feeling stuffy, I switched on the fan and dimmed the lights. The numbers of a digital clock glowed large in the dark, as if hovering in mid-air. Nobody was about to forget the time in this bee hive. It was 11:35 p.m., and counting.

After another 15 minutes of this, I'd had quite enough for the time being. As the hotel was open 24 hours a day, I ejected from my capsule, and headed out for a walk in the Tokyo night air.

I'd already seen, at a glance, everything there was to take in on my floor. There were perhaps ten men staying there at that point in the evening; others would show up later, I would discover, in various states of inebriation.

Down in the mini-lobby, I picked up an information booklet (pocket-size, in keeping with the spirit of the place), and headed out into *Dogenzaka* for a stroll. A few statistics in the booklet provided some food for numerical thought. They kept me company during my walk.

There were 10 floors, with 18 private rooms and 140 capsules. With 28 tubes on my floor, it figured that the capsules only took up five of the floors. Most of them were probably full on an average Friday or Saturday night, but this being the *Golden Week* holiday, many people were out of town, or not working, which accounted for the empty capsules.

I thought about the fourth floor, just in itself. It was a compact space. Back home in Canada, it could be used for two hotel rooms at the most, commanding somewhere between $50 to $150 a room. By contrast, a full house in the capsule hotel would pull in 28 times $35 on the fourth floor alone – or $980 for the use of the same floor space. I had a fleeting thought about going into the capsule-hotel business in Vancouver.

Of course, to earn such profits, you first have to find customers who will agree to sleep alongside 27 other people in tubular modules, protected only by a pull-down curtain. They'll also have to settle for one shower between the lot of them – a hard sell in America or Europe.

Then there's the fact that the man at the front desk had warned me about leaving my valuables in the locker. He'd imitated somebody using a crowbar as a lever, suggesting that I give them to him for safekeeping. As I hadn't seen any safety deposit boxes behind his desk, I had courteously declined, later tucking my wallet inside my pillow case. Even Tokyo is not quite the paradise of safety it used to be.

Still walking around the neighborhood, I made a mental note of a nearby coffee shop where I could have breakfast. Then I wandered back to my capsule, tucked myself in, and slept straight through the night – all watched over by the digital clock. One thing I had to give it top marks for: The place was quiet.

But that, I have little doubt, was a bit of a freak. When there's a full house in a Tokyo capsule hotel – especially during peak party season – you just know there's a lot of carousing, upchucking and drunken *karaoke* singing going on.

"No fair," said Maggie, on hearing of my fairly uneventful adventure, "you have to go again when it's full, if you're going to tell people what it's really like."

"No chance," I replied, "if they're really that interested, they can come to Tokyo and see for themselves."

I know I got off lucky, but I think I got the picture. If capsule hotels are the wave of the future in big-city hotel accommodations, I'm buying the biggest tent I can find and heading for the great outdoors.

To Opine or Not to Opine

Years ago, in India, I waited for three weeks in New Delhi for a bank transfer from Canada. Every day, Monday through Friday, I went into the bank and asked the same patient gentleman if my money had arrived. I, too, was patient, until Friday of the third week, that is - at which point I lost my cool.

"Ah, I've been coming in here for three weeks," I said slowly. "The money should have arrived at least two weeks ago. I received word from the sender in Canada that it would take three days. This bank is the most incompetent I've ever come across."

"Oh, sir," the Indian gentleman replied immediately, without losing an ounce of his composure, "I must remind you that that is only your opinion."

With one stroke, he took all the wind out of my youthful sails. Then he quietly suggested that I try several other banks, explaining that the money may somehow have been transferred there.

In fact, that's exactly what had happened. My much needed infusion of funds had arrived within three days as promised, and had been sitting in an entirely different bank waiting for me. His own bank's competence was not in question, but my strongly worded opinion surely was.

As with India, living in Japan has mirrored to me just how flippant and contentious we Westerners can sometimes be. We usually express our opinions with great confidence, whether they're actually supportable by fact or not. We frequently toss off a mixture of fact and fiction, as though our culture's approval of expressing opinions lends an aura of truth to anything that comes out of our mouths.

Jonathan Rauch made this observation about his countrymen in Japan: "Often, I suspect, Americans have more than their share of problems because so many are know-it-alls."

At the other end of the conversational galaxy in Japan lies a quite different experience. All Westerners know this one: waiting interminably for a response from a Japanese person, especially if what is sought is an opinion of some kind. There's often a long pause, a sucking in of breath, and a slow turning of the head that seems like a theatrical stalling ritual. This will usually terminate with *Chotto ne*, basically meaning, "I would really be sticking my neck out to give an opinion on that controversial subject."

Unlike Westerners, Japanese seem much less prone to *opinionitis* – at least when they're speaking with us. Then they have the opposite problem. Many seem reluctant to venture an opinion of any kind, or at least one that's different from everyone else's.

But there are positive sides to this that are not apparent at first. An American friend with a thoughtful Japanese girlfriend once said to me, "I've learned to ask her a question, and then sit back and wait five minutes for the answer. Usually what comes out is profound and well worth hearing."

How interesting! Perhaps because we're so often opinionated, we Westerners miss a lot of what the Japanese have to teach us. Namely, the advantages of an approach to dialogue that stresses connection and agreement over individual viewpoints.

Living in Japan alongside a small number of Westerners – with the Japanese as a backdrop – is like seeing yourself under a microscope again and again. Our tendency to pass judgment, and our need to be 'right,' often sets us up for conflict. As with my British boss at Soulful Software, I've found that the culture clash between Westerners in Japan rivals anything that goes on between Westerners and Japanese.

Of course, the Japanese may simply be more private about their judgments. In intimate groups, they can certainly complain and opinionize with the best of us. And in more public situations – especially 'after hours' – they can be tremendous talkers. Warmed by saké and beer in the Tokyo *isakaya*, everyone seems to be *O-shaberi* (chatterbox). But social interaction is still guided by a greater emphasis on avoiding divisiveness.

It's my sense that this has positive repercussions and advantages for the community at large. A Japanese university student of mine explained to me how towns in Japan have been traditionally divided up into small and very tight districts. All of these are then organized into larger groups, an arrangement that provides mutual-support networks at various levels.

Ken, my former colleague and friend at Shōrai-dai, experienced how this actually works when he and his wife moved to Tochigi. They soon learned that they were expected to take a gift to the 15 households in their designated *circle*. They also had to invite everyone over for a party, in order to become part of the neighborhood unit. Such rituals are not optional. There's scripted protocol behind 'getting along' with your neighbors in Japan. It becomes easy to see how opinions and preferences get in the way of such practices.

In our own more informal way, we do this in the West with associations like 'neighborhood watch.' But in more traditional Japan, you and your neighbors are glued together. I'm reminded of this every night in the winter, as I sit quietly working in my Tokyo apartment. Around 10:00 p.m. – like clockwork – I hear the *Hinoyō-jin* passing by. These are small groups of men who stroll around the neighborhood, clapping blocks of wood together to remind everyone to be careful of fire. Now that's community! Afterwards, they'll go and have a drink together.

By placing greater emphasis on getting along – and by not voicing opinions that could disrupt the harmony – Japanese people definitely seem to experience less 'overt' conflict. They go to great lengths to avoid confrontation of any kind, whereas many Westerners thrive on discussing conflicting views.

But I now notice how we often insist on the veracity of half-truths, tossing them off as though they were absolutes. From a little information on a subject, we're all too ready to form a judgment, and then argue for its correctness.

In fact, not having an opinion is often taken as a sign of weakness in the West. It's almost as though we're taught that holding an opinion with conviction is more important than being accurate.

One Japanese friend who moved to San Francisco told me how intimidated she felt in her second-language English class. The teacher insisted that everyone give their opinion about stories from the previous night's news. But if the students had even heard about them, they hadn't had time to decide what they thought. I suggested the response, "Hmm, I haven't formed an opinion on that just yet." She loved the idea.

Like me, my teacher friends in Japan complain that their students seldom venture an opinion. But one friend returned to Vancouver, and she soon found herself facing the opposite problem. Of loquacious students from Latin America and the Middle East, she said, "They're great learners, but I can't get them to stop talking."

Yet, I still prefer rambling commentary to none, even if part of it is shot from the hip. It makes for better conversation than dialogue that's devoid of a commitment to a point of view. The practice of discussing the issues of the day runs deep in the Western tradition of Plato and Aristotle.

Japanese seem more comfortable conforming to conventional thought. And when forming an opinion in English, they usually need much more time than impatient Westerners are willing to give them. That may be our loss.

I appreciate the positive qualities my Japanese friends bring to our social gatherings – a sense of ease, and a concern for everyone's well-being. They usually sustain a more mellow way of being than I do, try as I might. That lends a welcome balance to my sometimes overly cerebral ways.

Money Matters

It's definitely true: Japan is a pricey country. Year after year, Tokyo and Osaka are listed as the most expensive cities in the world. That said, bargain hunting is not outlawed here, and if you turn it into a kind of treasure hunt, it's surprising what can turn up. But there's no sense in talking about that before first dealing with the hard financial facts of life in Japan.

The details of the 'cash up front' required for renting an apartment in Tokyo are legendary. Just to step in the door, you have to fork over the equivalent of six months' rent, meaning $6,000 for a $1,000-a-month apartment.

$2,000 of that is so-called *key money*, a gift to the landlord for the privilege of renting the place, and $1,000 is a fee for the real estate agent. You'll never see that $3,000 again. Another $2,000 is a damage deposit, which you may have trouble getting back when the time comes. Lots of people do, though a rule of thumb is that the landlord starts by offering you half, and you negotiate from there. The final $1,000 is your first month's rent. Every two years, you're expected to pay an additional one month's rent, just to renew your lease.

There's one upside to all of this: Tenants' rights are very strong in Japan. Once you get in, it'll be very hard to get you out, at least not without generously compensating you for the move.

Of course, if your employer provides and subsidizes your apartment, you're on easy street, although I declined this offer with Soulful Software. I knew that quitting my job – at some later time – would then force me to find a new apartment. But as a foreigner, you'll almost certainly need a *hoshōnin* (guarantor), a Japanese person who'll guarantee payment on your behalf. This apartment 'bind,' just in itself, leads many foreigners down the road to disliking this country.

It also leads many into *gaijin houses*, one of which Krista and I lived in during our first months in Tokyo. Ours was called *Takenoko House*, meaning 'young bamboo.' It's a name every Japanese person I've mentioned it to has gotten a real kick out of.

We found it through the *gaijin* network, a necessity in Tokyo. Word about *Takenoko House* came along via a tip from my friend Kate, whom I knew from Montreal days. I was very grateful to her. It gave Krista and me a short-term place to live that required only one month's *key money*, no deposit and no agent fee.

Typical of *gaijin houses*, it was a ramshackle old house slated for demolition. The complicated process of working out an agreement between the owner of the house and the owner of the land was taking years. The negotiations also involved compensating Keiko, the Japanese woman who lived there and rented us our suites. The owners were going to have to pay Keiko off handsomely to get her to agree to move out. Meanwhile, she was subletting to us at a reasonable rate, which helped her and helped us too.

Gaijin houses have a reputation for being terrible places to live. But Randall lived in a terrific hostel for foreigners, called *Green Peace*, when he first got to Tokyo. It was run by a wonderful counter-cultural couple we grew very fond of. And *Takenoko House* was a green oasis in the desert, back when we knew nothing much except how overwhelming Tokyo was. It had many charms, not the least of which was the sense of community we all shared.

Many *gaijin houses* are made up of a mix of nationalities, including unorthodox Japanese. Ours was no exception. In addition to Keiko and Krista and me, there was a German named Rainer, who did work for Amnesty International. He lived in a room at the back of the house, and he actually had bamboo trees growing up through his wooden floorboards in the spring.

It was by sitting in our garden, during my first April in Tokyo, that I learned how quickly bamboo grows – 20 or 30 feet in a month. From one weekend to the next, it would be below your knees, and then twice your height!

We had one more resident, my pachinko-loving friend, Kathy. She was studying fashion design at the time. Some years later, she went back to Canada and played piano as a 'hired gun' with the *Crash Test Dummies*.

The house was spacious, with four completely separate rooms and a huge living room. Since all of us were very busy, we seldom saw anyone else except on weekends, at which time we really appreciated each other's company. In the winter months, we huddled around our kerosene heaters – or sometimes stood in the kitchen making breakfast, with all the burners on for extra heat. Then we did 'Japan talk,' sharing our latest, "You won't believe what happened!" I can easily get to feeling *natsukashii* about those early days in Tokyo.

Years after Krista and I had moved on from *Takenoko House*, we heard that the house had finally been torn down. Keiko, a Hawaii-marathon runner, had been proposed to at the age of 35 – a bit of a matrimonial miracle in Japan. Her husband-to-be was a Kyushu tea farmer, and Keiko soon headed off to join him at the other end of the country and start a new life. But she had her lump sum settlement from *Takenoko House* in hand. Perhaps the name of our *gaijin house* had blessed her with youthful good luck.

But if Tokyo's apartment costs seems outrageous, apparently it's worse in Osaka, where the initial outlay can be equivalent to 10 months' rent. Like Tokyo, however, there are communal houses, where foreign residents can cut their costs and get around the system.

It's the same story with many money issues here – there are usually cheaper alternatives. I went to Hong Kong once for 65,000 yen with Northwest Airlines. But, just out of curiosity, I checked with my agent on the price of a Japan Airlines (JAL) ticket. I did this because you always hear that many Japanese will only fly on JAL. This is no surprise – it's their national carrier. So most of the passengers will be Japanese, the food will be recognizable, and they'll feel safer and more comfortable. Nevertheless, it turned out that the least expensive ticket available was more than double the cost at 145,000 yen.

Other 'bargains' are popping up these days. A new phenomenon that started in the middle '90s is '100 yen shops.' You can now get the most amazing little deals on CD holders, soap dishes and plastic food containers, items that would have set you back 2,000 yen in the cash-rich '80s. Sometimes these discount shops just spring up on the sidewalk, at the corner of a busy intersection. I never thought I'd see the day in Tokyo – shades of the Middle East.

And how about reasonably priced meals? It's surely time the myth about Japan *always* being super expensive is debunked. You can pay 800 yen for a milkshake here, that's still true. But on the other hand, a *lunch setto* in Japan is usually a great deal – you can easily find a full meal for 800 yen.

Coffee in the '80s in Japan was 450 yen, but it later plunged to 180 yen with chains like *Doutor*. By the late '90s, you could sometimes find morning coffee on special at *Pronto* for 100 yen (80 cents) a cup.

Breakfast *morning setto* – toast with a hardboiled egg, salad and coffee – goes for 450 yen (about three to four bucks), exactly the same price as 10 years ago. If all else fails, you can go to Denny's. For about $5 (600 yen including tax, with no tip) you get everything they can put on your plate – juice, eggs, pancakes or toast, salad, coffee with refills, and no need for a tip. If you're on a budget, there are plenty of gems hidden in the rough, even in exorbitantly priced Tokyo.

Institutional Priorities

On renewing my two-year contract a second time at Shōrai-dai, I attended a ceremony in a large hall with other faculty members, all of whom were either being promoted or had been recently hired. As there was nothing else to do, I pulled out a pad and took notes. There were about 300 metal chairs on the floor – 15 rows and 20 columns deep – almost all filled with men in grey, blue and black suits. Each of us had been assigned a specific seat with our name on it, which had been carefully written on a label and stuck to the chair.

Prior to the start of the ceremony, the hall was totally silent, despite the presence of 300 people. Luckily, I'd been seated next to my American colleague, Jan, and we exchanged whispers. She and I both watched as row after row of men rose and went up to the front, one row at a time. One by one, they bowed to the university luminary doing the honors that day, and received their very official-looking document confirming their new position. As *gaijin*, we were the least important people in the room, but our turn finally came, and then the event was over.

Much is made of such ceremonies in Japan, whereas other areas of institutional life receive scant attention. On the positive side, one of the private universities I've taught at part time for a number of years, *Aoyama Gakuin*, maintains very high standards, and does not warrant such criticism. Its infrastructure and technical facilities are excellent, and the administration is clearly concerned with meeting the needs of its students. It's a trendsetter in Japanese universities.

Shōrai-dai is a less prestigious institution, though it has wonderfully spacious campuses and a huge student body. I learned from conversations with many Japanese that it's a well-known middle-status university, with a reputation for having students of average ability level. But it has higher aspirations. In recent years, the administration has had the means to construct other campuses in Europe and the U.S.

Knowing that, I always found it puzzling that in our campus near Tokyo, female janitors in their fifties were not provided with trash containers. Instead, they dragged around recycled cardboard boxes, rigged-up with string handles. Coat hangers sometimes served as toilet roll dispensers. The walls in many of the classrooms and hallways – drab and peeling – hadn't been painted in years.

To be fair, it must be pointed out that several modern buildings have now been constructed on our campus. At some point, a decision may have been reached to just 'make do' with the old ones until the new ones were ready. That's easy enough to understand, though it hardly explains scrimping on janitorial equipment.

As for technical support, such as televisions and V.C.R.s for classroom use, one might have had trouble recognizing that this university is located in Japan. After all, this is an incredibly advanced technological society, and one whose corporations have transformed the world's electronic industry. Yet, in the first five years of the 1990s, most of the equipment – tape recorders, televisions and V.C.R.s – was one or two decades old. The weighty video cameras looked to be the first ones ever made.

Along with the new buildings came state-of-the-art equipment. But thousands of students had to make do with outdated technical support for years. Sometimes, it's been hard to know where the needs of the learners fit into the administrative scheme of things.

At a week-long educational conference in the summer of '93 – set up by Shōrai-dai, and attended by 13 Japanese and four non-Japanese professionals – there were no word processors. In fact, there was just one old typewriter with a worn-out ribbon for all 17 of us. Yet great attention had been paid to organizing a dawn-to-dusk routine, a reflection of the nationwide administrative philosophy that 'the people' have to be guided at all times.

Fortunately, the Japanese director of the program, Tasogawa-san, was a very cool cat. On the first day, he set everyone free at 3:30 p.m., even though the schedule clearly said that we'd hold introductory ceremonies until 5:00. I looked around, and saw that the other Japanese were quite stunned. Breaking the *plan* like this is so rarely done; I'd seldom encountered it. Ah, if only he wielded great influence in his country!

The Japanese we worked with were high-school English teachers within the Shōrai-dai system, and our job was to introduce them to new methods of teaching. It came as no surprise to discover, over the course of the week, that their teaching lives are totally tied up in structure. The curriculum is all laid out. To a far greater extent than in the West, the teacher just follows the detailed administrative plan.

Our new techniques were great, they told us, but most felt they'd never be able to squeeze in an experiment to try them out. Almost every hour is accounted for. Classes are all geared towards preparing students for the entrance exams. It reminded me of the title of the book I was given when I got my job: *The Shōrai-dai Educational System*. The system's requirements routinely trump the people's needs.

Yet, it was so valuable to have a chance to really get to know these Japanese teachers. One man in his fifties astonished us by being an expert on the *Brothers Four*. He knew every song they'd ever recorded by heart.

Meeting him, I was reminded of the university student I taught who told me her father loved India, played the tabla every day, and wanted to be in Varanassi when he died. Japan has its wonderful oddballs – closet eccentrics who only *seem* to fit the mold.

Also at the conference, one woman, who was in her early forties, told me her heart-wrenching story late on our final evening together. Thirteen years before – at a time when her three children were aged one, two and three – her 29-year-old husband had collapsed in the shower one morning, and died of a heart attack.

His condition had been congenital, she confided to me. But she'd married him anyway, "out of the folly of youth." Her children were teenagers now, and she worked as a teacher to support them. She'd been away from them for a week at the conference, and pizza was on the menu for their reunion dinner the following night.

One evening, it occurred to me to depart from the relentless academic focus and teach a yoga technique called 'deep relaxation' to all the conference participants. I'd begun teaching yoga privately in Tokyo, and I loved sharing its benefits. We dimmed the lights, and soon had everyone lying down on their backs – breathing deeply, tensing and relaxing their muscles, and letting go.

One young male teacher came up to me afterwards and said that in all his life, he'd never relaxed like that before. Hearing that, I felt the whole week had been worthwhile. And since this is Japan, I later received thank-you cards from all the wonderful teachers we worked with at the conference.

The People and Their Society

To make my peace with Japanese society, I eventually began to make a clear distinction between 'the powers that be' and the people themselves. This enabled me to remain fundamentally positive about the Japanese people – not to mention their remarkable cultural traditions – even though I continued to chafe at the pervasive social control and the constraints the system imposes on people's lives and personalities.

On one trip back to Montreal, I met a former professor of mine for dinner. Like most everyone I meet, he asked me what I thought about Japan.

"Well," I told him confidently, "I separate the people and the system now, because I basically like the Japanese people very much, but I have serious concerns with the way things work in Japan."

"But can you really do that?" he queried, blowing a hole in my self-assured position. "Can you really separate people from the system that formed them?"

Ron was not saying my distinction was wrong. He was doing what he'd always done when I'd been his student and he was my thesis advisor – he was provoking inquiry.

He succeeded, and I began to second-guess myself. Are people completely responsible for the society they live in? Are Americans all accountable for the guns and violence in their society?

With my personal experience in Japan, the dilemma was this: Numerous books and articles written about this country have decried the negative side of the business and social face of Japan. Many of the points their authors make seemed to be entirely valid, but the projection of ugliness onto the Japanese people as a whole was abhorrent to me. One book came out that was actually titled *The Ugly Japanese* (obviously mimicking *The Ugly American*).

I find that it's not an easy thing to explain all of this to people who haven't lived in Japan. On the surface, it doesn't seem like much of an issue. Generally speaking, I find Japanese people easy to get along with, and I now count some as good friends. Most of my students have been friendly and well-disciplined young men and women, and except for an occasional class where the chemistry isn't there, we work well together.

Yet the fact that questioning the way things work in Japan seems to be taboo, or out of bounds, is something many Westerners, myself included, find fundamentally disturbing. Too often in the mainstream of this 'agreement culture,' it feels like there's a nationwide complicity of silence on all things controversial, as though there's a consensus reality that must be adhered to.

In her book *In the Realm of a Dying Emperor: A Portrait of Japan at Century's End*, Norma Field, a writer of American and Japanese parentage, interviews the outspoken then-mayor of Nagasaki, Motoshima Hitoshi, and they have this exchange:

Norma Field: Having spent this year in Japan, which I haven't done in a long time, I've been reminded of what a profoundly difficult place it is to live in.

Motoshima Hitoshi: Sure it is. You're always worried about embarrassing yourself, you spend your whole life worrying about what other people think.

Norma Field: And the act that takes the most courage is to say something awkward.

Motoshima Hitoshi: That's it.

Like many Westerners, and Japanese who will speak openly about it, I find the social ambience in Japan to be rigid and unresponsive to the creative and expressive needs of the individual. One only has to read *Straitjacket Society: An Insider's Irreverent View of Bureaucratic Japan* by Dr. Masau Miyamoto, for evidence that many Japanese – including film director Itami Juzo, who wrote the Foreword – feel the same. His book was welcomed by Japanese who experience similar frustrations with the constraints of their working lives, even though most feel unable to speak about it so publicly. They fear that they, like Dr. Miyamoto, would lose their jobs and their position in Japanese society.

Yet Ishihara Shintaro – who always speaks forcefully in defense of Japan – has also lambasted Japan's "warped bureaucratic logic," saying that "preserving dysfunctional practices in the name of Japan's cultural identity is contemptible."

On one trip home to Canada, I sat up and took notice of a television interview with James Fallows, because he affirmed some viewpoints I'd come to myself. He said he believed that individual Japanese were much like us in their efforts to get pleasure out of life. Then he added that, "There is a peacetime military structure on the whole of Japan, in my view, that constrains the choices people have."

As for examining such topics with this kind of forthrightness, some of my Japanese friends tend to be people who don't flinch at open discussions. Perhaps we often share compatible views, and that's why we're friends.

But when you live in Japan, you have to decide how you're going to respond to the many Japanese who put up walls at your first hint that Japan isn't perfect. As my friend Shiraz discovered, many such people seem to take any criticism of Japan personally. So what do you do? Do you reject them – and their extraordinary culture – along with the nationalism that taught them such knee-jerk defensiveness? Of course not.

To survive here, you learn to do what you'd do anywhere. Perhaps you politely agree to disagree, or you change the subject. I try to remember that however right I think I am, it's still only my opinion. Living in Japan, where opinions can seem like grenades lobbed into a marketplace, I finally came to the conclusion that being happy was more important to me than being right.

So can you make a distinction between people and their system? My experience in Japan has convinced me that sometimes, you have to. You take people as the Japanese do, one at a time – or *case by case* as everyone says here. To do otherwise is to blind yourself to much goodness in your fellow human beings. Ironically, many Japanese would never agree to such a distinction.

That brings the whole discussion around full circle. Ron's question raises an important point that can hardly be ignored. People *are* identified with their systems, and they're painted by others with its brush. My students, taught to have unquestioning faith in their government and system, go overseas and face questions they're completely unprepared to answer. They've simply never been given the green light to discuss controversial subjects. As a result, many difficult issues have been passed on to them unexamined and unresolved.

One story, in particular, drove this home to me. It was about a couple of 20-year-old Japanese women who went to Seoul, Korea on a shopping trip. On entering a store, they were spoken to in *Nihongo* by the proprietor – a sixtyish Korean man, who'd immediately recognized they were Japanese. With the best of intentions, they both proclaimed, as young Japanese frequently do, "Ah, *Nihongo wa jozu!*" (Your Japanese is good!). In response, the proprietor slapped the face of one of the frightened and bewildered girls.

How can one not feel sympathetic towards these uninformed and quite innocent young women? Their school curriculum has failed them. It has not provided them with an explanation of the repercussions of Japan's actions overseas, in this case their country's annexation of the Korean peninsula between 1910 and 1945.

These young women probably knew nothing of the fact that the Korean people were forced to learn the Japanese language in their schools during those years. Nor did they know that, in many cases, Koreans were forced to adopt Japanese names. The proprietor spoke Japanese because when he was their age, he'd had no choice but to speak it. Obviously, he resented their ignorance of history.

One can feel empathy for the people of a country without being an apologist for the shortcomings of their society. One can appreciate Americans for their open and friendly natures, while still believing that Vietnam was a disastrous mistake, or that the refusal of America's gun lobby to go along with tighter restrictions on gun ownership - especially in the face of repeated school shootings - is a disgrace.

In the final analysis, people are responsible for their social systems, and for eventually changing them, if change is what they really want. However Machiavellian its political/industrial complex may be, Japan is held by all the world to be a democratic nation. Only the Japanese people know, in their heart of hearts, if they are unacceptably constrained by their society, or content for things to stay the same. Meanwhile, I like a great many of the Japanese people I meet, and I accept them just as they are.

The Japan Far Beyond Tokyo

It's 6:30 on a beautiful February morning. I've just rung the breakfast gong at a Vipassana (mindfulness) meditation center in the Japanese countryside, about an hour and a half by train from Kyoto. I'm working here for 10 days, helping out with the cooking and doing some carpentry. It's wonderful to be away from Tokyo. The air here is lovely, fresh and crisp.

Suddenly, a huge truck pulls up on the narrow gravel road, temporarily dispelling the morning stillness with the sounds of its engine. The flatbed of the truck is loaded up with the drywall we ordered by phone only yesterday. The rectangular sheets are neatly piled up and securely tied.

The driver hops out to speak with us. He's short in stature, sprightly and cordial, almost chipper. He's been driving from Osaka since 4:00 a.m., it turns out, just to drop off our drywall for us on his way to work. He's wearing his freshly starched company uniform.

Three of us unload the shipment - an American, an Australian and me. We sign the necessary papers, and off he goes. The surrounding hills soon reclaim their mantle of silence, this being a back road with very little traffic.

"That's the great thing about Japan," says Peter, the Australian, a few moments later. "It's the way things should be."

"Can you imagine that situation back home?" he continues, meaning Australia, of course. "The guy would be grumpy and surly, making sure we knew he was doing us a big favor getting up so early in the morning."

"Well," I added, "he would never have gotten up that early in the first place, right? And we might not have seen that drywall for a week."

It's a very different world out here in the countryside, a place that a book about Tokyo cannot pretend to know much about. My experience has been largely that of the millions of Japanese whose lives, like mine, are confined to the country's busiest beehive. It's a city that now feels to me like a universe unto itself. The day may come when I've had enough of Tokyo, and move out here to discover more of the 'Real Japan' I've been missing.

Rural Japanese, like country people most everywhere, are generally more open, friendly, kindhearted and helpful. I recall having much the same experience during my year in London, England. I only had to hop on my motorbike and drive 20 miles out of the city to encounter noticeably more friendly British human beings.

But in Japan, some things – like the efficiency and the congenial manner of many of the people – are countrywide. They're on display in Tokyo, of course, or I wouldn't have known about them. But out here in the hinterland of *Mizuho-cho*, the polite and cooperative manner of our drywall delivery man really stands out. What else can you say? It's a side of Japan that's very impressive, and one that the Japanese are understandably proud of.

Tokyo Snapshots

I'm on a train – what else is new in Tokyo? A woman and man who look to be in their seventies, obviously strangers, are both trying to compel the other to take the one available seat. Finally, the old man consents. He sits down, and immediately squeezes himself into half of the space available, in order to make room for her. He pats the seat with the palm of his hand, insisting that she join him.

At first, she declines. Then she too relents, and sits down. They both smile and thank each other profusely, and then they grow quiet and seem to turn inward.

As I step off the train, I glance back at their contented faces. Playing out their gracious social ritual, they were both able to get what they wanted, while attending to the needs of the other. Both had a chance to give something of themselves in the process.

I'm reminded of another scene I witnessed one Sunday near the Tama River. A group of about 20 elderly people had formed a long line, and they were giving each other shoulder-and-neck massages. After a couple of minutes, everyone turned around and reciprocated, massaging the shoulders of the person who'd just done theirs.

It's an underlying, time-honoured principle of Japanese life, a current that runs deep and still guides the actions of its people at their best. I believe it goes something like this: As I take care of you, I know you'll take care of me, and in that way, we'll all be cared for.

∞

youngphotography

6

STILL I'M GONNA MISS YOU

Tokyo Time Flies

In my sixth year in Tokyo, my mother came to Asia with her longtime male companion, both of them in their seventies. They visited Hong Kong, Thailand and then Japan. Arriving during *Hanami* (cherry-blossom-viewing season) they liked Japan the best, and had nothing but good things to say about it. It's always refreshing to see how positively friends and relatives respond to this country. Short-term visitors generally have a very good time, especially if they have a family member here to put them up and negotiate their way through the culture.

In nearby Kamakura, we were guided around by two young Japanese men, who serve as volunteers for tourists in order to practice their English. The Japanese seem especially comfortable in the role of hosting foreign 'guests,' and they treat them extremely well. Add in the traditional respect for age, and tourists my mother's age usually find Japan to be a most hospitable place.

We caught a beautiful wedding ceremony at *Hachiman-gu Shrine*, watching as the bride and groom – both poised and radiant with happiness in a rickshaw-style throne – were carried up the dozens of steps leading into the shrine, like Cleopatra and her consort.

In Tokyo's Inogashira Park, mum and her companion were quickly invited to join some elderly Japanese men for drinks under the cherry blossoms. Although they found Tokyo to be tiring, they loved the orderliness, the neatness and the safety. The only real challenge they faced was Tokyo's lack of escalators in the older subway stations. It's sometimes a tough town for golden-agers to get around in.

A year later, mum suddenly grew gravely ill, though she lived for another year and a half. Throughout this period and the year following, I flew back across the Pacific Ocean six times, to lend my sister a hand with caring for our mother, and then to tend to her affairs after she'd passed on in January 1995, exactly two weeks after the Great Hanshin Earthquake in Kobe.

It was a time when all of Japan was in mourning. The names of the quake's victims were read and scrolled out on television, one by one. I mourned along with them, and remember well the image of one young girl, captured on CBS News. Weeping and kneeling down at the sight where her family home had once stood, she laid flowers, and mourned the loss of both of her parents. Little does she know, but she gave me courage to face my own personal loss.

Over a three-year period, I wrote much less, though I always took notes. Simply living the experience of being here became much more important than constantly writing about it. I didn't want to end up leaving Japan and realizing I'd been like the critic in E. B. White's poem:

> The critic leaves at curtain fall
> To find, in starting to review it,
> He scarcely saw the play at all
> For watching his reaction to it.

It was a valuable time of growing more comfortable with Japan, though I became much more of a drinker and barhopper than I normally am in order to achieve that sense of belonging. When in Tokyo ...

Being in Japan during the time my mother passed away, I gained a lot of respect for my bosses at Shōrai-dai University. Back in Canada for two weeks, I received three telegrams: one from the President of the university, and two others from my immediate superiors.

I've heard all manner of stories on the response of Japanese bosses to the death of a foreign staff member's relative. I can only speak about my experience. Suffice it to say, that I will always remember how sensitively I was treated, as I went through the grieving process of losing a second parent.

In accordance with Japanese custom, I was given several condolence gifts from the university, as well as from my bosses themselves. It amounted to a tidy sum of money, tucked inside special envelopes called *bushuugi-bukuro*. It helped to pay for my flight home for the memorial service. I'll always remember this gesture with gratitude. Japan is simply unrivaled when it comes to showing this kind of consideration.

Being on the third of renewable two-year contracts, I had actually given nine months' notice at Shōrai-dai, and was planning to return to Canada. But mum passed on before this period ended, and her male companion – a family friend for many years – also passed on soon after. It was a challenging time.

Meanwhile, new opportunities were coming along. I decided to remain longer in Tokyo, become a free-lance university teacher and a part-time writer. By this time, there was also a very sweet Japanese woman in my life, Hanae, whom Maggie had introduced me to, and that was reason enough to stay on.

Inside the Kobe Quake

Terry, my former boss at Soulful Software, was living with his family in Kobe on January 17, 1995 – the day of the Great Hanshin Earthquake. It had a magnitude of 7.1 on the Richter Scale and struck at 5:45 in the morning. I met Terry for lunch in Tokyo later that spring, and he told me their story.

It was pitch black in their basement apartment when the quake struck, waking them up with terrifying suddenness. It rocked their building, breaking all the glass in the windows. Terry, his Japanese wife and three children, decided to stay perfectly still for one full hour, until there was enough light to see. Otherwise, they'd have all cut their bare feet on the shattered glass that was everywhere on the floor. As they lay on their futon waiting for the light of morning to return, distant voices yelled, "*Tasukete! Tasukete!*" (Help! Help!)

By 6:45 a.m., once they understood their own situation, they were also calling for help. The door frame was bent, and the bars on the windows – designed to prevent entry by robbers – were now barring their own exit. Luckily, a local man was able to get them out, but once they were on the street, Terry quickly realized that Kobe was a disaster area.

He decided there was nothing to do but walk, until they'd walked right out of town. So walk they did, past burning gas mains and blazing houses. They walked until they could catch a bus that carried them still further away from the devastation. Finally, they got to a small airport, flew to Haneda in Tokyo, and went up to Saitama by train to stay with Terry's wife's parents.

Terry later spoke with his older Japanese neighbor, who'd been out jogging at the time of the quake. He said it was like a scene out of *Back to the Future*. The pavement suddenly ruptured, and he saw a searing flash of light below the surface. It shot past him, ripping open the earth along the fault line right through the center of Kobe.

Observing the social chaos that ensued, Terry's Japanese wife told him she finally understood what he'd been saying for so many years about the management muddle at Soulful Software. On a macro level, it was mirrored everywhere. Stories of disruptions abounded, caused by breakdowns in the chain of command. One city-government section had lost its *buchō* (division chief), and without his *hanko* (rubber stamp with his personal seal), nothing could be done. Despite the emergency, the lines of protocol had to be obeyed, even though they'd been torn apart.

Roughly four hours after the quake struck, Kobe was paralyzed. Yet, postmen could still be seen dutifully delivering the mail; it's easy to suppose that no one had given them other instructions. A few days into the crisis, American T.V. camera crews recorded one scene at an intersection. Power had been restored, and the signal lights were working again. But the men directing traffic carried right on doing so for another hour and a half, no doubt awaiting new orders.

In faraway Tokyo, the national government was caught asleep at the wheel. It was several days before they realized they had a catastrophe on their hands, something for which they later took a lot of heat. The prime minister at the time was reported as showing up in Kobe 48 hours later, wandering around the streets and saying the equivalent of "Cheer up."

Four days later, while the search continued for survivors still buried alive, railway personnel were out checking on the *shinkansen* tracks. It seemed macabre, but the train line across southern Honshu is Japan's main train artery, and the nation must go on.

Terry told me that three days after the quake, he and his wife were chatting at her parents' home in Saitama. They were wondering how others were doing back in Kobe. Among other things, they remembered that they'd rented some videos from their local video store. Terry decided to call long distance to chat with the guy and find out how he was. He also intended to explain that they were staying north of Tokyo for the time being, and wouldn't be able to return the videos anytime soon.

To his surprise, he learned that the owner was not willing to waive the overdue fee. As he recounted the story to me, we both laughed, because we've been in Japan long enough to know the score. It was just one more case of someone being so used to going 'by the book,' that he knows no other way to respond.

Meanwhile, the important thing was that Terry and his family were all alive and well. Five thousand people died in the Great Hanshin Quake. For months, dragging on into years, hundreds were placed in temporary housing. Many lives were shattered forever.

On my most recent trip to Kobe – four years after the quake – I was relieved to discover a city that's recovering remarkably well. I was very pleased, because Kobe is a beautiful seaside port. It's a city I grew to love early on in my time in Japan, through half a dozen visits I made there while working for Soulful Software. I suspect that many lessons have been learned from the disaster in Kobe about earthquake preparedness.

Many things about Japan's future are uncertain. But one constant is that the Japanese archipelago will continue to rock and roll. The Land of the Rising Sun is also the land of trembling terrain.

The English-Teaching Conundrum

In addition to working full time at Shōrai-dai for five years, I've now worked part time at six other universities in Japan. I figure I've taught about 6,000 students in a variety of programs and departments. One has to conclude that English is considered to be enormously important here, though most Japanese have a heck of a time learning how to speak it. Many of us take English for granted in the West, but it's one tough language for people from radically different language backgrounds to get a handle on.

For seven years, I've also taught part time in a private language school, *Athenée Française*. It's an excellent school that attracts adult learners of all ages who are seeking to improve their English or French. Most teachers love working there, because the learners are highly motivated. That's a sharp contrast with most of our university students.

Our program at *Athenée Française* also allows us to teach students frequently enough to make a difference – three or four classes a week, for example. As a result, they make great progress. Like most adult Japanese, they start out as 'false beginners' – loaded up with grammar, but tongue-tied. Many come out fluent three or four years later. Once Japanese people make an intentional decision to engage in a course of study, they can be incredibly focused. Their years of disciplined rote-learning stands them in good stead.

My experiences at universities other than Shōrai-dai, however, only served to confirm many of the impressions I formed in my first few years of teaching there. Many other teachers I know have come to similar conclusions. When it comes to teaching freshman university students to speak English in Japan, one colleague summed up the average student in a nutshell: "Risk-averse, low in initiative, with a fear of mistakes."

When English teachers here read accounts from the 1890s and the 1960s, we conclude that it's the same as it ever was in Japan, where foreign languages are very foreign indeed. Therein lies a real problem: Most Japanese appear to have a major psychological barrier to overcome before they can start speaking a second language. It's an issue with their Japanese identity, perhaps. ("If I speak English, I won't be Japanese anymore.") Or a problem with letting go of the need for controlled and scripted expression.

I've met Russians who arrive in Japan not speaking a word of Japanese or English. Yet within three months, their spoken Japanese is quite decent, and they speak English better than most Japanese. Despite having studied English since junior high school, most Japanese 'in Japan' have trouble coming out with a simple spontaneous greeting, let alone engaging in a conversation.

Fear of not having perfect pronunciation plays a major role in keeping many a Japanese mouth closed. Many believe that to speak English, they have to sound just like Americans. Every English teacher in Japan struggles to help students too tongue-tied to speak because of this perfectionism.

But the lion's share of the blame lies with the educational system. Grammar is the main focus in school, because it's more easily teachable by Japanese teachers who don't speak much English. Grammatical knowledge, unlike speaking skills, is also more easily testable on the entrance exams in multiple choice questions. Students sometimes face questions that border on the absurd on these exams. One question I read went: "She cannot drink wine at seven without being {a) hasty b) prepared c) eager d) incapable e) near} of getting dinner before eleven."

Diligently preparing for questions of this kind undoubtedly improves grammatical knowledge, but it does little to develop practical speaking skills. Later, at the university level, classes are set up so that most professors only get to see their students once a week, just as they would with a typical lecture-style course. I've occasionally been given the assignment of teaching English Conversation to classes of 70 students, a stressful and impossible task. Given such conditions, it's no surprise that the English speaking ability of many Japanese students remains at a low level.

Yet many of these same students can do a terrifically good job of memorizing a script, just as they do in speech contests. They can pass your 'speaking test' with flying colours, engaging in a well-rehearsed dialogue with a partner about their trip to Paris. At times, you'd swear a particular student was fluent! But one simple spontaneous question from the teacher, and the cat's out of the bag. The whole routine has been learned by rote.

Through questionnaires to hundreds of my students at Shōrai-dai, I learned that the majority have not read much, outside of their school curriculum and *manga*. This didn't really surprise me, since all their energy goes into preparing for the entrance exams. When asked to name the last book they read, or one book in Japanese or English that really made an impression on them, most struggled to come up with anything. They often conferred, and then wrote down something they'd all read in junior high school, such as the Japanese classic *Botchan* or an abridged version of it. Perhaps the situation is not all that different from many schools in the States and Canada now. For many young people, television and computers have taken over where books left off.

Students at first-rate universities like *Waseda* are still mostly unable to speak English, much as generations of English-Canadians have been unable to utter more than a few phrases of French, despite six or more years of studying it. But *Waseda* students are much more articulate with their written English, which is often excellent. Writing and reading have been emphasized since the *Meiji Era* (1868 to 1912), in Japan's efforts to learn from the West.

From time to time, I've received the most fascinating essays from students who can't speak a word of English. One young woman at *Waseda* carefully explained to me how the *kanji* characters for the word 'busy' literally mean 'dead heart.' This was her way of explaining her views on the destructive side of Japanese workaholism.

Many write up a storm in their essays, going on a passionate tirade about how much they loathed the oppression of *examination hell*. Would they want their children to go through that experience? There's seldom a dissenting opinion on that topic – definitely not. One Japanese woman sent a letter to *Time* magazine in which she described her country's education system as 'absurd.' I suspect many Japanese would agree with her.

But at least when they were back in high school, my university students had a clear goal to shoot for. Most lack any such purpose once they've reached university, and they often write about that. Yet, one thing I have to say in favor of Japan's examination system is this: It allows for a quite democratic selection of the best and the brightest. My *Gifu* student, whose family I visited out in the Japanese countryside, made it to *Waseda* – one of the best universities in the country. There's a meritocracy at work in the system that allowed her to do that.

Several other phenomena must be noted. Every now and then, I've run across a student who gives no evidence of being able to speak a word of English. This may go on for months, and I'll be totally fooled. Then one day, they'll suddenly demonstrate that they can speak extremely well. I'll test it out, and lo and behold, their ability is rock solid. There are definitely 'closet English-speakers' in Japan, people who are fluent but never let you know it.

There are also many people who can't speak at all, but who have excellent listening ability. When I'm talking in English with friends on the trains, I've learned to assume that the people around us may understand our every word.

When it comes to speaking *Nihongo*, Japanese in Tokyo would be wise to assume the same thing about Westerners. Sitting next to *gaijin* on the trains, most Japanese never imagine that we might be understanding everything they're saying. Sometimes we overhear quite unbelieveable things. But then, when they understand our conversations, I'm sure they hear the same from us.

Cautious Optimism

I think it was Kurt Vonnegut who said, "Opportunities to travel are dancing lessons from God." The Japanese would no doubt say it differently, but in the past decade, millions have been creating such opportunities for themselves every chance they get. Japan's young people are eager to reach out to the wide world their ancestors could not explore.

Whenever a university I've worked for has offered an overseas study program to its students, I've always encouraged them to take advantage of it. Some jump at the chance. Invariably, they come back changed, bubbling over about the new friends and discoveries they've made.

After returning, some have told me they think Japan is "strange" and "ridiculous." I assure them that my country has its own ways of being ridiculous. The hullabaloo over 'English sightings' on commercial signs, by the so-called Quebec Language Police, is a rival for just about anything I've seen in Japan.

But I don't forget that it was my exchange trip to Quebec, during my high-school years, that educated me about the feelings of the Québécois. That two-week journey beyond the barriers of 'English Canada' did much more than six years of studying French had done, to teach me about Canadians of French descent. As a result, I've been more understanding of their cultural aspirations ever since.

In a similar vein, after six or seven years of teaching in Japan, I began to feel that going overseas was the single most valuable experience my Japanese students could have. It would be much more useful than anything my classes, or even Japan, could do for them. Many young Japanese sense – as do their parents – that their quest for a spirited adventure and transformative learning experience is something they're not going to come by easily in their own country.

I once spent my lunch hour with two female students at *Aoyama Gakuin*. They were *returnees*, having lived overseas for a few years with their parents before returning to Japan. They confided to me how depressed they were about most of their classes and university life in general. They appreciated being able to talk with me – a foreign teacher – so openly about this. They told me they'd never feel comfortable about doing so with a male Japanese *sensei*.

These were extremely bright young women who'd made it into an excellent university, and then felt very disappointed by their experience. The fact that they were *returnees* made little difference: Their emotional lassitude was 'just par for the course.' My colleagues and I are constantly comparing notes, and many of our university students seem weary and disgruntled with their university experience.

Such feelings help to account for the tidal wave of millions of Japanese students pouring overseas to study, to do homestays, or to live for a year on working-holiday visas. Later, when it comes time for them to return to Japan, many say they don't look forward to it. Homestay families in the U.S., Canada, Australia and elsewhere have witnessed the same scene: young Japanese breaking down and crying at the airport. Something about their overseas experience has affected them deeply. They know that back in Japan, they'll again be more constrained emotionally.

Both in the education system and in the media, the traditional insularity of the Japanese point of view remains strong. My colleagues and I have always been puzzled at the reactions of our students – at least those who have never been overseas – when we broach topics related to Japan.

They'll often say, "How do you know about that?" Their astonishment reveals a deeply rooted assumption that we don't know much of anything about Japan, at least beyond *judo* and the *shinkansen*. Many students register shock on learning that we know all about such subjects as the *chikan* on the trains, or the women known euphemistically as *comfort women* – the former sex slaves of the Japanese Imperial forces. Environmental issues, such as the long-running saga of mercury poisoning in Minamata, are topics many young Japanese know little about.

It's as if they imagine that such information about Japan is unavailable to Westerners, even to those of us living in Japan and being bombarded every day by Japanese news. This mindset – the notion that Japan remains inaccessible to the West – still runs deep in the Japanese psyche.

But more and more people, especially the young, are now reaching far beyond the psychic constraints of the nation that was closed off for centuries. As a result, they are rapidly expanding their sense of themselves. They are 'getting the big picture' of what their country looks like in comparison with others.

The cross-cultural sharing brought about by international sister-city relationships is helping to break down barriers. The Internet is spawning an explosion of mutually beneficial cross-cultural contacts, and study-abroad programs continue to open doors for young people.

By venturing overseas, young Japanese get the opportunity to gain a much-needed objectivity, to recognize the things that are truly wonderful about their country, and to get a sense of the things they'd like to do differently. Young

Japanese are changing rapidly. Their biggest problem may be figuring out how to bring their new insights home, to a society that can't keep up with them.

Post-Sarin-Gas Tokyo

Two months after the Kobe earthquake came the horror of the sarin-gas attack in the Tokyo subway. It was carried out in March 1995 by the 'doomsday cult' – *Om Shinrikyo* (Supreme Truth) – and it shook Japanese society violently. The aftershocks will be felt for many years to come.

It so happened that I'd flown out of Tokyo the day before. I had returned to Canada for just four days, to deal with family matters related to our mother's passing. My nephew, Ryan, greeted me with the news that had shocked Japan and the world. Even Tokyo was no longer safe, it seemed. It was soon apparent that I'd serendipitously chosen a good time to be out of town.

For the Japanese people, the most frightening aspect of the sarin attack was the willingness cult members had shown to unquestioningly follow orders to murder innocent people. Potentially, they could have killed hundreds or thousands. People were also horrified to learn that their leader had managed to recruit members from Tokyo's top universities. Then there was the fact that the organization of the cult was eerily similar to government and corporate structures. A broad ripple of fear went through the whole country. Some commentators briefly questioned whether or not this reflected a sickness in society as a whole.

I made a point of discussing one aspect of the whole tragedy with my students. The first gas attack carried out by the cult had actually occurred earlier, in 1994. In a rural area of Japan, a mysterious gas leak during the night had killed seven people. A local man in his forties was then falsely accused, arrested and vilified. Many months later – following the Tokyo subway attack – it eventually became clear that he was totally innocent. I used this story to discuss the impact of the media with my students. I found that it was a shocking and embarrassing revelation to them that their media could be so wrong.

The 'shock waves' continued for some time, with periodic copycat attacks. For about six months to a year, there was an ever-present sense of fear and apprehension in the air. But after that, things started to settle down again in Tokyo, though I hesitate to say they 'returned to normal.'

Posters – with the faces of *Om Cult* members who remained at large – were plastered all around the city. Even four years later, those 'Wanted' posters were still up on walls everywhere. Sometimes, there would be a big X through the face of someone who'd been captured.

One Japanese acquaintance of mine made a passing comment about how much she detested those posters. Perhaps they were a daily reminder of a chapter in Japan's history she'd rather forget. An ongoing issue for Japanese society is the continued popularity of the cult, and the controversy over how to curtail its activities without undermining religious freedom.

In terms of public safety, Tokyo has put the sarin attack behind it now. It's still one of the safest cities of its size in the world, though the ubiquitous innocence I first encountered in the late '80s can be harder to find. The economic downturn of the '90s has led to an increase in various types of crime.

But I don't forget the day I left my wallet – loaded with I.D., credit cards and plenty of cash – at a ticket machine in Shinjuku Station, and charged off at a good pace. Within 30 seconds, a middle-aged Japanese woman was breathlessly tapping on my shoulder and returning it to me, safe and sound.

You can't always count on this – a colleague of mine had his wallet stolen from a teachers' lounge not long ago. But your odds are certainly better in this country than anywhere I've ever been.

In another absentminded moment a few years ago, I left my briefcase on the *Chiyoda Line* with my passport inside. After a few phone calls, I got on another train going in the same direction and went to the last station at the end of the line. There, in the Lost and Found Office, I soon found my briefcase. There was nothing missing. It had already been tagged and put on a shelf. The exact details of where and when it had been found were all written up in a big hardcover book. In situations like this, the words still come easily: Advantage Japan.

But now the magnificent Sanskrit word *Om* (or *Aum*, like *Amen*), meaning, 'The Word – the primordial sound of the universe, the eternal vibration underlying all that exists,' has a deadly association for the Japanese. Living in Japan as this came about, I thought of the *swastika*. Before it was appropriated and reversed by Hitler, it was an ancient symbol of peace and joy, signifying a turning inwards from the four corners to the center of one's being.

Interestingly enough, at many shrines and temples in Japan, the original swastika is still used as a symbol. This is something which has undoubtedly caused terrible confusion for many visitors to this country. I've long imagined that some Westerners probably misinterpret it as reflecting Japan's link with Nazism.

This is not the case at all. It reflects a correct understanding of the original meaning of this powerful and ancient symbol. It derives from the Sanskrit *svasti*, means 'well-being' and once served as a token of good luck. Its sacred meaning – the symbol was once described to me as a human being running for joy – needs to be restored in people's minds.

In a similar way, it's very unfortunate that the Japanese now associate *Om* with absolute terror. But many people here do understand the life-enhancing meaning of the ancient swastika. So I hope the tragedies wrought by Japan's Doomsday Cult can one day give way to an appreciation of the true meaning of this peaceful word *Om*. One only has to wander in the Himalayas to find it on stones and prayer wheels wherever you go.

Highway Mayhem

When it comes to aggressive violence, Japan – compared with America – is quite tame. People are much more likely to be 'passive aggressive.' But it certainly has its mad moments. My American motorcycling friend, Tom, confirmed that for me.

Tom was cruising along on the highway, somewhere outside of Tokyo. He then watched as a bizarre scene unfolded right in front of him. A man in a car was trying to pass a truck, but the truck driver wouldn't let him by. Every time the car made a move, he'd switch lanes to block its passage. The car driver kept trying, however, and he finally made a run for it in the inside lane.

Just as he pulled up alongside the truck – at 100 km per hour – the door on the truck driver's side swung open. Out came an arm and a baseball bat, pounding away at the car! Tom pulled over and rubbed his eyes in disbelief. Like many things Japanese, Japan-style road rage turned out to have its own unique approach.

Through a Newcomer's Eyes

On one return trip home, my girlfriend Hanae came with me. Through her eyes, I was able to see something of what a tourist – or immigrant – sees when they come to Canada. My years of being a *gaijin* in Japan were mirrored to me through her experience of being a newcomer in my own country. It was an eye-opener.

Hanae loved many things about Canada. Arriving in the middle of July, we dove right into an organized two-week trip through the Rockies with eight Europeans and an Aussie. The spaciousness and beauty of B.C. and Alberta delighted and astonished her, as it does most Japanese. Through her everyday encounters, Hanae quickly acquired a sense that Canadian society is "very flexible." We Canadians often take far too much for granted.

At the Cave and Basin Hot Spring in Jasper, she had some culture shock. In a Japanese *onsen*, you wash yourself thoroughly before going into the water. But in Canada, people just took a quick shower and climbed right in. In an *onsen*, people relax and soak. But in Canada they swam around the pool, and kids splashed water at each other! What was going on? Was it a swimming pool, or a hot spring bath? Did anybody know?

At the top of the cable car in Banff, we stood near enough a Japanese father and son to overhear a dialogue in Japanese. It had us both shaking our heads and laughing. The little Japanese boy, about five or six years old, pointed across the valley at one mountain and exclaimed, "Dad, it's so big!" His father – less impressed – replied, "Hmm, Mount Fuji is bigger."

Later, at The Butchart Gardens in Victoria, we overheard other comments from Japanese tourists that we completely agreed with. They loved the flowers and fountains, but were disappointed by how small the Japanese garden was. True enough, it certainly can't hold a candle to the authentic and spacious Japanese gardens I've wandered through in Japan. *Kenroku-en* in Kanazawa and *Ritsurin-kōen* in Takamatsu are splendid gardens.

In Kelowna, we watched the town's mayor, dressed casually in slacks and a short-sleeved shirt, officially open the B.C. Summer Games. He said, "Well, I'm going to keep this short. Let's get the games under way!" Accustomed to hearing long-winded speeches at such ceremonies, by mayors wearing dark suits and ties, Hanae was astonished at the informality in Canada.

Later, watching television, we saw the prime minister face comic confrontations with the flamboyant character Marg Delahunty (played by Mary Walsh) from C.B.C. T.V.'s *This Hour Has 22 Minutes*. Hanae was flabbergasted that such an encounter was allowed to happen.

When it came to restaurants, we both missed the consistency of good service in Japan; Canada was hit and miss. We often felt much less attended to, and yet somewhat preyed upon, by waiters seeking tips. In Vancouver's Gastown (which has some great restaurants), we took our chances with one Italian place that turned out to be an expensive tourist trap with tasteless food.

At our four-star hotel-restaurant near the Vancouver airport, we waited 25 minutes to order our meal, and after one hour, we were still waiting patiently to be served. I didn't want things to get uncomfortable, as this was Hanae's introduction to Canada. But when we finally spoke to the manager, she was unapologetic. We've never had such experiences in restaurants in Japan, and my impressions of the excellence of service in Tokyo were only reconfirmed. You blew it, Canada.

But in small town Victoria, Hanae was delighted at how shopkeepers initiated conversations and asked her about herself. As is the case for many English-speaking Japanese who visit Canada or the U.S., the naturalness of dialogue between strangers was a revelation to her.

So were the prices. We saw one special at *Canadian Tire*: $9 U.S. for a box of 12 bottles of Perrier, imported from France. Later, back in Tokyo, we priced the same dozen Perrier at Tokyo's *Kinokuniya*, my favorite import grocery store. It was quadruple the price – $36 U.S., proof to us both that there are a lot of wealthy middlemen in Japan.

And what about the everyday things a newcomer like Hanae sees, which Canadians seldom notice? In a lineup to a movie, I was fumbling in my pockets for the right change, and the people behind us were getting impatient.

"Hanae, do you have any coins?" I said quickly. Reacting to my sense of hurry, she pulled out her change purse, rifled through it and said, "Yeah, here we go. I've got two deer, a yacht and a beaver."

Sex and the Love Hotel

Writing in the 1940s, Ruth Benedict wrote, "We have many taboos on erotic pleasure which the Japanese do not have. It is an area about which they are not moralistic and we are. Sex, like any other 'human feeling,' they regard as thoroughly good in its minor place in life."

She probably could have written it yesterday. In Japan, sexual relations still fall outside of the zones of obligatory behavior that Japanese owe primary allegiance to. In a stressed-out culture that's private and circumspect when it comes to expressing emotions, a lot of bottled-up energy appears to get channeled into sexuality.

So what else is new? Well – for one thing – not being Christian, most Japanese don't grow up making a direct association between sex and guilt. At least, not in the same way people with Christian backgrounds do, often without even realizing it.

As a result, there's a playful side to much of flirtation and sexuality in Japan. That can be very refreshing, especially to those of us who grew up with Protestant or Catholic paranoia and repression around sex. As long as it's kept private and discreet, sex is a kind of social 'free zone' for Japanese of any age. And for younger Japanese, it's sometimes anything but private. During the hot summer evenings, hundreds of couples cuddle up together in parks in central Tokyo, hotels being way too expensive for their budget.

In the public realm, some former porn stars make an easy transition into becoming T.V. talk-show personalities. Their sexuality is celebrated. In one ceremony that still takes place in Japan, women walk through the streets carrying large artificial penises. It's a fertility rite, and they're hoping it'll bring them luck with having a child. I can just imagine how Western moral watchdogs would deal with that one.

When it comes to sexual orientation, I know American gays and lesbians who feel very comfortable here. They're much less likely to be harassed for their sexual preferences. As for heterosexuals, my friend George, with his characteristic good humour, once said to me, "A lot of young Japanese women will sleep with a guy about as easily as they'll play tennis with him. It's just that getting her to play tennis may take some doing."

This easygoing approach to sexuality – as a natural part of life – is hardly the whole story, however. Japanese social reality is always complex and multi-faceted. There are many other sides to sexuality that cover the whole gamut of experience.

These include such scenarios as middle-aged men seeking to fulfill fantasies denied them in their adolescence. I reckon they were too busy back then, since they were totally taken up with *examination hell*. So years later, they pay 20-something-aged women to act out their fantasies with them. The women pretend to be the junior-high-school girls their middle-aged clients never had a chance to touch in their youth.

You see the graphic advertisements all over Tokyo, with pictures or drawings of young women or girls dressed up in schoolgirl sailor-suit uniforms. The sexual-fantasy industry is big in Japan. The media treatment of women's bodies as consumer goods rivals anything in Western nations. Some of the weekly news magazines look like *Newsweek meets Playboy*.

When it comes to mature relationships, one hears and reads many stories about 'sexless marriages' and vengeful jealousy. It's not hard to conclude that all is far from well on many of the nation's futons and in its sexual psyche. There may be fewer feelings of 'guilt,' but ambivalence appears to be alive and well.

Amazingly, it took until 1999 for the birth control pill to be legalized. No, that's not a misprint. Advocates for women's rights had to fight for three decades, against all manner of resistance. One wonders if the newly developed birth control 'patch' – eliminating the need to take a pill – will take another few decades to gain Japanese government approval. Meanwhile, *Viagra* was approved within six months.

But though we often imagine ourselves to be sexually liberated in North America, many Japanese – not to mention the French, the Thais and many others – see it otherwise. They see the American approach to sexuality as being hypocritical and judgmental.

Watching the Monica Lewinsky soap opera unfold, I had plenty of company in being very disappointed with Bill Clinton. Personally, I think he's the most knowledgeable and articulate president the U.S. has had in a long time. His actions cost him his credibility with millions of people. But above all else, he simply proved himself to be all too human, and I think that's his and his wife's business. Those who put him through a circus-like inquisition over his private life seemed much more pathetic. As one Australian quipped after the whole affair was finally over and done with, "Thank God we got the criminals and they got the puritans."

In Japan, Clinton would have had to resign, not because the affair 'happened,' but because it was exposed publicly, and face was lost. I think most Japanese would agree that, so far as sexual relations between mutually consenting adults goes, Canada's brightest prime minister in my lifetime, Pierre Trudeau, got it right years ago. With his usual poetic flair, he quipped, "There's no place for the state in the bedrooms of the nation." Likewise the media.

In keeping with this spirit, sex in Japan remains a very private matter for the average person. In a tremendously overcrowded city like Tokyo, *love hotels* provide much needed personal space. For many people, they're the only places that are free from prying eyes and ears.

I've come to think of them as a great invention, a civilized acknowledgement that sex is a normal human need for which people need privacy. Between consenting adults, what goes on in *love hotels* is nobody else's business. Japanese visiting North America are often surprised to discover we don't have them.

The one Hanae and I went to, in Shibuya, didn't even require us to talk to a hotel clerk. On a wall in the lobby, pictures of the interiors of available rooms are lit up. They're arranged according to price and theme-setting, with choices such as rodeo, Cadillac, or mini-swimming pool. You press a button next to the picture you like, and out pops your key. Off you go to your secret love nest, often without seeing another person.

Two hours later – when you're ready to leave – you make a phone call to someone behind the scenes. They then send you the bill in a plastic tube propelled through an air tunnel! I believe they used the same system in Paris in the 19th century. You pop your money in and send it back; it soon returns with your change. If you've come by car, long flaps like those in car washes will hide your license plate from any media cameras. Japanese journalists sometimes search for a scoop on famous patrons.

Since so much of life in Japan is tied up in required public behavior, the discreet sexual rendezvous is a time-honored tradition. It's just about the only venue that's free from all the many constraints of public life. Not surprisingly, the *love hotel* business appears to continually thrive, through good times and bad.

Sex and Gender Politics

When it comes to sexuality, most Japanese pay homage to discretion. They're much less likely to run around talking about their sex lives than Americans are. What others think of you is far too important. In my view, they have a better handle on the division between public and private than we do.

But many Japanese will listen intently while a loquacious American pours out the details of his or her love life. Meanwhile, they'll usually reveal nothing about their own private affairs, but you can hardly hold that against them. It's usually the American who wants to do the yakking, and the Japanese are delighted to listen. They're very intrigued by such loose tongues.

As for the sex lives of young women, the Japanese media is fascinated by the topic. At one point, it portrayed those in their late teens and early twenties as having a variety of boyfriends for various purposes (car boy, gift boy, toy boy). Perhaps reflecting this, many young women earn a reputation among *gaijin* men for playing mind games or being impossible to 'read.'

But once they start to approach their middle twenties, most women quickly become very conservative and marriage-minded. By this age, they're much more likely to view sex as a prelude to a lifetime together. Western men who land in Japan with hopes of a fling with a Japanese woman would be well advised to remember this – or to be prepared for the possibility of a wildly emotional reaction to a breakup. Though increasing numbers are postponing the rigors of married life, marriage remains a very big deal for most Japanese women. It's still their main source of power, and the only long-term alternative to being single. As of the late '90s, less than 3% of Japanese couples live together without being married. By contrast, in Sweden, more than half the population is now living in a common-law arrangement.

Most marriages in Japan are still viewed as a social bond. The idea of a 'love marriage' was a foreign import. When you live here, you learn that it's quite common for sex to pretty much stop after the babies arrive. You also discover that extramarital relations have long been a routine part of the social landscape. They remain so to this day.

Provided that it remains hidden – and doesn't interfere with a man's family *giri* – sex outside of marriage is often tolerated. In one opinion poll I came across, 48% of people said extramarital affairs were "never okay." Though only 7% said they were "okay," 45% chose the option, "it depends."

Many North Americans, with a penchant for moral absolutes, strongly object to this side of Japanese culture. But setting them aside long enough to look at things from the Japanese point of view is a useful exercise. For one thing, we're obviously not strangers to extramarital affairs ourselves. And North America also has the carnage from its gender wars. There are the deadbeat dads, and the millions of single working mothers – abandoned or single by choice – struggling to make ends meet. One reads with amazement that more than half of American children now live in situations other than two-parent households.

These are situations which most Japanese would view as being intolerable. If there are children involved, sticking with the marriage is still an inescapable duty for most, regardless of the status of the couple's relationship. Obviously, we North Americans are in no position to lecture other cultures on how to keep their families together.

At the heart of those families is the strength of Japanese women. Mitsuko Shimomura, a well-known Japanese journalist, was quoted in *Newsweek* in

1998 as saying, "Japanese women have an inner strength that is perhaps not apparent to the casual observer."

That certainly describes most of the Japanese women I've gotten to know well – at least those in their late '20s or older. Unfortunately, some of my Western women friends in Japan end up settling for a simplistic view. They conclude that Japanese women – compelled to act like girls well into their womanhood – have candy floss for brains.

But hidden beneath surface appearances to the contrary (usually just the requirements of *tatemae*) lies real character. Japanese women often possess a pragmatic cleverness that I've grown to greatly respect.

In my personal life, I've discovered that Hanae – seemingly meek and mild – possesses incredible tenacity. I'm now convinced that Japanese women, given all the same advantages as their American sisters, would easily prove to be a professional match for them every step of the way.

Another quality I've grown to appreciate is a certain innocence and lightheartedness. It's something that's often mocked by Western women and men in Japan, who take it to be superficial. It can certainly be that, especially with younger Japanese women. But it can also be genuine, delightful, and refreshingly free from cynicism.

On Tokyo trains, it's often only the young women who show signs of life, standing out from the general torpor. In the humdrum atmosphere of university teachers' lounges, where I spend a lot of time, it's the good-natured disposition of the women that keeps everyone's spirits up. Although some of my Japanese male colleagues can be very friendly, many come across as somber and remote. Meanwhile, the women in charge of the lounge can be counted on for a cheerful exchange, in addition to tending to our myriad needs.

One day, I found myself pondering a certain scenario. I pictured myself as a landlord in Canada; then I thought about finding a tenant. I extended the scenario, and at one point, I imagined myself having to choose a tenant without meeting the person. Then I had this thought: What if the only thing I had to go on was that one prospective tenant was a Japanese woman and another was a North American woman?

I decided that I'd choose the Japanese woman every time. It's not that I'm under the illusion that they're all angels. But I realized that if I had to 'gamble' with a tenant, I believed the 'odds' of her being trustworthy were better.

Many Westerners find the social demeanor of Japanese women to be too acquiescent. It's helpful to remember the constraints their culture imposes on them. In situations where American women would feel free to let fly with a string of epithets, their Japanese sisters will strive to be accommodating.

Near major train stations in Tokyo, I've stood back and watched as woman after woman is propositioned by men in sunglasses and suits. These smooth operators only approach attractive young women. So I suspect they're trying to cajole them into appearing nude in raunchy magazines or porn videos.

In such a situation, an American or European woman would feel well within her rights to say, "Get lost," or something far cruder. At the very least, she wouldn't feel obliged to give the guy the time of day. But a sophisticated young Japanese woman feels she must handle it differently. Even with such gross solicitations, she feels obliged to decline the offer in a manner that's not abrupt or impolite. At all times, her actions must not reflect badly on her. Sometimes, I've watched these guys talk for three or four minutes before the woman succeeds in extricating herself.

During a discussion on 'passive smoking,' one of my university students said that she and her girlfriends could absolutely never ask a man, sitting next to them in a coffee shop, to stop smoking. Somehow, I don't see this situation changing dramatically anytime soon in Japan.

Yet, although the newest generation of Japanese high-school girls seem as conformist as ever, they're a rapidly evolving species. Behind the latest version of teenage goofiness and the ever-present love of *kawaii* (cuteness), there's a fierce determination to get what they want. Japan's ongoing patriarchal control is turning many women into restless warriors.

As for cross-cultural relationships between Japanese and foreigners, some couples weather the storms. But a greater number seem to get shipwrecked. Serious problems often arise because of the formidable complexities of Japanese family relations. There's the complex web of obligations, the language barrier, and other cultural differences that show up along the way.

One cross-cultural couple I know had no problems until their first child was born. Then they started fighting. Later on, they figured out that the conflict was due to radically different ideas about childrearing. Fortunately, they worked it out, and they're still happily married.

However, the main Japanese rulebook for life, with its three main principles – *enryo* (to restrain or refrain), *doryoku* (to make efforts), and *gaman* (to endure and be patient) – proves to be all too much for many Westerners. I read one letter to the editor, written by a woman with a Spanish-sounding name, that gave me pause. She said she'd married a Japanese man 15 years before, and she mentioned these three challenging principles in her letter.

She also added a fourth: *silence*. She explained that, in her view, this was a disturbing feature of modern Japanese society. She first expressed her respect for those Japanese who can endure life's difficulties by following the first three principles. Then she bemoaned the pervasiveness of the fourth, saying that problems and painful issues are just not discussed in Japan. Instead, silence reigns supreme.

In fact, divorce in marriages where both spouses are Japanese is quickly rising, but there's still quite a stigma attached to it. One group of divorced women I saw interviewed on television in the mid-'90s wore masks to hide their identities. A publication on divorce, which has sold well, is called *Elizabeth* (named after divorce-veteran Elizabeth Taylor). To give a magazine on divorce a title like that is vintage Japan: It's best to allude to things, without stating them, especially when they're beyond the pale.

I've been told hundreds of romantic stories living in Tokyo, and I'm also living my own. In this often lonely and alienating city, there's much talk of Cupid's adventures. You hear tales of happiness and heartbreak both, and they could make an entire book just in themselves. But I side with the Japanese about sexual love. Pillow talk is private prose, best shared between intimates and left written on their hearts.

The Trials of Being an Alien

Very occasionally, Japanese people will say quite surprising things around you. A colleague of mine interjected such a comment one day, during a discussion on Japan by the Westerners on staff.

"Japan is totalitarian," he said quite calmly. "We're all oppressed, so we oppress each other."

Watanabe-san knows his country infinitely better than I ever will. But I had to wonder – despite his fluency in English – if he understands the exact meaning of the word. Totalitarianism implies jack boots, terror and knocks on the door in the middle of the night. It's also invoked by many to describe China's actions in Tiananmen Square in 1989 and their handling of Tibet. As for Japan, historians might agree that such a description suited the fascist regime in place during the Fifteen Year War (1931 to 1945), but it hardly applies to post-war Japan. Perhaps Watanabe-san meant much the same thing as a number of Americans I've met in Tokyo mean, when they tell me America is becoming 'fascist,' and that's why they moved to Japan.

Or maybe he meant authoritarianism. If that's the case, I would need no convincing, especially on subjects such as textbook censorship. Likewise with the status of non-Japanese in Japan, most of whom are obliged to carry their fingerprinted *Alien Registration Card* at all times. I never leave home without it.

I learned from David Suzuki and Keibo Oiwa's book that in 1987, America's social-activist, Jesse Jackson, wrote to Japan's Justice Minister to protest this. He said it was similar to the pass laws in apartheid South Africa. Since then, some changes have slowly been introduced. The small pass booklet I had to carry when I first arrived in Japan has been replaced with a card, similar to a driver's license. It comes with a plastic cover that hides the fingerprint at the bottom, a typical Japanese way of dealing with something unpleasant. At long last, however, the government has finally agreed to put an end to the fingerprinting of foreign residents, starting in April 2000.

The *Alien Registration Law* of 1952 has made life very difficult for many minority groups, such as 'Resident Koreans.' Those who were brought to Japan as slave labour before the war were later denied citizenship by this law. Altogether too much fingerprinting has gone on in Japan, and many people have been abused and denigrated because of it. In Norma Field's words, "Resident Koreans have been fingerprinted, harassed, and treated as second-class citizens, the combined effect of government policy and ordinary prejudice."

Still, it's not insignificant that in all my years here, I've never once been asked to show my card. I may have been lucky, because many other foreigners have had a rougher time of it. But I've generally found the police in their tiny *koban* (police boxes) to be friendly and helpful, at least when I need something uncomplicated like directions.

In fact, I've found them to be easily as approachable, and less intimidating, than many of their counterparts in my country. Providing you remain scrupulously law abiding, Japan, while rough in its treatment of those it finds threatening, can be quite an accommodating place for foreigners it has no grievance with.

That said, if you have a genuine problem of your own to report, your local *koban* may not be much help. One Canadian I heard about was trying to sell used cars in Nagoya. The *yakuza* kept beating him up; they obviously felt he was infringing on their turf. He finally contacted the embassy, but the police wouldn't touch it.

One Western female colleague of ours had a Japanese man break into her apartment and stand over her bed, amusing himself, while she was sleeping. She woke up and screamed, and he fled. When she reported it, the police asked her if the man had kept his shoes on in the house. When she said 'yes,' they laughed and said he must have been a *gaijin*. Then they told her to forget about it, and to keep her windows and doors locked in future.

You definitely wouldn't want to end up in prison here, as another female colleague of ours did on a drug charge (hashish) in the autumn of 1996. It's too bad she didn't learn from Paul McCartney, who was also jailed here years ago on a similar charge. Coincidentally, her imprisonment coincided with a very harsh story on Japan's archaic prison system that appeared in *Time* magazine. On her arrest, she was allowed just one phone call. She was interrogated, and kept in jail for five weeks. As the story spread, I watched fear ripple through most everyone who knew her.

Only our colleague's closest friends were brave enough to visit her in jail. Most of us feared we'd be viewed as guilty through association, and possibly put under surveillance. Those who did visit her discovered that a Japanese guard was present at all times. They had to speak Japanese, or if they spoke English, every question and response had to be translated, one at a time, by an interpreter. The conversations were all recorded. It seemed to be a firsthand experience of the covert intimidation which journalists, such as Karel van Wolferen, allege that Japan exercises over its citizens.

A petition of support was started. At first, people were glacially slow to sign. However, once a critical number had been reached, the feeling of safety in numbers kicked in. Then hundreds of people put down their names, both non-Japanese and Japanese alike.

After five weeks, our colleague was released to await sentencing. With help from a very expensive lawyer, she was convicted a month later, but given a suspended sentence. Within three months, she was free to leave the country, which she promptly did. The last I heard, she's safely back in the States, though she continues to have nightmares of being behind bars.

There are plenty of comparisons that serve to make Japan look reasonable. Our co-worker would have faced serious charges in many places in the U.S., and might easily have spent a much longer time in prison. If she'd been arrested in Singapore or Malaysia, she wouldn't have had a prayer.

As a foreigner in Japan, you can write letters to the editor that are highly critical of this country, with little concern that it'll jeopardize your job. That could theoretically happen, but it's very unlikely (even though detailed files are kept on foreign residents). In Singapore, it's a different story. Some foreigners who have written such letters – critical of the government – have later learned that their visa will not be renewed.

Japan definitely flirts with totalitarianism, but backs off from it in the end. The term 'soft authoritarianism' is one label that's been adopted by some political scientists to describe many Asian governments. Of all the descriptions I've come across, it seems to suit Japan's bureaucratically run society best of all.

Politics, War, Candor and Cover-up

People have a democratic vote here, and their votes can make a difference. I learned this back in 1993. My view of Japan changed for the better in that year, when the Liberal Democratic Party (L.D.P.) was finally replaced (for a short time) by a new coalition led by Hosokawa Morihiro.

If I'd never come to Japan, I doubt if I'd ever have given much thought to Japanese politics. I certainly can't imagine that it would ever have grown to matter so much to me that Japan admit to its aggression in the 1930s and 1940s. I was born in the '50s, and I'm neither an historian nor a Japanese scholar. But simply through living here for a decade, I was inextricably drawn into examining the question of Japan's wartime actions more deeply.

In my first months in Japan, I ran up against some intense hostility from Japanese men that felt very uncomfortable. One man in Sendai literally went berserk in a *ramen* shop, raging at Krista and me in Japanese. We concluded that he was mentally unhinged. Another fellow, whom I met on the Yamanote Line in the late '80s, spoke English well. It was right around the time when the Canadian government paid compensation of $20,000 to each Japanese-Canadian who'd been put into internment camps during the war. On learning I was from Canada, the man in question spoke to me about this issue. He became accusatory and hostile. Everything was our fault, it seemed, and it was about time we'd atoned for it.

The longer I stayed here, the more I felt compelled to learn what lay behind official Japan's silence and the denial of its own aggression. At one point, I discovered that many Japanese defend Japan's actions, believing that this country broke the Western colonial grip on Asia.

That point of view certainly has validity; the Western colonial powers still have plenty to answer for. The journalist Robert Elegant interviewed one Indonesian politician who believed that, "An entire generation remembers the Japanese with gratitude... It was the end of the white man when we saw them as prisoners of war..."

But other Asian people, though initially hopeful that Japanese rule might be benevolent, were soon mortified by the treatment they received from their new masters. I took a tour through the museums in Singapore. It chronicled the brutality of the war years and served to further educate me. These museums serve the same purpose for thousands of Japanese tourists, who were taught little about it in school.

In the museum on Sentosa Island, we read that on capturing Singapore, Japanese soldiers quickly killed 20,000 Chinese males, fearing they might be spies. (It was puzzling to see that the panel with this information on it was not translated into Japanese - whereas all the others had been. I couldn't help but wonder if the exhibit's sponsorship by a well-known Japanese company had something to do with that.) Strangely, another museum in downtown Singapore cited the figure of 50,000 killed. It's easy to see how such glaring discrepancies fuel Japanese disputes over what actually took place during the war.

Still, the mood of the Singapore exhibitions was not evasive. Life under the Japanese was not to be envied. In a separate exhibit, in a fort at the far corner of Sentosa Island, I wandered through a gallery of drawings done by POWs. They were hanging on the concrete walls of rooms in which men had actually been held prisoner. At the very end of the gallery was a picture of the A-bomb mushroom cloud over Hiroshima. It had a caption that shocked me. It read, 'End of Empire.'

Stories of POWs exposed to Japanese military brutality have sometimes been written as a direct consequence of official Japanese forgetfulness. I heard of one book by a Canadian, Dr. Ken Cambon, who enlisted and went to Hong Kong in 1941 – just in time for the Japanese invasion. He ended up in Japan, at Niigata, in prisoner-of-war camp 5B. Although he survived his ordeal, many of his comrades did not. After the war, he returned to Canada where he became a doctor, ready to let bygones be bygones.

Then in 1982, his daughter came to Japan and went to Niigata. There, she was told by officials at City Hall that, "there had never been any Prisoner of War Camp in Niigata but there may have been one further down the coast."

On hearing this, her father wrote to the mayor of Niigata, who later responded that there had been a misunderstanding. He invited Dr. Cambon to come to Japan.

Ken Cambon then felt strongly enough to write a book about his wartime trauma, *Guest of Hirohito*, though he'd never intended to do so. He decided that the treatment he and his comrades had suffered in internment had to be acknowledged, so it could never be repeated. Ultimately, Dr. Cambon went back to Niigata, and he was welcomed most warmly.

It's clear that some Japanese in official circles – once pressured – do take steps to atone for atrocities committed during the war years. Dr. Cambon wrote about his gracious reception in Niigata in 1991. He also recounted the Japanese military's brutal treatment of those it conquered.

Over the years, in trips back to Canada, I've sought out a few firsthand accounts from other POW camp survivors. I wanted to get my own personal sense of what they went through. At one point, I was introduced to a remarkable man, Mr. Alex Jardine, by a friend in Victoria. I spoke with him for several hours and taped our conversation, with his permission.

I discovered that Alex Jardine had led an amazing life. Starting at age 15, he spent five years at sea, and from 1930 to 1932, the ship he was assigned to made several stops in Japan every six weeks. At that time, his uncle Bill was working in Yokohama, where he'd lived for many years. So every time young Alex's ship docked in Japan, he saw his uncle and wandered around Yokohama and Kobe.

Mr. Jardine has some very clear memories of those early years. One that he recounted to me involved meeting some young Japanese naval cadets. They struck him as unbelievably arrogant – "the military was all-powerful in those days" – but he learned something about them that shocked him: "When they went into barracks at night, they had to take it in turns to beat each other. It was part of their tradition to harden themselves for when they were disciplined. That was how they were disciplined, and they were not to flinch, or move, or anything while being beaten. Later on, I watched that in prison camp."

After joining the Royal Air Force in 1935, Alex Jardine was stationed in Singapore, which served as his base for years. From there, he flew around the world in 'Catalinas' and quickly rose in the ranks of the air force. After the Japanese invaded Singapore in 1942, he and others retreated to the south coast of Java. From March 1942 until the end of the war, he was held as a Prisoner-of-War. One of his fellow POWs was the writer, Laurens van der Post, with whom he worked on a prison-camp newspaper, which they called *Mark Time*.

Alex Jardine described Van der Post as being a man with a very gentle nature, "who had no business being in the military." Van der Post also "had this feeling for the Japanese," arising from his personal experience with them. Years before, in a coffee shop in South Africa which had a racist proprietor, he'd helped some Japanese seamen who were being refused service. In gratitude, they invited him on board their ship. He ended up sailing with them for several years, and developed an intimate knowledge of Japanese culture and language.

Mr. Jardine told me that at the end of the war, his fellow POWs all thought of their Japanese captors as brutes for the treatment they'd received at their hands. "Their cruelty was just awful," he said. Only Van der Post felt differently. He appreciated the Japanese in ways the others couldn't fathom. He understood the tyrannical side of their group mentality, and spoke of the need for forgiveness and reconciliation.

I had one other interesting encounter in Victoria B.C. On a walk along the ocean front, I happened upon Mrs. Helen Senior one morning, and she chatted readily about her wartime experiences. She told me she'd worked in Calcutta for British intelligence during the war years. Meanwhile, her husband had been captured by Japanese forces. He did forced labour in the coal mines along Japan's inland sea. Though nearly six feet tall, he weighed 93 pounds at war's end. He had lived for years on a diet of 350 grams of rice a day.

"Was he bitter?" I asked. "No, not at all," she assured me without hesitation.

Listening to her, I had the sense that it was simply taken for granted in those days that war was war; it had its own rules, which nobody could control. Her explanation sounded a lot like the Japanese use of *shōgenai*. But like Dr. Cambon, she also wanted the events of the war to be known. She worried that young Canadians and Americans are not being educated properly. She feared that they're ignorant of history, much like their young Japanese peers.

Hearing these accounts, it became clear to me that these people had no interest in revenge. But they did have a strong belief that the truth must be told. Survivors of POW camps simply wanted their suffering at the hands of the Japanese to be acknowledged. It must never be forgotten, let alone denied.

So it was that events in 1993 came to matter a great deal to me. They've been rendered especially poignant, given that nothing similar has happened again since that time. The veteran journalist, Ian Buruma, explains it best:

"Barely a year later, in the summer of 1993, four years after the fall of the Berlin Wall, it finally happened; the monopoly of the Liberal Democratic Party was broken by a coalition of young conservatives who had led the LDP, the socialist party, and Komeito, a Buddhist party. The new Prime Minister was Hosokawa Morihiro, the grandson of Prince Konoe Fumimaro, Prime Minister at the time of the Nanking Massacre in 1937 and of the signing of the Axis Pact in 1940. Konoe committed suicide in 1945, after being charged as a Class A war criminal. One of Hosokawa's first acts, as the new Prime Minister of Japan, was to state in public that Japan's military actions in the 1930s and 1940s amounted to 'an aggressive war and a wrong war.' It was only a beginning, but the signs were good."

Hosokawa-san's tenure as prime minister was short-lived. In spite of that, of all the 10 prime ministers who have come and gone in my decade in Tokyo, he will probably be the only one I'll remember 20 years from now.

The government bureaucracy in Japan wields enormous clout, and the prime minister's power is notoriously constrained by its wishes. But Hosokawa-san stepped out of the circle drawn for him by the bureaucrats. Speaking his mind in the face of very powerful opposition, he certainly earned my respect for his boldness.

Ishihara Shintaro quickly responded by saying that Hosokawa-san "deserved death" for his defaming of Japan. How ironic that was, given that Mr. Hosokawa's courageous acknowledgement of Japan's wartime actions was seen by many people – Japanese and non-Japanese both – as a possible new beginning, a chance to face and let go of the past.

It was Hosokawa-san who offered foreigners a way of sorting out and coming to terms with the extremes and contradictions Japan presented us with. Despite subsequent backpedaling by others in government, his words were now in the public record. They could hardly be retracted from people's memories.

Though I had no great personal stake in the war with Japan (my father served in Europe, and I grew up hearing about it), official Japan's denials and silence about its wartime aggression had made me angry for all those who suffered because of it. Personally speaking, it was really Mr. Hosokawa's statement of apology that dissolved the anger I felt, and moved me to forgive and forget. I now believe Laurens van der Post got it right – it's only through forgiving that we can heal the wounds of the past.

I suspect Hosokawa-san's statement meant a lot to a great many people. That includes millions of Japanese, who have waited decades for someone in their government to finally speak with such candor about the war.

A Need for Reconciliation

Years have gone by since Hosokawa-san's brief tenure as prime minister. Since that time, I've retained an interest in learning more about what actually happened during the period the Japanese refer to as the "Pacific War" in Asia.

The official Japanese pattern of denial can be inexplicable and profoundly exasperating. In her introduction to *The Rape of Nanking*, published in 1997, Iris Chang wrote, "Strongly motivating me throughout this long and difficult labor was the stubborn refusal of many prominent Japanese politicians, academics, and industrial leaders to admit, despite overwhelming evidence, that the Nanking massacre had even happened."

Given the experience of Iris Chang and others, historian John W. Dower's major new work about the Occupation, *Embracing Defeat: Japan in the Wake of World War II*, published in 1999, was timely. I learned of this book through Jeff Kingston's excellent review in *The Japan Times*, though I'm still ploughing my way through its 676 pages. In Kingston's words, it offers a possible explanation for the "collective amnesia in contemporary Japan concerning its checkered past in Asia."

Generally speaking, U.S. occupation policies in Japan are thought to have been very successful. But Dower faults the U.S. for its mishandling of the war-crimes trials, a process that led to the absolution of the Emperor. The effect of that on the average Japanese citizen was surely profound.

Kingston quotes Dower as pointing out that "if the man in whose name imperial Japan had conducted foreign and military policy for 20 years was not held accountable for the initiation or conduct of the war, why should anyone expect ordinary people to dwell on such matters, or to think seriously about their own personal responsibility?"

Given that Japanese people had been taught to revere the Emperor as a God and to die for him, the fact that the victors in the war 'let him off' must have carried enormous weight. At the time, ordinary Japanese were suffering through the bitterness of defeat. They were also enduring an occupation, by conquering American troops, for the first time in their history. They undoubtedly had all they could deal with just putting their lives together again in the devastated cities of Tokyo, Hiroshima and Nagasaki, and throughout Japan.

Add to this the general Japanese discomfort with controversy, and perhaps you have a recipe for wartime amnesia. The fact that it turned into outright denial in academic and government circles is still very disturbing to me. But it's less puzzling than it once was. I know from personal experience that Japanese are very reluctant to face difficult issues head-on. Obviously, there are some who would like to bury history altogether. But for others with no such intentions, direct criticism can still result in defensiveness.

Speaking about the Emperor's actual role in the war, Ian Buruma interprets it this way: "Whatever else he may have been, he was not a fascist dictator." Suggestions that he was the malevolent mastermind behind Japan's fascist regime would lead many Japanese, with no stake in denying the actions of Japan's military, to leap to his defense. As my father fought for God, King and country without questioning it, so the Japanese fought for their Emperor.

I also recognize that many ordinary Japanese did denounce their military in the first decades after the war. I recently watched Ozu Yasujiro's charming film, *An Autumn Afternoon*, released in 1962. In the film, Hirayama-san – a widower and father who is a wonderful character – is slowly coming to terms with needing to give up his daughter, Michiko, to marriage. In one scene, Hirayama-san meets another former naval man who served under him, and they discuss the difficulties they've faced as a result of the war. Sakamoto-san wonders why they lost the war, and what would have happened if they'd won.

> Hirayama-san: It's lucky we lost.
> Sakamoto-san: You think so? (pause) Yeah, could be.
> We're rid of all those arrogant fools.

Aside from Hosokawa-san, the Japanese governments of the 1990s (with the L.D.P. again back in power), have basically continued to avoid taking direct responsibility for the war. Japanese leaders undoubtedly took note that the American government has not rushed to apologize for Vietnam.

Government officials probably fear setting themselves up for endless litigation. Korean and Taiwanese war victims, such as the so-called *comfort women* (a long-running story in the news here), hired lawyers at one point, to make their case. The government attempted to pass the buck to Japanese corporations, asking them to set up a compensation fund. But what the women most wanted was an official apology.

Many decades after the fact, it seems obvious that only governments can adequately respond to such demands for redress. Young Japanese are hardly responsible for actions of the state taken before they were born (any more than young Americans are accountable for Vietnam), and they don't deserve to inherit the blame for them.

For the young generations of Japan, China and the rest of Asia, the Pacific War is now distant history. Most are busy looking towards the future. Young Japanese have about as much use for the Emperor as some young Brits (or Canadians) do for their Queen.

But the search for truth, and for Japan's contrition, is not likely to fade away, especially since countries like China and North Korea are renowned for their long memories. Even in the U.K., during the official visit of the Emperor and Empress of Japan to London in 1998, World War II veterans turned their backs on the parade. It's difficult to imagine how the deep wounds of war can finally be healed, other than through honest admissions, and recourse to Buddhist compassion and Christ-like forgiveness, on all sides.

Atonement and reconciliation for the wartime transgressions of the 20th century would be very good medicine for Asia and the world. They're probably vital for a peaceful future for Japan and its neighbors, especially if they hope to grow closer together – as Europe has – in an East Asian common market.

Learning the Unspoken Language

Japanese culture continually forces you to re-examine your own Western assumptions about communication. Perhaps hardest of all is the preference for unspoken, or indirect exchanges of information. Hand in hand with this is the preference for what we might call denial or falsehood, but which Japanese culture recognizes as the need to save face and avoid confrontation.

For many Japanese, directness seems to be paralyzing. My colleague Marianne talked once about being in coffee shops (doing paperwork) and observing young Japanese couples. Some sit across from each other in mournful silence, often for an hour or two, without saying a word.

"It's obvious that their relationship is ending, but neither person knows how to deal with it," she said. Then she laughed, admitting that sometimes she had to resist going over and shouting, "Hey, break up already!"

Indirectness is the much preferred style. A Canadian friend of mine hosts Japanese students in Canada in homestay programs. She told me a story that's a variation on a theme I've heard a number of times. A Japanese high-school girl came to stay with them for a year. During the first month, everything was fine. Then she suddenly went to the organizers of the program and asked for a new homestay family. She vanished into thin air and never contacted them again.

My friend never knew why. In the month she'd stayed with them, the Japanese girl and my friend's teenage daughter had gotten along well. Why had she not even left a forwarding address, they wondered? My friend was mystified, and her daughter felt betrayed, sensing that the Japanese girl's expressions of friendship had been false. I did my best to explain that the girl's failure to contact them was probably about loss of face. It shouldn't be taken personally.

It's obviously impossible to know the cause without knowing the details. There were other possible explanations: Reverse culture shock? A negative reaction at being asked to do chores? (This is a common problem, sometimes born of a fear of being placed in a subservient role, or because their mother has always done chores for them.) But not being able to deal with an uncomfortable issue directly is such a common Japanese trait, that the young girl's failure to contact them again did not surprise me at all.

Hanae has clarified many things about Japanese language and culture for me. She once explained the language to me this way: "Ours is an indirect culture. The purpose of our mother tongue is to speak indirectly or hide. We have to read between the lines, and guess the hidden meaning in what people say."

She gave me a good example. After she'd spoken on the phone at work one day, her boss said to her cheerfully, "*Denwa de genki!*" Literally, this meant, "Hey, you're very energetic when you're on the phone."

Hanae explained the hidden meaning. "We have to guess what our boss is really saying," she told me. "What he was telling me, with that comment, was that I'm too loud when I talk on the phone in the office."

Being indirect is a cultural law of the land, and you fail to observe it at your peril. A former colleague of mine accepted a position at a new university more than a year before it was to start operations. With six months left before the grand opening, he and his wife decided they only wanted to stay in Japan another couple of years. He was then offered a two-year contract with another institution, which he promptly accepted.

Believing that honesty is the best policy, he explained the situation to the administration of the new university. He expected that six months would be plenty of time for them to find a replacement. But that was not the main issue, it turned out, and there was quite a kerfuffle.

The upshot was the fact that he'd chosen another institution over theirs, and then he'd told them about it! "Why didn't you just make up something?" one frustrated administrator asked him.

All would have been well, if he'd only done the culturally appropriate thing – inventing an unrelated excuse such as, "My wife's mother is ill, and we have to return to the States." Even if the administration had later discovered what really happened, that wouldn't have mattered. The university's face would have been saved, and his lie would have been understood as an acceptable means to that end.

Japanese cultural waters can be very tough to navigate in, because what we might call white lies, or outright deception, are such a common currency of communication. It seems to be an issue of means and ends. The 'ends' of Japanese intention are usually honorable – to protect people from embarrassment. But when the 'means' go against your Western upbringing, cultures can clash – as my colleague discovered.

In *Straitjacket Society: An Insider's Irreverent View of Bureaucratic Japan*, Dr. Masao Miyamoto explains the 'code' and *doublespeak* of the bureaucrat. He suggests that, "The Japanese willingness to sanction lies is, I believe, a major source of cultural friction with Western countries that are founded on Christian culture, which teaches people to face the truth unflinchingly in all things."

I don't believe for a minute that Western countries should be given this much credit for straightforwardness. Yet, to a Westerner, it can often seem that Japanese culture runs aground – and mostly harms itself – because of its habit of evasiveness and an inability to face the truth.

I recall reading about a female Thai AIDS researcher at the international AIDS conference in Yokohama. She presented anecdotal research – interviews with hundreds of young Thai boys – which was quite compelling. She had found that many young Japanese female tourists routinely engage in unprotected sex in Thailand. She suggested that they need much better sex education.

How was this information received? The Thai researcher was lambasted by a middle-aged Japanese woman, who said this research impugned the morality of young Japanese women. She demanded a retraction!

At a certain point in time, I reached this simple conclusion: In Japan, pointing out that a boat is leaking, and may sink, usually gets you nowhere. Instead, you have to talk 'around' the problem. You have to speak about the advantages of a seaworthy vessel, without ever mentioning why one is suddenly needed. Of utmost importance is getting the message across without anyone losing their all-important face, because if 'face' is lost, the message will be lost along with it.

Acts of Endearment

In my years in Japan, I've become very appreciative of numerous little courtesies and gestures that Japanese people extend to others. Only a foreigner who's grown truly numb and bitter could fail to continue to notice, acknowledge and appreciate these wonderful acts of kindness.

After a get-together with Japanese people, I bow and wave, turn and go on my way. But after taking five or six steps, I always turn around again now, for one last goodbye. Sure as the sunrise, my Japanese friends will still be there for the second wave. It's a lovely gesture of attentiveness to friendship, a reminder that you're not quickly out of their hearts and minds, and replaced by the next event in their busy schedules.

At a party, someone will take photographs. Invariably, they'll get copies to me within three or four days, either in person or by mail. Small gestures count for a lot in Japan. I feel very appreciated here for things I do for people. In turn, I'm grateful for the little things my Japanese friends are continually doing for me.

When Maggie left Japan, I organized a *Sayonara* brunch for her at the Hilton. There were about 35 of us, at six or seven tables, at 5,000 yen a head. When it came time to pay the bill, I put it on my credit card (175,000 yen), and asked people to collect money at their tables and get it to me later. At home that night, I counted the cash - 185,000 yen - 10,000 yen extra. I paused to reflect on how often people in such situations wind up 'short' in North America. I knew, without any doubt, what had happened. An anonymous Japanese person had put in 10,000 extra, to pay for Maggie and me.

Splitting a bill at a restaurant with Japanese is always easy, because it's handled graciously. There's never any nickel-and-diming it by someone who had one drink less than everyone else. It's a simple thing, but very pleasing when it's so consistently the case.

When you're invited on a picnic, nobody ever has to say the word 'potluck.' Everyone automatically brings something, and there's always an abundance. More than enough thoughtfulness has always gone into making sure the whole group is taken care of.

At the private school I've taught at for years now, *Athenée Française*, my students have sometimes taken me out to the most wonderful restaurants. Occasionally, they've paid for me and bought me lovely gifts as well. I can't thank them enough for the kindness they've shown me. I'll always remember it with gratitude.

Then there was the elderly gentleman - probably an octogenarian - whom I encountered in the famous Dogo Hot Spring in *Matsuyama*, on the island of

Shikoku. As I sat luxuriating in the *onsen* water, called *Kami-no-yu* (Water of the Gods), he motioned me to come closer to him.

He was up to his neck in the water, relaxing alongside a mythical stone creature, out of whose mouth a jet of water was pouring. Without speaking a word, he proceeded to gently position me under its stream. Then he directed the water over my head. He did all this in a very attentive manner, like it was some kind of ritual for him. I imagine he believed the water of his beloved *onsen* would purify anything in me that needed healing (my Tokyo-weary spirit, perhaps).

There's an endearing innocence about these gestures that's touching. Perhaps when the Japanese people speak of the importance of having *atatakai kokoro* (a warm heart), this is what they mean.

Two Tokyo Tips

If someone tells me they're moving to Tokyo to work and asks for some advice, two tips come to mind. The first pops up without a moment's hesitation. I tell them to make a priority of minimizing time spent on the trains. I suggest they do whatever they can to achieve this - to get accommodation within walking - or bicycling - distance of their place of work, or to live as few train stops away as possible. Otherwise, as I've learned from experience, the trains may eat you alive.

This city has changed quite a lot in 10 years. But the commuter trains remain much the same as ever. They're efficient, but jam-packed. They're the city's most essential feature, and its greatest human challenge. For those of us who ride them everyday, our lives and attitudes are shaped and defined by the punishing hours of cramped captivity spent in commuting. Life on the trains has dominated my experience of Tokyo.

My own life in Tokyo was always much more intense than those of my colleagues at Shōrai-dai, because I lived in Chofu and had to commute every day. When we'd get together for dinner or for an evening of card games, I always had to factor in my two-hour commute home.

I met an Austrian woman at a party, who worked for her embassy. She lived upstairs from her office on the second floor. Every day, she walked down a flight of stairs with her morning coffee to get to her desk.

Needless to say, her Tokyo is not the Tokyo I've known during my time here, nor is it the Tokyo of the average Japanese. I'm now appreciative of the fact that I've endured, as the Japanese have to endure, because I'll always know what their lives are really like as a result.

I've also learned a lot about Japanese sensibilities through the hours I've logged on the trains. I remember one night, on the Yamanote Line, when a group of five Irishmen suddenly jumped in the train car I was on. They had guitars, a standup bass, a drum and washboards, and they started right in with a rollicking Irish foot-stomper. Despite the lightheartedness of the music, I suspect they traumatized half the Japanese on board!

Hardly anyone displayed any outer reaction, except for the middle-aged gentleman sitting next to me. Perhaps because I was dressed in a suit and tie, he felt comfortable sharing his feelings with me. Clearly distraught, he repeated the same thing several times in English, "Not here, not on the train!"

After years of riding these rails, I understood his feelings well. When you're lucky enough to get a seat, Tokyo trains provide a kind of quiet interlude in a relentlessly busy life.

Westerners often take great license doing such culturally inappropriate things in Japan. Even when we have the best of intentions, we sometimes cross way over the line of acceptable behavior, doing what comes naturally to us. All of that said, some of the Japanese on the train - especially the younger ones - may well have enjoyed the music.

It so happened that after the Irishmen finished playing, I got off the train at the same time they did, a couple of stops further down the line.

"They're all so sad!" one of them remarked to me, incredulously.

"You'd best get used to it if you plan to be here awhile," I replied. "Actually, some of them may have loved your music, but you'd never know it."

That's the second major tip I offer to newcomers: Get out of the habit of assuming the impressions that you - and other foreigners - form of this culture are accurate or complete. In Japan, there's a much wiser course to follow. That is to suspend judgment, and wait for more information. It's so helpful to take the stance that there's always more going on in people's hearts and minds than you - as a cultural outsider - know about.

When I reflect on my years in Japan, perhaps my biggest regret is that I didn't learn this sooner. I would have been happier and gotten over my culture shock earlier on. If my experience persuades a few *gaijin* and Japanese - who are struggling as I once was - to start giving each other the benefit of the doubt, I'll consider that writing this book was well worth the effort.

A good illustration of all of this comes by way of one group of first-year university students, whom I recently taught once a week for a year - from April through January. Since it was an unusually small group of 18 students, I had high hopes that we'd have a great class. I was sure we'd get to know each other well.

It wasn't to be. I pulled out every trick I knew, but the students were all very tight-lipped. Working with them felt like pulling teeth. But I didn't express any exasperation with them; I'd finally learned from experience that doing so seldom helps. I just kept on quietly working with them, class after class.

One day, about eight months into our session, we were working on the Eagles' song, *Desperado*. Since they wouldn't sing, I decided to pour my heart into it, and really belted it out. I had a good time entertaining myself, but they showed no response.

One week later, I got a thoughtful three-page letter from one young fellow in the class.

"I think you are feeling desperate about us," he wrote, adding that he knew they should speak English more, but they were all very shy.

The year ended without any change taking place. I had taught this group through 25 sessions, of an hour and a half each, with few signs that they were enjoying the class, or learning much of anything.

On the final day, after I'd said my farewells and wished them luck, I prepared to leave. Suddenly, one young woman rushed up to my desk with a strawberry shortcake. She offered her sincere thanks for my work with the class. I gratefully accepted, and shared it with friends in an Irish bar in *Ikebukuro* later that night.

Such situations are a dime a dozen at universities – and elsewhere – in Japan. One Italian professor in his seventies wrote to a magazine here called *The Hiragana Times*. He expressed himself most eloquently. He said the Japanese are "a truly wonderful people who are kind, gentle and think of other people before themselves." He went on to say how tragic it is that this goodness "doesn't come across." He believed this was because the Japanese are too busy and have poor communication skills. So they're frequently misunderstood by foreigners, who conclude that they're just "strange people."

Like the Italian professor, I know about that goodness – hidden behind a wall of silence. As with him, I've discovered that the Japanese have many wonderful qualities. So one day, I took the magazine clipping to a few classes to talk about the professor's observations and to get my students' reaction. They all read it quietly, and said not a word.

Hubris and Humility, East and West

Generally speaking, I've experienced Japanese men in authority to be pretty tolerant of Westerners. They're constantly dealing with attitudes and behavior that are strange and idiosyncratic to them. To use the British expression, many Westerners in Japan can be bloody-minded – stubborn in ways that are easily a match for Japanese stonewalling.

Japanese bosses also put up with a lot of nonsense. Foreign employees sometimes break contracts and leave the country without warning. They request a week off to return to their country for a wedding, and then extend it to three. You hear many such stories. There are undoubtedly a good number of Japanese who have 'had it up to here' with troublesome Westerners. The deceptions and broken promises definitely go both ways.

Japanese men often get a collective bad rap in the Western press. They're widely portrayed as being sexist for their treatment of women, or perverts because of phenomena such as *chikan* and *manga*. When they go overseas, they often come across badly.

In Canada, I spoke with one American from Atlanta. He told me that Japanese men who play at his golf course are seen as unfriendly. That's because they often fail to respond when American men say 'Good morning' to them around the club house. That's no surprise to me – or anyone who's read this book; most Japanese are seldom as friendly with strangers as Americans are.

But when you work in Japan, you also see another side. You see these men at home on their own turf. You often meet their wives and children. You recognize that they have challenging lives.

The men in positions of authority, under whom I've worked, have generally been very serious men, often to the point of seeming somber or severe. This is especially true of those born in the 1930s, who were shaped by the war years.

With them, you often get a sense of authoritarian control. But they'll rarely lose their patience with you publicly when you question things. They seem aware that Westerners are raised to opinionize, and to say what we think. Many also seem to understand that we're under pressure living in a foreign culture, and they make allowances for that.

I shudder a bit now, when I look back at all the Western assumptions I carried with me to Japan, assuming they were 'universals.' I can now reflect with more insight on conflicts that arose, and recognize times when I took a wrong turn.

One of my favourite Japanese proverbs is *Nana-korobi, hachi-oki*. It translates as, 'Fall down seven times, get up eight.' I like it very much, because it describes the life of many *gaijin* in Japan, myself included. It also suggests how the Japanese cope.

It was tough to adjust to this alien social landscape. I made some false starts in the early going. And all the way along, there was a fair bit of stumbling through, and making it up as I went along. Even the Japanese sometimes seem to be flying by the seat of their pants.

One Saturday morning, we all showed up at *Shōrai-dai* for our regular staff meeting. To our astonishment, N.H.K. (Japan's national television station) was there, all set to film the proceedings. Owing to a unique educational policy *Shōrai-dai* had just adopted, they had descended on us to get the scoop. For the *gaijin*, at least, it was a complete surprise, but within minutes we were being interviewed. Our 'talking heads' showed up on television the next morning, discussing university education in Japan.

When Canadians, Brits and Americans come over to Japan to work, we come toting our beliefs ("Things like this shouldn't happen!"), not to mention our Western personalities. It's kind of hard to leave them back home. So we automatically throw them into the new cultural stew, assuming they suit the recipe. At times, we stir the mixture on low to medium heat, so it's not surprising when it starts to simmer. When something like N.H.K.'s sudden appearance happens – the *gaijin* invariably do some grumbling.

In response, the Japanese bosses I've known generally come off well. When we ruffle feathers through our cross-cultural ignorance, they usually handle it with patience and composure. For that, many of us are grateful and respectful. Ken, my American colleague and friend while I was at Shōrai-dai, reflected on this once with the comment, "Japan teaches you humility."

When Canada's and my hockey hero, the Great One (Wayne Gretzky), announced his retirement, it occurred to me that he exemplified many of the qualities that Japanese and Canadians both respect. He was renowned for emphasizing teamwork and seeking excellence. He seldom boasted, and always put the needs of the team above himself. He had a *gambatte* spirit, pushing him to persevere and work hard at all times. Apparently, he was always on time for practice and ready to give 100%. The Great One also avoided conflict, and never got into fights on the ice. How very Japanese of you, Wayne!

Canadians, like Japanese, are generally less comfortable than Americans at blowing our own horns. Yet we marvel at the attitude of "Let's see what you can do," in the U.S.

Canadians (like Jim Carrey and Michael J. Fox) and Japanese (like pitcher Nomo Hideo) head to the States, because it's the land of opportunity. As all Japanese learned, the 1999 Academy Award winner for best dramatic short feature was a Japanese woman, who'd only been in the U.S. for eight years. In her acceptance speech, she was flabbergasted to be receiving this honor after such a short time in her adopted country. Such is America!

Such is also America's greater respect for the professional aspirations of the fairer sex. But even the U.S. lags well behind other countries like New Zealand, which entered the year 2000 with women leading all its political parties. By comparison, Japan remains decades behind. From Hanae, I've heard some disquieting stories about the demeaning treatment she's been subjected to by a few of her male bosses. Fortunately, others have been very supportive of her.

It's my sense that it's in their dealings with Western women that Japanese male bosses run into the most problems with their foreign staff. Some seem quite unable to get their minds around the idea that their American and European female employees will not take kindly to being treated as inferiors to men.

In addition to good stories of considerate and fair treatment, I've also heard more than a few accounts of bosses who have alienated their foreign female staff, through fear and intimidation. One female colleague of mine left Shōrai-dai very shaken by the treatment she'd received at the hands of two of the male bosses she'd worked under. Because of them, her feeling on leaving Japan was basically, 'Good Riddance.'

How to explain this? In the 1991 *Lonely Planet Guide for Japan*, the authors put it in simple language, "Women in Japan are, however, very much second class citizens." By the 1997 edition, this passage had been deleted, something I'd prefer to take as a hopeful sign that things are slowly changing.

Yet, there's no disputing that women in Japan are still at a distinct disadvantage professionally. For many Japanese men, the viewpoint that women are subordinates is not one they're going to relinquish easily. Yet, it's perplexing, because these are men who never fail to ask me how my *okusan* (wife) is. (They just assume I'm married.) Their wives are obviously very important to them.

When you're a teacher - even in a male-dominated society such as Japan's - you look for reasons to be hopeful, and you find them. One sensitive male *returnee* student of mine, Okaka Rintaro, wrote on the topic of male/female relations one day in our class. He expressed a sensible perspective all men could aspire to: "However hard women and men try, they can't build perfectly 'equal' relations (because they have fundamental differences). They can only build 'good relations' if there is consideration and forgiveness. That's all we can do, and that's enough."

Kipling Revised

Rudyard Kipling's view that "East is East, and West is West, and never the twain shall meet," while correct in his day, ought to be amended for the 21st century. It's now surely more accurate to say that, "East was East, and West was West, but now the twain have met."

People from every cultural background on earth are moving around the planet, such that more than 20% of the people of Vancouver, Canada are now reported to be of Asian ancestry. It's the same situation in hundreds of increasingly multicultural cities and towns in all corners of the globe.

My experience of adjusting to Tokyo has given me a firsthand look at what a Hong Kong Chinese, who speaks no English, goes through in emigrating to Vancouver. It's a valuable thing to know in a world that started the 20th century with one billion people, but began the 21st with six times that number. Tens of millions of us - at some point in our lives - are leaving the country we were born into and transplanting ourselves elsewhere. Our movements create change in our newly adopted cultures.

During my decade in Tokyo, the clash and merging of Japanese and

American cultures and ideologies have been omnipresent. I only have to turn on radio station InterFM to hear the American and Canadian deejays dissecting yet another aspect of Japanese culture. Meanwhile, textbooks for Japanese students are filled with descriptions of every facet of the American way of life.

In many ways, I now see Japan and the U.S. as being polar opposites, embodying behavioral and cultural extremes. Japan has its emphasis on cohesion and conformity. That gives rise to a phenomenally disciplined workforce with an emphasis on self-denial, which puts severe limits on individual expression. America has its 'go for it' individualism, leading to tremendous innovation and creativity, alongside brazen self-interest and rampant violence.

How do you reconcile such enormous differences, when people from radically different backgrounds mix together? It certainly isn't easy. During my time in Tokyo, what's helped me cope with this society's many constraints is the realization that on a daily basis, each interaction I have is reshaping my own attitudes, as well as those of the Japanese I meet. Opportunities are always coming along where I know I have something important to contribute, and just as often something to learn.

I had one conversation with a Japanese man in his thirties, who'd recently returned from a solo trip to Europe. He wanted to show me his photographs, and I happily obliged. Looking at a shot of him on the Matterhorn, high up in the Swiss Alps, I asked him who'd taken the photograph.

"Oh, a foreigner did," he said.

Instead of letting it pass, I mentioned to him that in Canada, we refer to people by their nationalities: Swiss, Chinese, German, etc. In fact, they do this in Japan for non-Western foreigners. But from his reaction, I could tell that this was a novel idea when it comes to *gaijin*. Unfortunately, the English word *foreigner* is still widely used in Japan, along with the Japanese word *gaijin*. I can't think of how else this will change unless the *foreigners* in Japan talk about it with the Japanese, in a non-threatening way.

This kind of exchange has been mutual; I've learned plenty from Japanese people. Ironically, they've taught me to be mindful about including others at all times (those within your group, that is). In Japan, you never pour a drink for yourself, and it's become second-nature for me to pour for the people next to me, and let them return the favour. It's a great custom. It reminds you of your interdependence every time you sit down to share a meal.

I've become equally accustomed to the practice of always waiting to eat until everyone's ready. The whole group says *Itadakimasu* in unison. It literally means, "I will receive." When people eat together, they closely attend to the sense of community. They focus on the experience of sharing together. It's a wonderful side of Japanese culture that I respect and love.

From my point of view, this intermingling of people and cultures is definitely a good thing. Another culture's rituals teach you new ways of appreciating life. From customs at odds with your own, you can learn tolerance. It's a quality that's high up on the list of those we're going to need to survive as a species.

This cross-pollination of cultures is also happening on a global scale, whether we like it or not. Rival ideologies in the world power game will surely do battle as long as separate human societies exist. But on a personal level, every time two people from different cultures overcome their differences, the world takes a step towards peace.

We can dig in our heels, defend our own cultural bias, and stay blind to the views of others. Or we can embrace a new world Kipling probably couldn't have imagined – one in which East meets West, both sides give some ground, and our lives are all enriched.

The Bureaucracy Grinds On

Anything regulated by bureaucrats in Japan is liable to wrap you up in reams of red tape or require, at the very least, plenty of patience. You can occasionally get lucky, but most of the time, things are not going to go as fast as you'd like. As the Japanese know well, your best option is to invoke the all-purpose word *shōgenai*, and then throw yourself at the mercy of the administrators.

I learned from personal experience that selling a car privately, and doing the paperwork to change ownership, is an unbelievably complex procedure. It can take days to walk through it. By comparison, doing this in Canada is a cakewalk, something I've come to appreciate.

Most Canadians and Americans think our systems are complex – little do they know. It's tempting to conclude that, in Japan, the whole procedure has been set up to discourage people. That is to say, it's designed to dissuade them from selling their used car to anyone other than a dealer, from whom they're buying a new one. If you go that route, the paperwork is all done for you.

It's a similar story with electronic products, in the sense that getting parts can take more time than it's worth. With both a television set and a camera tripod – made by huge and well-known international corporations – I found that procuring a simple replacement part took hours.

In both instances, I was first told that the parts weren't available, but I didn't give up. After a great amount of checking in thick parts manuals, the story changed. The problem was that parts would be very difficult to get. I persevered, and a half-hour later, I learned that the parts were available after all. Forms were filled out, and in both cases the parts arrived within a few days.

I came away from these experiences convinced that it's set up this way to discourage you, in hopes that you'll just buy a new one. In general, getting electronic goods repaired is far less common in Japan than in North America.

When it comes to starting up a new enterprise, I heard one story on a television program called *Today's Japan* about an inventive Japanese entrepreneur who developed a mini-car. It took him 60 trips to the local prefectural office, armed with new paperwork each time, to set up a small car company. Orders were coming in fast, but first he had to devote himself to jumping through these bureaucratic hoops.

So it's not just foreigners who endure endless grief trying to crack the Japanese market; stiff regulations apply to Japanese entrepreneurs as well. This is useful information for foreign companies and exporters, who have struggled for decades to cut through Japan's famous red tape. I heard one report from a spokesperson for *Starbucks*. She explained the highly detailed nature of the quality-control regulations they had to conform to, in order to set up in Japan. As Jonathan Rauch concluded: "Moreover, I do not think that the Japanese City Hall tries especially to thwart foreigners. Rather it tries to thwart newcomers."

The politician Ozawa Ichiro wrote a book some years ago called *Blueprint for a New Japan: The Rethinking of a Nation*. At that time, he commented in a speech at the National Press Club in Washington that Japan is a nation "where legal and administrative regulations penetrate every sector of our society, every nook and cranny of our lives."

So des ne (Isn't it so!), as everyone in Japan is fond of saying. But it's very hard to imagine how significant change in this bureaucratic colossus will come about, especially since Japan's bureaucrats surely deserve some of the credit for this country's successes. In contemplating change, they may be terrified of killing the goose that laid the once-golden egg.

In fact, as I watch my own country, Canada, lose more and more ground to foreign - especially American - ownership, I have some respect for the refusal of Japan's bureaucracy to be overly conciliatory to U.S. demands. They have no wish to lose any more control of their own destiny than they have to.

Back in Canada, I was dumbfounded to read a tiny newspaper story about a new condo complex on B.C.'s Saltspring Island. The report said that American and other foreign buyers were to be allowed first dibs on the units. A month later, Canadians would have their chance. Such a situation is unimaginable in Japan.

As for bureaucratic imbroglios that affect the average person, I've heard some stories from Westerners recently, of dealings with the computerized and backlogged bureaucracies of our own countries. These can be every bit as nightmarish as anything you'd find in Japan. After an extended visit back in America, Randall e-mailed me and said, "I now realize that a lot of what I didn't like about Japan is the same as what's happened everywhere in the world these past 10 years."

Such observations are a reminder to those of us holed up in Japan that techno-bureaucratic bottlenecks are worldwide phenomena now. Japan's bureaucracy is just more thorough and all-encompassing, and it really does seem to touch "every nook and cranny" of its citizens' lives. I've long suspected that's the reason so many Japanese seldom go a day without their saké.

The *Salaryman* Keeps Slogging on

Tokyo has its share of foreign musicians of all kinds. They play in the train stations and busk on the streets. In Hachiko Square in Shibuya one day, I saw a group of energetic Latin Americans in colorful ponchos playing Paul Simon's song, El Condor Pasa, with its famous refrain, "I'd rather be a hammer than a nail."

It was a poignant moment hearing this in Tokyo. The lyrics took on new significance, because of this country's most well-known and overused proverb, Deru kugi wa utareru – the nail that sticks up gets hammered down. (Add me to the long list of overusers.) It's a proverb Canadians can relate to, because tremendous individual success is something that's viewed with suspicion in Canada much more often than it's celebrated.

As I listened, I noticed a few tired and sad-eyed *salarymen*, who'd also stopped briefly to check out what was going on. They looked exhausted and uncomprehending. No doubt, they would also prefer to be hammers, rather than the nails they surely are.

On another afternoon inside Shibuya Station, a young Chinese student was pummeling away on a kind of horizontal harp, but one that was played like a xylophone. It was entrancing to listen to, and I lingered as long as I could. He had some Chinese tunes in his repertoire. But for the most part, he was playing lovely renditions of traditional Japanese songs on his marvelous instrument.

I watched and listened, along with three or four middle-aged Japanese women. They smiled and applauded at the end of each song, enthralled with the young man's performance. At one point, I asked one of them if they knew the name of the instrument. This spurred them all into an animated discussion. Eventually, they wrote down several kanji characters that I couldn't identify. They weren't even sure about the instrument's name in *Nihongo*, but they gave me their best guess. I thanked them, we exchanged laughter and smiles, and continued enjoying the music.

As we continued listening, disheveled-looking *salarymen* would stop to join the crowd from time to time. They were unsmiling, but clearly curious. I imagined that the familiarity of the Japanese tunes, played by this Chinese pied piper, had momentarily wrenched them from the trajectory of their frantic routines.

Gazing at him rather vacantly, some would stand with their arms folded across their chests. One or two had a barely discernible kind of wistfulness on their faces. It was as if they were trying to reconnect with something lost, something long ago and far away, something locked up deep inside them. Then in a flash, they would dash off, company men once more.

If you've ever worked alongside these men, you can't help but feel some empathy for them. I've seen firsthand how hard they work, and how tough their lives are. But I also know how much they respect dedication and mastery. So I wasn't surprised by what I saw on another occasion, as I listened to a young European violinist finish up a beautifully played piece with a flourish. An older company man, looking to be in his fifties, had been listening intently. With an appreciative smile, he bowed slowly and deeply to the musician, and then trundled off.

Hope Springs Eternal

My friend Maggie used to rent a small but comfortable apartment on the second floor of an old Japanese home in *Omori*, in central Tokyo. A gracious, elderly Japanese woman lived downstairs. Amazingly, the house had a 'well' in the garden. When I stayed over at Maggie's, we could hear the pumping of the handle in the morning as Mrs. Kobayashi drew water by hand.

The Tokyo that Maggie's landlady once knew as a child has largely vanished. It was obliterated by war, and then rebuilt in a frenzy of modernization. That led to buildings like the three-story walkup I now live in. It's in an older neighbourhood, *Bunkyo-ku*, where there are dozens of printing shops that run off thousands of flyers and newsletters every day.

My apartment, on the third floor, is a compact, six-*tatami*-mat room. It has sliding paper doors called *shōji* that open onto two corridors. One goes to the entrance, and the other to a narrow kitchen, which leads to a bathroom and shower. By Canadian standards, my apartment is minuscule. It's still amazing to me to note that the longer I've lived in Tokyo, the more normal such tiny apartments have grown to seem.

I love my little place, partly because it's the kind of setting Japanese couples with two children shared in the '50s. Living here, I get a better sense of what the lives of those who rebuilt this country after the war were like. My friend Maki clapped her hands with delight when she visited and exclaimed, "This is exactly the kind of place I grew up in!"

When I first moved in, my landlady, Kumagai-san, sat and had tea with me on my *tatami* mat. She told me she was 15 years old in 1945. She remembers being able to look right across the rubble of Tokyo in all directions, because so little was left standing.

How completely things have changed in just half a century. Kumagai-san is a diehard landlord, holding out against developers who want to buy and level her place. They'd like to put up another clone-apartment block.

A new one has just gone up across the street where a parking lot used to be. The neighbors hung banners out the windows of their houses to protest, but the development went ahead anyway. Now, the sunshine they used to get is entirely blocked by a 10-story building. It's located five feet in front of their front doors – such is progress.

It reminded me of a situation I watched unfold during my years of jogging alongside the Tama River. A row of old houses, with a beautiful view over the river, had been bought up for new development, but one family held out. To force them to sell, the developers basically buried their house. They brought in truckloads of earth and piled it up to the eaves troughs, all the way around the perimeter of the house. They left only enough space for the door. Then they put in asphalt on top. They opened up a temporary parking lot – above and around the roof of the house – while they waited for the family to give up.

Japan's phenomenal economic growth definitely came with a huge price. Industrialization has ravaged much of the countryside. Ironically, given the Japanese love of gardens, many of the beaches are a mess. On the ones I visit in Kamakura just south of Tokyo, plastic bottles, car tires and the detritus of a consumer lifestyle are strewn everywhere.

During one conference my university colleagues and I attended near Shimizu, located on Suruga Bay southwest of Tokyo, we were taken on a boat trip that was intended to be touristy. We assumed that meant it would be scenic, but though we sailed for quite a few miles along the coast, we saw only factories and belching smokestacks.

Reading Alex Kerr's *Lost Japan*, my heart grew sadder by the page, as I learned more about the destruction the recently pristine Japanese countryside has been subjected to. From David Suzuki and Keibo Oiwa, I learned that there are virtually no wild rivers left in Japan. They've all been 'domesticated.'

And yet, all is not lost. At Maggie's place in *Omori*, when we lifted the latch on Kobayashi-san's gate and walked through the garden in front of her home, our eyes immediately fell on beauty and orderliness. Great care is taken to maintain it. Passing through the front door and into her small *genkan*, we took delight in her tasteful flower arrangement. We'd then take off our shoes and line them up with the others, all neatly arranged in the *genkan*. You never wear outdoor shoes in a Japanese home. It's a sensible and hygienic custom many non-Japanese people retain on leaving Japan.

These contrasts are so striking. In one setting, there's relentless destruction and alarming indifference to nature. In another, there's evidence of great care and attention. Somehow, these extreme contradictions seem harder to fathom in Japan, perhaps because we grew up hearing of its exquisite beauty and refined aesthetic sense, and yearn for that respect to be widespread.

Fortunately, this love of beauty can still be found. You see it in homes and gardens like Kobayashi-san's. And you discover it in wonderful urban retreats like the peaceful Imperial Palace Gardens in *Chiyoda-ku*, across from *Otemon* intersection in Tokyo's business district. I've walked on those grounds while office workers – perched on benches – eat their *bentō* (lunch boxes) amidst flowers, birds and small waterfalls. This picturesque scene takes place in a huge park, surrounded by a moat, in the center of modern Tokyo.

But with the steamroller of 'progress' came a new way of thinking that dispensed with the old. This was poignantly revealed to me in my very first week at Soulful Software. I remember the day well. Our lovely young secretary accompanied me to the city office to pick up my alien registration card. We took a delightful little toy train, called the *Setagaya Line*, to get there. It actually stopped for cars at one point, at a busy intersection.

I was an unabashed train-lover before the daily commute in Tokyo dampened my ardor somewhat. So I became enthralled with the *Setagaya Line* from the moment we stepped inside. I commented on the marvelous wooden floors and paneling, the uniqueness of the low station platforms, and the narrow gauge of the rails.

But my secretary would have none of it. To all my expressions of pleasure, she responded again and again, "Oh no, it's old."

She seemed embarrassed. She may have thought I was just being polite, and was secretly chuckling at this old-fashioned technology. I certainly couldn't make any headway in persuading her that an old train like this had plenty of merit.

With all eyes on the 'new,' the older homes and buildings in neighborhoods like *Omori* and *Bunkyo-ku* are rapidly being bulldozed into the past. It's a planetary process, no doubt, happening in urban centers everywhere to a greater or lesser extent.

For the generations of Japanese to come, I find myself feeling concerned. I picture this country with the beauty of old Japan gone – replaced with convenience stores, video shops and pachinko parlors on every street corner. I find myself wondering if the courtesy, deference and respect for others – especially the elderly – will disappear along with it.

I offer my prayers that this will not happen. When I heard Kobayashi-san's well pumping water in a Tokyo garden in the early morning hours, I took heart. May the well not run dry.

Where Japan is a Refreshing Change

I'll always remember a story in the newspaper here about a middle-aged wheelchair-bound woman who had bad luck one day. She was accidentally left in a freight elevator overnight by the night watchman. She was trapped there for 14 hours. When she was discovered the next day, she was asked by Japanese reporters what she would do.

"I'm going to go home," she replied calmly.

"And aren't you going to sue?" asked one, knowing that an American would typically jump at the chance to file a lawsuit for emotional damages in such a case.

"There's been no harm done." she said. "Accidents happen sometimes."

That's something many Americans and Canadians seem to have almost forgotten. It's as if we've begun seeing all of life through a lens of fault-finding, legal advantage and self-interest. On the one hand, lawsuits can be a good thing, an effective deterrent against unacceptable behavior. The Japanese are finally discovering this with cases of genuine sexual harassment. But when an American woman sued the world's most famous hamburger chain because she'd burned herself with its coffee, the U.S. stepped fully into the Land of Legalese and Legal Oz.

With many small matters, the Japanese retain a perspective that we've lost. Sometimes a drunk businessman will piss against a wall on a public street in Tokyo. In legalistic North America, such a thing could land a man on page 3 of the newspaper now, and ruin his career. He could well be publicly humiliated, 'blamed' and 'charged.' In Japan, the police would just put him on the train and send him home.

During *Omikoshi* season, you see groups of Japanese men walking through the streets, carrying a heavy portable shrine on their shoulders. They shout, grunt and sweat their way along in a ritualistic demonstration of their combined masculine power. They wear skimpy little upper-body outfits, and some have their bare asses showing. Nobody gives it a second thought.

It's one of the ironies I love to ponder. This most bureaucratic and rule-bound of nations can also be incredibly sensible and appropriate in its responses to natural human foibles and expressiveness. In the latitude it provides its police and tax officials to make case-by-case decisions, it demonstrates good common sense. They're often empowered with the means to make 'light' of first offences, or to weigh the seriousness and triviality of an event and judge accordingly, without being strictly bound by the letter of the law.

You can find a similar sense of perspective in the actions of ordinary Japanese, as with the remarkable woman in the wheelchair. In some ways, our law-bound and lawyer-driven societies are fast becoming more rigid than theirs.

Nagano: Japan on the World's Stage

When Japan hosted the winter Olympics in February 1998, the planners put on a terrific show, as those of us living here knew they would. Nobody rises to the occasion of welcoming famous foreign guests quite like the Japanese. And when it came to hosting the entire world, they made sure everyone pulled out all the stops.

The new *shinkansen* from Tokyo was built especially for the Olympics. Washing your hands on the train could all be done without touching a thing. You put your hands under the electronic tap, and one sensor gave you a spurt of soap, another delivered water, and a third sensor dried your hands.

In Nagano City, I saw something I'd never seen anywhere in Japan - buses with hydraulic lifts for people in wheelchairs. It's often said that nothing changes Japan faster than *gaiatsu* - foreign criticism. Or, in this case, anticipation and avoidance of it. *Gaiatsu* can definitely bring changes for the better, though the people of Nagano Prefecture will be paying for decades for this party, just as Montrealers have done, for their Olympics, since 1976.

My colleagues and I watched on T.V. as all of Nagano stadium sang Beethoven's *Ode to Joy*. Their performance was linked with other choirs in various places around the world. I felt a surge of energy at our global interconnectedness. Yet something didn't feel quite right about the fact that every single Japanese in the stadium had learned the German words and was singing them fervently. Everywhere the camera panned, people were holding forth like they'd all known the *Ode to Joy* since early childhood.

My friend and colleague, George, had the same reaction. I think we both wanted to say it was wonderful. But it was also eerie - a kind of designer spontaneity. Of course, every city that's ever hosted the Olympics, or even just a G7 Conference, has used masquerade to put its best foot forward - moving its homeless and painting its slums. But on the center stage of satellite television, the Japanese proved to be unrivaled at presenting a unified image to the world.

Meanwhile, back in Tokyo, the overwhelming majority of my adult students at *Athenée Française* were quite unmoved by the Olympics. In every one of my classes, most people really couldn't have cared less. It was all happening just north of Tokyo, only an hour and a half by express train, but it might as well have been taking place in another country. They had more important things on their minds.

That said, I did find two eager students who were super-keen. One had lived in L.A., and she'd been to N.H.L. games there. So the three of us went up to Nagano together for the day to watch a Canada/U.S. hockey game.

We had a great time, but we sure paid for it. We shelled out 50,000 yen ($450 U.S.) each for tickets from a Canadian scalper. But we got to watch the Canucks beat the Yanks 4 - 1. It was worth every yen to hear the large contingent of raucous Americans deflate, and then lay into us every time we cheered a Canadian goal – how they hate to lose.

Many months later, I returned to Nagano for a day to get a sense of what the town was really like. By then, the Olympic hoopla was long since over. I decided I wanted to spend more time at *Zenkō-ji*, Nagano's remarkable temple, that dates back to the 7th century. It's one of the finest temples I've visited in Japan, and it was well worth returning for.

Walking up a narrow street full of noodle restaurants and gift shops, you approach the temple by passing through several large gates. These are guarded by fierce-looking entities carved in stone, reminding you to leave any negative thoughts outside. The journey up the hill culminates in the impressive *San-mon* Gate. Nearby, you can read about the temple's liberal philosophy on a wooden sign. Men and women from all Buddhist sects, and from all other traditions, are most welcome.

I got there around noon, and I slowly walked through *Zenkō-ji's* famous tunnel, which is completely dark and passes under the temple's inner sanctum. Groups of excited junior-high-school children were all talking and shouting, as kids anywhere might do in such a setting. It felt more like a haunted house at Disneyland than an ancient Buddhist temple.

So later in the day, I returned in the quiet of the evening. Just after sunset, I sat near the huge incense cauldron, in front of the *Hondō* (Main Hall), for about half an hour. It was very still, and I savored the moment, enjoying a welcome respite from the chaos of Tokyo. Every few minutes, someone would come by and pay homage – a middle-aged businessman, a jogger, a schoolgirl, a working woman who smiled innocently at me as she passed.

Each person would go up to the front of *Zenkō-ji*, place their palms together, and bow their head in a moment of prayer. Their faith affirmed, they'd quickly go on their busy way. It was a wonderful evening under a sky full of stars, near a Japanese temple that draws on more than a thousand years of history. Here was a side of Japan I could love and revere.

I sat awhile longer, and then it was time to return to Tokyo. By the time I started on down the hill to the station, I felt a sense of contentment. Far beyond the reach of modern media imagery, this was the real Japan of everyday Japanese people.

The Disastrous Decade

Just as the 1980s belonged to Japan, the amazingly resilient Americans roared back along the 'information highway' and reclaimed the 1990s. Meanwhile, for the Land of the Rising Sun, the 10 years leading up to the millennium will probably be remembered as a disastrous decade. While the American stock market skyrocketed with Alan Greenspan's "irrational exuberance" – eclipsing the triumphs of Japan's economy in the '80s – the once feared *Nikkei* stock index collapsed, and lay flat for the whole decade. It almost seemed as though it was cut off from the life force of the rest of the world.

In terms of stock market evaluations, at the end of the 1980s, seven of the top ten companies in the world were Japanese. Ten years later, Japan had only four in the top 100. Concern in the U.S. over Japan's chronic trade surplus was replaced by talk over China's, and everyone was left to wonder what on earth had happened to Japan. Did anyone even remember that this nation had so recently seemed unstoppable?

Those of us who lived through this period in Japan pieced together our own sense of what went wrong. Through journalists and economists, we all heard stories of government and corporate collusion and corruption. For years on end, newspaper headlines in Japan routinely focused on the latest officials arrested for taking bribes. Going through my notes, I came upon a comment by Masamura Kimihiro – a professor at Senshu University – who pointed out, "It is difficult to distinguish between gifts and bribes in Japan. Capitalizing on the ambiguity, many Japanese tend to give gifts expecting something in return later."

There was endless talk of stimulating the domestic economy, and the usual procrastination about opening up the Japanese market to more foreign imports. Then there were the admissions of bad loans. The numbers kept rising, eventually reaching a trillion U.S. dollars and counting, a 'savings and loans' crisis of gargantuan proportions.

True to form, it took years for the Japanese government to admit to this. One Japanese acquaintance, who now lives in Canada, explained it her way with a laugh, saying, "Japanese people hide until they can't hide anymore."

But there was less and less hiding in Japan. More and more of my students were not finding full-time jobs after their four years of university. The reliability of the old system was giving way to widespread uncertainty. Ritual suicides began happening left and right, with bank directors and government officials hanging themselves in hotel rooms. Delays on the *Chuo Line* in Tokyo started to become a routine event. For whatever reason, it became the line of choice for those wishing to end it all by leaping in front of an oncoming train.

Perhaps unrelated to the recession, Juzo Itami, my favorite Japanese film director, killed himself in December 1997. I felt a wince of pain and confusion, not understanding the Japanese proclivity for suicide. As Robert Elegant once said of Japan, "self-destruction is exalted as it is nowhere else."

The following year, 33,000 Japanese took their own lives, a large increase. It struck me that whereas Americans, at the breaking point, might 'go postal' and shoot up a restaurant, Japanese would be more likely to take their frustration out on themselves. Americans explode; Japanese implode.

Remembering my Soulful Software colleagues, I knew that many company men are totally devoted to their corporate families. Older employees can't really imagine an identity separate from the jobs they've had all their lives. No doubt, there were other psychological factors at work as well, having to do with shame and loss of face.

The long recession has brought changes for everyone. At one point, I learned that Soulful Software was asking employees to take one or two days off a month, without pay. It was something that was unheard of in the days I worked for them.

In the spring of 1999, I wandered around Tokyo's trendsetting *Shibuya* district. It was quite obvious that high-school dropouts, with nothing to lose, were starting to hang out in greater numbers. More and more were reported to be engaging in petty crime, like shoplifting and purse grabbing. For the teenage girls with their six-inch heels, bronze tanning-studio skin, and *keitai denwa* (cell phones), sex for money with middle-aged men, *enjokosai*, was becoming disturbingly commonplace.

The slovenly look of many kids was 'studied' – a paper-tiger rebellion as always in Japan – but there was a distinctly tougher feel to these teenagers, especially with the dropouts. I found myself bemoaning a loss of innocence in the decade I'd been a Japan-watcher.

Yet, there were some bright notes. One was a striking increase in the number of Japanese street performers, something I'd never seen in Tokyo; they had always been *gaijin* before. Suddenly there were small gatherings of kids with guitars and music sheets, sitting and playing on street corners. This was not only happening in Tokyo, but in cities across the country. If you're a music lover as I am, you know that can't be bad – especially in a society that's in short supply of such spontaneous expressiveness.

Surprising things were happening at Shibuya Station's famous meeting spot – the statue of *Hachiko*, a famously loyal dog who waited there for his master for seven years, not knowing that he'd passed on. A young all-male dance troupe from the *Kansai* region (Osaka, Kobe, Kyoto) amazed me one afternoon. They performed Japanese-style rap next to *Hachiko* with great energy and abandon.

Over the years, I'd occasionally seen small groups of young men (and women) privately practicing rap-choreography, with boom boxes in parks, at 11:30 at night. But in all my years of meeting friends at *Hachiko*, I'd never seen such a thing there, let alone on a weekday – at 3:30 on a Friday afternoon. Some young Japanese were clearly showing new signs of life. Their country's worst downturn since the war was spawning some risk-taking. When the young performers finished, they handed out leaflets advertising themselves. One of these guys, with a big smile on his face, sported a T-shirt with a message in very understandable English: *Only the Strong Survive*.

At one terrific Tokyo coffee house, *Ben's Cafe* – near Waseda University in *Takadanobaba* – you could now stumble into all manner of creative happenings. Ben, a transplanted New Yorker, began hosting Sunday night poetry readings, art showings and calligraphy demonstrations. With Ben's 'Greenwich Village exuberance' supporting them, some young Japanese were getting the chance to let their expressive hair down. One got the sense of a small, but growing creative community, a sorely missing element in Tokyo life.

Yet these were still basically the exceptions, the blades of grass through the cracks in the social concrete. As a teacher and casual observer of Japanese society, I have my own subjective and intuitive 'take' on the decade of the '90s in Japan. Living and working in Tokyo for many years, you get your own sense of how things are with the people. You get a feeling of how the country works, and what's good about it. You also see indications of what's wrong all around you.

In my role as an educator, I never stopped getting the impression that something vital was missing in my university students. All of them were fortunate, in the sense that they'd successfully made it through *examination hell*. So they had a much better chance at a future, unlike the dropouts in Shibuya, who faced a social black hole. This is a country that offers few second chances to such kids. Yet an inordinate number of my 'successful' university students seemed disenchanted with life.

In my classes, there were certainly those who shone like bright stars and lit my day. But there were too few of them. It felt as though the life force of the rest had been compressed inside them, from too many years of pressure in the classroom.

Entrusted with the responsibility of teaching these young people, I never ceased doing my level best to earn my pay by motivating and encouraging them. I learned to always get them into groups of four, because they invariably fared better in groups – no surprise, in such a group-oriented society.

I often used brainstorming techniques like mindmapping, because they undercut student perfectionism and released their innate creativity. We sometimes looked at issues that had been left unexamined in their high-school classes. We studied topics like the dangers of smoking, AIDS and safe sex. They definitely appreciated the chance to get straight information about these 'hidden' subjects. Music - and song sheets with missing lyrics - became staples for listening practice in my classes, because they served to motivate, lift spirits, and focus student attention better than anything else. Absolutely anything by the Beatles worked like magic.

Again and again, I felt I won the day with many of my classes. I believe they appreciated my efforts, and I grew very fond of many of my Japanese students. I'm going to miss them. Yet it was always an uphill battle, working against an inner lethargy that is uncomfortably pervasive at Japan's universities. In thinking about why Japan had lost power and experienced a 'disastrous decade,' I felt this had to somehow factor into the explanation.

The End of the Line

One day, as I approached the 'one decade' mark in Tokyo, I read a letter to *The Japan Times* which contained the following:

> Japan is morally diseased, chronically dishonest and spiritually empty. The nation is a morass of selfish pride and materialistic cupidity. It is virtually impossible to persuade Japan to come to its senses. All one can do is attempt to rescue as many young victims as possible by giving them the warm-hearted love and strong guidance they crave for.
> Gavin Bantock (29 years in Japan).

Reading this was very disturbing for me. It's not that the letter was so unusual. The English daily newspapers have been filled with such diatribes for the whole time I've been in Japan. What shook me up was that I easily understood the frustration that could lead someone to write such a letter to the editor.

For years, my strongest motivation with my students had stemmed from a similar feeling. Like Gavin Bantock, I also sensed that what these frequently dispirited young people most needed was endless encouragement, and a sense of meaning. By focusing on giving them that, I felt I'd made a lot of headway. From the many wonderful thank-you cards I'd received, I knew I'd inspired some to believe their lives could be better and they could make a difference.

I recognized the writer's name. He was the author of a textbook I was familiar with, entitled, *Towards Wisdom: How to Live in the Sunshine.*

"So here's a man who's been in this country for *three* decades," I thought, "and look at the shape he's in!"

His letter helped me to come to a firm decision. To teach well, your heart has to be in it. Mine always had been, and it sounded as if Gavin Bantock's had too. But one decade of working and teaching in Tokyo was quite enough. If I were to stay on any longer, burnout loomed on the horizon.

As for Gavin Bantock's other conclusions about Japan, I was done with bending myself out of shape about the ills of Japanese society. What didn't work for me, might well work for Japan. And some things about this country did work for me – it wasn't all bad, for God's sake! As for the things that seemed intolerable, launching into daily harangues about them was definitely a poor substitute for peace of mind.

But the country was stuck in recession, and people were more glum than usual. I'd gotten into the habit of turning on American Armed Forces Radio on Saturday mornings, to catch *Car Talk* on N.P.R. There's seldom any Canadian news in Japan – the foreign media are mostly American. One day, it struck me that my main interest in the program was simply that I wanted to cheer myself up. I loved hearing the hilarious laughter of the two American brothers who do the show. The signs were all there; it was time to go home and immerse myself in my own culture again.

The disastrous decade was taking its toll on everyone, and I wasn't alone in wondering if this country would ever bounce back from its malaise. Japan has often been referred to as a closed system in terms of trade, but I don't think it stops there. When a friend talked to me about Systems Theory – explaining how a closed system starts feeding on itself and then begins to atrophy – that description made me think of Japan. Cut off psychically from the rest of the world for 250 years, this powerful country got into the habit of excluding energy not its own. Centuries-old habits die hard.

Yet all through the '90s, Japanese people have continued to race to the airports by the millions, as fast as their paychecks could carry them. It's my sense that they're often looking for transfusions of energy from the outside world. Until very recently, that world was remote and inaccessible. Now it's just a quick plane trip away. Listening to 'medical intuitive' Dr. Carolyn Myss – author of *Anatomy of the Spirit* – speak about 'tribal permission' versus 'self-permission,' I reflected on the fact that most Japanese have only just begun to give themselves some personal nurturing, and to step out from under the tyrannies of their tribe.

My longtime friend Ayako – long ago laid off from her bankrupt shipping firm – recently sent me an e-mail message describing her new job. The recession has only made matters worse for many of this country's uncomplaining citizens, because those with a job feel they're lucky to have one. If there's a Murphy's Law for Japan, it's probably this: Working time expands to fill time available to work.

Ayako's e-mail message to me says it all: "As you can see from the date of this message (Sunday), I work at weekends too. Usually I work from 8:00 a.m.

to 9:00 p.m. I wonder how can I still be alive. The new job is quite hard, but I enjoy a part of that. That's why I can keep this kind of hard life." [sic]

In Stephen R. Covey's book, *The 7 Habits of Highly Effective People*, I came across a little passage that spoke to my feelings about conscripted Japanese workaholism. Covey advocates a win/win scenario for companies and their employees. But he recognizes that all too often, systems win and people lose. In his words, "So often the problem is in the system, not in the people. If you put good people in bad systems, you get bad results. You have to water the flowers you want to grow."

My friend Ayako is a great person, and a wonderful flower. For me, she exemplifies the very best of Japan. She and millions of other Japanese like her deserve a lot more watering than they're getting.

By contrast, my former student and friend, Hideo, works for Sun Microsystems in Tokyo. This enlightened company rewarded all of its worldwide employees by inviting them to Paris for a celebration. This included a gala three-day costume ball! Hideo dressed as a samurai, and his wife donned a kimono. They later sent me photos. They had a great time, and they tacked on four more days so they could make it into a week-long holiday.

Hideo marveled at this, telling me that a Japanese company would never do such a thing! The upshot of all this is that Hideo is one happy employee. He'll work very hard for his company out of gratitude, as well as loyalty. There's a clear lesson here, if anyone in corporate Japan is listening.

My two bits' worth is this: Obviously financial mismanagement, bad bank loans, the real estate collapse, and lack of effective leadership are behind much of this country's difficulties in the '90s. But a decade is a long time for a country as powerful as Japan to flounder as it has. On a spiritual or metaphysical level, there are intangible factors at work that you never read about in an 'economic analysis.' Japan in the '90s is proof to me that you can only put so much pressure on people. You can't relentlessly control and exhaust the citizens of a nation, to the extent that's been done here, and expect it to flourish indefinitely.

This economic giant may yet come roaring back, once the nation's trajectory has been reset and the Info-Tech Revolution has been fully embraced. The many countries who have grown dependent on Japan's economic power are counting on it. But as far as educational reform goes, only Keio University's Fujisawa campus (written up in *Time* magazine and the *Economist*), has really risen to the challenge of the Information Age, at least to date.

And what about the Japanese people themselves? A torrent of creative energy could be unleashed in this country, if the social gridlock on these hardworking people were loosened somewhat. That, however, would require making a social priority out of giving people a better life.

Up to now, much 'lip service' has been given to this idea in Japan. Making it a priority would require actually enforcing the laws regarding maximum working hours, so that people like Ayako don't end up working 13-hour days, seven days a week. It would mean forcing companies to pay their employees for overtime work, and to make it 'voluntary.' It would require protecting people from overwork, and safeguarding their leisure time.

In Tokyo, a genuinely enlightened municipal government could easily work out a plan for companies to have staggered starting times, and to use flextime. With a single stroke, commuter congestion would be reduced dramatically, and Tokyo's citizens could lighten their emotional load.

At least in part, Japan collapsed because so many of its people are exhausted on every level. One wonders how many of the leaders of this nation – the culture that introduced Zen to the world – remember the idea that 'less is more.' Paradoxically, a less stressful and less hardworking life for Ayako – and the tens of millions of her fellow Japanese – might do more to bring about Japan's renewal than any amount of overwork could ever do.

Looking on the Bright Side

As the new millennium gets under way, most of Japan's so-called *salarymen* have much the same look they had back in the 1980s. They still wear the same corporate uniform – conservative suits, ties and starched white shirts. But on 'Casual Fridays,' many now dress down, and colorful shirts are more acceptable. Many of Tokyo's *office ladies* still wear their company's conservative blue or gray uniforms, but others now dress much more flamboyantly. Corporate workers in the second-wealthiest nation on earth are finally being allowed to show some flair.

Near Tokyo Station, in the spring of 1999, I saw a group of three young company women walking along at lunchtime. They were all wearing flaming pink and blue blouses with black skirts. Their 'uniforms' were identical, but these women looked very classy – like flight attendants for an exotic airline. It was such a welcome change from the drab colours *office ladies* always used to wear.

Japan's efforts at 'internationalization' are often criticized for only being on the surface. But in practical ways, significant change has taken place, and credit should be given for this. When I first wandered through Shinjuku Station's labyrinth of tunnels in the fall of 1987, there wasn't a word of English to be found anywhere. I remember being overwhelmed at one point, caught up in a tidal wave of humanity with no idea how to get where I was going. I finally caught a glimpse of some blond hair, and I made a beeline for its owner to get directions.

Just over a decade later, there are computerized and liquid-crystal displays everywhere you look – all bilingual. Despite its monstrous size, Shinjuku Station is now much more manageable for Tokyo's English-speaking population, small though it is. Unilingual Americans might have more trouble getting around in Quebec than they would in Tokyo.

The train stations on the Yamanote Line are somewhat more humanized now. Instead of buzzers and alarm bells, announcing that the doors are about to close and making everyone feel like laboratory rats, a melody is more the rule these days. Most stations have their own signature tune.

Many of the cars on the *Yamanote Line* have 24 small television screens that show advertisements. I'm not at all sure this is an improvement of any kind – it would have caused Orwell to wonder – but it's impressive. Meanwhile, the glossy-poster ads for beer, notebook computers, *onsen* and wedding ceremonies are as ubiquitous as ever.

Westerners often complain about Narita Airport, but in my experience, luggage delivery from the plane to the carousel is now fast and efficient. The lines at Customs generally move quickly. Getting from the airport to downtown Tokyo is much easier than when I first arrived in Japan. It still takes over an hour, but the Narita Express is a technological delight. It has in-train vending machines, telephones and liquid-crystal displays that trace your progress on a map.

In small but noticeable ways, Japanese social manner has changed quite radically during the past decade. Many young Japanese seem more self-assured around Westerners, and they're so much more at ease making physical contact with each other. A colleague and I actually saw a young couple necking on a park bench in broad daylight a while back. That was a 'first' in Tokyo!

When I first arrived in Japan, people would often point to their nose and say *Watashi?* (Are you speaking to me?) Compared to how pervasive this custom used to be, it's now almost disappeared. I suspect young Japanese discovered that the practice seemed strange to foreigners, and they just dropped it.

On the job front, an increasing number of my fourth-year university students are being hired on one-year contracts, renewable if economic conditions improve. Others have had to settle for jobs in the hospitality industry, far beneath what they'd hoped for. But this shift away from the security – and banality – of lifetime employment is something I always felt would be a good development for Japan, at least in the long run. And the uncertainty of the times is spawning a new generation of entrepreneurs, who are breaking out on their own with 'Internet start-ups.' So it's possible to look on all of this positively, even though the short-term outlook is worrisome for most of my students.

Some of them have headed to Australia on working-holiday visas. But rather than feeling carefree and ready for adventure, they've often done this with misgivings. Most have feared they'll never get another chance at a full-time job. Going directly from university into the Japanese workforce has always been the acceptable course of action. Traditionally, when you broke out of an accepted pattern in Japan, it didn't work in your favor.

In the early '90s, I met one young fellow in his mid-20s who'd spent two years with the Japanese Peace Corps. On his return, far from getting credit for having an adventurous and idealistic spirit, he found he wasn't even in the running for full-time employment.

One fluently bilingual Japanese woman in her mid-20s told me her story. After getting her Master's degree in the U.S., Akiko spent a very frustrating year trying to find work in Tokyo. Again and again, during interviews, she was grilled with the standard questions, such as "What does your father do?" Then she was told she was "overqualified."

Akiko suspected differently, believing that the real problem was that she was a *woman* who was *qualified*. That threatened Japanese men. Eventually, she gave up, and landed a six-month contract with the U.N. in Switzerland.

But it's not been all bleak for women, nor for men who break new ground. Hanae struck gold by taking a two-week course in Microsoft applications when we were in Canada in 1995. As a result, she's had steady work in Tokyo ever since. It was contract work at first, but it eventually led to a full-time job with a subsidiary of an American company. She's very overworked, but she plans vacations six months in advance, gets permission to take them, and suffers no repercussions.

Some of the male titans who run Japan are recognizing and harnessing the creative talents of young men and women who have broken out of the mold. As the number of young people who don't fit the old respectable patterns keeps increasing, hiring practices are starting to reflect those new realities.

The son of my longtime friends, the Takanos, joined *Mitsubishi* after his university years. But after two years, he did the previously unthinkable. He quit his job with a prestige company and got a new position at a newspaper. I hear from his father that he's much happier.

Like people everywhere, the Japanese of Tokyo keep changing, and so does their society. This is a country that's inspired Westerners to write books with such wrenching titles as *The Blighted Blossom*, *The Hollow Doll* and *Lost Japan*. But in making my own small contribution to understanding this complex and difficult society, I found that one feeling won out over all the others. That was my desire to do justice to the many ordinary and likable Japanese I've met and gotten to know here, who have shown me much goodwill.

I always encourage people to visit this country. I once read that only 2.5% of the American public have traveled outside of the U.S., Canada or Mexico, meaning that more than 97.5% of Americans – and probably a similar percentage of my fellow Canadians – have never been to Asia. Of all the tourist destinations available nowadays, Japan is easily one of the safest in the world. Though coming here does require stepping into a radically different culture, there are many rewards for doing so.

With their indomitable spirit, the Japanese people soldier on, and they need to be better understood by the rest of the world. As the 21st century gets underway, there's plenty of uncertainty in the air, but a few things are very clear. One is that Japan is a major player in our future. We can count on it.

How We Need You: Let's Count the Ways

Despite its problems in the 1990s, the country that gave us pokémon remains the world's second-largest economy. In the last 25 years of the 20th century, an economic 'sea change' took place, reminiscent of the period in the '60s when the British pound surrendered to the dollar. Between 1975 and 2000, the value of one U.S. dollar, relative to the Japanese yen, plummeted from 360 to 100 yen. The Canadian dollar went down even further in value, from 360 to 70 yen. For the yen, it was an astonishing rise.

Japan remains a nation with incredible potential. Its positive contributions are integral to the survival of our endangered planet. The Land of the Rising Sun must definitely be part of the solution if we're going to reverse course environmentally.

It may turn out that Japan will never regain the phenomenal momentum it had in the 1980s, that China will surpass it as the Asian country to be reckoned with. Yet, in my own wildest hopes, Japan in the early 21st century will undergo one of its famed paradigm shifts, similar to the transformations that began in 1868, and later in 1945. Japan could become a pacesetter in crucial areas, and fulfill the meaning of its *Heisei Era*, which began in 1989. *Heisei* means 'inner tranquility attained, leads to outer peace.' What a magnificent name for an era; all the more so, if it has real meaning.

I express these hopes partly so that I can answer the often-asked question, "Do you like Japan?" in the form of a challenge. My answer has now become this: Yes, I do, and I see a Japan, 20 or 30 years from now, which has remade itself into a world leader of ecological responsibility, drawing on its own ancient, Shinto wisdom about nature, to confront our mounting environmental crisis. Just as this country's car manufacturers revolutionized the industry through an emphasis on quality, I envisage a Japan that will do it again, this time by mass-producing environmentally friendly cars. In fact, in 1999, Toyota, Nissan and Honda showed clear signs of getting the ball rolling. Nissan introduced its methanol fuel cell vehicle, producing exhaust gas that's close to being as clean as air, and Toyota was ready with its own 'hybrid' vehicle.

Honda unveiled its own low-pollution car, the *Insight*, the most fuel-efficient car that's ever been mass-produced. Using an electric motor and battery to share duties with the engine, the car has a new catalytic converter that reduces exhaust emissions dramatically.

This is an area in which Japan could take the lead, and pull the world along with it, shaming the energy-guzzling Yanks and Canucks into doing the same. The 1999 version of Canada's *Lemon-Aid Guide* has this to say, "Today American cars' quality control is about where Japanese cars' was in the mid-80s." It's Japan that's in position to set the standard and create the market for low-pollution vehicles.

It's not a day too soon. The ozone layer is depleting, and the major cities of planet earth are choking. As long as we're going to insist on using cars, we desperately need manufacturing giants like Japan to succeed in transforming the automobile industry. The skyrocketing numbers of children who have developed asthma from air pollution, in cities like New Delhi and Mexico City - not to mention Tokyo - are proof that drastic change is needed.

As for their nuclear industry, the Japanese people figured out in the '90s that they deserve better than they're getting. The accident that took place at a uranium processing plant northeast of Tokyo, in 1999, caused ordinary people to question their government's regulation of its nuclear industry. If there's a silver lining to the incident, it's that Japan didn't have to have a Chernobyl to get a wake-up call. An earthquake-prone country the size of California with 51 nuclear power plants needs - at the very least - to tighten up safety procedures, and maximize the amount of energy it can harness from the wind and the sun.

Do I like Japan? Yes, and I see a Japan, 20 or 30 years from now, whose industrial might has been harnessed to mass-produce biodegradable bottles for products like shampoo and soft drinks, thereby putting a halt to the growing mountains of plastic and aluminum in landfills.

The technology is now available, but nations with the necessary infrastructure and manufacturing power need to take bold steps. It's only a matter of time until we have no choice but to make these changes, if we are actually going to secure a future for our fragile planet.

Japan could provide a model for change, by redirecting industry on a massive scale towards the sustainable use of finite resources. By making this a priority, this country could prod the United States and other industrialized nations into doing the same. The opportunity is there. What better way for Japan to gain the respect of the world (and secure its long-sought seat on the U.N. security council), than by making this Herculean effort for the sake of the planet, thereby demonstrating its understanding that we're all in this together?

There was one exercise I used to love doing with some of my university students - at least the ones who could manage to do most of it in English.

Working in groups, as always, I'd get them to brainstorm and write down ways in which Japanese people are unique. They had no problem with this, being so very familiar with thinking along these lines. There was *ikebana* (flower arrangement), *soba* (buckwheat noodles), *origami* (the art of paper folding), *taiko* drumming and dozens of other things. This is, after all, a country with close to several thousand years of history and tradition.

Then I'd ask them to think of ways in which Japanese people are much the same as people right round the world. This usually stumped them at first, as it might with students anywhere. But I only had to make a few suggestions to get most of them going.

"For example," I'd say, "we all need to breathe, or we're gone in five minutes, and we all need fresh water to drink."

Very quickly, most of them were off to the races. They came up with long lists of things, both serious and frivolous: We're all born of mothers, we all speak a language, we all have cultural traditions, we all need sleep, our bodies eventually die, and on and on.

By the end of the exercise, I felt sure that my students had a more inclusive way of looking at their fellow human beings, one that might translate into their thinking more globally. I hoped it would lead to their understanding, for example, that the hole in the ozone layer affects us all equally – that we'll only survive as a species if we can learn to work co-operatively on such problems. Too much emphasis is placed on differences in our school systems, and not enough on the ways in which we're all fundamentally the same.

Years ago, during a radio interview in Canada, I heard an artist, whose name I can't recall, say something I instantly committed to memory: "I don't love everyone and never could," he said, "but I still think trying to love, or at least understand as many people as you can, offers the best hope for the future of life on this planet."

It was a message I tried to convey day in and day out to my Japanese students. These young people have, for the most part, been educated to think of Japan as separate and different. But I always sensed that the idea of adopting a global perspective was something most of them readily responded to.

In its own sphere of influence, Japan has extended enormous amounts of aid to countries like China, Indonesia and Thailand, as Southeast Asia struggles to build the infrastructure we take for granted in the West. Although this country operates out of self-interest like nations everywhere, I think that some of this assistance has been Japan's indirect way of overcoming its 20th-century transgressions.

Nations such as South Korea remain wary, but they know they need their powerful neighbor for their own survival. The rest of the world feels much the same. Japan's contributions are not only needed; they're vitally important. It's only by working together as a global community that we can succeed in the tremendous task of making the shift to sustainable growth, and laying the ground for our mutual survival.

Dreams of the Open Range

I feel very lucky to be a Canadian, especially after my years in Tokyo. We're very fortunate people. Sometimes in daydreams here, I've imagined myself flying out of Narita to Vancouver with Hanae, buying a car, starting to drive and just carrying on right across the country.

I imagine driving around Stanley Park in Vancouver, amazed that such an enormous park sits right in the heart of the city. In my mind's eye, we cruise up into the Rockies and take in their splendor. We carry on down into Alberta, where I spent my childhood, visit some old friends and acquaintances, and then keep rolling across the prairies. I appreciate the spaciousness and beauty of the countryside like never before.

We soak up the golden light of a wheat-field sunrise. I check out a red grain elevator as if I'd never seen one before. We stick our heads out the window to feel the warm prairie wind on our faces, and fill up our spirits with that galactic blue sky. We drive and drive, and it just goes on and on.

We drive through the vast and deep-green woodlands of Ontario, and I hear Gordon Lightfoot singing about Canada's forests - "too silent to be real." After 10 years in Tokyo, it all looks so precious, something nobody should ever take for granted.

We keep on driving up to Montreal, where I spent eight good years. I speak my fractured French, sip *café au lait* and savor a croissant on St. Denis Street with my Québécois friends. I take a moment to feel very proud of our multicultural society. After years in a much more homogeneous nation, I celebrate the vitality of diversity.

We drive across the equivalent of 27 Japans, and we marvel at the fact that all of this is one country. Hanae tells me that Canadians have got it made; I come home to the Canada of my dreams.

Then I snap out of my reverie. I recognize that geographically, the dream is real. But I quickly acknowledge that the reason thousands of Canadians have come to Tokyo is to get work they couldn't find back home. I remember once seeing a headline in *The Japan Times* in the early '90s: *Unemployment surges to 2.7%!* The wording may have been the work of English-speaking editors having a little fun, but the statistics reminded me of why I've always had plenty of work in Japan. Even as things have gotten tighter in the '90s, there have still been lots of jobs for foreigners like me.

Meanwhile, just as I've been changed by Japan, Canada has kept rapidly changing in my years away. On trips home, my illusions of a perfect Canada – versus an imperfect Japan – gradually vanished. It's still the country the U.N. liked enough to pick as the best country in the world to live in, six years in a row. But the downside was all too evident. Cities like Toronto and Vancouver were filled with social problems of every description: rampant car theft and home break-ins, poor single mothers, drug-addicted teenage prostitutes on street corners, motorcycle gang warfare, chronic homelessness and aggressive panhandlers.

I remember my surprise at having to routinely ask for the key – or the combination-lock code on one occasion – to restaurant and office washrooms. I've never once had to get a key to use a public washroom in Japan.

One Christmas Eve in a department store in B.C., I waited 20 minutes while the cashier – hired the day before with no training, it turned out – tried unsuccessfully to get the cash register open. As a long line formed, I reflected on the fact that such a scenario just wouldn't happen in Japan. And as for getting a response of "Oh, whatever..." from a clerk who'd given me the wrong change, that was unimaginable. I no longer had any trouble understanding how my Soulful Software colleague had gotten the impression that "Americans never say they're sorry."

Then there were the genuine nightmares, the most horrific being the slaughter of 14 women at Montreal's École Polytechnique in 1989, by an enraged and hateful anti-feminist. I was in Japan at the time, and it was many years before I fully understood the impact this terrible event had on Canadian society.

My Canadian friend, Bronwyn, with whom I'd studied in Montreal, spent three years working at Shōrai-dai, and then married a Japanese man. They returned to her hometown, Toronto, where they had their first child. Within a few years, they'd returned to Japan, and she called me up.

"Canada's not the country I grew up in anymore," she said, explaining why they'd returned. "I told my husband about a Toronto that no longer exists. It's more and more like a big U.S. city everyday, but people have gotten used to it. You only notice the difference when you've been away for a few years. There's so much more violence and homelessness now. We never really felt safe when we went out, and we just think our child will have a better life in Japan."

I remember being quite taken aback at first. Most of my Western friends had always said we wouldn't want children of ours to go beyond elementary school in Japan. Yet here was a whole different take on things by a Canadian whose views I respected.

Part of their problem was surely reverse culture shock and the difficulties Bronwyn's husband had getting work. I'd read an article in Japan about the many challenges facing Japanese who'd relocated to Toronto. Some of their issues were a lot like the ones I faced in Tokyo, though getting work had never been one of them.

But I didn't have to reflect for long to understand Bronwyn's feelings about the safety of Tokyo. I'd been changed by that as well. Whenever I'd read stories about young hooligans in Canada and the U.S. going on a rampage – because their team had won a championship – I always pondered the fact that such things never happen in Japan. Compared with the civility and refinement of sumo wrestling, the brutality of hockey was an embarrassment.

As for homeless people, Tokyo has its share - roughly 6,000 at the end of the '90s. For years, they camped in cardboard-box villages in stations like Shinjuku, until the police finally tore them down. But I know from visits to Toronto and Vancouver that the situation in Canada is certainly no better. It struck me that the social manner of the homeless in Japan and Canada says a lot about our cultural values. Homeless Japanese have too much pride to panhandle; they seldom bother anyone. By contrast, many young Canadians and Americans on the street have no qualms about aggressively petitioning every passerby.

And what of politics and social harmony? The world knows well that Canada has been in a decades-long tug-of-war about whether it'll even hold together or not. The *wa* (or harmony) of Japan is partly an illusion, but something about it is quite real. You come across much more verbal sparring and mean-spirited aggressiveness in North America than you do in Japan. An attitude of respect for others, though often impersonal in nature, is a side of the Japanese social landscape I've grown to appreciate.

But like Japan, Canada continues to be a great nation. And it has 27 times as much space to live, work and play in. "Miles from nowhere" is a place you can still find. You can disappear in the woods if you really want to, paddle around the 116-kilometer Bowron Lake chain in northern B.C., or just drive through ever-shifting terrain for weeks on end. It was soon going to be time to go home and rediscover my imperfect country.

History Lessons in Nagasaki

I'd always known I'd eventually get to Nagasaki. I was drawn there, much as I'd been pulled to visit Hiroshima in my first weeks in Japan. That had been a profoundly sobering experience, walking silently past the burned-out shell of the A-Bomb Dome, once the Industrial Promotion Building, until the world's first nuclear bomb exploded right above it. Ten years later, near the end of my years in Japan, I made it to Nagasaki. My three days there were a small revelation.

From the moment I arrived, at 10:30 p.m. on the train from Fukuoka, I felt good about Nagasaki. As I was about to get off, I noticed a young woman sleeping, unaware that we'd reached our destination. So as not to startle her, I whispered gently, "*Nagasaki eki des.*" (This is Nagasaki station.)

She awoke quickly and smiled, thanking me. A few moments later, when I was just out of the station and getting my bearings, she came by and looked my way again, giving me a warm and appreciative smile. She then sauntered off at a leisurely pace.

"Hey," I thought, "I like this town."

Located on Kyushu, the southernmost of Japan's four largest islands, Nagasaki felt friendly, and continued to feel that way throughout my stay. I'd always heard that Kyushu people are very friendly, and so it was. By the end of three days, I knew that the island of Kyushu is a place I'd like to see more of.

Nagasaki is so manageable. I trundled out of the station, up and over the walkway above the street cars, and reached my hotel on foot within 10 minutes. Early next morning, I quickly found a great little spot for *morning setto*. The proprietor brewed each cup of coffee he served individually, with its own filter. He showed me reproductions of old maps of Nagasaki that were hanging on his coffee shop wall, which illustrated how the area had looked in the 17th century. He was relaxed and had time to talk. It was such a welcome contrast with Tokyo.

Off I went to the excellent Dejima Museum to learn more about Japan's early contacts with the West. With a background of 10 years of living as a *gaijin* among the Japanese, I found it fascinating to learn more about how this country first dealt with foreign influences. Understanding the Japanese attitude towards the foreigners in their midst is a little easier when the realities of Dejima are right before your eyes.

Dejima, an artificial fan-shaped island, was built in 1634. Its purpose was to isolate the Portuguese living in Nagasaki and to prevent the further spread of Christianity. It was less than 15,000 square meters in size, and it was joined to the town by a short bridge. In the Dejima Museum, the visitor reads, "This stone bridge was the only link between Dejima and the town of Nagasaki and the gate was guarded at all times."

The museum provides the visitor with an outdoor scaled-down model of the island. This does a terrific job of conveying what Nagasaki looked like with this foreign appendage attached to its banks. As I wandered around, a group of young school children approached me a bit timidly.

"Where are you from?" they asked.

"I'm from Canada," I said.

"Oh, do you like Japan?" asked one young boy.

"Yes, very much," I replied.

"Oh, good," they exclaimed with delight, clapping their hands.

Could they take some photos of all of us together? Sure – smiles, joy and laughter all round.

The Portuguese only lasted five years on Dejima, before being kicked out of Japan altogether, on the heels of the Shimabara Rebellion of 1637. The Shogun, Tokugawa, had already banned Christianity in 1587, fearing Christians inside the Shogunate. But now the authorities had really had enough.

In time, Dutch traders were asked to move their trading post from Hirado to Dejima, and they remained there from 1641 to 1859. It was a period during which the island of Dejima was Japan's only open window to the West.

Dejima served as a prototype model for Japan's evolving approach to dealing with the unpredictability of outsiders. Most of the time, there were about 15 Dutchmen on the island, along with Japanese officials, who lived there as well. Dutch women were not allowed on Dejima, but the museum's exhibit explains that there was "a room for entertainment by the pleasure girls." Some of the relationships that sprang up between Dutch men and Japanese women are duly recorded in the museum's annals – famous first affairs with foreigners.

As for ordinary Japanese, "no one was allowed to have contact." Many Japanese living in Nagasaki and throughout Japan developed a fascination for forbidden foreign influences. For more than 200 years, the Dutch served as transit traders between Japan and East Asia. Japan traded its silver and gold and later its copper, along with ceramics and lacquer. In return, it bought silk and sugar. European painters were greatly influenced by the *Ukiyoe* style of Hokusai and Hiroshige, and all of this trade and cultural exchange was funnelled through Dejima.

The Dutch company was controlled by Nagasaki's governors. In the Dejima Museum, you get a sense of the control the Japanese authorities wielded by examining three framed scrolls. They mark, with a red dot, every single visit of a Dutch ship to Nagasaki between 1600 and 1859. From the first unplanned visit of the ship *De Liefde* in 1600, the list proceeds chronologically year by year:

1673: six red dots for six Dutch ships; 1706: five Dutch ships; 1745: three ships.

Similarly, between 1633 and 1850, the long treks by representatives of the Dutch company to pay homage to the Shogunate in *Edo* (now Tokyo), were all monitored and chronicled. Close tabs were kept on the movements of foreigners.

Wandering through the museum, you see tables laden with European-style food and dishes, showing how the foreign inhabitants of Dejima lived. You also learn interesting tidbits: The Japanese word *kimono* was actually adopted from the Portuguese word *kimon*.

By sealing itself off in the 17th century, Japan protected itself from colonization by foreign powers in a way that was quite unique in the world. Its Shoguns established a psychological model of learning from things foreign, without allowing them to have a dominant influence. In this way, they prevented a takeover by Europeans. They also established an approach to dealing with outsiders on their own terms, elements of which persist to this day.

Throughout the world, Christian nations with great navies were knocking over countries one after another, bringing in missionaries who were closely followed by mercantilists. By ruthlessly suppressing Christianity and 'containing' foreign influence, Japan retained its own sovereignty, at the cost of plunging itself into a dark period of isolation and oppression.

In 1605, this Buddhist island nation had 750,000 Christians. Four hundred years later, less than double that number choose such an identity, a mere 1% of the population. In fact, I've met very few Japanese in all my years here who speak of 'religion' as having a vitally important place in their lives, and almost all of those have been Christians, or members of a fringe religious sect. Though you hear that Japanese are born 'Shinto' and die 'Buddhist,' most people come across as being quite wary of organized religion. Instead, they choose a strong cultural identity, great reverence for their ancestors, and an appreciation for the spirit of life itself.

I have mixed feelings about the Japanese leaders who recognized the danger of powerful foreign ideologies and shut them out. On the one hand, life under Tokugawa rule (1600-1867) was apparently rigid and suffocating, and its effects can be seen to this day. But from another perspective, the Japanese – unlike Native Americans – were able to pull up the drawbridge in the 17th century and protect their own culture from invasion. Strict rule and unquestioning obedience were the hallmarks of the Tokugawa period, but the arts did continue to develop. Were it not for the tribal approach taken with Dejima, the unique set of islands the world knows as modern Japan would surely be a radically different nation.

A Special Encounter

The April morning I visited the Dejima Museum was a hot one. I lingered there in its cool exhibit rooms for several hours and then carried on walking. Nagasaki is a small enough city to permit visitors to do most of their sightseeing on foot. That day, a serendipitous encounter awaited me. Without it, my account of my years in Japan would have been greatly diminished.

On the advice of my *Lonely Planet Guidebook*, I headed up and across *Oranda-zaka*, the so-called Dutch Slopes. They were once sprinkled with wooden homes of Dutch design, and many still remain. Here and there, I saw large houses that once served as embassies, or way stations for sailors on leave, resting up while their ship was being repaired in the harbor below.

The old houses in this area were inhabited by the first foreigners to live in the fishing village of Nagasaki after 1859, once the Americans had pried the country open, and the island of Dejima had been closed forever. Replacing Dejima were the foreign quarters of Nagasaki, Yokohama and Hakodate in Hokkaido. These were 'cultural islands,' as Dejima had been, but they were now within mainland Japan itself.

I continued on towards the Glover Garden area - named after the inventive Scotsman Thomas Glover, the man who constructed the first rail line in Japan. I then climbed a hill, going up from the *Ishibashi* tram stop. Walking through narrow laneways and past curious shopkeepers, I ascended concrete stairways built into the hill. A few of them led to overgrown thickets, from which I had to backtrack.

As I meandered my way up and around the hill, between rows of small houses and gardens that sprang out of the hillside, I began to glance down and across the city of Nagasaki. The higher up I got, the more astonished I became at the beauty of the town's location, nestled amongst its splendid green hills and perched at the mouth of Nagasaki harbour. Tiny islands hung in the misty distance beyond it, looking like exquisite mirages, or little green paradises in a scroll painting.

And while marveling at the greens of the hills and the blues of Nagasaki harbor in the springtime, how could I not be conscious of what took place here in August 1945? As I gazed across the quiet beauty of modern Nagasaki, a continuous awareness of its quite recent catastrophe hovered just beneath my appreciation of the moment. I found myself trying to imagine what on earth it must have been like, on the day that mushroom cloud exploded - between the hills near the *Urakami* train station - just four kilometers north of where I stood.

Yet, I had resisted going to the A-bomb exhibit right away. I first wanted to gather my own sense of the kind of city Nagasaki is today. That had seemed to be the right way to go about it: first the present time; then the distant historical past; finally, the great horror of more recent times.

Searching for the high point of the Glover Garden Area, I decided at a certain point that I was probably lost. I sensed that I might be around the wrong side of the hill. Just as that thought popped into my mind, along came an energetic-looking man in his sixties, bounding along with a little boy who was running in front of him. I smiled at the boy and said, "*Konichiwa*" (Hello) to them both. Then I asked the man if he might help me find the Mitsubishi No. 2 Dock Building, with its display of ships built in its Nagasaki shipyard.

"It's right there behind you," he replied cheerfully in *Nihongo*. He spoke, I would discover, virtually no English. "I'll take you there."

His name was Fujiwara Michio, and he soon became my guide. He and I, and his five-year-old grandson, Kenta, spent most of the rest of that Tuesday afternoon together. I felt lucky to have stumbled across him. I also felt privileged to get to know him and learn about his life.

Gazing down over the city that had always been his home, Fujiwara-san began his story. He told me that he'd been a boy of 13 on the day the A-bomb exploded over Nagasaki. He described the colossal boom that had thundered through these hills at 11:02 a.m. on August 9, while he sat in his home at the bottom of this very hill. He and his family were 3.3 kilometers away from the epicenter of the blast that killed 75,000 of Nagasaki's 240,000 people. It injured 75,000 more, and condemned an estimated similar number to a slower death, resulting from the long-term effects of radiation.

Fujiwara-san remembers tying up his shoelaces, and then rushing outside to see what was happening. He was confronted with one of the 20th century's most horrific images – the mushroom cloud rising up over his family's devastated city. He demonstrated to me how the shock wave from the blast had struck his body, pushing him back with awesome force.

As Fujiwara-san told me his story, I didn't sense any bitterness. He's the most easy-going of men, and at one point he assured me, with an enthusiastic laugh, that he plans to live to be 100.

"I love Americans and Canadians," he said.

I detected no falseness in him at all. He seemed to be one of the sweetest and most fun-loving men of his age I've ever met. As for what took place in Nagasaki in 1945, the feeling he conveyed was that 'it happened the way it happened, that's all.' Moment by moment, being with him was an ongoing lesson for me in transcending the pain of the past, learning to accept life as it unfolds, and getting on with it.

Little Kenta bounded around us as we walked and talked that first day. He was ever so well behaved and respectful of his *Ojiisan* (grandfather). Eventually, we ran across Kenta's seven-year-old sister, Ayumi, coming home from school.

Then we all climbed up to Fujiwara-san's home, which turned out to be right on top of this small mountain, *Nabekamuri yama*. There, we had coffee and gazed quietly over the splendid town of Nagasaki.

At one point, we went outside again, and he showed me two steel rings protruding from the concrete foundation on either side of the house. During Kyushu's fierce typhoon season, the house has to be fastened down with wire, so it doesn't blow off the mountain!

Fujiwara-san later drove me down the hill to *Sofuku-ji*, the magnificent old Chinese temple dating from 1629. It's the first in a row of temples in Nagasaki which every visitor to Japan ought to see. They sit near a canal (*Nakajimagawa Stream*), which has a series of little stone bridges crossing over it. These once served as entryways to the temples.

My new friend in Nagasaki then dropped me off, insisting that I call him again the next morning. I promised I would. Meeting this cheerful and enlightened man had made my day.

Nagasaki Touches My Heart

The next morning, I headed north on the street car from Japan Railways' Nagasaki Station. I was on my way to Matsuyama to visit the Hypocenter Park, the A-Bomb Museum and the Peace Park. Unlike the day before, it was a cloudy Wednesday, which suited the somber mood I was in as I prepared for what lay ahead.

A huge sculpture of a mother, holding her wounded child, greeted me as I entered the Hypocenter Park. It's accompanied by the simplest of inscriptions: 1945 8.9 11:02.

The effect is powerful. Alongside it is a well-worded message from 'The Mayor of Nagasaki,' dated July 1997. The mayor remains nameless, perhaps because of the assassination attempt on Motoshima Hitoshi, who was Nagasaki's mayor in 1990. He paid dearly for his statement that the Emperor bore responsibility for the war.

In his message, the mayor explains that the child in the sculpture represents not only the victims of the A-bomb – 70% of whom were children, women and senior citizens – but also Japan itself in 1945. In its helplessness, this country was aided in rebuilding itself by other nations, who were horrified by the bomb's destructiveness.

The combined effect of the monument and the mayor's message was powerfully moving. I walked on and came upon another smaller monument to the 10,000 Koreans killed by the A-bomb attack on Nagasaki. This memorial had been financed by a group calling itself 'The Nagasaki Association to Protect Human Rights of Koreans in Japan' and was equally moving.

On a small plaque, I read about the suffering of over 2 million Koreans, who were "forcibly brought to Japan and put to slavery ... under atrocious conditions" after Japan's annexation of Korea in 1910. Then came the words: "Here we apologize to Korea and the Koreans for the immeasurable suffering that we inflicted upon them."

Citizens' groups such as this Association need to be publicly commended for their conscience and their courage. Living in Japan, I have come to understand how difficult it is for such groups to persevere in their intent and achieve their goals. The erection of this monument (with its accompanying declaration) in 1979 was undoubtedly preceded by many years of dedicated struggle. As Japan has taught me to bow to people I respect, I bow deeply to all those responsible for creating this healing monument.

I soon moved on into the A-bomb museum, the one white guy in a sea of young, Japanese junior-high-school children. I'd been through the museum in Hiroshima years before, so I had a sense of what lay ahead. But the pictures of Nagasaki's devastation were so catastrophic that I soon felt very shaken up.

The children around me paid me no mind. They busily scribbled down notes for their classes and took it all in. They were quietly attentive and sometimes seemed stunned by what they were seeing.

At first, I was startled to notice that in the first main exhibit area, entitled "Events leading up to the Nagasaki Atomic Bombing," the first entry reads as follows: "1943, May 5: The Japanese fleet at Truk Bay is proposed as an atomic bomb target at a meeting of the Military Planning Committee."

I soon realized that this display was simply an explanation of how the city of Nagasaki became a target. In one of those immensely consequential weather-related flukes of history, the city was chosen at the last minute because the original target, Kokura – on the northeast corner of Kyushu – was clouded over. There was good reason for Nagasaki to be on the target list, however. As Ian Buruma points out, "The Mitsubishi factories in Nagasaki produced the bulk of Japanese armaments."

In the next room, there's a longer chronology of the war, starting with: 1931 – Manchurian Incident occurs in September; 1937 – War with China begins in July.

Japan has long been criticized for downplaying its aggressive role in the '30s with such passive expressions as *occurs* and *begins*. Though my Japanese reading ability was woefully inadequate to understand how this was expressed in Japanese, Norma Field relieved my ignorance by writing on the same topic. As a teenager visiting the bomb exhibit, she'd noted that the Japanese signs always deleted "the most gruesome details."

Returning years later, she wrote, "I am eager to see if there are any hints of the new impetus I have heard about, to situate the bombs in the context of a war of aggression waged by Japan. There are none. I tell myself I can understand, it would be difficult to incorporate such a perspective in a city that had suffered directly and massively."

I once read a Japanese journalist's translation of the explanation in *Nihongo* in the Hiroshima A-bomb museum. It was equally evasive, apparently, and the journalist himself lamented his nation's inability to come to terms with its own past.

In Nagasaki, no linkage is made between the actions of Japan's military in Manchuria and Nanking and the blockade of Japan's raw materials and fuel supply by the ABCD Line (America, Britain, China and the Dutch). That was the embargo that propelled Japan to ally itself with Nazi Germany, and soon after that, to attack Pearl Harbor. All of this provides the background to the American bombing of Nagasaki.

With no examination of the chain of cause and effect, one is left to wonder how many young Japanese leave the exhibit with a disturbing impression: Americans dropped nuclear bombs on Nagasaki (and Hiroshima) with little or no provocation.

I left the A-bomb museum feeling like I'd been through a shredder. But a walk back across the Hypocenter and up into the Peace Park, with its fountain of doves and the Nagasaki Peace Statue, left me feeling somewhat better. As I looked around, I happily acknowledged a modern miracle: In spite of all the horrors endured here, Nagasaki had survived, and it was now a thriving modern city.

I caught the tram back to my hotel near Nagasaki Station and called Fujiwara-san. He came straight on down in his five-speed Daihatsu Mira minicar to pick me up. We then sped off to the top of Mount Inasa, Nagasaki's highest point, to have lunch together.

On the way up, we chatted and laughed. Fujiwara-san's bright spirit quickly started to lighten my mood. I noticed that the city of Nagasaki has devised an excellent variation on speed bumps: gently-rolling curves in the pavement, that slow you down without jolting you. I quickly dubbed them *speed waves.*

After our cruise up to a parking lot, and a short cable-car ride, we were soon at the top of the mountain, gazing over Fujiwara-san's city. It was so good to see him again after my morning alone in the A-bomb museum. As we ate lunch – which he insisted on paying for – he pointed out various sites in the city. His upbeat nature and lightheartedness were irresistible.

"Hey," I kept reminding myself, "this remarkable man lived through it. I just had to go through the museum."

After lunch, out on the roof of the restaurant, I commented on the fact that the wind was blowing out to sea. Fujiwara-san then told me that on the day of the bombing, it had been blowing inland. This had protected him and his family from radiation poisoning.

But all of his friends had died, he told me, quite matter-of-factly. He himself has an 'A-bomb Victim Card,' which he showed me later that evening. He's listed as having suffered a #1 & #2 level of exposure. Yet, he's a healthy man, and he's raised three healthy children, all with children of their own. Perhaps the wind, on that fateful day, made all the difference.

I mentioned to him that I'd once read an article about some research conducted at McGill University. That study suggested that Japanese who'd been on a traditional diet fared much better after the atomic blasts. It was determined that certain Japanese foods – miso and seaweed if my memory is correct – actually expel radiation from the body. He chuckled, and told me he'd eaten that way every day of his life.

At one point, our conversation became very somber. Fujiwara-san recalled how he walked to the epicenter two days after the bombing, on August 11, 1945. There, he saw dying people everywhere, begging for water. I knew from photographs in the A-Bomb museum that the scene was one of total devastation. It must have been like something out of Dante's Inferno. Fujiwara-san described for me how some people, on receiving a sip of water, choked and died instantly.

I know from the writings of Jonathan Schell, the author of *Fate of the Earth*, that as the 20th century ended, "some 31,000 nuclear weapons remained in the world." According to Schell, the end of the Cold War lulled us into a false sense of security in the 1990s. We have to remain vigilant, he believes, teaching the younger generations about the unspeakable horrors that these weapons unleash, and working for their eventual abolition.

Following my guide book's suggestion, Fujiwara-san drove us down the mountain to visit the *Fukusai-ji Zen Temple*. This is an incredibly unusual place. The temple is constructed in the shape of a large turtle, with a huge statue of the Goddess of mercy, Kannon, astride the turtle's back.

We no sooner entered it than a speed-rapping Japanese woman, probably in her fifties, suddenly appeared and appointed herself as our guide. She whisked us through the temple at breakneck speed.

A Foucault pendulum hung from the ceiling of the main hall and extended right down through an opening – about 20 feet across – to the floor below us. There, the ball of the pendulum swung in continual motion. It was the centerpiece of this Zen temple! It was quite mystifying. Our guide took us down below, where we read explanations about the tilt of the earth's axis. It seemed strangely out of place in a Zen temple, and there was no knowing why it was there. Perhaps it's a Zen *koan* made manifest, designed to get cerebral types like me to go beyond our logical minds.

But this was a very serious temple. Back on the main floor once again, we were shown a large metal ball representing the earth, with a chunk taken out of it - like a slice of pie. Beneath the ball were the ashes of thousands of A-bomb victims and Japanese soldiers lost in battle. I could easily have stood there for 15 minutes contemplating that powerful display, but our guide was in perpetual motion like the pendulum. She soon moved us on to another room in the temple containing artifacts of war.

Noticing how fast she spoke, Fujiwara-san kept catching my eye as if to say, "Wow, this woman is too much." His genial and lively disposition seemed to prevail at all times.

We soon left that temple, and talk of 1945 gave way to the present moment. We headed off to find somewhere to have tea, but as the places we tried were closed for the afternoon, we ended up eating *tofu donatsu* (tofu donuts) at Mister Donut. This became a source of much hilarity later in the evening.

We then went to meet Fujiwara-san's wonderfully cheerful *Okusan* (wife). She'd been a girl of four in 1945, he later told me. Now she works in a small company with just a few employees. Her somewhat older husband has been retired for three years, and he seems to fill his time being a very active grandfather. His wife assured us that she'd make us a lovely meal that evening.

Though they'd insisted that I spend the night with them, I didn't want to put them out. I asked Fujiwara-san to drop me at the local hostel. We went back and forth about this for some time. Finally, we agreed that if the hostel were open, I'd stay there. If not, I'd happily be their guest.

We soon discovered that the place had closed down. Fujiwara-san was delighted, and he immediately whisked us off to a small restaurant that served *champon*, a local noodle speciality. He introduced me to the proprietor - someone in his extended family - and asked her to just give us a sample.

Instead, she served us both a huge steaming bowl. Already half filled-up with tofu donuts, we ate it anyway. It was so delicious, and I certainly didn't want to be rude. The proprietor would not accept any money, of course. Japanese in such a position are the most gracious people I've ever met.

Stuffed like turkeys, we next drove to the *hoikuen* (daycare center) to pick up two more of Fujiwara-san's seven grandchildren. These were his daughter Shiori's darling girls, Yui, 5, and Riho, 4. We had a wonderfully happy afternoon drive through the sunny streets of Nagasaki, and Yui later recruited me to help put her toy train together in the living room. From time to time, she'd come up close to my face and lick my big Western nose. Then she'd run off with a smile and a giggle.

I spent the whole evening with this wonderful family, and I felt warmly welcomed into their hearts and home. Fujiwara-san's wife sang sweetly in the kitchen as she prepared us dinner. At one point, their son Kazuhito-san, Kenta and Ayumi's father, showed up with a bottle of saké.

While Fujiwara-san roared with laughter about the effect of the tofu donuts on his digestive system, we somehow managed to eat dinner. He mimed squashing them into one compartment in his stomach, next to the *champon*, to make room for his wife's delicious meal.

Kazuhito ("Call me Kaz") and I drank plenty of saké that evening, and we got to know each other. At one point, Fujiwara-san motioned for me to come up to the top of the house to look at the stars. There were plenty of them on that splendid night, shining down on Nagasaki and its surrounding hills. My new Japanese friend pointed out the mountain next to theirs.

"It's called *Hishitoriyama*," he told me. "That means *Star-Taker Mountain*."

"What a magical name for a mountain," I thought, musing on this magical evening, spent amongst very special people. They kindly set me up on a thick futon with a fluffy comforter, in their shrine room. Fujiwara-san bowed to the shrine, and then spoke briefly about his ancestors to me, before retiring for the night.

The next morning, he drove me to Nagasaki Station. It was tough to bid farewell to this gentle and most courageous of men. Here was a master of forgiveness, a man whose city had been obliterated and whose friends had all been killed in the most horrific bombing in the history of humankind. And yet, in three days with him, I never detected even a trace of bitterness or anger. I had much to learn from this man and his family. For me, they were now synonymous with Nagasaki, its beautiful green hills, electric trams and kindhearted people.

The truth is, we were both a little choked up as we said goodbye. After the alienation of Tokyo, it was such sweet relief to once again touch hearts with Japanese people. Just as with my student's family in Gifu, I felt welcomed into Fujiwara-san's Nagasaki home, in a way that's as heartwarming as anything I've ever known.

Debriefing in Thailand

At the end of my 10 years in Tokyo, I first went to Thailand to meet my foster child near Kon Ken. I also visited the island of Ko Samui to mellow out at a spa. They had great Thai-style vegetarian food, herbal steam baths and Thai massage. It was heavenly, and I decided to stay for a few weeks and do a cleansing fast. I had finally left Japan, but I would soon discover that it hadn't left me.

Along came Colin, an American in his forties, who'd spent eight years in the Land of Wa before returning to the U.S. Now, he was on his way back to Japan, to the town of Hamamatsu, to work for another year or two. With so many shared points of reference, we hit it off immediately and talked our way through our many *gaijin* experiences.

After a few days, we noticed a Japanese woman at the spa, who looked to be about 30 years of age. I found it interesting to note my reactions: I both did and didn't want to talk with her.

I recalled that during my first three or four years in Japan, whenever I was outside of the country and met Japanese people traveling abroad, I tried to strike up a conversation out of friendliness. I felt a sense of connection because I was living in their country. But eventually, I pretty much stopped that, except when I got a clear hint that it might be welcome. I'd concluded that you're best off being introduced to Japanese people, since they're most comfortable with that.

In Canada and elsewhere, I'd had some delightful chance encounters with Japanese, who'd since become my friends. But many Japanese tourists seemed ill at ease once they found out I'd lived in their country for years. Strangely, it didn't seem to make them warm to me, as it always would with an Iranian when I said I'd lived in Iran.

A few times, I experimented by playing dumb and pretending I'd never been to Japan. Conversations usually went better! I finally concluded that many Japanese on holiday want to forget all about Japan for a while. The last thing they want to do is meet a foreigner who knows a bit about their country and wants to talk about it.

I caught word from someone that the woman at the spa was from Hiroshima, a city I'd enjoyed visiting. A solo Japanese woman in Thailand was a bit unusual, and I was curious. Yet I continued to resist my natural impulse to approach her.

Then one night after dinner, I saw that Colin had engaged her. Eavesdropping on their conversation, I could tell that she'd asked him what he thought about Japan.

I'd long since discovered that when asked this question, if I just replied, "Good country, nice people," there was often an unmistakable sense of relief, coupled with a breathy *Arigato gozaimas* (Thank you very much). Even on a day when I felt otherwise, I often chose to say this, just to maintain a pleasant rapport. You often sense an insecurity in Japanese people when they ask this question, as though they're very afraid of the answer and actually assume that foreigners dislike Japan.

But Colin had waded into controversial waters. He was saying much of what I would say if I were in a mood to be straightforward. Yes, he appreciated many things about the people and the culture, but he had problems with certain aspects of Japanese society – such as the social gridlock it forced on its citizens.

"Well, that's your problem," I overheard her say, quite emphatically. Hey, this woman had a bit of gumption!

I knew better, but I couldn't help myself; I jumped in with both feet.

"Well, I guess it's my problem, too," I said. "I lived there for 10 years, and I feel pretty much as Colin does."

She was taken aback, but we introduced ourselves. Her name was Yuko. We then talked a while, along much the same lines as her conversation with Colin.

"You can't love the people and not the country," she insisted. I responded by saying that I have plenty of problems with my own country – the ongoing battle over Quebec separation, whereas we could all just speak two languages and get along; a tax system that discourages investment; a government that too often caves in to U.S. demands.

"Oh," she said with certainty, "you don't love your country!"

Growing exasperated, I replied, "Of course I love my country. I don't have to accept absolutely everything about my country to love it."

This, Yuko simply couldn't understand. Very little in her education had adequately prepared her to think in those terms. Japan does not teach its people to deal in such shades of gray. If there was one thing I'd learned about Japanese society in my years there, that was it! And it was getting late, and I was tired and ready for bed.

The next morning at breakfast, I noticed Yuko at the next table, talking animatedly with an American woman. It was only 7:30 a.m., but she was already hard at it, defending Japan.

I overheard the American woman, obviously a teacher, saying, "Well, all I can tell you is that the Japanese kids in my classes in the States were less creative than the other kids."

It actually pained me to see this going on. I felt I'd been a part of creating the turmoil in this young woman. I thought for a moment and then hastily pulled out a sheet of paper. I wrote down three headings: things I love about the Japanese people; problems I have with the Japanese social structure; reasons I'm hopeful about Japan's future. I then listed about 10 points under each heading, and filled up several pages.

After I finished, I went over to Yuko's table and gave her what I'd written. I explained that I wanted her to understand my feelings and not to be confused. She gratefully accepted my letter and read it through quite quickly.

I'm not sure how much she'd read before looking up at me, beaming. She then exclaimed, "You *do* love Japan!"

It occurred to me that this experience encapsulated the thing I'd most done battle with throughout my time in the Land of the Rising Sun. Was there any point in a comeback? No, no point at all, and that just didn't matter. Yuko was happy, her discomfort with my mixed feelings laid to rest. Sure now that I loved her country unequivocally, she was busy writing out her address in Hiroshima for me. Why on earth would I put a damper on her happiness? Not to mention my own.

I cry uncle, Yuko. No qualifiers; I love Japan. There's a lot to love.

author's collection

EPILOGUE

I finally left Tokyo after living in that frenetic city for over a decade. In my last two years there, I found myself enjoying most of my teaching assignments more than ever. It's as though I finally found the wavelength Japanese university students are on, and taught accordingly. I had learned to appeal to their strengths and never challenge them unrealistically. So it felt like it was the right time to leave – on a very good note.

During those last two years, I taught a couple of classes made up mostly of *returnees*, and I worked with the same students two years in a row. That had never happened before, but things had been slowly changing in Japan over the years I'd been there. In one class there was a student from France and another from Egypt. There were about 30 students in each class, and I developed a real bond with those two groups. It was students like them who kept me in Tokyo much longer than I'd ever anticipated staying.

Yes, they were often hard to motivate, as many university students in Japan are. Some skipped classes, drifted in late and lacked motivation. But that's simply the way Japan is for young people at that age – *shōgenai*. Most of them were also very pleasant young people with the most congenial of natures, and it was my pleasure to teach and encourage them. More than anything else, they needed encouragement. I knew I would miss them all, and now, back in Canada, indeed I do.

Too often, I'd observed Westerners departing Japan with a sense of anger and disgust, projecting all their negative feelings onto the country that had hosted them. Their parting shots in the letters to the editor were all too often devoid of warmth or gratitude. I felt very saddened by that, yet I knew very well from my own trials how that could come about.

For myself, at some point along the line I made a promise to myself: I would not leave Japan until I'd made my peace with this country and I could leave on the best possible terms.

At a deeper level than I'd ever understood it before, Tokyo confronted me with the truth of that pithy little saying of Jon Kabat-Zinn's: "Wherever you go there you are." Living in Japan, I developed a gut-level sense that we all carry our baggage with us, until we decide to drop it. In Tokyo, the commonest scenario of all is this: Westerner comes to Japan with issues; Japan soon becomes 'the issue.'

Looking back, I can now see how the mirror of Tokyo constantly showed me my strengths and my weaknesses. It also reflected back to me my own direct role in dwelling on the negative or reclaiming the higher ground. 'Shit happens' – as they say – no matter where you go. How we respond to it is always up to us.

In the end, a CD entitled *The Pearl*, by the wonderfully talented American singer Susan Osborne, made all the difference in the world. I really thank her from the bottom of my heart. For me, she is *subarashii* (magnificent and wonderful). I had already known and loved Susan's music from her days with the Paul Winter Consort. But it was a happy day when I discovered that she'd also recorded three CDs of Japanese music.

In the liner notes to *The Pearl*, she spoke about her connection to Japan with such heartfelt love. And then there was the music! Listening to the songs again and again, I began re-experiencing the warm and wonderful feelings I'd had in my first weeks in Japan. I remembered the thrill I'd felt on first seeing the 'floating' vermilion *torii* gate, rising out of the waters next to Miya-jima Island, near Hiroshima, at the entrance to the famous shrine there.

Memories and feelings that I'd lost touch with, living in Tokyo, came flooding back. It dawned on me that it was a musical feeling which had first put Japan on my radar screen as a child. I'd loved the bouncy, bittersweet melody of the *Sukiyaki Song*, which became a big hit in North America. For some years, that song was pretty much the only thing I knew about Japan.

In those last months in my tiny apartment in *Bunkyo-ku* in central Tokyo,

I sometimes listened to Susan Osborne's songs and found myself sobbing. I was overwhelmed and quite surprised by what they evoked in my heart: deep feelings of the kind that move the Japanese to say *natsukashii* – the interweaving of the pleasant and the sad. I knew that I was finally leaving Japan, after 10 tumultuous years in Tokyo. I also knew that despite all the stress, aggravation and reactivity I'd gone through – a good deal of it self-imposed – I, too, like Susan Osborne, loved some intangible essence of Japan, more deeply than I'd realized.

I played one of her songs for a few groups of students to end our year together. It's a beautifully moving version of a song Japanese people all know well and sing at graduation time, with Susan Osborne's modified English lyrics expressing a universal spirit. Entitled 'Graduation' (*Sotsugyo*), this musical gem holds and conveys a powerful emotional energy. The words evoke a mystical image of our "blue green planet" hurtling through space, with all of us, "Companion travellers ... whether stranger, foe or friend," sharing the journey together.

I won't soon forget one brave young 18-year-old lad who came up to see me after the song was over. He'd been clearly moved, and it was not easy for him, with his buddies all around teasing him for having such tender feelings!

But he was not deterred by the peer pressure. From his words, I understood something clearly: He now knew that I loved something deep within his culture's heart, that he also knew and loved. He felt connected with me now because of that, and he always would, he told me. He would never forget it, he added, and I don't doubt that. It was a humbling moment – a very Japanese moment. I'd encourage anyone who is drawn to things Japanese, or who's spent time in Japan, to listen to the song that brought it about.

Through its traditional music, I felt connected with the soul of Japan. But in my last years in Tokyo, health issues played a major role in my decision to return to Canada. I developed serious allergies to *futon* and *tatami* dust and I'm not sure what else. The smoke-filled coffee shops and diesel fuel emissions sure didn't help. During my worst bouts, I had chronic wheezing and sneezed hundreds of times a day. I decided Tokyo was finally rejecting me.

Eight months after leaving Japan, I found myself settling into my new life in Victoria, B.C., writing and singing again in a high-spirited choir. It felt good to be back, and my allergies soon cleared up. But reverse culture shock was challenging. It felt very strange to be living in a mostly 'white' culture again, so accustomed had I become to being surrounded by Japanese faces.

One night, I found myself really missing Japan and ended up at the video store renting *The Makioka Sisters*, a film highly praised by Pauline Kael. A quiet masterpiece, it moved me almost as deeply as Susan Osborne's music had done. Filmed in 1983 and set in the Osaka of 1938, it spoke to me of a Japan that still exists deep in the hearts of its people, despite the devastation wrought by war and industry in the 20th century.

As the commuter trials of Tokyo recede into memory, I'm warming to my new life and friends in Canada. But I retain much fondness for my friends and students in Japan. I sense I'll be drawn back to their island shores again one day to discover whole other sides to their country that I've yet to touch. But Tokyo? With gratitude and no regrets, I bid you farewell.

author's collection

GLOSSARY

atatakai kokoro: warm heart

amae: a unique kind of dependency that underlies many relationships in Japan

bentō: boxed lunch (a macron over a vowel indicates a long vowel sound)

Bonenkai: 'forget the year' parties

Bon odori: popular dance during the August Festival of Obon (cf. Obon)

bosozoku: motorcycle rebels who race through the streets in packs late at night

buchō: division chief in a company

burakumin: untouchable class in Japan; deemed "unclean" in Buddhist and Shinto tradition as a result of being descended from butchers, morticians and leather workers.

byōin: hospital

chikan: molesters who grope women on trains

chotto: a little (as in time); *Chotto matte kudasai* means "Please wait a minute"; also a multi-purpose expression, used to show agreement or to deflect a question by communicating that it's uncomfortable to talk about it

daigaku: university

daijōbu: all right, safe (**tabun daijōbu** means "It may be okay").

denki: electricity, light

densha: train

denwa: phone

doryoku: to make efforts

enryo: to restrain or refrain

gaiatsu: foreign criticism

gaijin: a non-Japanese person or foreigner; literally 'outside person' (*gai* means "outside" and *jin* means "person"); Japanese use it mainly to refer to Westerners, but primarily Caucasians, which makes it a controversial term. With non-Western foreigners, there is more often a reference to the country of origin, as in Firipin-jin (Filipino) or Kankoku-jin (Korean).

gaman: to endure and be patient

Gambatte kudasai!: Hang in there! Do your best! Carry on! Good luck!

geisha: professional female entertainer or escort (the literal meaning is 'person of the arts')

genkan: the little entranceway or vestibule in a Japanese home or dwelling where you leave your shoes; it also serves as a buffer against the outside world (literal meaning: 'hidden barrier')

genki: lively, full of energy and vitality, high spirits

giri-ninjō: conflict between obligation, social duty and repaying debts of gratitude (as through gift giving) versus following the dictates of the heart

gomen nasai: a form of apology ("I'm very sorry"); used interchangeably for this purpose with *sumimasen*

gomi: garbage (as in discarded items)

hai: yes (**ie** means 'no')

Hanami: blossom-viewing season (February through April): plum blossoms in February, peach in March and cherry blossoms in late March and early April.

hazukashii: embarrassed, ashamed

Heisei: the era which began in 1989; it means 'inner tranquility attained, leads to outer peace.'

hiragana: one of the two phonetic systems used to transcribe syllables in Japanese

hoikuen: daycare centre for young children

honne: one's real feelings; the private self beneath the public presentation; true intentions (cf. *tatemae*)

hoshōnin: guarantor

Ijime: bullying or malicious teasing

ikebana: the art of flower arrangement

isakaya: large pubs that serve food

ishin denshin: knowing other people's thoughts without speaking; heart-to-heart communication

Itadakimasu: expression intoned in unison before meals, literally "I will receive."

juku: cram schools

jun ken po: 'paper, rock, scissors,' often used to decide who goes first in Japan

kanji: Chinese calligraphic characters used in Japanese script

Kanrinin: guard or doorman

Kanto: Tokyo and its surrounding area, often called the Kanto Plain

karōshi: death from overwork

katakana: one of the two phonetic systems for writing Japanese, used primarily for transcribing foreign 'loan words' into syllabic Japanese

kawaii: cute

keigo: verb inflection to show appropriate deference

koan: a Zen Buddhist riddle that defies logic; used to achieve sudden enlightenment

koban: police box

kokusaika: internationalization

mama-san: a woman in charge of a nightclub, bar or restaurant

manga: Japanese cartoons

meishi: business card

muzukashii: difficult, troublesome, complicated; often used as a way of saying 'no'

natsukashisa: (popular form: **natsukashii**) an expression of nostalgia; a feeling viewed very favorably in Japan that is both pleasant and sad; homesickness

nengajo: New Year's cards

ningen: human being

ninjin: carrot

Nihon or Nippon: Japanese for Japan; literally means 'source of the sun.'

Nihongo: The Japanese language

noren: hanging cloth, indicating that a *sento* or shop is open for business

Obon: a mid-August event; Buddhist Festival of the Dead (cf. Bon odori)

o-furo: traditional Japanese bath

ojiisan: grandfather

okusan: wife

OL: *office lady*; the stereotypical young, unmarried woman working for a company in an office job

Omiage: (also written as *o-miyage*) souvenir, usually bought for others on returning from a trip

omiai: a formal meeting of prospective marriage partners, their parents and the so-called go-between; a test encounter to see if the young man and woman feel suited; traditional first step of an arranged marriage

onsen: hot spring, mineral spa

oshibori: steaming hot towels provided to customers in restaurants

O Shogatsu: New Year

pachinko: vertical pinball machines, hugely popular in Japan

rōmaji: the phonetic transcription of Japanese into the Roman alphabet

ryokan: a traditional Japanese inn

-san: a gender-neutral suffix appended to both first and family names to show respect (the nearest equivalent in English is "Mr." or "Ms.")

sarariiman: "salaried" male employee; *salaryman* or businessman; the stereotypical Japanese company white-collar worker

sempai/kohei: relationship between superior/subordinate at work or senior/junior at school

sensei: teacher or professor; respectful title addressed to someone with greater knowledge or a person in authority

Shinjuru: 'new species' of young people who reject traditional patterns of Japanese life

Shinto: Japan's indigenous religion (Way of the Gods), much influenced by Buddhism. *Kami* (divine power) is imminent in everything, at all times. So all things matter, and any moment can be a doorway to realization.

shōgenai: (popular form of **shikataganai**) – a very common phrase, meaning "it can't be helped," and reflecting a resigned sense of acceptance of that which cannot be changed or understood

shoji: sliding doors with a latticed wooden frame, covered on one side with a sheet of soft paper, serving to divide an open space into rooms and corridors (known as *fusuma* when both sides are covered with several layers of paper)

shinkansen: the famous "bullet train" that races around Japan at speeds rivaled only by high speed trains in France

soba: buckwheat noodles

sotsugyo: graduation

subarashii: wonderful, splendid, magnificent

sumimasen: an everyday form of apology ("I'm sorry") which also serves as "Excuse me" or "Thank you"

tatemae: public face; surface appearances; the appropriate presentation of the social self; the expected way to interact in various social circumstances (cf. *honne*)

tatami: large, thick straw mats, used as a unit of room measurement and serving as a floor in traditional Japanese rooms

tomodachi: friend

torii: entrance gate to a Shinto shrine

wakaru: to understand (opposite: **wakaranai**), comprehend, accept

yakitori: grilled chicken

yakuza: Japanese mafia; gangster (literally: a demeaning term suggesting vulgarity and worthlessness)

yasumi: holiday, day off, break

yukata: cotton summer kimono, very casual style

Zen: A Japanese school of Buddhism, brought to Japan from China in the 12th century, which teaches the path to enlightenment through one-pointedness of mind and the attainment of inner knowing.

NOTES

Introduction

Page #

v "Oh Tokyo – I never can sleep in your arms": Bruce Cockburn, *Tokyo*, from the CD *Humans* (Golden Mountain Music Corp. & High Romance Music Ltd., 1980).

Chapter 1: Claustrophobics Need Not Apply

6 "Camptown Races": Stephen Foster, *A Treasury of Stephen Foster* (New York: Random House, 1946), p. 63.

12 " 'another favored indulgence' ": Ruth Benedict, *The Chrysanthemum and the Sword* (Boston: Houghton Mifflin Company, 1946), p. 180.

35 " 'Japan's complex wholesale and retail distribution' ": Ishihara Shintaro, *The Japan That Can Say No: Why Japan Will Be First Among Equals* (New York: Simon and Schuster, 1991), p. 94.
41 " 'Joke-Jitsu' ": Allen Klein, *The Healing Power of Humor* (Los Angeles: Jeremy P. Tarcher, Inc. 1989), p. 48.

Chapter 2: Settling into the System

45 " 'Japan Air Lines personnel' ": *The Japan Times*, December 9, 1989.
57 " 'even after excluding people' ": *Economist*, Vol. 316, Issue 7662, July 7, 1990.
59 " 'The fact that a man often suffers intensely' ": Ruth Benedict, *The Chrysanthemum and the Sword* (Boston: Houghton Mifflin Company, 1946), p. 192.
65 "Into the Denki Furo": Jeff Greenwald, *Travelers' Tales Guides (Japan): true stories of life on the road*, eds. Donald W. George & Amy Greimann Carlson (Redwood City, CA: Traveler's Tales, Inc. 1999), reprinted from *I Should Have Stayed Home: The Worst Trips of Great Writers*, RDR Books, 1994.
70 " 'We can neutralize your brain' " Paul Simon, *The Big Bright Green Pleasure Machine* from the CD *Simon & Garfunkel: Parsley, Sage, Rosemary and Thyme* (BMI, Columbia Records, 1965).
79 "Seidensticker syndrome" quoted in *Lonely Planet Travel Survival Kit: Japan* (Hawthorn, Victoria, Australia: Lonely Planet Publications Pty Ltd., 1991), p. 26.
79 " 'Among other foreigners I found a polarization' ": Jonathan Rauch, *The Outnation: A Search for the Soul of Japan* (Boston: Little, Brown and Company, 1992), p. 104.
79 " 'The reverse side has' ": David Galef, Editor and Translator, *Even Monkeys Fall From Trees* (Tokyo: Tuttle Books, 1987), p. 48.

Chapter 3: The Honeymoon Draws to a End

122 " 'Saving face is the reason' ": Kasumi, *The Way of the Urban Samurai* (Boston: Charles E. Tuttle, Inc., 1992), p. 15.
144 " 'vying for approval' ": Robert Elegant, *Pacific Destiny: Inside Asia Today* (New York: Crown Publishers, 1990), p. 158.
148 " 'You can choose to live a dead life' ": Yoko Ono, *People* Magazine, March 28, 1994.
159 " 'Say what you mean' ": The Moody Blues from the CD *Keys to the Kingdom* (Polydor Ltd., 1991).

Chapter 4: Up Against the Social Contract

168 " 'For if we don't find the next whiskey bar' ": Weill-Brecht (Witmark ASCAP) from the CD *The Doors* (Electra Records, 1967).

183 " 'These debts are regarded' ": Ruth Benedict, *The Chrysanthemum and the Sword* (Boston: Houghton Mifflin Company, 1946), p. 116.
194 " 'uglification ... Everywhere music's turning into noise' " : *The Unbearable Lightness of Being* (Orion Pictures Corp. 1988).
222 " 'streets crammed with people' ": David Suzuki, *Shared Vision* (Vancouver, B.C., Sept. 1994).
222 Rick Kennedy, *Little Adventures in Tokyo: 39 Thrills for the Urban Explorer* (Berkeley, California: Stone Bridge Press, 1998).

Chapter 5: Coming To Terms With Tokyo

227 "Vitamin H": Allen Klein, *The Healing Power of Humor* (Los Angeles: Jeremy P. Tarcher, Inc., 1989).
232 " 'I do not know why believing' ": Ruth Benedict, *The Chrysanthemum and the Sword* (Boston: Houghton Mifflin Company, 1946), p. 14.
238 " 'a story of wasted intellectual resources' ": Jonathan Rauch, *The Outnation: A Search for the Soul of Japan* (Boston: Little, Brown and Company, 1992), p. 134.
248 "not logical": Karel van Wolferen, *The Enigma of Japanese Power* (Tokyo: Tuttle Books, 1993), p. 346.
253 " 'I might be just beginning' ": Enya, *Anywhere Is*, from the CD *The Memory of Trees* (Warner Music U.K. Ltd., 1995).
254 " 'the constant reminders of the perceived racial gap' ": James Fallows, *Looking at the Sun: The Rise of the New East Asian Economic and Political System* (New York: Pantheon, 1994), p. 103.
254 " 'discrimination is still widespread in Japan' ": Ishihara Shintaro, *The JapanThat Can Say No: Why Japan Will Be First Among Equals* (New York: Simon and Schuster, 1991), p. 79.
254 " 'Japanese should not forget that Caucasians' ": ibid, p. 27.
254 " 'persistent and widespread, especially against members' ": *The Vancouver Sun*, on an Amnesty International report, September 25, 1999.
255 " 'I always believed in the superiority' ": *Memoirs: Pierre Elliott Trudeau* (CBC Television Documentary, 1993).
255 " 'When human beings encounter' ": David Suzuki & Keibo Oiwa, *The Japan we never knew: a journey of discovery* (Don Mills. Ont., Stoddard, 1996), p. 153.

257 " 'Several classmates also offered support' ": Hiroko Noro, *Focus on Women* (Victoria, B.C.), January 1999.

260 "are ruthless in commerce": Robert Elegant, *Pacific Destiny: Inside Asia Today* (New York: Crown Publishers, 1990), p. 104.

265 " 'The Johnny Walker wisdom' ": Leonard Cohen, *Closing Time*, from the CD *The Future* (Sony Music Entertainment Inc., 1992).

267 " 'whose efforts to make public' ": Ian Buruma, *The Wages of Guilt: Memories of War in Germany and Japan* (New York: Meridian Books, 1993), p. 116.

279 " 'Japan's consensus is not formed' ": Robert Elegant, *Pacific Destiny: Inside Asia Today* (New York: Crown Publishers, 1990), p. 160.

296 " 'Having spent this year in Japan' ": Norma Field, *In the Realm of a Dying Emperor: A Portrait of Japan at Century's End* (New York: Pantheon Books, 1991), p. 255.

296 " 'warped bureaucratic logic' ": Ishihara Shintaro, *The Japan That Can Say No: Why Japan Will Be First Among Equals* (New York: Simon and Schuster, 1991), p. 99.

296 " 'preserving dysfunctional practices' ": ibid., p. 99.

297 " 'there is a peace-time military structure' ": James Fallows, C.B.C. Television, Interview on *Venture*, March 27, 1994.

Chapter 6: Still I'm Gonna Miss You

302 " 'The critic leaves at curtain' ": Elwyn Brooks White, *Critic* (from *Definitions*), *Norton Book of Light Verse*, ed. Russell Baker (New York: Norton, 1986), p. 189.

314 " 'We have many taboos' ": Ruth Benedict, *The Chrysanthemum and the Sword* (Boston: Houghton Mifflin Company, 1946), p. 183.

318 " 'Japanese women have an inner strength' ": *Newsweek*, 1998. (Additional source: *New Perspectives Quarterly*, Special Issue 98, Vol. 15, Issue 3, p. 61, July 1, 1998).

321 "I learned from David Suzuki": David Suzuki & Keibo Oiwa, *The Japan we never knew: a journey of discovery* (Don Mills. Ont.: Stoddard, 1996), p. 166.

321 " 'Resident Koreans have been fingerprinted' ": Norma Fields, *In the Realm of a Dying Emperor: A Portrait of Japan at Century's End* (New York: Pantheon Books, 1991), p. 217.

322 "a very harsh story on Japan's prison system": *Hard Times* by Gibney Jr., Frank; & Tashiro Hiroko (*Time* Australia, Time Inc. Issue 44, October 28, 1996), p. 36.

323	" 'An entire generation remembers' ": Robert Elegant, *Pacific Destiny: Inside Asia Today* (New York: Crown Publishers, 1990), p. 9.
324	" 'there had never been any' ": Ken Cambon, M.D., *Guest of Hirohito* (Vancouver, B.C.: PW Press, 1990), p. 119.
325	" 'the military was all-powerful' ": Interview with Alex Jardine (Victoria, B.C., November 17, 1998).
326	" 'Barely a year later' ": Ian Buruma, *The Wages of Guilt: Memories of War in Germany and Japan* (New York: Meridian Books, 1993), p. 297.
326	" 'deserved death' ": quoted by James Fallows in *Looking at the Sun: The Rise of the New East Asian Economic and Political System* (New York: Pantheon, 1994), p. 412.
327	" 'Strongly motivating me' ": Iris Chang, *The Rape of Nanking* (New York: Basic Books, 1997), p. 12.
327	" 'collective amnesia in contemporary Japan' ": Jeff Kingston, *Dazzling Portrait of the Occupation. The Japan Times*, May II, 1999.
327	" 'if the man in whose name imperial Japan' ": ibid., quoted from John W. Dower, *Embracing Defeat: Japan in the Wake of World War 11* (New York: W.W. Norton, 1999).
328	" 'Whatever else he may have been' ": Ian Buruma, *The Wages of Guilt: Memories of War in Germany and Japan* (New York: Meridian Books, 1993), p. 63.
328	" 'It's lucky we lost' ": *An Autumn Afternoon*, Ozu Yasujiro (Shochiku Co., Ltd., 1962; New Yorker Film Artwork, 1991).
331	" 'The Japanese willingness to sanction lies' ": Miyamoto Masao, M.D. *Straitjacket Society: An Insider's Irreverent View of Bureaucratic Japan* (New York: Kodansha, 1994), p. 124
335	" 'a truly wonderful people' ": *Hiragana Times*, January 1996.
338	" 'Women in Japan' ": *Lonely Planet Travel Survival Kit: Japan.* (Hawthorn, Vic. Australia: Lonely Planet Publications Pty Ltd., 1991), p. 86.
341	"Starbucks": *Morning Edition* (National Public Radio), September 14, 1999.
341	" 'Moreover, I do not think' ": Jonathan Rauch, *The Outnation: A Search for the Soul of Japan* (Boston: Little, Brown and Company, 1992), p. 123.
349	"In terms of stock market evaluations": *Morning Edition* (National Public Radio), November 16, 1999.
349	" 'It is difficult to distinguish' ": Masamura Kimihiro, *The Daily Yomiuri*, November 23, 1993.
350	" 'self-destruction is exalted' ": Robert Elegant, *Pacific Destiny: Inside Asia Today* (New York: Crown Publishers, 1990), p. 100.
352	" 'Japan is morally diseased' ": *The Japan Times*, December 15, 1997.
353	"He was the author": Gavin Bantock, *Towards Wisdom: How to Live in the Sunshine* (Tokyo: Kinseido, 1989).

353 "tribal permission": Caroline Myss, *Anatomy of the Spirit* (New York: Crown Publishers, Inc., 1996).
354 " 'So often the problem is in the system' ": Stephen R. Covey, *The 7 Habits of Highly Effective People : Restoring the Character Ethic* (New York: Fireside Books, Simon and Schuster, 1989), p. 232.
359 "Honda unveiled its own": Business Briefs: *Asahi Evening News*, May 14, 1999.
359 " 'Today American cars' quality' ": *Lemon-Aid: Used Cars* (Toronto: Stoddard Publishing Company Ltd. 1998), p. 4.
370 " 'The Mitsubishi factories in Nagasaki' ": Ian Buruma, *The Wages of Guilt: Memories of War in Germany and Japan* (New York: Meridian Books, 1993), p. 100.
371 " 'the most gruesome details' ": Norma Field, *In the Realm of a Dying Emperor: A Portrait of Japan at Century's End* (New York: Pantheon Books, 1991), p. 232.
372 " 'some 31,000 nuclear weapons' ": Jonathan Schell, *The Unfinished Twentieth Century : What We Have Forgotten About Nuclear Weapons* (in *Harper's* Magazine, January 2000), p. 43.

Epilogue

380 "Wherever you Go": Jon Kabat-Zinn, *Wherever You Go There You Are* (New York: Hyperion, 1994).
381 " 'blue green planet . . Companion travellers' ": Susan Osborne, from the song *Graduation* on the CDs *The Pearl* (Pony Canyon Inc., 1996) and *Waraku: The Best of Japan* (Pony Canyon, Inc., 1998).

About the Author

After living and working in England, Iran and India, Bruce McCormack returned to Canada and settled in Montreal, where he got a Master's Degree in Applied Linguistics from Concordia University. In 1987, he headed off to Japan, just in time to catch the last years of the Japanese 'bubble economy.' He worked at a Japanese company and seven universities during his decade in Tokyo. He also did a lot of thinking and writing about The Land of Wa (meaning 'Harmony'); hence the thickness of this book. He loves to travel and has visited close to 30 countries. He currently lives in Victoria, B.C., on Canada's West Coast, where he writes, teaches, hikes, and sings in the Gettin' Higher Choir. As far as he can tell, laughter and singing are the best cross-cultural bridges we have for bringing people together across borders.